CONFORMITY AND CONFLICT

CONFORMITY AND CONFLICT

Readings in cultural anthropology

FIFTH EDITION

Edited by
JAMES P. SPRADLEY
DAVID W. McCURDY
Macalester College

Little, Brown and Company
Boston   Toronto
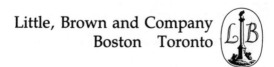

Library of Congress Cataloging in Publication Data
Main entry under title:

Conformity and Conflict.

Includes bibliographical references.
1. Ethnology—Addresses, essays, lectures.
2. Social history—Addresses, essays, lectures.
I. Spradley, James P. II. McCurdy, David W.
GN325.C69   1983   306   83-18700
ISBN 0-316-80774-5

Library of Congress Catalog Card Number 83-18700

ISBN 0-316-80774-5

9 8 7 6 5 4 3 2 1

BP

Published simultaneously in Canada
by Little, Brown & Company (Canada) Limited

Printed in the United States of America

To Barbara Spradley and Carolyn McCurdy

Preface

Cultural anthropology has a twofold mission: to understand other cultures and to communicate that understanding. Fourteen years ago, in preparing the first edition of this book, we sought to make communication easier and more enjoyable for teachers and students alike. We focused on the twin themes stated in the title — conformity, or order, and conflict, or change — while organizing selections into traditional topics. We balanced the coverage of cultures between non-Western and Western (including American), so students could make their own cultural comparisons and see the relation between anthropology and their lives. We searched extensively for scholarly articles written with insight and clarity. Students and teachers in hundreds of colleges and universities responded enthusiastically to our efforts, and a pattern was set that carried through three subsequent editions.

This new fifth edition retains the features of the earlier editions: the focus on themes, the coverage of Western cultures, and the combination of professionalism and readability in the selections. As in past editions, we have revamped topics and added or subtracted selections in response to the suggestions of teachers and students across the country. This edition includes at least one new article in every section, with the greatest additions appearing in the chapters on language and communication, sex roles, cultural ecology, economic systems, and religion, magic, and world view. Sixteen of the thirty-five articles are new, all of them reflecting careful research and literate craftsmanship. A complimentary instructor's manual, which offers abstracts of each selection along with essay, true or false, and multiple choice questions, is available from the publisher to instructors requesting it on school letterhead.

Many people have made suggestions and contributed toward this edition of *Conformity and Conflict*. In particular we would like to express appreciation to Bradford Gray, Warner Hutchinson, Julia Winston, Jeffrey Heine, Wendy Homa, Laurie Kroshus, and the many instructors and students whose suggestions have guided us.

Contents

Cargo cults are social movements based on the belief that ancestors will
return and bring Western goods, or "cargo," with them; these cults have
swept new Guinea and its adjacent islands in response to disorientation
caused by Western influence.

Psychotherapy in Africa is more effective when psychiatrists and
traditional healers work hand-in-hand.

The Yanomamö face cultural extinction because of interference from
intruders in quest of uranium.

Tourists descend on the quiet island of Bali and show disrespect for all
that its inhabitants hold sacred.

CONFORMITY AND CONFLICT

I

Culture and the contemporary world

Many students associate cultural anthropology with the study of primitive peoples. They picture the anthropologist as that slightly peculiar person who, dressed in khaki shorts and pith helmet, lives among some exotic tribe in order to record the group's bizarre and not altogether pleasant customs. Like most stereotypes, this one is not completely true but it does reflect anthropology's traditional interest in describing the culture of less complex societies. In the last century, when anthropology became a recognized discipline, its members collected and analyzed the growing number of reports on non-Western peoples by missionaries, travelers, and colonial administrators. This tradition continued into the twentieth century, although the collection of data was refined by actual fieldwork. Impressed by the variety of human behavior, anthropologists sought to record these cultures that were vanishing before the onslaught of Western civilization. Such studies continue among remote groups, and reports of this research are regularly found in professional journals.

During recent decades, however, anthropologists have developed wider interests. As primitive groups have been obliterated or assimilated, anthropologists have increasingly studied subcultures within more complex societies. Certainly World War II and the Cold War stimulated this trend. The United States government employed anthropologists to describe societies in whose territories we fought. The Cold War years, marked by competition with the Russians for influence in developing nations, led to studies of peasant life styles and culture change.

Today, however, our position in the world has changed. Americans are less welcome in developing nations. Concurrently, problems in our own country have multiplied and taken the center stage of national concern. It is not surprising that anthropologists have extended their attention to subcultures within our own society.

But what can anthropology contribute to an understanding of American life? After all, other social scientists have been doing research in this country for years. Is there anything special about anthropology? In many ways the answer to this question is no. The various social sciences often share the same interests. Yet, as a result of their intensive cross-cultural experience, anthropologists have developed a unique perspective on the nature and the significance of *culture*. This view has emerged from over a century of fieldwork among populations whose behavior was dramatically different from the anthropologists' own. Why, for example, did Iroquois women participate with apparent relish in the gruesome torture of prisoners? How could Bhil tribesmen put chili powder in the eyes of witches, blindfold them, and swing them over a smoky fire by their feet? What possessed Kwakiutl chiefs to destroy their wealth publicly at potlatch ceremonies? Why did Rajput widows cast themselves upon their husbands' funeral pyres? Why did Nagas engage in raids to acquire human heads? In every case, anthropologists were impressed by the fact that this "bizarre" behavior was intentional and meaningful to the participants. Bhils wanted to swing witches; to them it was appropriate. Kwakiutl chiefs made careful investments to increase the wealth they destroyed. These acts were planned; people had a notion of what they were going to do before they did it, and others shared their expectations.

CULTURE

The acquired knowledge that people use to interpret their world and generate social behavior is called *culture*. Culture is not behavior itself, but the knowledge used to construct and understand behavior. It is learned as children grow up in society and discover how their parents, and others around them, interpret the world. In our society we learn to distinguish objects such as cars, windows, houses, children, and food; to recognize attributes like sharp, hot, beautiful, and humid; to classify and perform different kinds of acts; to evaluate what is good and bad and to judge when an unusual action is appropriate or inappropriate. How often have you heard parents explain something about life to a child? Why do you think children are forever asking why? During socialization children learn a culture, and because they learn it from others, they share it with others, a fact that makes human social existence possible.

Culture is thus the system of knowledge by which people design their own actions and interpret the behavior of others. It tells an American that eating with one's mouth closed is proper, while an Indian knows that to be polite one must chew with one's mouth open. There is nothing preordained about cultural categories; they are arbitrary. The same act can have different meanings in various cultures. For example, when adolescent Hindu boys walk holding hands, it signifies friendship, while to Americans the same act may suggest homosexuality. This arbitrariness is particularly important to remember if we are to understand our own complex society. We tend to think that the norms we follow represent the "natural" way human beings do things. Those who behave otherwise are judged morally wrong. This viewpoint is *ethnocentric*, which means that people think their own culture represents the best, or at least the most appropriate, way for human beings to live.

Although in our complex society we share many cultural norms with everyone, each of us belongs to a number of groups possessing exclusive cultural knowledge. We share some categories and plans with family members alone. And our occupational group, ethnic group, voluntary society, and age group each has its distinctive culture. Instead of assuming that another's behavior is reasonable to him, that it is motivated by a different set of cultural norms, we frequently assume that he has intentionally violated accepted conventions. In their attempt to build bridges of understanding across cultural barriers, anthropologists have identified the universality of ethnocentrism many years ago. The study of subcultures in our own society is another attempt to further mutual understanding, as some of the selections in this volume indicate.

How do anthropologists discover and map another culture? Are their methods applicable in the United States? Typically anthropologists live among the people of the society that interests them. They learn the culture by observing, asking questions, and participating in daily activities — a process resembling childhood socialization or enculturation. Obviously, the anthropologist cannot become a child, and must try to learn the norms in a strange group despite his or her foreign appearance and advanced age. Those who study in the United States have followed a similar procedure.

More than anything else, the study of culture separates anthropologists from other social scientists. Other scholars do not ignore culture; they assume their subjects have it, but their main interest is to account for human behavior by plotting correlations among variables. Some social scientists have explained the rise in the American divorce rate as a function of industrialization; this hypothesis can be tested by seeing if higher divorce rates are associated with industrialization and mobility. Anthropologists share a concern for this kind of explanation; for example, many have employed the Human Relations Area Files, a collection of ethnographies describing several hundred societies, as data for testing more general hypotheses. Almost every anthropologist starts with an *ethnography*, the description of a particular culture, and such studies are required to understand the complexity within American society.

As anthropologists have encountered, studied, and compared the world's societies, they have learned more about the concept of culture itself. As we have seen, culture is the knowledge people use to generate behavior, not behavior itself; it is arbitrary, learned, and shared. In addition, culture is adaptive. Human beings cope with their natural and social environment by means of their traditional knowledge. Culture allows for rapid adaptation because it is flexible and permits the invention of new strategies — although change often appears to be painfully slow to those who are in a hurry for it. By the same token, the adaptive nature of culture accounts for the enormous variety of the world's distinct societies.

Culture is a system of interrelated parts. If Americans were to give up automobiles, then other modes of travel, places for courtship, marks of status, and sources of income would have to be found. Culture meets personal needs; through it, people seek security and a sense of control over experience. Indeed, every tradition includes ways to cure the sick, to prepare for the unexpected, and to support the individual. In a complex society with many ways of life in contact with each other, change is persistent. It may be illusion to think that people can control the course of change, or can modify the resulting culture conflict. But if we can understand human cultures — including our own — the illusion may become reality.

CULTURE AND VALUES

It is easy for people to feel that their own way of life is natural and God-given. One's culture is not like a suit of clothing that can be discarded easily or exchanged for each new life style that comes along. It is rather like a security blanket, and though to some it may appear worn and tattered, outmoded and ridiculous, it has great meaning to its owner. Although there are many reasons for this fact, one of the most important is the value-laden nature of what we learn as members of society. Whether it is acquired in a tribal band, a peasant village, or an urban neighborhood, each culture is like a giant iceberg. Beneath the surface of rules, norms, and behavior patterns there is a system of values. Some of these premises are easily stated by members of a society, while others are outside their awareness. Because many difficulties in the modern world involve values, we must examine this concept in some detail.

A value is an arbitrary conception of what is *desirable* in human experience. During socialization every child is exposed to a constant barrage of evaluations — the arbitrary "rating system" of his culture. Nearly everything he learns is labeled in terms of its desirability. The value attached to each bit of information may result from the pain of a hot stove, the look of disapproval from a parent, the smile of appreciation from a teacher, or some specific verbal instruction. When a parent tells a child, "You should go to college and get a good education," he is expressing a value. Those who do not conform to society's rating system are identified with derogatory labels or are punished in a more severe way. When a Tlingit Indian says to his nephew, "You should marry your father's sister," he is expressing one of the core values of his culture. When a young couple saves income for future emergencies, they are conforming to the American value that the future is more important than the present. When a tramp urinates in an alley, he is violating the value attached to privacy. All these concepts of what is desirable combine cognitive and affective meanings. Individuals internalize their ideas about right and wrong, good and bad, and invest them with strong feelings.

Why do values constitute an inevitable part of all human experience? That human potential is at odds with the requirements of social life is well known. Behavior within the realm of possibility is often outside the realm of necessity. There are numerous ways to resolve the conflict between what people *can do* by themselves, and what they *must do* as members of society. It is a popular notion that prisons and other correctional institutions are the primary means by which our society enforces conformity, but this is not the case. Socialization may be ineffective for a few who require such drastic action, but for the vast majority in any society, conformity results from the internalization of values. As we learn through imitation, identification, and instruction, values are internalized. They provide security and contribute to a sense of personal and social identity. For this reason, individuals in every society cling tenaciously to the values they have acquired and feel threatened when confronted with others who live according to different conceptions of what is desirable.

CULTURAL RELATIVISM

A misconception about values has been spawned by science and, in particular, by the anthropological doctrine of cultural relativism. Some have maintained that it is possible to separate values from facts, and since science is limited to facts, it is possible to do "value-free" research. By an exercise in mental gymnastics, the very scholars who admit the influence of values in the behavior of others sometimes deny it for themselves. Preferences operate whenever an individual must *select* one action from a multitude of possible courses. Anyone who decides to observe one thing and not another is making that decision on the basis of an implicit or explicit conception of desirability. Science is an activity that makes many value judgments — including which approaches to information gathering are the best. When biologists decide to examine the structure of the DNA molecule using an empirical approach, rather than a mystical, intuitive, or religious one, they are doing so with reference to their sense of what is desirable. Even the decision to study DNA rather than some other substance involves an exercise of values. When doing research on human behavior, the influence of one's values is undeniable. The "objective observer" who is detached from the subject matter, who refrains from allowing values to influence observations, is a myth. This fact does not suggest a retreat from the *quest for objectivity*. It does not mean that social scientists are free to disparage the customs encountered in other societies, or to impose their morals on those being studied. Skilled anthropologists are aware of their own values and then approach other cultures with tolerance and respect. They *identify* rather than *deny* the influence of their own viewpoints. They strive to achieve the ideal of value-free research but realize that it would be naive to assume such a goal possible.

Cultural relativism rests on the premise that it is possible to remain aloof and free from making value judgments. Put simply, this doctrine is based on four interrelated propositions.

1. Each person's value system is a result of his or her experience, i.e., it is learned.
2. The values that individuals learn differ from one society to another because of different learning experiences.
3. Values, therefore, are relative to the society in which they occur.
4. There are no universal values but we should respect the values of each of the world's cultures.

Cultural relativism has enabled the uninformed to understand what appears to be strange and immoral behavior. Although we may not believe it is good to kill infants, for example, we have found it intelligible in the context of a native Australian band. Although Americans generally believe in the desirability of monogamous marriage (or at least serial monogamy), we have found the practice of polygamy in other societies to be comprehensible when related to their cultures. This view presents numerous difficulties. Does one respect a society that believes it best to murder six million of its members who happen to be Jewish? How do anthropologists respect the values of a headhunting tribe when their own heads are at stake?

Moreover, all the statements in this doctrine of relativism are either based on implicit values (i.e., empiricism), or they are outright statements of desirability. The belief that it is good to *respect* the ideals of each of the world's cultures is itself a "relative" value. An extreme relativism is based on the philosophy that it is best to "let everyone do his or her own thing." Given unlimited resources and space this might have been possible, but in the modern world this philosophy represents a retreat from the realities facing us. It absolves the believer from the responsibility of finding some way to resolve conflicts among the world's different value systems. What is needed today is not a "live and let live" policy but a commitment to a higher, more inclusive, value system, and this requires changes that are extremely difficult to achieve.

CONFORMITY AND CONFLICT

Every social system is a moral order; shared values act as the mortar binding together the structure of each human community. Rewards and punishments are based on commonly held values; those persons achieving high status do so in terms of cultural rating systems. These values are expressed in symbolic ways — through food, clothing, wealth, language, behavior — all of which carry implicit messages about good and bad. The pervasiveness of values gives each person a sense of belonging, a sense of being a member of a community, the feeling of joining other human beings who share a commitment to the good life. But the moral nature of every culture has two sides — it facilitates adaptation and survival on the one hand, but it often generates conflict and destruction on the other. Let us examine each of these possibilities.

For almost a million years, people have successfully adapted to a variety of terrestrial environments. From the frozen tundra to the steaming jungle, people have built their homes, reared their children, performed their rituals, and buried their dead. In recent years we have escaped the thin layer of atmosphere surrounding the earth to live, if only for a few days, in outer space and beneath the ocean. All these achievements have been possible because of a unique endowment, our capacity for culture. Wherever people wandered, they developed patterns for organizing behavior, using natural resources, relating to others, and creating a meaningful life. A genetic inheritance did not channel behavior into specialized responses but instead provided a reservoir of plasticity that was shaped by values into one of the many ways to be human. Children in every society do not learn the entire range of potential human behavior — they are taught to *conform* to a very limited number of behavior patterns that are appropriate to a particular society. Human survival depends on cultural conformity, which requires that every individual become a specialist, be committed to a few values, and acquire knowledge and skills of a single society.

This very specialization has led to diversity, resulting in a myriad of contrasting cultures. This volume contains only a small sample of the different symbolic worlds created by people in their attempt to cope with the common problems of human existence. We will see how the generosity of the American Christmas spirit stands in contrast to the daily sharing among the Bushmen. Chicago suburbanites and natives of the Brazilian jungle both adorn their bodies with paint, clothing, and rings, but neither can comprehend how the other defines these symbols. All elements of human experience — kinship, marriage, age, race, sexuality, food, warfare — are socially defined and valued. The difficulty of moving from one cultural world to another is immense.

Cultural diversity has fascinated people for centuries. The study of strange and exotic peoples has attracted the curious for many generations. In the isolation of a remote jungle village or South Sea island, anthropologists found a natural laboratory for carrying out research. Their research reports often seemed more like novels than scientific studies and were read by both professionals and laymen; seldom did any reader feel threatened by the strange behavior of far-off "savages."

But isolation rapidly disappeared, sometimes by virtue of the anthropologists' intrusion! Exploration gave way to colonization, trade, and the massive troop movements of modern warfare. Today it is impossible to find groups of people who are isolated from the remainder of the world. Instead we have a conglomeration of cultures within a single nation, and often within a single city. Anthropologists need only walk down the street from the university to encounter those who have learned a culture unlike their own. Individuals with different language styles, sexual practices, religious rituals, and a host of other strange behavior patterns sit in their classrooms or play with their children on the urban playgrounds. Anthropology today is a science concerned with understanding how people can survive in a world where village, hamlet, city, and nation are all *multicultural*. In isolation, each value system was interesting. Crowded into close and intimate contact, these distinct culture patterns often lead to conflict, oppression, and warfare. Barbara Ward has eloquently summed up our situation:

In the last few decades, mankind has been overcome by the most change in its entire history. Modern science and techology have created so close a network of communication, transport, economic interdependence — and potential nuclear destruction — that planet earth, on its journey through infinity, has acquired the intimacy, the fellowship, and the vulnerability of a spaceship.[1]

In a sense, our greatest resource for adapting to different environments — the capacity to create different cultures — has become the source of greatest danger. Diversity is required for survival in the ecological niches of earth, but it can be destructive when all people suddenly find themselves in the same niche. Numerous species have become extinct because of their inability to adapt to a changing *natural* environment. Culture was the survival kit that enabled us to meet fluctuating natural conditions with flexibility, but now we are faced with a radically altered *human* environment. Successful adaptation will require changes that fly in the face of thousands of years of cultural specialization. Our ingenuity has been used to develop unique cultures, but thus far we have failed to develop satisfactory patterns and rules for articulating these differences. Can we survive in a world where our neighbors and even our children have different cultures? Can we adapt to the close, intimate fellowship of a spaceship when each group of passengers lives by different values?

TOWARD A MULTICULTURAL SOCIETY

What is required? In the first place, instead of suppressing cultural diversity by stressing assmilation into the mainstream of American life, we must recognize the extent to which our culture is pluralistic. We must accept the fact that groups within our society are committed to disparate and sometimes conflicting values. The second requirement for a truly multicultural society is that we continuously examine the *consequences* of each value system. What is the long-range effect of our commitment to a "gospel of growth"? What are the results of a belief in male superiority? How do our values of privacy affect those without homes? What is the consequence for minority groups when all students are taught to use "standard English"? As we study American culture we must discover the effect of our dominant values on every sector of life. The ideals that have made this country what it is have also been destructive to some citizens. In our efforts to assimilate ethnic groups, we have destroyed their pride and self-identity. In our attempt to offer the advantages of education to American Indians, we have induced them to become failures because our schools are not able to educate for di-

[1] Barbara Ward, *Spaceship Earth* (New York: Columbia University Press, 1966), p. vii.

versity. In order to demonstrate the tolerance built into American values, we have created the "culturally deprived," but the sophistication of labels does not conceal our prejudice. The absence of men in the families of the urban poor is a logical consequence of welfare institutions created from a single value system. The consumer suffers from dangerous products because in our culture productive enterprise is more important than consumer protection. We have only begun to understand some of the consequences of our values, and during the next few decades our survival will demand that the study of values be given top priority.

Finally, the most difficult task for the contemporary world is to induce people to relinquish those values with destructive consequences. This will not be simple, and it probably will not occur without a better understanding of the nature and the function of the world's many value systems. People's capacity to learn has not yet reached its full potential. In every society, children learn to shift from *egocentric* behavior to *ethnocentric* behavior. In deference to desirable community standards, individuals give up those things they desire, and life in a particular society becomes secure and meaningful, with conventional values acting as warp and woof of social interaction.

Can we now learn to shift from *ethnocentric* to *homocentric* behavior? Can we relinquish values desirable from the standpoint of a single community but destructive to the wider world? This change will require a system of ideals greater than the conventions of any localized culture. The change will necessitate a morality that can articulate conflicting value systems and create a climate of tolerance, respect, and cooperation. Only then can we begin to create a culture that will be truly adaptive in today's world.

II

Culture and fieldwork

Culture is learned. At the moment of birth, the human being lacks a culture — a system of beliefs, knowledge, patterns of customary behavior. But from that moment until we die, each of us participates in a kind of universal schooling that teaches us our native culture. Laughing and smiling are genetic responses, but the infant soon learns when to smile, when to laugh, and even how to laugh. Crying is an inborn behavior, but every infant soon learns the rules for crying in a particular culture.

During the first few years of life, cultural learning proceeds at an intense and rapid rate. Informally, without thinking about it, children in every society learn their native language, kinship terms, family structure, how and when to eat, etiquette for everyday life, what goals are worth achieving, and hundreds of other things. Culture is a kind of social heredity: passed on from one generation to the next, it is acquired through learning.

The customs we acquire as members of a society have a curious effect on us. Though we find them difficult to learn, with practice we conform and eventually we come to feel that these customs are right and natural. In time, the explicit rules for customary behavior fade from awareness. Most people are not conscious of the culture that guides their behavior. Conformity is effortless; it feels comfortable and secure. For example, each of us speaks a native language fluently, yet we are usually unable to state the rules of its grammar. Similarly, people abide by the rest of their culture with confidence, yet they lack a knowledge of its structure. We say then that culture has a tacit, taken-for-granted quality.

It is no accident that anthropologists, interested in understanding culture, have sought out groups with very different life-styles. They have purposely chosen to study in these natural laboratories because they realize that conformity to their own culture acts as a blinder to the study of its patterns. Even the nonconformist rejects little — perhaps a few words, the prevalent style of clothing, the length of hair, or the spending patterns. But when compared with members of non-Western cultures, it is evident that even the most blatant nonconformist thinks, talks, and acts according to our cultural rules. Furthermore, those who withdraw from America's cultural mainstream in an attempt to achieve a radically different life-style only create a new kind of conformity within their special groups.

When people learn about another culture's way of life, its practices seem strange, curious, even bizarre. The first two articles in this section describe the experience of anthropologists who had intense personal encounters with cross-cultural misunderstanding. It is only as we take on the native's point of view and enter into another culture that we begin to make sense of what once appeared strange. Misunderstanding is an inevitable consequence of cultural differences, and leads to bewilderment, anxiety, and sometimes despair — a condition called *culture shock*. But this shock of recognition can also produce insight into a universal phenomenon — conformity to culture. As anthropologists increase their study of complex societies, they should be reminded of the lessons they learned by studying cultures that differ radically from their own.

To understand and describe an alien culture, anthropologists engage in fieldwork. Because culture is so all-inclusive, because it involves every area of life, anthropologists seek to immerse themselves in the culture they want to study. Fieldwork means living with people, eating their food, learning their language, listening to gossip, watching them discipline children, and seeing them work in traditional occupations. The researchers make observations, record interviews, and chart genealogies. All these activities can be done with detachment and scientific objectivity — but a gap will remain in the researchers' data. Anthropologists identify with, participate in, and imaginatively enter into the lives of those studied. To achieve an understanding of experience from the natives' point of view, to see life from the perspective of another culture, anthropologists themselves become a kind of research instrument. The essence of fieldwork is immersion in an alien way of life, as insider yet outsider, as stranger yet friend.

Anthropologists employ many strategies during field research to understand another culture better. But all strategies and all research ultimately rest on the cooperation of informants. An informant is neither a subject in a scientific experiment nor a respondent who answers the investigator's questions. An informant is a teacher who has a special kind of pupil — a professional anthropologist. In this unique relationship a transformation occurs in the anthropologist's understanding of an alien culture. It is the informant who transforms the anthropologist from a tourist into an ethnographer. The informant may be a child who explains how to play hopscotch, a cocktail waitress who teaches the anthropologist to serve drinks and to encourage customers to leave tips, an elderly man who teaches the anthropologist to build an igloo, or a grandmother who explains the intricacies of Zapotec kinship. Almost any individual who has acquired a repertoire of cultural behavior can become an informant.

Because fieldwork requires involvement in the lives of people, because it depends on intimate personal relationships, it always raises important ethical issues. Informants often confide personal matters to the anthropologist. And the anthropologist may acquire information that could bring harm to those studied if outsiders learned of it. What is the anthropologist's responsibility to informants? How much should the anthropologist tell the people about the purposes of the study? What if the anthropologist discovers illegal activities? What if military authorities ask the anthropologist for information about population size or political leadership in the village? When publishing reports, should the anthropologist keep the name of the village and the names of informants anonymous? These are only some of the ethical issues involved in carrying out a fieldwork project.

Eating Christmas in the Kalahari

RICHARD BORSHAY LEE

*What happens when an anthropologist living among the bushmen of
Africa decides to be generous and to share a large animal with
everyone at Christmastime? This compelling account of the
misunderstanding and confusion that resulted takes the reader deeper
into the nature of culture. Richard Lee carefully traces how the
natives perceived his generosity and taught the anthropologist
something about his own culture.*

The !Kung Bushmen's knowledge of Christmas is thirdhand. The London Missionary Society brought the holiday to the southern Tswana tribes in the early nineteenth century. Later, native catechists spread the idea far and wide among the Bantu-speaking pastoralists, even in the remotest corners of the Kalahari Desert. The Bushmen's idea of the Christmas story, stripped to its essentials, is "praise the birth of white man's god-chief"; what keeps their interest in the holiday high is the Tswana-Herero custom of slaughtering an ox for his Bushmen neighbors as an annual goodwill gesture. Since the 1930's, part of the Bushmen's annual round of activities has included a December congregation at the cattle posts for trading, marriage brokering, and several days of trance-dance feasting at which the local Tswana headman is host.

As a social anthropologist working with !Kung Bushmen, I found that the Christmas ox custom suited my purposes. I had come to the Kalahari to study the hunting and gathering subsistence economy of the !Kung, and to accomplish this it was essential not to provide them with food, share my own food, or interfere in any way with their food-

Originally published as "A Naturalist at Large: Eating Christmas in the Kalahari." With permission from *Natural History*, Vol. 78, No. 10; Copyright the American Museum of Natural History, 1969.

gathering activities. While liberal handouts of tobacco and medical supplies were appreciated, they were scarcely adequate to erase the glaring disparity in wealth between the anthropologist, who maintained a two-month inventory of canned goods, and the Bushmen, who rarely had a day's supply of food on hand. My approach, while paying off in terms of data, left me open to frequent accusations of stinginess and hard-heartedness. By their lights, I was a miser.

The Christmas ox was to be my way of saying thank you for the cooperation of the past year; and since it was to be our last Christmas in the field, I determined to slaughter the largest, meatiest ox that money could buy, insuring that the feast and trance dance would be a success.

Through December I kept my eyes open at the wells as the cattle were brought down for watering. Several animals were offered, but none had quite the grossness that I had in mind. Then, ten days before the holiday, a Herero friend led an ox of astonishing size and mass up to our camp. It was solid black, stood five feet high at the shoulder, had a five-foot span of horns, and must have weighed 1,200 pounds on the hoof. Food consumption calculations are my specialty, and I quickly figured that bones and viscera aside, there was enough meat — at least four pounds — for every man, woman, and child of the 150 Bushmen in the vicinity of /ai/ai who were expected at the feast.

Having found the right animal at last, I paid the Herero £20 ($56) and asked him to keep the beast with his herd until Christmas day. The next morning word spread among the people that the big solid black one was the ox chosen by /ontah (my Bushman name; it means, roughly, "whitey") for the Christmas feast. That afternoon I received the first delegation. Ben!a, an outspoken sixty-year-old mother of five, came to the point slowly.

"Where were you planning to eat Christmas?"

"Right here at /ai/ai," I replied.

"Alone or with others?"

"I expect to invite all the people to eat Christmas with me."

"Eat what?"

"I have purchased Yehave's black ox, and I am going to slaughter and cook it."

"That's what we were told at the well but refused to believe it until we heard it from yourself."

"Well, it's the black one," I replied expansively, although wondering what she was driving at.

"Oh, no!" Ben!a groaned, turning to her group. "They were right." Turning back to me she asked, "Do you expect us to eat that bag of bones?"

"Bag of bones! It's the biggest ox at /ai/ai."

"Big, yes, but old. And thin. Everybody knows there's no meat on that old ox. What did you expect us to eat off it, the horns?"

Everybody chuckled at Ben!a's one-liner as they walked away, but all I could manage was a weak grin.

That evening it was the turn of the young men. They came to sit at our evening fire. /gaugo, about my age, spoke to me man-to-man.

"/ontah, you have always been square with us," he lied. "What has happened to change your heart? That sack of guts and bones of Yehave's will hardly feed one camp, let alone all the Bushmen around /ai/ai." And he proceeded to enumerate the seven camps in the /ai/ai vicinity, family by family. "Perhaps you have forgotten that we are not few, but many. Or are you too blind to tell the difference between a proper cow and an old wreck? That ox is thin to the point of death."

"Look, you guys," I retorted, "that is a beautiful animal, and I'm sure you will eat it with pleasure at Christmas."

"Of course we will eat it; it's food. But it won't fill us up to the point where we will have enough strength to dance. We will eat and go home to bed with stomachs rumbling."

That night as we turned in, I asked my wife, Nancy: "What did you think of the black ox?"

"It looked enormous to me. Why?"

"Well, about eight different people have told me I got gypped; that the ox is nothing but bones."

"What's the angle?" Nancy asked. "Did they have a better one to sell?"

"No, they just said that it was going to be a grim Christmas because there won't be enough meat to go around. Maybe I'll get an independent judge to look at the beast in the morning."

Bright and early, Halingisi, a Tswana cattle owner, appeared at our camp. But before I could ask him to give me his opinion on Yehave's black ox, he gave me the eye signal that indicated a confidential chat. We left the camp and sat down.

"/ontah, I'm surprised at you: you've lived here for three years and still haven't learned anything about cattle."

"But what else can a person do but choose the biggest, strongest animal one can find?" I retorted.

"Look, just because an animal is big doesn't mean that it has plenty of meat on it. The black one was a beauty when it was younger, but now it is thin to the point of death."

"Well I've already bought it. What can I do at this stage?"

"Bought it already? I thought you were just considering it. Well, you'll have to kill it and serve it, I suppose. But don't expect much of a dance to follow."

My spirits dropped rapidly. I could believe that Ben!a and /gaugo just might be putting me on about the black ox, but Halingisi seemed to be an impartial critic. I went around that day feeling as though I had bought a lemon of a used car.

In the afternoon it was Tomazo's turn. Tomazo is a fine hunter, a top trance performer . . . and one of my most reliable informants. He approached the subject of the Christmas cow as part of my continuing Bushman education.

"My friend, the way it is with us Bushmen," he began, "is that we love meat. And even more than that, we love fat. When we hunt we always search for the fat ones, the ones dripping with layers of white fat: fat that turns into a clear, thick oil in the cooking pot, fat that slides down your gullet, fills your stomach and gives you a roaring diarrhea," he rhapsodized.

"So, feeling as we do," he continued, "it gives us pain to be served such a scrawny thing as Yehave's black ox. It is big, yes, and no doubt its giant bones are good for soup, but fat is what we really crave and so we will eat Christmas this year with a heavy heart."

The prospect of a gloomy Christmas now had me worried, so I asked Tomazo what I could do about it.

"Look for a fat one, a young one . . . smaller, but fat. Fat enough to make us //gom ('evacuate the bowels'), then we will be happy."

My suspicions were aroused when Tomazo said that he happened to know of a young, fat, barren cow that the owner was willing to part with. Was Tomazo working on commission, I wondered? But I dispelled this unworthy thought when we approached the Herero owner of the cow in question and found that he had decided not to sell.

The scrawny wreck of a Christmas ox now became the talk of the /ai/ai water hole and was the first news told to the outlying groups as they began to come in from the bush for the feast. What finally convinced me that real trouble might be brewing was the visit from u!au, an old conservative with a reputation for fierceness. His nickname meant spear and referred to an incident thirty years ago in which he had speared a man to death. He had an intense manner; fixing me with his eyes, he said in clipped tones:

"I have only just heard about the black ox today, or else I would have come here earlier. /ontah, do you honestly think you can serve meat like that to people and avoid a fight?" He paused, letting the implications sink in. "I don't mean fight you, /ontah; you are a white man. I mean a fight between Bushmen. There are many fierce ones here, and with such a small quantity of meat to distribute, how can you give everybody a fair share? Someone is sure to accuse another of taking too much or hogging all the choice pieces. Then you will see what happens when some go hungry while others eat."

The possibility of at least a serious argument struck me as all too real. I had witnessed the tension that surrounds the distribution of meat from a kudu or gemsbok kill, and had documented many arguments that sprang up from a real or imagined slight in meat distribution. The owners of a kill may spend up to two hours arranging and rearranging the piles of meat under the gaze of a circle of recipients before handing them out. And I also knew that the Christmas feast at /ai/ai would be bringing together groups that had feuded in the past.

Convinced now of the gravity of the situation, I went in earnest to search for a second cow; but all my inquiries failed to turn one up.

The Christmas feast was evidently going to be a disaster, and the incessant complaints about the meagerness of the ox had already taken the fun out of it for me. Moreover, I was getting bored with the wisecracks, and after losing my temper a few times, I resolved to serve the beast anyway. If the meat fell short, the hell with it. In the Bushmen idiom, I announced to all who would listen:

"I am a poor man and blind. If I have chosen one that is too old and too thin, we will eat it anyway and see if there is enough meat there to quiet the rumbling of our stomachs."

On hearing this speech, Ben!a offered me a rare word of comfort. "It's thin," she said philosophically, "but the bones will make a good soup."

At dawn Christmas morning, instinct told me to turn over the butchering and cooking to a friend and take off with Nancy to spend Christmas alone in the bush. But curiosity kept me from retreating. I wanted to see what such a scrawny ox looked like on butchering, and if there *was* going to be a fight, I wanted to catch every word of it. Anthropologists are incurable that way.

The great beast was driven up to our dancing ground, and a shot in the forehead dropped it in its tracks. Then, freshly cut branches were heaped around the fallen carcass to receive the meat. Ten men volunteered to help with the cutting. I asked /gaugo to make the breast bone cut. This cut, which begins the butchering process for most large game, offers easy access for removal of the viscera. But it also allows the hunter to spot-check the amount of fat on the animal. A fat game animal carries a white layer up to an inch thick on the chest, while in a thin one, the knife will quickly cut to bone. All eyes fixed on his hand as /gaugo, dwarfed by the great carcass, knelt to the breast. The first cut opened a pool of solid white in the black skin. The second and third cut widened and deepened the creamy white. Still no bone. It was pure fat; it must have been two inches thick.

"Hey /gau," I burst out, "that ox is loaded with fat. What's this about the ox being too thin to bother eating? Are you out of your mind?"

"Fat?" /gau shot back, "You call that fat? This wreck is thin, sick, dead!" And he broke out laughing. So did everyone else. They rolled on the ground, paralyzed with laughter. Everybody laughed except me; I was thinking.

I ran back to the tent and burst in just as Nancy was getting up. "Hey, the black ox. It's fat as hell! They were kidding about it being too thin to eat. It was a joke or something. A put-on. Everyone is really delighted with it!"

"Some joke," my wife replied. "It was so funny that you were ready to pack up and leave /ai/ai."

If it had indeed been a joke, it had been an extraordinarily convincing one, and tinged, I thought, with more than a touch of malice as many jokes are. Nevertheless, that it was a joke lifted my spirits considerably, and I returned to the butchering site where the shape of the ox was rapidly disappearing under the axes and knives of the butchers. The atmosphere had become festive. Grinning broadly, their arms covered with blood well past the elbow, men packed chunks of meat into the big cast-iron cooking pots, fifty pounds to the load, and muttered and chuckled all the while about the thinness and worthlessness of the animal and /ontah's poor judgment.

We danced and ate that ox two days and two nights; we cooked and distributed fourteen potfuls of meat and no one went home hungry and no fights broke out.

But the "joke" stayed in my mind. I had a growing feeling that something important had happened in my relationship with the Bushmen and that the clue lay in the meaning of the joke. Several days later, when most of the people had dispersed back to the bush camps, I raised the question with Hakekgose, a Tswana man who had grown up among the !Kung, married a !Kung girl, and who probably knew their culture better than any other non-Bushman.

"With us whites," I began, "Christmas is supposed to be the day of friendship and brotherly love. What I can't figure out is why the Bushmen went to such lengths to criticize and belittle the ox I had bought for the feast. The animal was perfectly good and their jokes and wisecracks practically ruined the holiday for me."

"So it really did bother you," said Hakekgose. "Well, that's the way they always talk. When I take my rifle and go hunting with them, if I miss, they laugh at me for the rest of the day. But even if I hit and bring one down, it's no better. To them, the kill is always too small or too old or too thin; and as we sit down on the kill site to cook and eat the liver, they keep grumbling, even with their mouths full of meat. They say things like, 'Oh this is awful! What a worthless animal! Whatever made me think that this Tswana rascal could hunt!' "

"Is this the way outsiders are treated?" I asked.

"No, it is their custom; they talk that way to each other too. Go and ask them."

/gaugo had been one of the most enthusiastic in making me feel bad about the merit of the Christmas ox. I sought him out first.

"Why did you tell me the black ox was worthless, when you could see that it was loaded with fat and meat?"

"It is our way," he said smiling. "We always like to fool people about that. Say there is a Bushman who has been hunting. He must not come home and announce like a braggard, 'I have killed a big one in the bush!' He must first sit down in silence until I or someone else comes up to his fire and asks, 'What did you see today?' He replies quietly, 'Ah, I'm no good for hunting. I saw nothing at all [pause] just a little tiny one.' Then I smile to myself," /gaugo continued, "because I know he has killed something big.

"In the morning we make up a party of four or five people to cut up and carry the meat back to the camp. When we arrive at the kill we examine it and cry out, 'You mean to say you have dragged us all the way out here in order to make us cart home your pile of bones? Oh, if I had known it was this thin I wouldn't have come.' Another one pipes up, 'People, to think I gave up a nice day in the shade for this. At home we may be hungry but at least we have nice cool water to drink.' If the horns are big, someone says, 'Did you think that somehow you were going to boil down the horns for soup?'

"To all this you must respond in kind. 'I agree,' you say, 'this one is not worth the effort; let's just cook the liver for strength and leave the rest for the hyenas. It is not too late to hunt today and even a duiker or a steenbok would be better than this mess.'

"Then you set to work nevertheless; butcher the animal, carry the meat back to the camp and everyone eats," /gaugo concluded.

Things were beginning to make sense. Next, I went to Tomazo. He corroborated /gaugo's story of the obligatory insults over a kill and added a few details of his own.

"But," I asked, "why insult a man after he has gone to all that trouble to track and kill an animal and when he is going to share the meat with you so that your children will have something to eat?"

"Arrogance," was his cryptic answer.

"Arrogance?"

"Yes, when a young man kills much meat he comes to think of

himself as a chief or a big man, and he thinks of the rest of us as his servants or inferiors. We can't accept this. We refuse one who boasts, for someday his pride will make him kill somebody. So we always speak of his meat as worthless. This way we cool his heart and make him gentle."

"But why didn't you tell me this before?" I asked Tomazo with some heat.

"Because you never asked me," said Tomazo, echoing the refrain that has come to haunt every field ethnographer.

The pieces now fell into place. I had known for a long time that in situations of social conflict with Bushmen I held all the cards. I was the only source of tobacco in a thousand square miles, and I was not incapable of cutting an individual off for noncooperation. Though my boycott never lasted longer than a few days, it was an indication of my strength. People resented my presence at the water hole, yet simultaneously dreaded my leaving. In short I was a perfect target for the charge of arrogance and for the Bushmen tactic of enforcing humility.

I had been taught an object lesson by the Bushmen; it had come from an unexpected corner and had hurt me in a vulnerable area. For the big black ox was to be the one totally generous, unstinting act of my year at /ai/ai and I was quite unprepared for the reaction I received.

As I read it, their message was this: There are no totally generous acts. All "acts" have an element of calculation. One black ox slaughtered at Christmas does not wipe out a year of careful manipulation of gifts given to serve your own ends. After all, to kill an animal and share the meat with people is really no more than Bushmen do for each other every day and with far less fanfare.

In the end, I had to admire how the Bushmen had played out the farce — collectively straight-faced to the end. Curiously, the episode reminded me of the *Good Soldier Schweik* and his marvelous encounters with authority. Like Schweik, the Bushmen had retained a thoroughgoing skepticism of good intentions. Was it this independence of spirit, I wondered, that had kept them culturally viable in the face of generations of contact with more powerful societies, both black and white? The thought that the Bushmen were alive and well in the Kalahari was strangely comforting. Perhaps, armed with that independence and with their superb knowledge of their environment, they might yet survive the future.

2

Shakespeare in the bush

LAURA BOHANNAN

*Cultural anthropologists are all concerned with meaning, with the
difficult task of translation from one language to another. In this
classic of anthropology, Laura Bohannan shows the difficulty of
translating the meaning of* Hamlet *to the Tiv in West Africa. She
forcefully demonstrates the way in which different cultures provide
distinct and separate worlds of meaning for those who have learned
to live by them.*

Just before I left Oxford for the Tiv in West Africa, conversation turned
to the season at Stratford. "You Americans," said a friend, "often have
difficulty with Shakespeare. He was, after all, a very English poet, and
one can easily misinterpret the universal by misunderstanding the particular."

I protested that human nature is pretty much the same the whole
world over; at least the general plot and motivation of the greater trag-
edies would always be clear — everywhere — although some details of
custom might have to be explained and difficulties of translation might
produce other slight changes. To end an argument we could not conclude, my friend gave me a copy of *Hamlet* to study in the African bush:
it would, he hoped, lift my mind above its primitive surroundings, and
possibly I might, by prolonged meditation, achieve the grace of correct
interpretation.

It was my second field trip to that African tribe, and I thought
myself ready to live in one of its remote sections — an area difficult to
cross even on foot. I eventually settled on the hillock of a very knowledgeable old man, the head of a homestead of some hundred and forty
people, all of whom were either his close relatives or their wives and

children. Like the other elders of the vicinity, the old man spent most of his time performing ceremonies seldom seen these days in the more accessible parts of the tribe. I was delighted. Soon there would be three months of enforced isolation and leisure, between the harvest that takes place just before the rising of the swamps and the clearing of new farms when the water goes down. Then, I thought, they would have even more time to perform ceremonies and explain them to me.

I was quite mistaken. Most of the ceremonies demanded the presence of elders from several homesteads. As the swamps rose, the old men found it too difficult to walk from one homestead to the next, and the ceremonies gradually ceased. As the swamps rose even higher, all activities but one came to an end. The women brewed beer from maize and millet. Men, women, and children sat on their hillocks and drank it.

People began to drink at dawn. By midmorning the whole homestead was singing, dancing, and drumming. When it rained, people had to sit inside their huts: there they drank and sang or they drank and told stories. In any case, by noon or before, I either had to join the party or retire to my own hut and my books. "One does not discuss serious matters when there is beer. Come, drink with us." Since I lacked their capacity for the thick native beer, I spent more and more time with *Hamlet*. Before the end of the second month, grace descended on me. I was quite sure that *Hamlet* had only one possible interpretation, and that one universally obvious.

Early every morning, in the hope of having some serious talk before the beer party, I used to call on the old man at his reception hut — a circle of posts supporting a thatched roof above a low mud wall to keep out wind and rain. One day I crawled through the low doorway and found most of the men of the homestead sitting huddled in their ragged cloths on stools, low plank beds, and reclining chairs, warming themselves against the chill of the rain around a smoky fire. In the center were three pots of beer. The party had started.

The old man greeted me cordially. "Sit down and drink." I accepted a large calabash full of beer, poured some into a small drinking gourd, and tossed it down. Then I poured some more into the same gourd for the man second in seniority to my host before I handed my calabash over to a young man for further distribution. Important people shouldn't ladle beer themselves.

"It is better like this," the old man said, looking at me approvingly and plucking at the thatch that had caught in my hair. "You should sit and drink with us more often. Your servants tell me that when you are not with us, you sit inside your hut looking at a paper."

The old man was acquainted with four kinds of "papers": tax

receipts, bride price receipts, court fee receipts, and letters. The messenger who brought him letters from the chief used them mainly as a badge of office, for he always knew what was in them and told the old man. Personal letters for the few who had relatives in the government or mission stations were kept until someone went to a large market where there was a letter writer and reader. Since my arrival, letters were brought to me to be read. A few men also brought me bride price receipts, privately, with requests to change the figures to a higher sum. I found moral arguments were of no avail, since in-laws are fair game, and the technical hazards of forgery difficult to explain to an illiterate people. I did not wish them to think me silly enough to look at any such papers for days on end, and I hastily explained that my "paper" was one of the "things of long ago" of my country.

"Ah," said the old man. "Tell us."

I protested that I was not a storyteller. Storytelling is a skilled art among them; their standards are high, and the audiences critical — and vocal in their criticism. I protested in vain. This morning they wanted to hear a story while they drank. They threatened to tell me no more stories until I told them one of mine. Finally, the old man promised that no one would criticize my style "for we know you are struggling with our language." "But," put in one of the elders, "you must explain what we do not understand, as we do when we tell you our stories." Realizing that here was my chance to prove *Hamlet* universally intelligible, I agreed.

The old man handed me some more beer to help me on with my storytelling. Men filled their long wooden pipes and knocked coals from the fire to place in the pipe bowls; then, puffing contentedly, they sat back to listen. I began in the proper style, "Not yesterday, not yesterday, but long ago, a thing occurred. One night three men were keeping watch outside the homestead of the great chief, when suddenly they saw the former chief approach them."

"Why was he no longer their chief?"

"He was dead," I explained. "That is why they were troubled and afraid when they saw him."

"Impossible," began one of the elders, handing his pipe on to his neighbor, who interrupted, "Of course it wasn't the dead chief. It was an omen sent by a witch. Go on."

Slightly shaken, I continued. "One of these three was a man who knew things" — the closest translation for scholar, but unfortunately it also meant witch. The second elder looked triumphantly at the first. "So he spoke to the dead chief saying, 'Tell us what we must do so you may rest in your grave,' but the dead chief did not answer. He vanished, and they could see him no more. Then the man who knew things —

his name was Horatio — said this event was the affair of the dead chief's son, Hamlet."

There was a general shaking of heads round the circle. "Had the dead chief no living brothers? Or was this son the chief?"

"No," I replied. "That is, he had one living brother who became the chief when the elder brother died."

The old men muttered: such omens were matters for chiefs and elders, not for youngsters; no good could come of going behind a chief's back; clearly Horatio was not a man who knew things.

"Yes, he was," I insisted, shooing a chicken away from my beer. "In our country the son is next to the father. The dead chief's younger brother had become the great chief. He had also married his elder brother's widow only about a month after the funeral."

"He did well," the old man beamed and announced to the others, "I told you that if we knew more about Europeans, we would find they really were very like us. In our country also," he added to me, "the younger brother marries the elder brother's widow and becomes the father of his children. Now, if your uncle, who married your widowed mother, is your father's full brother, then he will be a real father to you. Did Hamlet's father and uncle have one mother?"

His question barely penetrated my mind; I was too upset and thrown too far off balance by having one of the most important elements of *Hamlet* knocked straight out of the picture. Rather uncertainly I said that I thought they had the same mother, but I wasn't sure — the story didn't say. The old man told me severely that these genealogical details made all the difference and that when I got home I must ask the elders about it. He shouted out the door to one of his younger wives to bring his goatskin bag.

Determined to save what I could of the mother motif, I took a deep breath and began again. "The son Hamlet was very sad because his mother had married again so quickly. There was no need for her to do so, and it is our custom for a widow not to go to her next husband until she has mourned for two years."

"Two years is too long," objected the wife, who had appeared with the old man's battered goatskin bag. "Who will hoe your farms for you while you have no husband?"

"Hamlet," I retorted without thinking, "was old enough to hoe his mother's farms himself. There was no need for her to remarry." No one looked convinced. I gave up. "His mother and the great chief told Hamlet not to be sad, for the great chief himself would be a father to

Hamlet. Furthermore, Hamlet would be the next chief: therefore he must stay to learn the things of a chief. Hamlet agreed to remain, and all the rest went off to drink beer."

While I paused, perplexed at how to render Hamlet's disgusted soliloquy to an audience convinced that Claudius and Gertrude had behaved in the best possible manner, one of the younger men asked me who had married the other wives of the dead chief.

"He had no other wives," I told him.

"But a chief must have many wives! How else can he brew beer and prepare food for all his guests?"

I said firmly that in our country even chiefs had only one wife, that they had servants to do their work, and that they paid them from tax money.

It was better, they returned, for a chief to have many wives and sons who would help him hoe his farms and feed his people; then everyone loved the chief who gave much and took nothing — taxes were a bad thing.

I agreed with the last comment, but for the rest fell back on their favorite way of fobbing off my questions: "That is the way it is done, so that is how we do it."

I decided to skip the soliloquy. Even if Claudius was here thought quite right to marry his brother's widow, there remained the poison motif, and I knew they would disapprove of fratricide. More hopefully I resumed, "That night Hamlet kept watch with the three who had seen his dead father. The dead chief again appeared, and although the others were afraid, Hamlet followed his dead father off to one side. When they were alone, Hamlet's dead father spoke."

"Omens can't talk!" The old man was emphatic.

"Hamlet's dead father wasn't an omen. Seeing him might have been an omen, but he was not." My audience looked as confused as I sounded. "It *was* Hamlet's dead father. It was a thing we call a 'ghost.' " I had to use the English word, for unlike many of the neighboring tribes, these people didn't believe in the survival after death of any individuating part of the personality.

"What is a 'ghost?' An omen?"

"No, a 'ghost' is someone who is dead but who walks around and can talk, and people can hear him and see him but not touch him."

They objected. "One can touch zombis."

"No, no! It was not a dead body the witches had animated to sacrifice and eat. No one else made Hamlet's dead father walk. He did it himself."

"Dead men can't walk," protested my audience as one man.

I was quite willing to compromise. "A 'ghost' is the dead man's shadow."

But again they objected. "Dead men cast no shadows."

"They do in my country," I snapped.

The old man quelled the babble of disbelief that arose immediately and told me with that insincere, but courteous, agreement one extends to the fancies of the young, ignorant, and superstitious, "No doubt in your country the dead can also walk without being zombis." From the depths of his bag he produced a withered fragment of kola nut, bit off one end to show it wasn't poisoned, and handed me the rest as a peace offering.

"Anyhow," I resumed, "Hamlet's dead father said that his own brother, the one who became chief, had poisoned him. He wanted Hamlet to avenge him. Hamlet believed this in his heart, for he did not like his father's brother." I took another swallow of beer. "In the country of the great chief, living in the same homestead, for it was a very large one, was an important elder who was often with the chief to advise and help him. His name was Polonius. Hamlet was courting his daughter, but her father and her brother . . . [I cast hastily about for some tribal analogy] warned her not to let Hamlet visit her when she was alone on her farm, for he would be a great chief and so could not marry her."

"Why not?" asked the wife, who had settled down on the edge of the old man's chair. He frowned at her for asking stupid questions and growled, "They lived in the same homestead."

"That was not the reason," I informed them. "Polonius was a stranger who lived in the homestead because he helped the chief, not because he was a relative."

"Then why couldn't Hamlet marry her?"

"He could have," I explained, "but Polonius didn't think he would. After all, Hamlet was a man of great importance who ought to marry a chief's daughter, for in his country a man could have only one wife. Polonius was afraid that if Hamlet made love to his daughter, then no one else would give a high price for her."

"That might be true," remarked one of the shrewder elders, "but a chief's son would give his mistress's father enough presents and patronage to more than make up the difference. Polonius sounds like a fool to me."

"Many people think he was," I agreed. "Meanwhile Polonius sent his son Laertes off to Paris to learn the things of that country, for it was the homestead of a very great chief indeed. Because he was afraid that Laertes might waste a lot of money on beer and women and gambling, or get into trouble by fighting, he sent one of his servants to Paris secretly, to spy out what Laertes was doing. One day Hamlet came upon Polonius's daughter Ophelia. He behaved so oddly he frightened her. Indeed" — I was fumbling for words to express the dubious quality of Hamlet's madness — "the chief and many others had also noticed that when Hamlet talked one could understand the words but not what they meant. Many people thought that he had become mad." My audience suddenly became much more attentive. "The great chief wanted to know what was wrong with Hamlet, so he sent for two of Hamlet's age mates [school friends would have taken long explanation] to talk to Hamlet and find out what troubled his heart. Hamlet, seeing that they had been bribed by the chief to betray him, told them nothing. Polonius, however, insisted that Hamlet was mad because he had been forbidden to see Ophelia, whom he loved."

"Why," inquired a bewildered voice, "should anyone bewitch Hamlet on that account?"

"Bewitch him?"

"Yes, only witchcraft can make anyone mad, unless, of course, one sees the beings that lurk in the forest."

I stopped being a storyteller, took out my notebook and demanded to be told more about these two causes of madness. Even while they spoke and I jotted notes, I tried to calculate the effect of this new factor on the plot. Hamlet had not been exposed to the beings that lurk in the forest. Only his relatives in the male line could bewitch him. Barring relatives not mentioned by Shakespeare, it had to be Claudius who was attempting to harm him. And, of course, it was.

For the moment I staved off questions by saying that the great chief also refused to believe that Hamlet was mad for the love of Ophelia and nothing else. "He was sure that something much more important was troubling Hamlet's heart."

"Now Hamlet's age mates," I continued, "had brought with them a famous storyteller. Hamlet decided to have this man tell the chief and all his homestead a story about a man who had poisoned his brother because he desired his brother's wife and wished to be chief himself. Hamlet was sure the great chief could not hear the story without making a sign if he was indeed guilty, and then he would discover whether his dead father had told him the truth."

The old man interrupted, with deep cunning, "Why should a father lie to his son?" he asked.

I hedged: "Hamlet wasn't sure that it really was his dead father." It was impossible to say anything, in that language, about devil-inspired visions.

"You mean," he said, "it actually was an omen, and he knew

witches sometimes send false ones. Hamlet was a fool not to go to one skilled in reading omens and divining the truth in the first place. A man-who-sees-the-truth could have told him how his father died, if he really had been poisoned, and if there was witchcraft in it; then Hamlet could have called the elders to settle the matter."

The shrewd elder ventured to disagree. "Because his father's brother was a great chief, one-who-sees-the-truth might therefore have been afraid to tell it. I think it was for that reason that a friend of Hamlet's father — a witch and an elder — sent an omen so his friend's son would know. Was the omen true?"

"Yes," I said, abandoning ghosts and the devil; a witch-sent omen it would have to be. "It was true, for when the storyteller was telling his tale before all the homestead, the great chief rose in fear. Afraid that Hamlet knew his secret he planned to have him killed."

The stage set of the next bit presented some difficulties of translation. I began cautiously. "The great chief told Hamlet's mother to find out from her son what he knew. But because a woman's children are always first in her heart, he had the important elder Polonius hide behind a cloth that hung against the wall of Hamlet's mother's sleeping hut. Hamlet started to scold his mother for what she had done."

There was a shocked murmur from everyone. A man should never scold his mother.

"She called out in fear, and Polonius moved behind the cloth. Shouting, 'A rat!' Hamlet took his machete and slashed through the cloth." I paused for dramatic effect. "He had killed Polonius!"

The old men looked at each other in supreme disgust. "That Polonius truly was a fool and a man who knew nothing! What child would not know enough to shout, 'It's me!' " With a pang, I remembered that these people are ardent hunters, always armed with bow, arrow, and machete; at the first rustle in the grass an arrow is aimed and ready, and the hunter shouts "Game!" If no human voice answers immediately, the arrow speeds on its way. Like a good hunter Hamlet had shouted, "A rat!"

I rushed in to save Polonius's reputation. "Polonius did speak. Hamlet heard him. But he thought it was the chief and wished to kill him to avenge his father. He had meant to kill him earlier that evening . . . ." I broke down, unable to describe to these pagans, who had no belief in individual afterlife, the difference between dying at one's prayers and dying "unhousell'd, disappointed, unaneled."

This time I had shocked my audience seriously. "For a man to raise his hand against his father's brother and the one who has become his father — that is a terrible thing. The elders ought to let such a man be bewitched."

I nibbled at my kola nut in some perplexity, then pointed out that after all the man had killed Hamlet's father.

"No," pronounced the old man, speaking less to me than to the young men sitting behind the elders. "If your father's brother has killed your father, you must appeal to your father's age mates; *they* may avenge him. No man may use violence against his senior relatives." Another thought struck him. "But if his father's brother had indeed been wicked enough to bewitch Hamlet and make him mad that would be a good story indeed, for it would be his fault that Hamlet, being mad, no longer had any sense and thus was ready to kill his father's brother."

There was a murmur of applause. *Hamlet* was again a good story to them, but it no longer seemed quite the same story to me. As I thought over the coming complications of plot and motive, I lost courage and decided to skim over dangerous ground quickly.

"The great chief," I went on, "was not sorry that Hamlet had killed Polonius. It gave him a reason to send Hamlet away, with his two treacherous age mates, with letters to a chief of a far country, saying that Hamlet should be killed. But Hamlet changed the writing on their papers, so that the chief killed his age mates instead." I encountered a reproachful glare from one of the men whom I had told undetectable forgery was not merely immoral but beyond human skill. I looked the other way.

"Before Hamlet could return, Laertes came back for his father's funeral. The great chief told him Hamlet had killed Polonius. Laertes swore to kill Hamlet because of this, and because his sister Ophelia, hearing her father had been killed by the man she loved, went mad and drowned in the river."

"Have you already forgotten what we told you?" The old man was reproachful. "One cannot take vengeance on a madman; Hamlet killed Polonius in his madness. As for the girl, she not only went mad, she was drowned. Only witches can make people drown. Water itself can't hurt anything. It is merely something one drinks and bathes in."

I began to get cross. "If you don't like the story, I'll stop."

The old man made soothing noises and himself poured me some more beer. "You tell the story well, and we are listening. But it is clear that the elders of your country have never told you what the story really means. No, don't interrupt! We believe you when you say your marriage customs are different, or your clothes and weapons. But people are the same everywhere; therefore, there are always witches and it is we, the elders, who know how witches work. We told you it was the great chief who wished to kill Hamlet, and now your own words have proved us right. Who were Ophelia's male relatives?"

"There were only her father and her brother." Hamlet was clearly out of my hands.

"There must have been many more; this also you must ask of your elders when you get back to your country. From what you tell us, since Polonius was dead, it must have been Laertes who killed Ophelia, although I do not see the reason for it."

We had emptied one pot of beer, and the old men argued the point with slightly tipsy interest. Finally one of them demanded of me, "What did the servant of Polonius say on his return?"

With difficulty I recollected Reynaldo and his mission. "I don't think he did return before Polonius was killed."

"Listen," said the elder, "and I will tell you how it was and how your story will go, then you may tell me if I am right. Polonius knew his son would get into trouble, and so he did. He had many fines to pay for fighting, and debts from gambling. But he had only two ways of getting money quickly. One was to marry off his sister at once, but it is difficult to find a man who will marry a woman desired by the son of a chief. For if the chief's heir commits adultery with your wife, what can you do? Only a fool calls a case against a man who will someday be his judge. Therefore Laertes had to take the second way: he killed his sister by witchcraft, drowning her so he could secretly sell her body to the witches."

I raised an objection. "They found her body and buried it. Indeed Laertes jumped into the grave to see his sister once more — so, you see, the body was truly there. Hamlet, who had just come back, jumped in after him."

"What did I tell you?" The elder appealed to the others. "Laertes was up to no good with his sister's body. Hamlet prevented him, because the chief's heir, like a chief, does not wish any other man to grow rich and powerful. Laertes would be angry, because he would have killed his sister without benefit to himself. In our country he would try to kill Hamlet for that reason. Is this not what happened?"

"More or less," I admitted. "When the great chief found Hamlet was still alive, he encouraged Laertes to try to kill Hamlet and arranged a fight with machetes between them. In the fight both the young men were wounded to death. Hamlet's mother drank the poisoned beer that the chief meant for Hamlet in case he won the fight. When he saw his mother die of poison, Hamlet, dying, managed to kill his father's brother with his machete."

"You see, I was right!" exclaimed the elder.

"That was a very good story," added the old man, "and you told it with very few mistakes. There was just one more error, at the very end. The poison Hamlet's mother drank was obviously meant for the survivor of the fight, whichever it was. If Laertes had won, the great chief would have poisoned him, for no one would know that he arranged Hamlet's death. Then, too, he need not fear Laertes' witchcraft; it takes a strong heart to kill one's only sister by witchcraft.

"Sometime," concluded the old man, gathering his ragged toga about him, "you must tell us some more stories of your country. We, who are elders, will instruct you in their true meaning, so that when you return to your own land your elders will see that you have not been sitting in the bush, but among those who know things and who have taught you wisdom."

3

Kapluna daughter:
Adopted by the Eskimo

JEAN L. BRIGGS

*Initially, the anthropologist is a stranger, often a threatening one, to
the people she wants to live with and study. One step toward
gaining acceptance is achieved when the anthropologist assumes a
role defined as believable and nonthreatening in the eyes of the people
she wishes to study. Jean Briggs found acceptance in the form of
fictive kinship — by playing the role of daughter. Although playing
this role had its frustrations and limitations, it allowed for her
assimilation into the Eskimo community, and taught her aspects of
their culture which could be learned in no other way.*

"It's very cold down there — *very cold*. If I were going to be at Back
River this winter, I would like to adopt you and try to keep you alive."
My Eskimo visitor, Uunai, dramatized her words with shivers as
we sat drinking tea in the warm nursing station in Gjoa Haven. It was
only mid-August, but already the wind that intruded through the cracks
in the window frame was bitter, and the ground was white with a
dusting of new snow. Last winter's ice, great broken sheets of it, still
clogged the harbor, so that the plane I was waiting for was unable to
get through to us. I was on my way to spend a year and a half with the
Utkuhikhalingmiut, a small group of Eskimos who lived in Chantrey
Inlet at the mouth of the Back River on the northern rim of the American
continent. They were the most remote group of Eskimos that I could
find on the map of the Canadian Arctic, a people who in many ways
lived much as they had in the days before *kaplunas* (white men) appeared
in the north. They were nomadic; they lived in snowhouses in winter,

Reprinted from Peggy Golde, editor, *Women in the Field*; copyright © 1970 by Aldine
Publishing Company. Reprinted by permission of the author.

in tents in summer; and their diet consisted very largely of fish — trout
and whitefish — supplemented now and again by a few caribou.

Uunai's words presaged the most important influence on the course
of my life at Back River, namely my adoption as a "daughter" in the
household of an Utkuhikhalingmiut family. I want to describe an aspect
of that relationship here, with the aim of illustrating some of the difficulties that a host community or family may encounter in its hospitable
efforts to incorporate a foreigner.

I arrived in Chantrey Inlet at the end of August, 1963 on a plane
that the Canadian government sent in once a year to collect the three
or four schoolchildren who wished to go to Inuvik. I had with me letters
of introduction from the Anglican deacon and his wife in Gjoa Haven.
Nakliguhuktuq and Ikayuqtuq were Eskimos from the eastern Arctic
who served as missionaries not only to the Anglican Eskimos in Gjoa
Haven, but also to the Utkuhikhalingmiut. The letters — written in the
syllabic script in which the Utkuhikhalingmiut, like most other Canadian
Eskimos, are literate — noted that I would like to live with the Utkuhikhalingmiut for a year or so, learning the Eskimo language and skills:
how to scrape skins and sew them, how to catch fish and preserve them
or boil the oil out of them for use in lighting and heating the winter
iglus. They asked the Eskimos to help me with words and fish and
promised that in return I would help them with tea and kerosene. They
told the people that I was kind and that they should not be shy and
afraid of me — "She's a little bit shy herself" — and assured them that
they need not feel (as they often do feel toward kaplunas) that they had
to comply with my every wish. They said, finally, that I wished to be
adopted into an Eskimo family and to live with them in their iglu as a
daughter.

CHOOSING A FATHER

I had a number of reasons for wishing to be adopted, and there
were several precedents for adoption as well: four other kaplunas of my
acquaintance, both scholars and laymen, who had wintered with Eskimos had done so as "sons," sharing the iglus of their Eskimo families.
Living in the iglu would be warmer than living alone, I thought (Ikayuqtuq and Nakliguhuktuq agreed); and I thought vaguely that it might
be "safer" if one family had specific responsibility for me. The idea had
romantic appeal too; I saw it as a fulfillment of a childhood wish to "be"
an Eskimo, and I expected no rapport problems, since on two previous
trips to the Alaskan Arctic I had identified strongly with the Eskimo
villagers with whom I had lived. To be sure, there were also arguments
against adoption: I had qualms concerning the loss of an "objective"
position in the community, drains on my supplies that would result

from contributing to the maintenance of a family household and loss of privacy with resultant difficulties in working. Still, when the moment of decision came, the balance lay in favor of adoption.

There were two suitable fathers among the Utkuhikhalingmiut (that is, two household heads who had wives alive and at home), and these two were both more than eager to adopt me. One, however — an intelligent, vigorous man named Inuttiaq — far outdid the other in the imagination and persistence with which he "courted" me as a daughter. Not only were he and his family extremely solicitous, but he was also a jolly and ingenious language teacher. Most gratifying of all, both he and his wife, Allaq, were astonishingly quick to understand my halting attempts to communicate. There was no question which family I preferred. Fortunately, Inuttiaq also occupied a much more central position among the Utkuhikhalingmiut than did Nilak, the other possible father. He had many more close kin and was also the Anglican lay leader of the group. I was convinced that both anthropology and I would benefit more if I were adopted by Inuttiaq.

WINTER

From the moment that the adoption was settled, I was "Inuttiaq's daughter" in the camp. Inuttiaq and his relatives with much amusement drilled me in the use of kin terms appropriate to my position, just as they drilled his three-year-old daughter, who was learning to speak. They took charge of my material welfare and of my education in language and skills. Allaq also to some extent took charge of my daily activities, as it was proper that a mother should. She told me what the day's job for the women of the family was going to be: gathering birch twigs for fuel, scraping caribou hides in preparation for the making of winter clothing or skinning the fish bellies out of which oil was to be boiled. The decision to participate or not was left to me, but if I did join the women — and I usually did — she made sure that my share of the work was well within the limits of my ability and stamina. "We will be walking very far tomorrow to get birch twigs," she would say. "You will be too tired." If I went anyway, it was always silently arranged that my load should be the lightest, and if I wandered out of sight of the other women in my search for birch bushes, someone always followed behind — sent by Allaq, as I discovered months later — to make sure that I didn't get lost.

I felt increasingly comfortable with my family and found their solicitude immensely warming. At the same time, I dreaded the loss of privacy that the winter move into their iglu would bring. Curiously, the effect of the move when it came in October was the opposite of what I had expected. I basked in the protectiveness of Inuttiaq's household;

and what solitude I needed I found on the river in the mornings, when I jigged for salmon trout through the ice with Inuttiaq, or, to my surprise, in the iglu itself in the afternoons, when the room was full of visitors and I retired into myself, lulled and shielded by the flow of quiet, incomprehensible speech.

BEHAVING

The family's continuing graciousness was very seductive. I came to expect the courtesies that I received and even to resent it a bit when they were not forthcoming, though at the same time I told myself that such feelings were shameful. However, as time passed and I became an established presence in the household, I was less and less often accorded special privileges, except insofar as my ineptitude made services necessary. Allaq still mended my skin boots for me and stretched them when they shrank in drying; my stitches were not small enough and my jaws not strong enough. She continued to fillet my fish when it was frozen nearly as hard as wood. But in other respects Allaq, and especially Inuttiaq — who was far less shy than his wife — more and more attempted to assimilate me into a proper adult parent-daughter relationship. I was expected to help with the household work to the best of my ability — to make tea or bannock and to fetch water — and I was expected to obey unquestioningly when Inuttiaq told me to do something or made a decision on my behalf.

Unfortunately, I found it impossible to learn to behave in every respect like an Utkuhikhalingmiut daughter. Inuttiaq lectured me in general terms on the subject of filial obedience, and once in a while I think he tried to shame me into good behavior by offering himself as a model of virtue — volunteering, for example, to make bannock for me if I were slow in making it for him — but to little avail. Sometimes I was genuinely blind and deaf to his lessons, unaccustomed as I was to Utkuhikhalingmiut subtlety. At other times I saw what was wanted but resisted for reasons I will describe in a moment. Inevitably, conflicts, covert but pervasive, developed, both regarding the performance of household chores and regarding the related matter of obedience to Inuttiaq.

ASSUMPTIONS IN CONFLICT

The causes of the conflicts were three. First was the fact that some feminine skills were hard for me to learn. Overtly my Utkahikhalingmiut parents were very tolerant of the lack of skill that they rightly attributed to kapluna ignorance and perhaps also to kapluna lack of intelligence, or *ihuma*. However, perhaps because of an assumption that kaplunas were unable to learn, if I was at all slow to understand Allaq's instructions and demonstrations, she easily gave up trying to teach me, preferring instead to continue to serve me. And though she stretched my boots and cut my fish in the most cheerful manner, after a while her added chores may well have been burdensome to her.

A second cause of the conflicts was that some of Inuttiaq's and Allaq's assumptions about the nature of parental and daughterly virtue were at variance with mine; in consequence not only did I have to learn new patterns, I also had to unlearn old ones. Hardest of all to learn was unquestioning obedience to paternal authority. Sometimes I could not help resisting, privately but intensely, when Inuttiaq told me to "make tea," to "go home," to "hurry up" or to "pray." I was irritated even by the fact that after the first weeks of gracious formality had passed he began to address me in the imperative form, which is often used in speaking to women, children and young people. Rationally I knew that I should have welcomed this sign of "acceptance," but I could not be pleased. My irritation was due partly to the fact that subordination threatened my accustomed — and highly valued — independence, but it was aggravated by a fear that the restrictions placed on me interfered with my work.

And herein lay the third cause of the conflicts: I found it hard sometimes to be simultaneously a docile and helpful daughter and a conscientious anthropologist. Though Allaq appeared to accept my domestic clumsiness as inevitable, she may have felt less tolerant on the occasions when it was not lack of skill that prevented me from helping her, but anxiety over the pocketful of trouser-smudged, disorganized field notes that cried out to be typed. A number of times, when I could have helped to gut fish or to carry in snow to repair the sleeping platform or floor or could have offered to fetch water or make tea, I sat and wrote instead or sorted vocabulary — tiny slips of paper spread precariously over my sleeping bag and lap. It was sometimes professional anxiety that prompted me to disobey Inuttiaq too; and I am sure that on such occasions, as on others, he must have found my insubordination not only "bad," but completely incomprehensible. My behavior at moving time is an example. My gear, minimal though it was by kapluna standards, placed a severe strain on Inuttiaq when we moved camp. Whereas the sleds of others were loaded to little more than knee height, the load on Inuttiaq's sled was shoulder-high. From his point of view it was only reasonable that he should instruct me to leave my heavy tape recorder and my metal box of field notes on the top of a small knoll, as the Utkuhikhalingmiut cached their own belongings, while we moved downstream, not to return until after the flood season. I, however, questioned whether the water might rise over the knoll, and Inuttiaq's silent scrutiny seemed to say that he considered my inquiry a reflection on his judgment.

I do not mean to create the impression that life in Inuttiaq's household during that first winter was continuous turmoil. There were many days, even weeks, when I, at least, felt the situation to be very peaceful and enjoyable. I was grateful for the warmth of my parents' company and care; it was good to feel that I belonged somewhere, that I was part of a family, even on a make-believe basis. But the rewards of my presence for Inuttiaq and his real family were of a different, and probably of a lesser, order. Because Inuttiaq's purchases in Gjoa Haven were supplemented by mine, our household was richer than others in store goods: tea, tobacco, flour, jam, dry milk, raisins and kerosene. But apart from these material benefits, and at first perhaps the novelty (and prestige?) of having a kapluna daughter, it is hard to see what Inuttiaq's family gained in return for the burden they carried. I played "Tavern in the Town" and "Santa Lucia" on my recorder; Inuttiaq enjoyed that and once in a while asked me to play for guests. I helped inefficiently in the mornings to remove the whitefish from the family nets and to drag them home, harnessed with Allaq to the sled. I assisted — erratically, as I have mentioned — with the other domestic chores; and in late winter, when the sun returned and Inuttiaq began again to jig for salmon trout, I usually fished with him. That is all that occurs to me, and a trivial contribution it must have been from my family's point of view.

SATAN AND SELF-CONTROL

It was hard for me to know at the time, however, just what their reactions to me were, because the tensions that existed were nearly all covert. Hostility among Utkuhikhalingmiut is ignored or turned into a joke; at worst it becomes the subject of gossip behind the offender's back. I, too, did my best to smother my annoyance with frustration, but my attempts were not wholly successful. My training in self-control was less perfect than theirs, and at the same time the strains were greater than those I was accustomed to dealing with in my own world. Moreover, the most potentially gratifying of the outlets utilized by the Utkuhikhalingmiut — gossip — was not open to me as an anthropologist. I did my best to learn with the children when they were taught to turn annoyance into amusement, but laughter didn't come easily.

The Utkuhikhalingmiut are acutely sensitive to subtle indications of mood. They heard the coldness in my voice when I said, "I don't understand," noted the length of a solitary walk I took across the tundra or the fact that I went to bed early and read with my back turned to the others. Later, Inuttiaq might give me a lecture — phrased, as always, in the most general terms — about the fate of those who lose their tempers: Satan uses them for firewood. Or he might offer me an especially choice bit of fish — whether to shame me or to appease me I don't know. The contrast between my irritability and the surface equanimity of others gave me many uncomfortable moments, but I persuaded myself that the effects of my lapses were shortlived. When I laughed again and heard others laugh with me, or when they seemed to accept the generous gestures with which I tried to make amends, I was reassured that no damage had been done. I was wrong. But it was only when I returned to Gjoa Haven on my way home a year later that I learned how severe the tensions had become between November and January of that first winter. Then the deacon's wife, Ikajuqtuq, told me of the report Inuttiaq had made of me in January when he went in to Gjoa Haven to trade: "She is not happy. She gets angry very easily, and I don't think she likes us anymore." Shortly after Inuttiaq's return from Gjoa Haven in January, conflict erupted into the open.

"THE IGLUS ARE COLD"

The two weeks of Inuttiaq's absence in Gjoa Haven had been an especially trying period for me. I had looked forward to them as a much needed interlude in which to type and organize my swelling pile of penciled notes. When Inuttiaq was at home, it was often difficult to maintain the iglu temperature within the range of 27 to 31 degrees at which typing was feasible. If I tried to type during the daylight hours of the morning, when the outdoor work was done, my fingers and carbon paper froze as a result of Inuttiaq's drafty comings and goings at jobs that seemed to necessitate propping the door open. But in the sociable afternoon and evening hours the snow dome dripped in the heat and occasionally deposited lumps of slush into my typewriter, and the iglu steamed so that my work was lost in a wet fog as a result of Inuttiaq's demands for tea, boiled fox, bannock and soup in rapid succession. Many were the frustrated moments when I heartily wished him gone; but it was only when he *was* gone that I discovered how completely our comfort depended on his presence. "When the men are away the iglus are cold," the women said; and it was true. The morning drafts that had plagued me before were nothing compared with the chill that resulted when nobody came and went at all. It was partly, of course, that Inuttiaq had taken with him one of our two primus stoves and one of the two kerosene storm lanterns, which ordinarily heated the iglu. But Allaq's behavior during her husband's absence intensified the cold. She never boiled fish, rarely brewed tea and never lit the lamp to dry clothes — any of which activities would have warmed the iglu. She merely sat in her corner of the sleeping platform, blew on her hands and remarked that the iglu was cold. It was; it was 20 degrees colder than when Inuttiaq was at home. I fretted and fumed in silent frustration and determined that when he came back I would take drastic steps to improve my working conditions.

I broached the subject to Inuttiaq a few days after his return to camp. He listened attentively to my explanation. I told him that I had thought about going to live for a while in the empty wooden building that stood on a peninsula a few miles from camp. The government had built it as a nursing station, but it had never been used except by me as a cache for my useless belongings. It had a kerosene stove, which would make it luxuriously comfortable — unless the stove was as erratic as the one in the similar nursing station in Gjoa Haven, with which I had once had an unfortunate experience. Inuttiaq agreed that the stove was unpredictable. Instead, he suggested that he take me to the nursing station every morning and fetch me again at night, so that I would not freeze. As often before, he reassured me: "Because you are alone here, you are someone to be taken care of." And, as often before, his solicitude warmed me. "Taking me to the nursing station every day will be a lot of work for you," I said. The round trip took an hour and a half by dog sled, not counting the time and effort involved in harnessing and un-harnessing the team. He agreed that it would be a lot of work. "Could you perhaps build me a small iglu?" I asked. It would take only an hour or two to build a tiny iglu near our own, which I could use as an "office"; then he need concern himself no further. Lulled by the assurance he had just given me of his desire to take care of me and by the knowledge that the request I made was not time-consuming, I was the more disa-greeably startled when he replied with unusual vigor, "I build no iglus. I have to check the nets."

A DAUGHTER'S TENT

The rage of frustration seized me. He had not given me the true reason for his refusal. It only took two hours to check the nets every second or third day; on the other days, Inuttiaq did nothing at all except eat, drink, visit and repair an occasional tool. He was offended, but I could not imagine why. Whether Inuttiaq read my face I do not know, but he softened his refusal immediately: "Shall Ipuituq or Tutaq" — he named two of the younger men — "build an iglu for you?" Perhaps it would be demeaning for a man of Inuttiaq's status, a mature house-holder, to build an iglu for a mere daughter. There was something in Inuttiaq's reaction that I did not understand, and a cautioning voice told me to contain my ethnocentric judgment and my anger. I thought of the small double-walled tent that I had brought with me for emergency use. It was stored in the nursing station. "They say my tent is very warm in winter," I said. Inuttiaq smoked silently. After a while he asked,

"Shall they build you an iglu tomorrow?" My voice shook with exasperation: "Who knows?" I turned my head, rummaging — for nothing — in my knapsack until the intensity of my feeling should subside.

Later, when Inuttiaq was smoking his last pipe in bed, I raised the subject again, my manner, I hoped, a successful facsimile of cheerfulness and firmness. "I would like to try the tent and see whether it's warm, as I have heard. We can bring it here, and then if it's not warm, I won't freeze; I'll come indoors." Allaq laughed, Inuttiaq accepted my suggestion, and I relaxed with relief, restored to real cheer by Inuttiaq's offer to fetch the tent from the nursing station the following day — if it stormed — so that he could not go on the trapping trip he had planned.

My cheer was premature. Two days later the tent had still not been fetched, though Inuttiaq had not gone trapping. I decided to walk to the nursing station. I had no intention of fetching the tent myself — it would have been impossible; but I needed a few hours alone, and vaguely I knew that the direction of my walk would be to Inuttiaq a sign, however futile, that I was in earnest about my tent.

But I did not dream that he would respond as charitably as he did. I had just arrived at the nursing station and was searching among my few books for a novel to comfort me in my frustration when I heard the squeak of sled runners on the snow outside and a familiar voice speaking to the dogs: *"Hoooo* [whoa]." Inuttiaq appeared in the doorway. I smiled. He smiled. "Will you want your tent?"

Gratitude and relief erased my anger as Inuttiaq picked up the tent and carried it to the sled. "You were walking," he said, in answer to my thanks. "I felt protective toward you."

It was a truce we had reached, however, not a peace, though I did not realize it at once. Since it was nearly dark when we reached camp, Inuttiaq laid the tent on top of the iglu for the night, to keep it from the dogs. Next morning I went with Inuttiaq to jig for trout up-river, and when we returned I thought that finally the time was ripe for setting up the tent. Not wanting to push Inuttiaq's benevolence too far, and remembering the force of his response to my query about iglu-building, I asked, "Shall I ask Ipuituq to help me put up my tent?" "Yes," said Inuttiaq. There was no warmth in his face; he did not smile, though he did tell me to keep my fur trousers on for warmth while I put up the tent. I obeyed, but the wind had risen while we drank our homecoming tea, so that even in fur trousers tent-raising was not feasible that day or the next.

When the wind died two days later, Inuttiaq and I went fishing again, most companionably. Relations seemed so amicable, in fact, that this time on our return I was emboldened to say directly, without mention of Ipuituq, "I would like to put up my tent."

Naïvely I thought that Inuttiaq would offer to help. He did not. His face was again unsmiling as he answered, "Put it up."

My anger was triggered again. "By myself?" I inquired rudely.

"Yes," said Inuttiaq, equally rudely.

"Thank you very much." I heard the coldness in my voice but did not try to soften it.

Inuttiaq, expressionless, looked at me for a moment then summoned two young men who were nearby and who came, with a cheer that was in marked contrast to his own manner, to help me set up the tent.

Although Inuttiaq thought it ridiculous anyway to set up a tent in winter, I think now that he was also personally affronted by my request. One clue to his reaction I find in a question that I hardly heard at the time: he had wanted to know, after the tent was up, whether I planned to sleep in it or only to work there, and I think he may have felt that my demand for a tent was a sign that I was dissatisfied with him as a father, with his concern for my welfare.

In any case, his behavior was a curious blend of opposites. He chose the site for my tent with care, correcting my own choice with a more practiced eye to prowling dogs and prevailing wind. He offered advice on heating the tent, and he filled my primus stove so that it would be ready for me to use when my two assistants and I had finished setting up the tent. And when I moved my writing things out of his iglu, he told me that if I liked, I might write instead of going fishing. "If I catch a fish, you will eat," he assured me. But he turned his back on the actual raising of the tent and went home to eat and drink tea.

NEVER IN ANGER

On the following day I saw his displeasure in another form. It was Sunday morning and storming; our entrance was buried under drifting snow. Since there could be no church service, Inuttiaq and Allaq had each, separately and in mumbling undertones, read a passage from the Bible. Then Inuttiaq began to read from the prayer book the story of creation, and he asked if I would like to learn. I agreed, the more eagerly because I feared that he had perceived my skepticism toward his religious beliefs and that this was another hidden source of conflict between us. He lectured me at length. The story of creation was followed by the story of Adam and Eve (whose sin was responsible for the division of mankind into kaplunas and Eskimos), and this story was in turn followed by an exposition of proper Christian behavior: the keeping of the Sabbath — and of one's temper. "God is loving," said Inuttiaq, "but only to believers. Satan is angry. People will go to heaven only if they do not get angry or answer back when they are scolded." He told me that one should not be attached to earthly belongings, as I was: "One should devote himself only to God's word." Most striking of all was the way Inuttiaq ended his sermon to me. "Nakliguhuktuq made me king of the Utkuhikhalingmiut," he said. "He wrote that to me. He told me that if people — including you — don't want to believe what I tell them and don't want to learn about Christianity, then I should write to him, and he will come quickly and scold them. If people don't want to believe Nakliguhuktuq either, then . . . a bigger leader, a kapluna, the king in Cambridge Bay [the government center for the central Arctic], will come in a plane with a big and well-made whip and will whip people. It will hurt a lot."

Much of this I had heard before, but this version was more dramatic than previous ones. It made me see more clearly than I had before something of Inuttiaq's view of kaplunas generally. I heard the hostility directed against myself as well, but again he had softened the latter by blending it with warmth, in the manner that I found so confusing. He knew that I believed in God, he said, because I helped people, I gave things to people — not just to one or two, which God doesn't want, but to everybody.

The rest of the winter passed more peacefully, at least on the surface. I spent much of the time working in my tent, and there was no more overt hostility. But I am no longer sure that my peace of mind was justified. In retrospect, it seems possible that the warm and solicitous acts my family continued to perform were neither rewards for improved behavior on my part nor evidence of a generous willingness to accept me in spite of my thorny qualities, but, rather, attempts to extract or blunt some of the thorns. If I knew I was cared for, I might not get angry so easily. I thought I heard similar logic in the admonition Inuttiaq once in a while gave his six-year-old daughter when she sulked: "Stop crying, you are loved." Another possible motive may have been a desire to shame me, by virtuous example, into reforming. Perhaps these kind acts even had the effect of nullifying Inuttiaq's and Allaq's own prickly feelings, permitting them to prove to themselves that — as Inuttiaq once said — they didn't get angry, only I did.

INCORRIGIBLE

But whatever the interpretation of these incidents, it is clear to me now that there existed more of an undercurrent of tension in my relationship with Inuttiaq and Allaq than I perceived at the time. I began to suspect its presence in the spring, when our iglu melted and I moved — at Inuttiaq's order — back into my own tent; Allaq almost never visited me, as she had done the first days after my arrival in Chantrey Inlet. More important, these winter tensions, I think, added their residue of hostility to a crisis situation that developed at the end of the summer. This introduced a new phase in my relations, not merely with Inuttiaq and Allaq, but with all the other Utkuhikhalingmiut as well — a phase in which I ceased to be treated as an educable child and was instead treated as an incorrigible offender, who had unfortunately to be endured but who could not be incorporated into the social life of the group.

The crisis was brought about by the visit to Chantrey Inlet of a party of kapluna sports fishermen. Every July and August in recent years Chantrey Inlet has been visited by sportsmen from the provinces and from the United States who charter bush planes from private sports airlines and fly up to the Arctic for a week's fishing. Every year the sportsmen ask permission to borrow the Eskimos' canoes, which were given to them by the Canadian government after the famine of 1958 and are indispensable to their economy. In 1958 the disappearance of the caribou herds from the Chantrey Inlet area forced the Eskimos to begin to rely much more completely on fish than they had formerly done. This meant accumulating and storing quantities of fish during seasons when they were plentiful, and to facilitate this, the government introduced fish nets and canoes. Originally there had been six canoes, one for each of the Utkuhikhalingmiut families, but by the time I arrived in Chantrey Inlet only two of these remained in usable condition.

IN ANGER

The first parties that came asked, through me, if they might borrow both canoes, and the Utkuhikhalingmiut, who for various reasons rarely, if ever, refuse such requests, acquiesced, at some cost to themselves. They sat stranded on the shore, unable to fish, unable to fetch the occasional bird that they shot on the water, unable to fetch a resupply of sugar for their tea from the cache on the nearby island and worst of all, perhaps, unable to visit the odd strangers who were camped out of sight across the river. Ultimately these kaplunas left and were replaced by another group, which asked to borrow only one canoe. But relief was short-lived; trolling up and down the unfamiliar river in the late twilight, the kaplunas were unfortunate enough to run the canoe on a rock and tear a large hole in the canvas, whereupon they returned the canoe and announced to the men through sign language that since that craft was unusable they were now obliged to borrow the other — Inuttiaq's. When I arrived on the scene, the kaplunas were attaching their outboard to the canoe as Inuttiaq and the other Utkuhikhalingmiut men watched.

I exploded. Unsmilingly and in a cold voice I told the kaplunas' guide some of the hardships that I foresaw if his men damaged the second canoe. Then, armed with the memory that Innutiaq had earlier, before the arrival of this party of kaplunas, instructed me in vivid language never again to allow anyone to borrow his canoe, I told the kaplunas that the owner of that second canoe did not wish to lend it.

The kapluna guide was not unreasonable; he agreed at once that the loan of the boat was the owner's option: "It's his canoe, after all." Slightly mollified, I turned to Inuttiaq who stood nearby, expressionless like the other Utkuhikhalingmiut. "Do you want me to tell him you don't want to lend your canoe?" I asked in Eskimo. "He will not borrow it if you say you don't want to lend it."

Inuttiaq's expression dismayed me, but I didn't know how to read it. I knew only that it registered strong feeling, as did his voice, which was unusually loud: "Let him have his will!"

"WE WISH SHE WOULD LEAVE"

That incident brought to a head months of uneasiness on the part of the Utkuhikhalingmiut concerning my volatility. I had spoken unbidden and in anger; that much the Eskimos knew. The words they couldn't understand, but it didn't matter; the intrusion and the anger itself were inexcusable. The punishment was so subtle a form of ostracism that I would have continued to think that my difficulties were all of my own imagining had I not come into possession of a letter that Allaq's father, Pala, had written to the deacon, Nakliguhuktuq, the day after the kaplunas left. Pala had intended to send it out on the plane that was daily expected to come and pick up the schoolchildren; he had kept it for a time, but then — fearing that when the plane finally came, he would forget the letter — he had given it to me to hold along with my own correspondence. The letter was in syllabics, of course; in an amoral spirit I decided to read it, to test my skill in reading Eskimo. I did not anticipate the contents: "Yiini [that was my name] lied to the kaplunas. She gets angry very easily. She ought not to be here studying Eskimos. She is very annoying; because she scolds and one is tempted to scold her. She gets angry easily. Because she is so annoying, we wish more and more that she would leave."

But it was not until October, when the autumn iglus were built, that the change in the Eskimos' feelings really became apparent. I was not at all sure that Inuttiaq would invite me to move in with his family again as he had done the year before, but I need not have worried; his hostility did not take such a crass form. However, the quality of life in the iglu was in striking contrast with the previous year. Whereas then Inuttiaq's iglu had been the social center of the camp, now family and visitors congregated next door, in Allaq's father's iglu. Inuttiaq and Allaq — the children too — spent the better part of every day at Pala's. Even in the early mornings, when the family awoke, and at night when we were preparing for bed, I was isolated. It was as though I were not there. If I made a remark to Inuttiaq or Allaq, the person addressed responded with his usual smile, but I had to initiate almost all communication. As a rule, if I did not speak, no one spoke to me. If I offered to fetch water or make tea (which I seldom did), my offer was usually accepted, but no one ever asked me to perform these services. The pointedness of this avoidance was driven home one day when we were cooking. I do not recall what was being made or who had initiated the cooking; I think it likely that I had done so, since the primus stood on the floor in front of me, instead of in its usual place near Allaq. Nevertheless, when the pressure began to run down, unnoticed by me, Inuttiaq turned not to me but to Allaq to order her to pump up the primus. And she had to get up and come over to my side of the iglu to pump up the stove! Had he spoken to me, I would only have had to lean over to do it. Too late I realized the dignity inherent in the Utkuhikhalingmiut pattern of authority, in which the woman is obedient to the man. I envied Allaq the satisfaction of knowing that she was appreciated because she did well and docilely what Inuttiaq told her to do.

One day, about a week after we had moved into the autumn iglus, Inuttiaq suggested that when we moved into winter iglus later on, I should be physically walled off to a degree. Often when Utkuhikhalingmiut build their permanent winter iglus, they attach to one side a small chamber, called a *hiqluaq*, in which to store the fish they net. The hiqluaq opens into the interior of the iglu by way of a hole just big enough to crawl through. Inuttiaq's idea was to build such a chamber for me to live in; after I left, he would use it in the orthodox manner, for fish storage.

But in spite of all these tensions, I was still treated with the most impeccable semblance of solicitude. I was amazed that it should be so — that although my company was anathema, nevertheless people still took care to give me plentiful amounts of the foods I liked best, to warn me away from thin ice and to caution me when my nose began to freeze. The Utkuhikhalingmiut saw themselves — and wanted me to see them — as virtuously solicitous, no matter what provocations I might give them to be otherwise. Allaq's sister expressed this ethos of concern explicitly in a letter to Ikayuqtuq in Gjoa Haven: "Because she is the only kapluna here and a woman as well, we have tried to be good to her . . . and though she is sometimes very annoying . . . we still try to help her."

It was at the end of August that the incident with the kapluna fishermen occurred, and it was the end of November before I was finally able to explain myself to the Utkuhikhalingmiut. I had wanted from the beginning, of course, to confront them with an explanation of my behavior, but I had feared that such un-Eskimo directness would only shock them the more. Instead, I had written my version of the story to

Ikayuqtuq, had told her about my attempt to protect the Utkuhikha-lingmiut from the impositions of the kaplunas and asked her if she could help to explain my behavior to the Eskimos. My letter went out to Gjoa Haven, along with Pala's, when the school plane came in September. Unfortunately there was no way in which Ikayuqtuq could reply until the strait froze in November, enabling the men to make the long trip out to Gjoa Haven to trade. But when Inuttiaq, accompanied as usual by Allaq's brother, Mannik, finally went out, they brought back from the deacon and his wife a response that surpassed my most sanguine expectations. Inuttiaq reported to his family: "Nakliguhuktuq says that the kaplunas almost shot us when Yiini wasn't there." The exaggeration was characteristic of Inuttiaq's lurid style of fantasy. He turned to me: "Did you write that to Nakliguhuktuq?" I denied it — and later, in Gjoa Haven, Nakliguhuktuq denied having made such a statement to Inut-tiaq — but I did confirm the gist of Inuttiaq's report: that I had tried to protect the Eskimos. I described what it was that I had written to Ika-yuqtuq, and I explained something of the reasons for my anger at the kaplunas.

WALL OF ICE

The effect was magical. The wall of ice that had stood between me and the community suddenly disappeared. I became consultant on the moral qualities of fishing guides; people talked to me voluntarily, offered me vocabulary, included me in their jokes and in their anecdotes of the day's activities; and Inuttiaq informed me that the next day he and I were going fishing. Most heartwarming of all is the memory of an after-noon soon after the men had returned. The iglu was filled with visitors, and the hum of the primus on which tea was brewing mingled with the low voices of Inuttiaq and his guests. I knew every detail of the scene even as I bent over my writing, and I paid no attention until suddenly my mind caught on the sound of my name: "I consider Yiini a member of my family again." Was that what Inuttiaq had said? I looked up, inquiring. "I consider you a family member again," he repeated. His diction was clear, as it was only when he wanted to be sure that I understood. And he called me "daughter," as he had not done since August.

Not that I had suddenly become a wholly acceptable housemate; that could never be. I was not and could never become an Utkuhikha-lingmiutaq, nor could I ever be a "daughter" to Inuttiaq and Allaq as they understood that role. Inuttiaq made this quite clear one day about this time when we were both sitting, silently working, in the iglu. "I think you're a leader in your country," he said suddenly. The remark had no obvious context; it must mean, I thought, that he had never reconciled himself to my intractable behavior. There was also the slightly wild look that I caught in his eye when I said I thought that I might someday return to Chantrey Inlet. The look vanished when Allaq explained that I meant to return after I had been to my own country, not merely to Gjoa Haven. "Yes," he said then, "we will adopt you again, or others may want to — Nilaak, perhaps, or Mannik, if he marries." And later, when we were talking about the possibility of other "learners" coming to Chantrey Inlet, Inuttiaq said, "We would be happier to have a woman come than a man — a woman like you, who doesn't want to be a wife. Maybe *you* are the only acceptable kapluna."

But it was the letters that Allaq and Inuttiaq wrote me when I left Chantrey Inlet in January that expressed most vividly and succinctly what it meant to them to have a kapluna daughter. They both said, "I didn't think I'd care when you left, but I did."

STRANGER, CHILD, SIMPLETON

I observed three more or less distinct phases in the Utkuhikhalingmiut's view of me. During the first period I was a stranger and a guest, and I was treated with the formal courtesy and deference that the Utkuhikhalingmiut ordinarily accord to such persons. I was referred to as a kapluna, a white person, and addressed by my personal name — "Yiini" in the Eskimos' speech. Much of the time during this period the Eskimos must have been at a loss what to make of my behavior, and often when I did something that under other circumstances they might have defined as reprehensible — when I went to bed early, nursing a bad humor, or when I was silent in depression — they gave me the benefit of the doubt; they asked me if I were tired and considerately lessened my work load or withdrew so that I might "sleep."

Gradually, however, this first phase gave way to a second, in which my immediate family (though not others in the community) treated me in some respects as a daughter and a child. My parents replaced the name "Yiini" with the term "daughter" when speaking, and sometimes when referring to me; and my two small sisters called me "elder sister." Inuttiaq — though never Allaq — also began to use the imperative forms of speech that he used in addressing his other daughters and his wife. Even an appropriate age was invented for me: I had to be younger than Allaq — if only by one season — though all the evidence pointed to my being in fact slightly older than she was. Both parents directed my daily activities, and I was expected to obey them as a daughter should. When I did not, efforts were made to teach me better behavior through lecturing or shaming, the former a technique that was otherwise only used in teaching small children. My moodiness was no longer interpreted charitably, and efforts were made to educate me out of that behavior too.

Categorization of me as a "child" was probably determined by a combination of factors: I had introduced myself as one who wanted to "learn" from the Utkuhikhalingmiut, and I had asked to be adopted as a "daughter"; I was also obviously ignorant of Utkuhikhalingmiut proprieties and skills. The fact that I am a woman may also have facilitated my categorization as a child in several respects. For one thing, among the Utkuhikhalingmiut a woman's technical skill — skin-sewing — is very difficult to learn. I never mastered more than the most rudimentary, clumsy stitching; my work was so poor that when I mended my skin boots, Allaq considered it necessary to redo the job. Moreover, in order to be considered properly adult, a woman must have children, and I had none. For these reasons the role of an adult woman was virtually closed to me, whereas had I been a man, I might have earned an adult role as a fisherman and hunter, as some male kaplunas who have lived among Eskimos appear to have done. Finally, the fact that I am physically weaker than a man and thus unthreatening may have made it easier for the Utkuhikhalingmiut to view my ill temper, as I think they did, like that of a child. Had I been a man, I think they might have seen my temper as dangerous, even potentially lethal — anything but childish.

The third phase, in which I was treated as an incorrigible offender, replaced the "child" phase, I think, when it became apparent to the Utkuhikhalingmiut that I was uneducable. Inuttiaq no longer lectured me or used any other method to teach me. I was called "Yiini" again instead of "daughter," and daughterly services were no longer asked of me. In fact, nothing at all was demanded of me. Though my physical needs for warmth, food and protection from danger were still taken care of, socially I was simply "not there." There was one other person in the community who was similarly ostracized: a woman of about my age, who appeared to be of subnormal intelligence. Almost all of her personal qualities — her imperfect speech, clumsy gestures and domestic incompetence — were subject to comment behind her back, but hostility in her case, as in mine, centered on her volatility — the fact that she was easily upset and was unable to exercise proper restraint in the expression of her feelings. She too was considered uneducable, and I am sure that, like her, I was privately labeled simpleminded.

HOSTS AND ANTHROPOLOGISTS

In more general terms the sequence of judgments passed on me seemed to be: strange; educable; uneducable in important ways. And each phase, each judgment, was associated with a role familiar to the Utkuhikhalingmiut: stranger; child; simpleton — each role being identifiable in terms of the way I was addressed, the kinds of behavior that

were expected of me, the interpretations that were placed on my misbehavior and the methods that were used to control that misbehavior.

Although an anthropologist must have a recognized role or roles
in order to make it possible to interact with him sensibly and predictably,
nevertheless it will be evident from what I have described of my own
case that the assignment of a role may create as many problems as it
solves for both the anthropologist and his hosts. When Inuttiaq undertook to adopt me, I think he assumed that I would naturally behave as
he was accustomed to having daughters behave. He knew, of course,
that as a kapluna I was ignorant of the Eskimo skills that adult daughters
have usually mastered, but it is easier to recognize cross-cultural differences in technology and language than differences in the structuring of
interpersonal relations; one is far more inclined to think of the latter as
given in "human nature."

He was wrong, of course, in assuming that my behavior would be
that of an Utkuhikhalingmiut daughter. Consequently his first hypothesis was replaced by a second: that kaplunas don't (or Yiini doesn't)
know how to behave correctly but can learn. For various reasons, none
of which were, I think, recognized by Inuttiaq, I didn't learn easily. The
first reason why learning must be difficult is that the intruder faces a
double task. On the one hand he must discover what has to be learned —
that is, what exactly is wrong with his "normal" behavior and what the
proper behavior should be. And on the other hand he must overcome
resistance to doing what is required — resistance caused by the interference of his old patterns of role behavior. Such interference may be
expected to be particularly marked when the role to be learned bears
the same name ("daughter") as a role one is accustomed to playing in
one's own culture.

Learning will also be difficult and imperfect because the anthropologist is not completely committed to the role he is playing vis-à-vis
his hosts. For one thing, he must try to learn all kinds of facts about the
community, many of which it may be inappropriate for someone in his
assumed native role to know. He must try to maintain sufficient distance
from the culture he is studying and from himself so that he can record
"objectively" and, hopefully, use his reactions to his experiences as
sources of data. And he must try to record and participate simultaneously. The latter problem has been amply illustrated in my case as I
have described it above.

It was because of these difficulties and others that Inuttiaq's second
hypothesis — that I was educable — proved to a large extent wrong.
And so he arrived at his third hypothesis (shared, as I have said, by the
rest of the community), to the effect that I was a defective person: "bad"
and "simpleminded."

This analysis of the relationship between my Eskimo family and me is, of course, far from complete. It is obvious that difficulties of conceptualization are only one of the problems that beset relationships of any kind. It is obvious also that most relationships — and the one described here is no exception — have strongly positive features as well, or they would cease to exist. Nevertheless, the account that I have presented here may serve as a basis for discussion of the general issues of anthropological role-playing.

4

Trouble in the tank:
Ethics in urban fieldwork

JAMES P. SPRADLEY

All anthropologists fill a double role: anthropologist and citizen.
What should anthropologists do when, in the course of doing
research, they discover patterns of discrimination, inequities,
injustices, or inhumane treatment of the people they study? Because
anthropologists have access to information that is hidden to many
other people, do they thereby have a special responsibility? Should
they interfere in the operations of the society studied? And, perhaps
most important, how should they make known to the general public
what they discover? All these questions emerged in the course of
studying skid road alchoholics, or tramps, a study James Spradley
carried out in Seattle, Washington. In this article, he takes us
through the experience of research selection and then through the
decision to publish data in a way that most anthropologists avoid.
Another report from this urban anthropology research project appears
as article 23 in this volume.

I

The faculty meeting began promptly at eight o'clock. On that Thursday morning in early June of 1967, I was beginning to think around the edges of a decision that would eventually grow into a series of ethical dilemmas. The chairman took his customary place at the head of the long seminar table and started the meeting.

"Grand Rounds will meet in Health Sciences 405 this morning at ten. It's a classic case of schizophrenia. Dr. Johnson will present the case and I hope you can all come." A moment of silence followed while he

From pp. 17–31 in James P. Spradley and Michael A. Rynkiewich, *Ethics and Anthropology: Dilemmas in Fieldwork.* Copyright © 1976 by John Wiley & Sons, Inc. By permission.

sorted through some papers in front of him. Then, while the other faculty members discussed the Summer Research Training Program for medical students, my thoughts drifted away to my own research program.

I had been on the faculty of the Department of Psychiatry at the University of Washington for nearly a year, yet I still felt somewhat like an outsider. Everyone else seemed to know what was expected of them and I often wished for the security of well-defined responsibilities. My training had not prepared me to give psychological tests or engage in therapy; I had no desire to become a junior psychiatrist. I taught one course in the spring and offered lectures on culture and illness from time to time. Beyond that I was free to become involved in the training of future psychologists, psychiatrists, and physicians. I could participate in patient-related activities such as group therapy. I could also carry out research that was related to mental illness, provided I gathered the data in the greater metropolitan area of Seattle. I felt most comfortable doing research and other faculty understood that role. I was eager to begin a new project since I had recently completed research on a Kwakiutl Indian chief in British Columbia. But, I discovered, the choice to do research only presented me with a new set of alternatives and the necessity to make other choices.

The faculty meeting ended and I edged my way to the door and walked quickly up the long hallway toward the elevator. The Psychiatry Department occupied one wing of the seventh floor of the University Hospital. The two elevators stood opposite the nurses' station and beyond them lay the other wing with patients. The doors opened and a stream of people flowed out; I stepped in, pushed the button for the third floor — Department of Pediatrics — and leaned against the back of the elevator to wait. I knew that whatever I decided to study could easily continue for a number of years. I wanted a project that was interesting, challenging, and thoroughly anthropological. Perhaps a study of the Greek immigrant community in Seattle would meet these criteria; it could even lead someday to research in Greece. I thought of other alternatives like the spiritualist counselors and religious leaders who attracted clients from all over the city. I wondered if I studied their methods could I compare them to curing rituals in Africa or Asia? I might study the social structure of a psychiatric ward in any of a number of hospitals, a project similar to what William Caudill, another anthropologist, had done more than 10 years earlier.

As the elevator stopped at the fourth floor to pick up a nurse, I thought about the most likely possibility, a study of urban Indians. Many Native Americans had moved to Seattle from rural reservations and I could investigate their strategies for adapting to city life. A government agency that helped to relocate Native Americans from Alaska had an office near the University of Washington and when I approached the director about a possible study he seemed receptive, even enthusiastic.

But each week brought new ideas, new opportunities. The latest was an alcoholism treatment center. I saw the third floor light come on and when the doors opened I stepped out, went past the waiting area and down the hallway to the Department of Pediatrics. I had decided to see if Jim Oakland, a psychologist who worked there, had time for a cup of coffee in the hospital cafeteria. I wanted to talk to him about the possibilities and problems of studying an alcoholism treatment center.

Jim Oakland and I had taught together at Seattle Pacific College a few years earlier while we both did graduate work in different departments at the University of Washington. We frequently talked about our respective jobs and research interests. He had administered some psychological tests to James Sewid, the Kwakiutl chief whose life history I had recently completed. From time to time I had made suggestions on the social and cultural aspects of his work in developing norms for the Edwards Personality Inventory. His office door was ajar and I pushed it open. "Do you have time for coffee? I want to tell you my latest idea for research." Without a hesitation, he jumped to his feet, reached for his coat, and we were on our way to the first floor of the hospital.

As we sipped coffee in a quiet corner of the busy cafeteria I told him what I knew. "There's a new residential treatment center for skid road alcoholics opening sometime this summer. The King County Sheriff's Department will operate the center; they plan to take drunks arrested in Seattle and keep them at the center for treatment instead of giving them a jail sentence. I don't know much about the details but it would be a chance to get in on the ground floor, the start of the treatment center, and study its culture as it develops."

Jim listened with interest and then asked, "How would you go about doing the research?"

"I would drive out to the treatment center; the buildings are under construction now a few miles outside the city. I'd go maybe three or four days a week, maybe more, to observe and talk with the patients and staff. It would be like studying a small society. The drunks will undergo several months of treatment and I'd want to participate in the various kinds of therapy, observe the work program, eat meals with them, and just hang around to gather data on the informal aspects of the center. I might develop some questionnaires later on and use some personality tests. I'd do an ethnography of the treatment center — my goal would be to describe its culture."

"But why do an ethnography of an alcoholism treatment institution?" he asked. "What kind of contribution will it make? Do you have any larger goals in such a study?" His question went to the heart of my own values and I paused before answering. "Well, in addition to the pure scientific goals, I may be able to learn some things that could improve the treatment milieu and lead to a more effective program. I don't know much about alcoholism but the skid road drunk is the hardest to cure and most approaches haven't worked very well. Maybe I can make some contribution there."

We continued talking for nearly an hour about possible problems, about the goals of such a study, the strategies for collecting data, the ways it might lead to improved treatment, and how I felt about this study in contrast to the others I had considered. We talked again during the next week and by the middle of June all signs pointed toward a study of the alcoholism treatment center.

II

The cool, damp days of June gave way to the bright sun of early summer. Before I made a final decision on the project I tried to find out more about the planned treatment center, reviewed some of the literature on studying institutions, and worked out ideas for gathering data. A colleague in the Department of Psychiatry told me that a Mr. Ron Fagan, newly appointed director of the center, was the kind of person I would find receptive to research. I called Mr. Fagan and made an appointment to see him. A thin, soft-spoken man in his early fifties, he greeted me warmly; his informal manner put me at ease immediately. He began talking about alcoholics and his hopes for the new facility that he called "Cedar Hills Alcoholism Treatment Center." Although he did not fully understand what approach I would take as an anthropologist, he said that at one time he had collaborated on an alcoholism research project with a sociologist from the university. He believed in the importance of such research. He would welcome the kind of study I wanted to do.

Before we finished talking I knew I would learn a great deal from Mr. Fagan. I also sensed that his work involved far more than a job. He had a lifelong dream to help the alcoholic, especially the "low bottom drunk" from skid road. He recalled his own experiences as we talked, how he had been on skid road in Seattle and San Francisco and other cities around the country, the struggle with drinking, his attempts to stop the vicious cycle, finally hitting bottom and finding help through Alcoholics Anonymous. Since his recovery he had worked in a variety of settings to help alcoholics.

I learned that each year the Seattle police arrested more than 10,000 drunks, sending a steady stream of men to the city jail. After a few weeks or months to dry out, most ended up back on the streets only to find themselves arrested again. It was a revolving door. Ron emphasized that this system did little more than dry out the drunk and keep him away from the bottle for a few weeks. It treated the symptom, not the cause. The men needed help, not punishment. Alcoholism was a disease that could be treated and Cedar Hills would use the best treatment approaches yet developed, everything from medical care and group therapy to Alcoholics Anonymous. Of course they would not have room for all the drunks arrested each year but would select those most likely to respond to treatment. Ron said he would start hiring staff and selecting patients in the next few weeks and I could start my research almost immediately. He offered to let me sit in on interviews with prospective patients and record the development of selection procedures. It would only require the permission of Sheriff Jack Porter, the person ultimately responsible for the center. Confident of the Sheriff's support, Ron said he would arrange for an appointment. I agreed to prepare a brief written proposal.

On July 18 I sent the proposal to Sheriff Jack Porter. It stated my purpose: "This research project will focus on how Cedar Hills functions as a treatment center for alcoholics. A study will be made of the development of the center, the formal and informal organization of staff and patients, the daily activities of each, various types of therapy utilized, and the meaning of the center to its patients, staff, and visitors."

Three days later I sat in a comfortable, overstuffed chair in Sheriff Porter's spacious office with Ron Fagan. He agreed with Ron that my study of Cedar Hills was a good idea and thought it could add to developing an effective treatment program. I pointed out that such a study could add to our understanding of new institutions, provide a basis for evaluating various therapeutic approaches, and that publications on the study could help to inform the community about the center. I then asked him what kind of institution he had in mind at Cedar Hills.

"I feel we must have a custodial type rehabilitation center. Successful treatment of alcoholics demands an institution," he said, leaning forward slightly in his chair. "What do you mean by *custodial* rehabilitation center?" I asked. "There are many other types of institutions but it is necessary to have one with a controlled environment. As long as you have alcoholics and as long as the police have to handle them — somebody has to do it. We have the alcoholics and because no one else is doing it we felt we should attempt some type of rehabilitation program."

As he talked I sensed his deep commitment to reshaping the lives of repeated offenders, to changing the archaic system that only dispensed punishment. My image of a tough cop who had risen to the top in Washington State's most populated county began to fade. He talked of the work release program he had developed for county jail prisoners so they could continue on regular jobs while serving time. He expanded on his ideas for the treatment center: "I think our treatment at Cedar Hills should be as sophisticated as possible. A work program is important in therapy. A work program is also important for returning money to the taxpayer. But work is secondary; cure is the most important. I feel there is value in Alcoholics Anonymous, various therapeutic approaches, and that vocational rehabilitation is very important. If Cedar Hills hasn't changed in six months," he said, emphasizing each word, "we will have to take another good look at it. It must keep changing. We must have some follow-up. If we can follow up on 50 percent of the men who go through Cedar Hills, that is better than others are doing."

I left that meeting deeply impressed with these men who were working to make the effective treatment of chronic alcoholics a reality. I felt exhilarated, filled with anticipation of the research about to begin. Confusion over too many alternatives had given way in a few short weeks to a firm decision to study Cedar Hills Alcoholism Treatment Center. I felt good because I had selected a unique cultural milieu for research. I knew it was a project that could have direct application to a social science problem of immense proportions. At the same time I did not plan to become an applied anthropologist; I would not try to change institutions or individuals. I had even told Ron Fagan that in order to keep from influencing the development of Cedar Hills I would have to withhold much of what I observed until after the study was completed. During the next two years I was to become more deeply involved with transients and drunks from skid road than I could ever have imagined on that warm summer afternoon as I left Sheriff Jack Porter's office.

III

Before July ended I was deep into fieldwork. The treatment center, now nearing completion, still had no patients. In the mornings I visited the criminal court in Seattle to watch the daily parade of drunks, to hear their pleas of "Guilty," and to record the sentences handed out by the judge. Ron Fagan and a newly hired counselor were there to watch and select patients. I interviewed them both to learn their reasons for selecting some men and rejecting others. I visited Cedar Hills and gathered information on the history of the new center. My field notes grew as I wrote down everything I could from my observations and interviews.

By the end of the first week in August a group of men had been selected; they waited in the city jail for their transfer to the county treatment center. Each would receive a six-month sentence; those who responded to treatment quickly could expect an early release. I sensed an air of anticipation among the staff because, at last, the waiting would end and they could get down to the hard task of rehabilitating these derelicts from skid road. But then, at the last minute, a bureaucratic snarl developed over the source of funds to purchase food for the men taken from the Seattle city jail to the King County treatment center. I talked with the staff and others, listened to their frustrations, and recorded their reactions to the news that these first patients would never arrive at Cedar Hills. Some felt the delay was due to the long-time rivalry between the city and county police departments. Another month passed before the problem was solved and a new group of patients selected.

On the morning of September 14, I left home earlier than usual. I drove to the Public Safety Building in downtown Seattle where I met Bill Adams, a police officer who had recently joined the treatment center staff; together we would transport the first six patients to Cedar Hills. At last I could talk to patients, find out the reasons they volunteered for treatment, listen to how they felt about the new center, and hopefully come to understand their lives as alcoholics. The elevator brought the men from the jail on the seventh floor to the basement where they were escorted into a paddy wagon. We drove out of the police garage and headed south. More than 30 minutes later we pulled into the grounds of Cedar Hills. The new buildings and landscaping seemed a sharp contrast to the adjacent county dump, the acres of surrounding woods, and the six transients from skid road.

I still vividly remember one small incident that happened about ten o'clock that morning, although at the time it seemed almost too insignificant to record. Standing around in the basement of the multipurpose building trying to appear unobtrusive, I talked with these patients as they checked-in their meager belongings and received green uniforms to wear while at the center. Several talked about the city jail: "Sure is crowded in there, lotta men are sleeping on the floor," one said. "The food was really terrible," added an older man. "I haven't had coffee in two weeks because I haven't been able to drink the coffee in there." Then two of the others began complaining that the police officers who arrested them had stolen their money. For an instant I felt vaguely uncomfortable, aware that Bill Adams and Sergeant Ron Colvin were listening to these complaints. One patient recalled: "I had a $20 bill when I was arrested and when I asked for the money in my property there was none." The other man claimed he had $22 when picked up for drunk but it also had disappeared. As the discussion ended and the men began to leave for their dormitory, Sergeant Colvin assured me that the money probably hadn't been taken. "These men are drunk when arrested and don't really know what they have in the way of money. This kind of complaint is rather common."

The days that followed brought more patients and Cedar Hills came alive with activity. I interviewed informants and participated in staff meetings, patient orientations, meals, card games, informal bull sessions, and always I made long and detailed notes on what I learned. Late in September I joined a group of new patients for coffee in the dining room. They were discussing the laws in some states that protected alcoholics from repeated arrests for drunkenness; the topic shifted to conditions in drunk tanks in various jails around the country. One man said bitterly, "I don't see how any judge could ever go to bed at night without a guilty conscience after sentencing these men." Another spoke with deep resentment: "Throwing a man in jail over and over again just makes him that much more bitter each time." An hour later I overheard two of these same men talking about their own arrest a few days earlier. It had occurred at the same time and they had gone to jail together. The police officer had ordered them to turn their pockets inside out, ostensibly looking for knives and any items of personal property. One had $17, the other $23, but when they were released from jail to come to Cedar Hills they got nothing back. They noticed I had overheard their complaints and one said, "You'd better not tell on us!" I assured them that I did not work for Cedar Hills and would not tell anyone. Then he said, "In this jail they don't even give you a receipt for the money they take." Only later would I come to fully appreciate the significance of this statement.

During the next few weeks my role as neutral but interested observer became accepted; more and more patients sought me out to talk — and almost always their concern focused on conditions in the jail. If a staff member approached during such a conversation, the subject changed or became very general. But when I was alone with individuals or groups of men, they talked freely, expressing their deep resentment of the power of the police. They spoke from long years of experience; many had served "life sentences on the installment plan," as one man called it. They told me about thefts and beatings, about policemen who roamed around skid road waiting and looking for drunks to pick them up on the least provocation. Out of deep and angry feelings older men decried the drunk tank that they found almost unbearable, often forced to sleep there for several nights at a time on the cold cement floor. Others had witnessed drunks being robbed and beaten by policemen on skid road and in the jail. They stressed the impossibility of ever "beating a drunk charge" so that nearly everyone entered guilty pleas even when innocent. One man recalled, "I was picked up one time for panhandling or begging; I asked a man for a cigarette and they arrested me and brought me in to be booked but the officer in charge just said, 'Well, you haven't been picked up in this jail before, we'll just put down you were drunk.' "

About this time I went to one of the counselors at Cedar Hills, a recovered alcholic himself who, in years past, had spent many weeks

in jail on drunk arrests. One morning in late September we drove together from Seattle to Cedar Hills. "When you were drinking and running and in jail," I asked, "were you ever mistreated by the police? I'm
wondering if we can believe the stories the men report." I knew he
would willingly tell me of his own experience; he also knew personally
hundreds of other men he had worked with in Alcoholics Anonymous.
After a moment he replied: "Yes, one time I was in an elevator and I
said something that wasn't nice and the policeman started to beat me
up. And as to getting rolled, that is very true, drunks are rolled by the
police all the time." We talked for some time about the difficult problems
these men faced with the police in Seattle and in other cities. And as
we continued to drive the last few miles to Cedar Hills I began to feel
vaguely unsure about the direction of my research.

IV

October brought a warm Indian summer to Seattle; the trees turned
from green to red to gold and the university came alive again with
returning students. I continued to gather data on Cedar Hills but now
I struggled almost daily with the question I had comfortably resolved
during the previous summer: "What should I study?" Should I go on
investigating this new institution for the treatment and rehabilitation of
alcoholics? Or should I study the much older system for the arrest and
incarceration of drunks? Would it be right to use Cedar Hills as a base
for interviewing informants about life in jail? If I did change the focus
of my research and study the experiences of drunks with the Seattle
Police, would it be right to hide this fact from Sheriff Jack Porter? Ron
Fagan might accept this shift in my research goals but the Sheriff could
hardly allow it. If I began systematic interviews about the jail I would
still have to continue some research on Cedar Hills so as not to arouse
suspicion among the security officers who worked at the treatment center. On the other hand, maybe I should ignore the stories about the
police and stick to my original research goals. After all, I couldn't study
everything; sooner or later I had to draw the line and exclude some
things that could be investigated.

Jim Oakland knew of what I had learned during those first months
of research and one day over lunch I told him, "I'm wondering if I
should focus on interviews with patients about the jail, concentrating
on their experiences there rather than on the treatment center? Or should
I ignore the jail? I don't think I can study both and do justice to my
original proposal." I half expected the next question for it was one I had
thought about often. "How do you know these stories about the police
and the jail are true?" he asked. "Most people would see your informants
as merely bums and derelicts who can't be taken seriously."

"I'm not sure they are true," I told him. "In fact, up to now I've only thought of them as complaints that would have to be investigated. But I feel sure that something is going on at the jail that few people in Seattle know about. The whole system of arresting drunks seems to breed injustice. They make nearly 12,000 arrests each year and some men spend as much as six months in jail simply for appearing drunk in public. They could bail out for $20 every time if they only had the money. If conditions are half as bad as some men say, then it's a hell of a place. Almost all the men who come for treatment have spent years in and out of jail and they seem far more concerned about the police and doing time in jail than about their drinking. Some of them aren't alcoholics; they volunteer for Cedar Hills just to escape doing hard time in jail. It can't help but have a profound influence on any treatment program. It may be true, as one informant told me, 'After 30 days in jail, you owe yourself a drunk.' I wonder if there's some way to change the laws or something; I don't know, but as long as they keep arresting these men, any kind of treatment program will fight a losing battle." Jim agreed and as we left he encouraged me to seriously consider more concentrated research on the collective experience of these men with the police and in jail.

An unexpected event occurred a few days later to help me decide. On Tuesday, October 31, I sat in court waiting for things to begin. The bailiff rapped his gavel loudly several times; everyone stood in silence. "The Municipal Court Number One of Seattle is now in session. The Honorable James Noe presiding." I knew the procedure by heart and sat down to begin taking notes as I had done on many other mornings. I heard the city attorney begin the process: "Delmar Luden, you have been charged with drunk in public, how do you plead?" "Guilty." After a quick review of his previous record the judge announced, "Thirty days committed." It took 10 seconds from start to finish for Mr. Luden to have his day in court. Stephen Brady followed with a two-day suspended sentence. I wrote rapidly as the tempo picked up — the same charge, the same plea, and always the sentences. Suddenly the fourteenth name caught my attention — Charles Roberts. I looked more closely and saw a former patient from Cedar Hills walk from the holding tank into the courtroom and stand before the judge. Only a few days earlier I had talked with this man about the jail, his past, the treatment program, and his hopes for the future. I avoided looking directly at him for fear he might recognize me sitting there in the audience as a spectator watching him. Judge Noe asked a clerk to notify Cedar Hills and then said, "Mr. Roberts, we are going to continue your case until Thursday morning for sentencing. $500 bail." Charles Roberts walked dejected from the courtroom.

In the months to come other patients would follow like a steady stream going from the treatment center back to skid road, picked up there by the paddy wagon, and taken back to the drunk tank. I knew I could never sit in court again as a detached observer; I would never again see only faceless drunks pleading guilty and receiving their sentences. I could not view these men as merely candidates for an alcoholism treatment center. From now on they would stand there as individuals, men I had listened to, laughed with, shared meals together. Most important, now I knew some of the conditions they would suffer as they took their sentences, turned away from the judge, and walked back into the jail in quiet desperation. As I left the courtroom that day I wondered more than ever about the sign that had stared down at me for months from high over the judge's bench: EQUAL JUSTICE FOR ALL UNDER THE LAW.

V

Almost a year had passed when, one warm September afternoon in 1968, I returned to my office to find a message: "Call Dr. Fred Anderson, Associate Dean of the Medical School." I dialed the number and a secretary answered. "This is Jim Spradley in Psychiatry," I said. "I'm returning Dr. Anderson's call." She sounded as if she expected my voice and said, "Oh, yes, Dr. Spradley, could you come in tomorrow morning at 9:30?" "Yes," I said, "I probably could, what is it about?" She said she would check if I could hold a moment. I'd never met the Associate Dean and I thought it must be some general meeting or perhaps a committee. The secretary's voice came back on the line, "It's about the problems with the police department." I hung up the phone, leaned back in my chair, and picked up an old issue of the Seattle *Post-Intelligencer* that lay on my desk. "I wonder what he'll have to say?" I thought to myself as my eyes scanned the three-week-old headlines: SEATTLE'S DRUNK TANK: A PLACE OF FILTH, STENCH, HUMAN DEGRADATION. I started reading again that paper of August 13, 1968.

> Seen through the eyes of a Skid Road alcoholic, Seattle's City Jail is an overcrowded jungle of concrete and steel.
> It is a place of filth, sleeplessness and human degradation.
> It is a place where you are lucky to get enough to eat or adequate medical attention.
> It is a place where the poor stay longer and suffer more.
> This is the sordid picture drawn in an 88-page report just completed by Dr. James P. Spradley, assistant professor of psychiatry and anthropologist at the University of Washington.
> The report is based on interviews during the past year with 101 Skid Road men who have been arrested at least once for public drunkenness.

Spradley undertook the research project to find out if there is any therapeutic value in arresting an alcoholic and throwing him in jail.

He found that the men he questioned looked on their jail experience as much more detrimental than therapeutic. Of the alcoholics he surveyed:

— 83 percent said they had spent at least one night in the jail's drunk tank when it was so crowded they couldn't lie down.

— 93 percent reported that there is only one cup in the drunk tank from which those confined there may drink.

— 98 percent said they had never been given a receipt for money or property taken from them when they were booked into the jail, and 40 percent said police had taken money from their effects while they were in jail.

— 56 percent rated medical care they received in jail as very poor and 46 percent said they had not been able to get medical attention they needed while they were in the drunk tank. . . .

The article continued with more statistics and quotes from the men interviewed. I skipped to the second page of the paper and scanned the other stories: POLICE ABUSE ON SKID ROAD? read one. Another said, SOME ALCOHOLICS THINK POLICE ARREST THEM TO GET TRUSTIES. At the top of the page a small item gave me the most satisfaction. It read,

New emphasis on rehabilitation
The survey of Skid Road alcoholics by Dr. James P. Spradley was made public yesterday only four days after the City Council's Public Safety Committee recommended establishment of a detoxification center for handling public drunks.

Councilman Tim Hill said the purpose of the proposed ordinance is to change the handling of indigent alcoholics from a police matter to a public health procedure.

"The new emphasis," he said, "is on treatment and rehabilitation."

I folded the paper, placed it with a stack of others at the back of my desk, picked up my briefcase and headed for my car, thinking all the while about Dr. Anderson and my appointment the following day.

It was shortly after nine o'clock the next morning when I drove into the staff parking lot at the University Hospital. As I headed for the Dean's office I thought about the repetitious courtroom drama being enacted at that very moment in downtown Seattle. I wondered how many of the men I would recognize if I had been there this morning. I smiled to myself as I thought about Judge James Noe's recent comment: "Immediately following the news story of your research report the number of drunks on the court docket dropped off significantly," he had said, and then added with a twinkle in his eye, "Maybe that was the only way they could keep the jail clean enough for all the visitors coming through."

Dr. Anderson's secretary showed me to his office and he rose to shake my hand; a soft-spoken physician in his middle fifties, he seemed friendly and interested. "Well," he said, getting right to the point, "I'd like to discuss with you your study of the alcoholic. I've read it and I think it's quite a good study, but I'd be interested in discussing with you how this might be handled in the future to prevent this kind of thing that took place." My pulse quickened and I asked him, "What do you mean, *prevent*?" I tried to appear calm and unconcerned but I was beginning to feel warm and my voice sounded defensive. "Well," he answered, "I mean, perhaps there is some other way it could be handled that might have made it better, perhaps it would have been better to have it delivered at a scientific meeting and then it would have gotten out that way."

By this time I was angry but I tried not to show it. "I can't agree," I said, my voice rising slightly. "If I'd presented the report at a scientific meeting or published it in some journal hardly anyone would have read it and it wouldn't have done much good." I could see the next question coming. "By the way, how did the papers get your report?" Calmly, without hesitating, I looked directly at him and said, "I gave it to them." His mouth dropped open and he looked at me in disbelief.

And so I told him how I had been a member of the Ad Hoc Committee for the Indigent Public Intoxicant set up by Councilman Tim Hill who wanted me to contribute the perspective of the Skid Road Alcoholic. We had met for months to plan a detoxification center as an alternative to jailing men found drunk in public. Judge James Noe was a member of the committee; so was an inspector from the police department, one or two physicians, and others involved in work with alcoholics. I explained how the committee had been under the pressure of a possible Supreme Court ruling, the case of *Powell* v. *Texas*, how everyone expected the decision would make all drunk laws unconstitutional, and how they agreed that Seattle should set up a detoxification program to prepare for the coming change. Then, early in the summer, the Supreme Court had ruled against Powell, leaving all the state and local drunk laws intact. When our committee had met after that, many members voiced the opinion that now we did not have to plan a detoxification center. Even the physicians on the committee agreed; one man from the University Medical School had said, "I find it hard put to think that any other facility is going to be able to offer better care, other than the bar bit, than the jail." That meeting had convinced me that I should finish up my report and release it. I gave copies to the members of the committee, sent one to the Mayor of Seattle, to the Police Department, to the criminal court, and to members of the Seattle City Council. I had then called the editor of the Seattle *Post-Intelligencer* and gave him a copy.

He listened with interest to my long explanation and then zeroed in on the report itself. "I read the report and I used to work in King County emergency ward. I know the conditions, a lot of men dying in the drunk tank, and I learned quite a bit from your paper, especially about the bail system, and that sort of thing. But I noticed you always commented, even though the statistics might be that only 20 percent experienced some negative feature, you still make a comment in your paper. The bias is toward the negative side of the picture."

By now I was more relaxed and I agreed with him. "That very likely is true," I said, "but no one can do scientific research completely free from bias. I attempted to be impartial but I certainly don't feel that I achieved it fully. I'm willing to take the responsibility for that. But you have to understand that this report was prepared to shed light on a specific issue. The argument today is over whether the jail is therapeutic or not; the Supreme Court decision was based, in part, on the view that jailing a drunk has a therapeutic value for him. In view of this opinion and the fact that many people contend that jails *are* therapeutic, I felt we should hear from those who had repeatedly experienced being jailed for public drunkenness. I presented my data in terms of this issue and I say that in the report."

We talked on for some time about the report and the problem of alcoholics. Dr. Anderson said he was sympathetic with my approach in many ways and that it had not been his idea to call me in. As we drew near the end of our discussion I asked him, "How do you think it might have been handled differently?" He thought for a moment and then said, "Well, perhaps not releasing it to the press as you did. If you could have allowed it to slip out to the press through the subcommittee, then you would have preserved your own kind of scholarly identity in the University."

VI

As people who devote their professional lives to understanding man, anthropologists bear a positive responsibility to speak out publicly, both individually and collectively, on what they know and what they believe as a result of their professional expertise gained in the study of human beings. That is, they bear a professional responsibility to contribute to an "adequate definition of reality" upon which public opinion and public policy may be based.

— Principles of Professional Responsibility
American Anthropological Association

III

Language and communication

Culture is a system of symbols that allow us to represent and communicate our experience. We are surrounded by symbols — the flag, a new automobile, a diamond ring, billboard pictures, and, of course, spoken and written words. Each symbol has a special meaning in our society.

A symbol is anything that stands for something else. Almost anything we experience can come to have symbolic meaning. Every symbol has a referent that it calls to our attention. The term *mother-in-law* refers to a certain kind of relative, the mother of a person's spouse. When we communicate with symbols, we call attention not only to the referent but also to numerous connotations of the symbol. In our culture *mother-in-law* connotes a person who is difficult to get along with, who meddles in the affairs of her married daughter or son, and who is to be avoided. Human beings have the capacity to assign meaning to anything in our experience in an arbitrary fashion. This fact gives rise to limitless possibilities for communication.

Symbols greatly simplify the task of communiction. Once we learn that a word like *barn*, for example, stands for a certain type of building, we can communicate about a whole range of specific buildings that fit into the category. And we can communicate about barns in their absence;

we can even invent flying barns and dream about barns. Symbols make it possible to communicate the immense variety of human experience, whether past or present, tangible or intangible, good or bad.

Many channels are available to human beings for symbolic communication — sound, sight, touch, and smell. Language, our most highly developed communication system, uses the channel of sound (or for some deaf people, sight). Linguists have developed techniques for discovering the rules for the formation of sound symbols (phonology), their combination (grammar), and their interpretation (semantics).

To think that language is the only means for communication would be a mistake. In every society people use a wide range of things for communication — clothes, gestures, artifacts, the arrangement of space. In their study of language and communication, anthropologists are going beyond descriptions of sound and grammar to study meaning and style. Beneath the surface of language are hidden meanings built into the very structure of linguistic communication. A person's manner of speaking communicates as well as the words. In the following selections we examine the way that culture, language, and bodily adornment communicate in different cultural settings.

5

Student slang for college courses

PAUL A. ESCHHOLZ and
ALFRED F. ROSA

Slang is an "inside language" that lies below more formal verbal expression. In part, it functions to facilitate communication by providing short, easy-to-remember words and phrases in place of more cumbersome discourse. But it may also permit its speakers freely to express their feelings about large, impersonal, formally structured social settings. In this article, Paul Eschholz and Alfred Rosa discuss the way students at a large university generate slang names for their courses. By using shortening, acronymy, rhyming pairs, punning, and borrowing, they inject a humor into course naming that reflects a growing cynicism about their college experience.

College slang has a subcategory that consists of the names students give their courses. Richard K. Seymour, in briefly discussing such items, states that "a very frequent type of semantic transfer is that of facetious descriptions of courses to the names of the big courses."* Seymour, however, deals only with a few names for courses taken by large numbers of students or for the whole curriculum of a department or school. The use of such names as *dirt farming* for "History of American Democracy" or *God* for courses in a divinity school (to cite two of his examples) is a noteworthy departure from clipped forms such as *bio, econ, psych, chem, poli sci,* and *trig* that traditionally have been used by high school and college students.

Originally published as "Course Names: Another Aspect of College Slang," *American Speech*, Vol. 45, 1970, pp. 85–90. © 1973 The University of Alabama Press. Reprinted by permission.
    *"Collegiate Slang: Aspects of Word Formation and Semantic Change," *Publication of the American Dialect Society* 51 (April 1969):20.

With the belief that the phenomenon of students giving bynames to courses is widespread and complex, we set out to study the whole area more extensively, albeit in a limited context. During the past two years we have gathered by questionnaire a large sample of students' names for courses so that we could see more particularly what the data would reveal. The course names were used at the University of Vermont during the academic years 1970–1972, and our informants were students in the "Introduction to the English Language" course offered by the English Department and in an interdepartmental linguistics course. These students provided us with 263 different course names, which were then discussed in our classes in an effort to eliminate any idiosyncratic terms.

Our study of this data revealed that students use familiar patterns in creating slang names for courses. In addition, their names seem to reveal their biases about and attitudes toward particular courses and toward education in general. A wide variety of word-formation processes (such as shortening, acronymy, reduplication, rhyme formation, punning, derivation, blending, and alliteration) is exhibited in our data. The following is a description of these processes with examples, although categorizing is often difficult because several processes are at work in the formation of a course name. The names used in the following discussion are representative of larger categories of data in our study.

Shortening

Brevity is the soul of slang; the short word is easier to remember, is more forceful, and is more frequently used. In addition to the traditional clipped forms mentioned earlier that are still in use today, such as *Trig* for *Trigonometry* and *Calc* for *Calculus*, students have provided new clipped forms for individual courses:

Anal/enəl/	Fundamental Concepts of Mathematical Analysis
	Analytic Geometry and Calculus
Oral Interp	Oral Interpretation of Literature
Con Law	Constitutional Law
Cart	Cartography
Hip Lit	Literature of the Counter-Culture
Brit Lit	British Literature
Stat	Elementary Statistics
Comp and Con	(French) Composition and Conversation
Astrogut	Introductory Meteorology

The only two important words left intact in this list are *oral* and *law*, short words. *Hip* and *gut* are substitutions for *counter-culture* and *introductory*, respectively. In *Astrogut*, we see not only a clipping (Astronomy) but also a compounding. Also worthy of note are the assonance, rhyme, and alliteration in *Hip Lit*, *Brit Lit*, and *Comp and Con*.

ACRONYMY

The proliferation of new organizations and institutions with long, complicated names has spawned a great number of initialisms and acronyms — abbreviations made up of the initials of the original multiword titles. Every year at the University of Vermont the students have their own version of Sadie Hawkins week, when the girls pay all expenses on dates. While it is formally titled "Men's Economic Recovery Program," students affectionately refer to it as *MERP* Week. Student organizations that utilize an easy-to-remember acronym for their names include *DART* (Drug Abuse Research Team) and *BEAM* (Burlington Ecumenical Action Ministry). Although acronyms are more often used for students' social and political organizations, several have found their way into the titles of courses. A still frequent abbreviation is *ROTC* (Reserve Officers Training Corps), which may be pronounced either as an initialism /ar o ti si/ or an acronym /ratsi/ with the spelling variations *R.O.T.C.* and *Rotsy*. A frequently used initialism is *R&R* (Readings and Research), which enjoys widespread popularity because such a course is offered in many departments. Quite possibly this initialism is a carry-over from the Army's "Rest and Recreation." A less frequently used but interesting acronym is *FOC*/fak/ (Foundations of Oral Communication). Students playfully reverse the acronym procedure to yield such variations of the original course name as "Fools Obsessed with Communication" and "Fun on Campus." Whereas government and business, which are responsible for the creation of a great number of acronyms, tend to think in acronymic terms when naming new organizations and agencies, college faculty and administration rarely name courses with such abbreviations in mind. This may explain the sparsity of acronyms for course names; more often than not they seem to be accidental.

RHYMING PAIR FORMATION

Students often use pairs of names to designate their courses. The basic formula for pairs of nouns or verbs, "X and Y" or "X for Y," can be used in several ways. Often the key words rhyme:

Priests and Beasts	Introduction to the Study of Western Religion
Trees and Bees	Dendrology
Socks and Jocks	General Physical Education
Slums and Bums	Urban Local Government

Nuts and Sluts	Abnormal Psychology
Gabs and Blabs	Foundations of Oral Communication
Stars and Mars	The Solar System
Struck and Fuck	(Zoology) General Structure and Functions
Trees and Leaves	Dendrology
Hicks and Sticks	Rural Local Government
Stones and Bones	(Anthropology) World Pre-History
Places and Spaces	World Geography
Cuts and Guts	Principles of Biology
Flicks and Tricks	Development of the Motion Picture
Weeds and Seeds	Introduction to Plant Biology
Trains and Planes	Transportation and Public Utilities
Maps and Naps	Introduction to Physical Geography
Spaces and Races	Introduction to Human Geography
Rocks for Jocks	Introductory Geology
Drugs for Thugs	(Psychology) The Drug Culture
Choke and Croak	First Aid and Safety Education
Cut'em and Gut'em	Mammalian Anatomy and Physiology
Bag'em and Tag'em	Field Zoology
Seed and Breed	Advanced Livestock Production

Several rhyme formations that follow the analogy of "hit the pit" (go to the all-night study area in the basement of the library) include *Mug the Bug* (Principles of Pest Control) and *Play with Clay* ([Art] Basic Design).

A variation on the rhyming pair formation, without the conjunction, is reduplication. Examples are: *Blabber Jabber* (Public Speaking), *Mumble Jumble* (Public Speaking), and *Frig Trig* (Plane Trigonometry).

NONRHYMING COORDINATIONS

Although rhymed pairs are popular because they are easy to remember and have an aura of nursery-school childishness about them, some courses do not easily lend themselves to the rhyming process. The formula of coordinated nouns or verbs is nevertheless used:

Secants and Sines	Plane Trigonometry
Cowboys and Indians	(English) Regional Writing in America
Paper and Pulp	Forest Products
Wind and Rain	Climate
Ice and Snow	Glacial Geology
Needles and Pins	Clothing Selection and Construction

Needles and Thread	Tailoring
Nuts and Bolts	Household Equipment
Tricks and Puzzles	Fundamentals of Mathematics
Food and Nuts	Basic Concepts of Nutrition
Hills and Curves	Highway Geometric Design
Prove'em and Learn'em	Fundamental Concepts of Mathematics
Think and Write	Written Expression
Touch and Go	(Psychology) Sensory Perception
Divide and Multiply	Mechanisms of Cell Division
Show and Tell	Public Speaking

ANALOGICAL DERIVATION

The word ending *-ology* "science or study of" is a familiar constituent of college course names (for example, Immunology, Virology, Sedimentary Petrology, Advanced Paleontology); students by analogy have utilized this ending in devising new names for courses. For example, students have taken the forms *cow* and *barf* and applied them to courses entitled "Introductory Dairy Technology" and "Principles of Biology" respectively; to these they have added *-ology* to lend a degree of facetious respectability and academic stuffiness to the new names. The results are humorous incongruities: *Cowology* and *Barfology*. Another example of the same process is the appellation *zerology*, which students apply to any course that is, in their own terms, "a nothing course."

PUNNING

A play on words is manifested in the following examples:

Where's my fodder?	Fundamentals of Livestock Feeding
Stumping	Introduction to Forestry
Super Bull	Animal Breeding
Confusion	Chinese Religion and Thought
Gut Course	Principles of Biology
Bach to Rock	Survey of Musical Literature

Stumping operates on three levels: the literal "reducing to or removing stumps," the oratorical "speaking as from a stump," and the academic "challenging or perplexing." *Confusion* plays upon the name of Confucius. The last two puns are particularly interesting. *Gut Course*, a label usually reserved for easy or basic courses, is ironically applied to a course that has usually been considered difficult at the University of Vermont. This particular use derives from the subject matter of the course and is related to pair formations *Cut'em and Gut'em* and *Cuts of*

Guts. Bach to Rock is a good pun because it gives a sense of the historical orientation of the course and seems to be related to the expressions "Back to Back" and "Back to Bach."

SYNECDOCHE

Naming a course on the basis of a characteristic part is a form of synecdochic creation. Although synecdoche is evident in some of the other categories, especially pair formation, there are many other examples:

Cottage Cheese	Manufactured Dairy Products
Hoof and Mouth	Animal Diseases
Threads	Introduction to Textiles and Clothing
Loom	Weaving
Secants and Sines	Plane Trigonometry
God	Introduction to the Study of Religion
Sheet Folding	Introductory Nursing
Bedpan	Intermediate Nursing
Diaper Rash	Maternal-Child Nursing
Cat	Mammalian Anatomy and Physiology
Milk	Milk Processing
Steel	(Civil Engineering) Advanced Structural Design
Strength	(Civil Engineering) Mechanics of Materials
Cement	Reinforced Concrete
Water	Hydraulics
Crap	Sanitary Engineering
Clay	Introduction to Ceramics

While synecdoche often uses an important part that is directly associated with the subject to stand for the whole, students may take an unattractive, distasteful, and seemingly insignificant aspect of the course as the part to signify the whole, as in *Bedpan, Sheet Folding, Cottage Cheese,* and *Threads.*

BORROWING

One major category of course names comes from the world of advertising and television. Students borrow program names, the names of famous personalities, and key advertising phrases; they feel that such names are particularly apt for the impression that certain courses give.

Get Smart	(Education) The Slow Learner

Sea Hunt	Geological Oceanography
Edge of Night	Medieval European Civilization
The Lighted Path	Introductory Meteorology
Another World	The Solar System
As the World Turns	History of the United States
Our Changing World	Contemporary History
Ding-Dong Time	(Religion) Myth, Symbol, and Ritual
F Troop	Introduction to Tactics: American Military History
Bright Promise	(Sociology) Social Movements
All in the Family	(Sociology) The Family
Smokey the Bear	Forest Fire Control
Mickey Mouse Math	College Algebra
Roberts' Rules	Parliamentary Procedure
Robin Hood	General Physical Education: Archery
Newton's Menagerie	General Physics
Politics with Tricky Dicky	(Political Science) The National Executive
Blood, Sweat, and Tears	Mammalian Anatomy and Physiology
The Un-Math	Plane Analytic Geometry and Calculus
TV Guide	Advanced Television Production
Fight Now, Pay Later	American Foreign Policy
A & P	Mammalian Anatomy and Physiology
The Elephant and the Ass	Political Parties

The analogy that students make between television programs and courses has some validity. Just like serial television programs, college courses have a main character, a supporting cast, a theme, regular meetings, a generally similar yearly schedule, and a major statement for each installment.

CONCLUSION

Student bynames for courses, as examples of purely collegiate slang, express student attitudes, which seem to us to be satiric and anti-intellectual. Most of the course names solicited from students reflect their negative or cynical attitudes toward specific courses, education, and society in general. More important, these names are indicative of what appears to be a new wave of criticism directed at higher education. With greater public scrutiny of education has come the cry for accountability and more practicality, if not relevance, in courses, and this trend is also quite evident in our study. Although there are exceptions, in general we found courses that seemed to students to have a practical or utilitarian purpose did not elicit pejorative names.

The items include the vulgar and the witty, with a great deal of skepticism and satire throughout. In addition to the names already cited, the following ones are representative of student attitudes: *Physucks, FOC-off, Grow Your Own Grass, Supergut, American Gutterment, Sadistics, Orgasmic Chem, Flunk Fast, Sex for Credit, Bull for Credit,* and *Dunderology.* Although there has always been a strain of anti-intellectualism in American culture, this trend seems to be more pronounced today.

Much of the slang that college students use can also be found in other subcultures. It is, however, unlikely that the names students give their courses have any use outside the college ambience. Such names, tied as they are to the academic side of college life, seem to be genuine examples of college slang.

6

Odds and endos:
The language of bicycle motocross racing

JEFFREY E. NASH

*Most people are aware of the direct communicative functions of
language. Linguistic rules generate the utterances by which we
regularly exchange our thoughts. But language may also have other
functions for society, as we see in this article by Jeffrey Nash.
Describing the argot of US bicycle motocross (BMX) racers, he
shows how this special language not only facilitates efficient
communication, but also serves to intensify group visibility, generate
a greater sense of group identification, and symbolize prestige. The
BMX argot has a dual structure containing a complex technical
language and a slang. This structure permits BMX racers to interact
with important outsiders while they maintain their own special
identity.*

We normally associate language with nations or ethnic groups. Italian
is spoken by Italians, English by the English, Hindi by North Indians.
These tongues are shared by all members of such groups, providing the
basis for communication in daily life.

But many of the world's nations are large and complex societies
made up of a variety of groups, many of which have formed in response
to economic specialization, common interest, and other shared needs.
Members of such subgroups are part of the larger society, and speak its
language. But the smaller groups also tend to develop special languages,
ones that are clearly derived from national language but which include
special terms and special meanings. Such sublanguages are often termed
argots.

In our own society, we encounter argots almost everywhere we go. Stockbrokers speak of "cold calls" and "waffles" when they wish to refer to phoning strangers and the money they get when they start a new job. Tramps "flop" when they go to sleep at night. Students "cut" class when they miss one on purpose, and take a "gut" or "sluff" course when they want to find an easy one.

Bicycle motocross racers, or BMXers, also have a special argot, just as do many other people who participate in recreational and sports scenes. BMXers speak of "endos" when their bike flips over forward either by accident while racing or as a part of skilled trick maneuver. They suffer a "medical" when they hurt themselves in accidents. But why do BMXers or other members of subgroups in complex societies develop special argots? Is not the national language a sufficient means of expression? The answer to this question lies in the several functions that the language serves. Like most languages, argots reflect the special needs found in the cultural world of their speakers. For BMXers, this means that the argot must permit them to name and talk about the special technical aspects of their sport; and it must also meet social needs, such as enhancing a sense of group membership and permitting involvement with others, such as business people, parents, and new recruits, while allowing insiders the advantage of remaining special and elite.

BICYCLE MOTOCROSS RACING

Motocross racing originated in Europe, where it continues as a physically demanding sport involving motorcycles. Races are run on closed dirt courses that include sharp turns, jumps, mud, severe bumps, loose dirt, and ridges. Just keeping the highly specialized motorcycles upright at competitive speed on such a course takes substantial skill and physical stamina.

Motorcycle motocross is also found in the United States, although it has never attained the popularity here that it enjoys in Europe. Motocross racing is regularly shown on television sports programs and may be seen in many parts of the country both at outdoor tracks and indoor arenas. It has attracted a growing number of motorcycle enthusiasts and participants, so that today several of the world's leading, top-ranked competitors are from North America.

The growing popularity of motorcycle motocross attracted the attention of large numbers of children who, using bicycles, began to imitate what they saw motorcyclists doing on the track. Young riders sought out rougher terrain, learned to jump, and developed proficiency controlling their bikes in the rough. Their activities first came to be formalized as organized bicycle motocross in southern California during the early 1970s. Today BMX can be found almost everywhere in the United States. It usually involves boys between eight and seventeen who own and race specially constructed bicycles called BMX bikes. Like motorcyclists, they race over dirt tracks laid out like regular motocross tracks, with jumps, sharp turns, and bumps. The sale of special BMX bicycles, competition clothing, and racing accessories has become a multimillion dollar business, influencing styles of dress and the values of young people all across America.

CULTURE AND LANGUAGE

BMX forms a microculture within the larger American context, just as do the cultures of tramps and stockbrokers. Participants in BMX share a complex system of cultural knowledge about bicycles, equipment, riding techniques, and all the other activities and things that make up their cultural scene. As do all cultural groups, they use language to communicate with each other about these things; but unlike members of the general public, they use a special argot to do so. When BMXers talk about racing, they use phrases such as "wire the start," "get the hole shot," "wipe out," "get medical," and "cross up." They may say that they "dusted the pack," or "swooped" a competitor at the "zookers." They may complain that they "tweated" something, "slipped" a pedal, or perhaps worst of all, were "cherry picked."

Presumably BMXers could say these things in standard American English. They could say that "they got a fast start out of the gate and had the lead into the first turn" (the hole shot), or that "they fell off their bike and got hurt" (a medical trash). They could note that "they broke a piece of equipment" (tweated it), or that "they lost a race because an older boy lied about his age in order to race in a younger age category" (got cherry picked).

But they don't. To BMXers, standard English represents the larger conventional society. It is the language of school, the talk of the conventional world. It simply will not do for the purposes of BMX. BMX talk is precise and descriptive. It allows for fine distinctions among equipment; the ability to speak it is essential to membership in the cultural scene. But just how does BMX argot function for members of this racing group?

NAMING

BMX meets the special need to name things specific to this form of bicycle racing. The sport has evolved an enormous inventory of equipment. A complete list of terms for equipment results in a sizable glossary: BMX bikes are component systems, and BMX racers put them together piece by piece, looking for the "perfect" combination, or as they say, "the dialed-in bike." For each component there may be scores of brands to choose from: there are, for example, well over fifty different types of frames and each has its own name as we see in Figure I.

There are also an equal number of forks and parts of frames. Even minor features of the frame, such as "dropouts" and "gussets," are named.

FIGURE I. *Folk taxonomy of frames*

Frames				
20 inchers			Cruisers (big wheels 24" and 26")	Pit frames (16")
OK frames	Good frames	Minis		
Patterson	Coke	GT	Laguana	Traker
Procraft	Machine	JMC	Cal Cruiser	Hutch
Power Light	Mongoose	CW	SE Floval	Mongoose
Redline	Moose	Harbor Light	Flyer	CYC
Kabuki	Goose	Little Hole	OM Flyer	SE
Rampar	National Pro	Shot	Bassett	Kakubi
Predator	Quadangle	Little Shoot	Redline	Raleigh
SX 1000-	Rebel	Out	GT	
2000	CW	SE Ripper	Hutch	
Cycle Pro	Pro File	Kuwahara	Tahoe	
Eagle	Diamond		Torke	
RRS	Back		Mongoose	
Cyc Stormer	Hutch		CW	
DG	Puch			
Murray	Tahoe			
Race, Inc.	Shimano			
Basher	Jag			
Pan	MCS			
P. K. Ripper	GT			
Torker	Cook Bro.			
Traker	Ross			
Scorpion	Haro			
	Kuwahara			
	Star			
	Robinson			
	JMC			
	BXC			

The argot also names other aspects of bicycle motocross such as the larger number of tracks available for racing, as we see in Figure II. These tracks are judged by features that are important to BMX racers (see Figure III). Hence, the Richfield track is ABA (sanctioned by the American Bicycle Association), has a steep left turn after the first jump (a "rad" left orientation), and has decent "whoopdeedoos" (three jumps in a row).

BMX argot not only names these special features; it permits them to be efficiently communicated. With the inside language, one can compress a larger amount of information into a short utterance. "Gear 45X16, use a two pedal start and hang low in the first berm," is an efficient way of saying "put a 45 tooth sprocket on the front crank, a 16 tooth free wheel on the rear hub, start the race by balancing the bicycle with both feet on the pedals and ride the first steep turn by staying off the embankment." BMXers need a special argot to communicate clearly and efficiently.

FIGURE II. *Folk taxonomy of tracks (ABA sanctioned tracks)*

ABA sanctioned tracks			
Northstar	*Lake Elmo*	*Out of town*	*Inside*
Prior Lake Shorewood Richfield Eden Prairie Brooklyn Park		Austin Gamehaven Mankato Iowa Circuit	Auditorium Armory Civic Center

FIGURE III. *Folk taxonomy of features of tracks*

Features of tracks			
Turns	*Jumps*	*Flats*	*Starts*
European Hair Pin S Turns Berms	Whoopdeedoos Moonwalkers Table Tops Double Jumps Saddles Ant Hills Zookers Bumps Waps Steps	Bonzais Hills Straights	Voiced Lights Fast Slow

GROUP IDENTIFICATION

In addition to its communicative functions, language, including argots such as BMX, functions to increase a sense of group identification, to mark group boundaries, and to instill a sense of group pride. The need to belong to special groups is especially acute for children in the United States. Many scholars have suggested that the rise of peer group cultures in our complex society is at least a partial adaptation to changes in traditional institutions. For example, families relocate often, reorganize when both parents obtain jobs, and divide when parents are divorced. As children find it more and more difficult to feel part of a family group, they turn to other young people who are also uprooted. The formation of children's groups such as BMX racers is the result.

BMX language is an efficient way to mark boundaries of the group. To an outsider, words like "zookers," "whoopdeedoos," and "ant hills" are a foreign language. On the other hand, when a BMXer advises a fellow racer that a "berm" on a particular track is a place where "you can get medical," not only is he telling his friends that the turn is dangerous, he is also reaffirming a sense of membership by speaking a shared inside language. Take a conversation between two young racers, Jim and John. Jim says, "Hey, you chasing points?" (Are you racing as often as possible to pile up points toward your year-end standings in your district?) John replies, "Nah, but I'm goin' to the triple pointer" (I am going to the upcoming race that awards triple points for 1st, 2nd, 3rd, and 4th place finishes.) Jim points out, "That's a real rad track. You can wire the starts, but you'll bum out on the berms. There's an awesome European there you can really get medical on." (The track is very good. You can get fast starts there. But some of the turns are dangerous).

Using the argot gives these two racers a shared feeling of mutual experience and belonging. It permits them to compare their sense of being special and to test their degree of involvement in BMX. At the same time, a non-BMXer, listening to Jim and John talk, would be reminded of his alienation from the culture, although he might be impressed by the inside knowledge of the speakers.

DEALING WITH OUTSIDERS

Members of every group must relate systematically to outsiders, particularly those whose activities directly affect the welfare of group members or who must eventually be recruited to the group. This is certainly true for BMX racers, for their scene depends on interaction with equipment suppliers and parents, particularly fathers. It must also permit entrance into the group by new members. These needs are reflected in the structure of the argot.

BMX argot allows for the need to communicate with outsiders and to bring new recruits into the group by displaying a dual structure. There is an inside slang — illustrated by the conversation between Jim and John — that is almost exclusively spoken by the racers themselves. But there is the vast technical language also described earlier that is spoken by both insiders and those closest to the scene. This multiple language feature, which characterizes a large number of argots in the United States, gives outsiders a sense of belonging to the scene without actually becoming full members. It also provides potential recruits with a stepping stone toward full membership.

Take the relationship with the manufacturers and sellers of BMX equipment. Manufacturers and promoters actually introduce many of the terms for new pieces of equipment. A company such as Schwinn or Murray may introduce a new frame or handlebar, giving them names ("Predator" or "Vector") that become part of BMX vocabulary. When BMX racers buy equipment, they can use the technical part of the argot to conduct transactions. The language functions as a medium through which economic exchanges can be made with shop owners. Both racers and owners know, for example, that only "SR" makes a long seat post.

Parents are even more important to BMXers. The average BMX racer is male and between ten and fifteen years of age. Standard BMX bikes cost at least $275.00 and fully outfitted racing machines may cost up to $1,000.00. In addition, tracks are often located quite far apart. To be active in the race scene, a BMXer needs large sums of money and reliable transportation. Parents and other relatives represent the main source of such support.

To gain the support of their parents, BMXers must conform to certain values and rules laid down by these adults. Parents support the BMX activities of their children with their time and money, but the young racers must participate in the organized racing activities stressing competition, a willingness to cooperate with racing organizations, personal dedication, and other things of value to adults.

BMX argot symbolizes the reciprocal relationship between parents and their children. It says that parents, particularly fathers, are part of the scene. It permits effective communication between fathers and sons, and it enables a father to identify with his son's racing aspirations without holding full membership. For example, a typical conversation finds a BMX racer asking his father for money to buy a new piece of equipment:

> BMXer: Hey, Dad, do you think I can ride a three piece crank?
> Dad: I don't know, I guess so.
> BMXer: Profile has this new set up that's real tough. Larry cranks on it an' never busted it up.

Dad: How much?
BMXer: $158.00
Dad: What's the weight?
BMXer: Real light.
Dad: Friday we'll go to Mr. B's and look at 'em.
BMXer: Great, maybe they'll help my starts.

In this conversation, the racer's father can use the technical aspect of BMX argot to question his son's reasoning about buying this expensive piece of equipment. The argot reflects the father's knowledge about the scene, thus certifying his membership in it; and at the same time it permits him to think he is exercising his adult judgment in his son's affairs. He does not speak the inside slang that would indicate his full participation in the scene, but what he can say is enough to involve him in the all-important purchase of expensive equipment and leaves him feeling good about it. One BMXer summed up this father-son relationship, as well as the importance of slang for real membership in BMX, by saying:

> We put up with that stuff — organization, trophies, talk about good sportsmanship, and the value of competition. Sure the races are fun, and I get off on chasing points. But real BMX — that's just being with your buddies down at the track. Just sittin' on the bike, doin' a little showboatin' and findin' out where everybody is at. That's real BMX to me.

Another function of the dual construction of BMX relates to the recruitment of new members. BMX slang is difficult for a stranger to understand at all. But the technical language is more accessible. Any boy or girl who can buy the latest BMX magazine or newspaper can learn some of the usual terms for equipment, tracks, and other aspects of the sport. These will be many of the same terms used by those who really race; learning them can give an outsider a sense of membership that initiates him into the culture.

True insiders, however, those who actually race, will often remind newcomers that they haven't attained full membership yet, for there are many levels of involvement in BMX. Language again is a primary tool for achieving this end as the following conversation indicates. Mark asks the new kid on the block what kind of bike he has. The boy replies, "A Predator," using part of the technical BMX vocabulary to indicate a standard factory bicycle that does not convey a deep commitment to BMX. Mark continues, "You race?" to which the boy responds, "Nah." Mark indicates his own deep commitment to BMX now by saying, "I have a Hutch with bear trap pedals, and CW bars." Faced with this insider talk, the boy can only reply, "Oh."

In short, BMX talk may impress its listeners in opposite ways. A listener may be put off by the talk, increasing his distance from the scene and reinforcing the exclusivity of the racing group. Or the listener may be impressed by the argot. For example, saying, "Man, that JT is awesome with CW bars, Hutch bear traps, and graphite mags," may impress a naive youngster and lure him into the BMX scene, not drive him away.

CONCLUSION

BMX talk is an argot, a sublanguage associated with a special group found within a larger, more complex society. It functions to name the special cultural categories that make up the cultural knowledge of the group, and it permits precise and economical conversation among group members. It also meets several social needs. It marks group members, giving them a sense of sharing common interests and experiences while separating them from outsiders. It signals commitment — elite status — and by its unintelligibility, it sustains an attractive and mysterious aura about group members.

Like most languages and argots, BMX talk is divided into levels. One, the more technical side of the language, permits BMXers to interact with commercial outlets and to involve parents, especially fathers, paying for their equipment and related costs of BMX. It may also enable aspiring BMXers to gain entrance into the group. The second level, best described as a slang, helps racers identify and maintain a highly committed inside group of BMXers, the "real" members of the scene.

The BMX argot, and by extension, other languages, serve to achieve much more than simple referential meaning. They symbolize social connections, often adapting their form to the structures of particular groups. In this sense, they are essential to the construction and maintenance of social order.

7

The sounds of silence

EDWARD T. HALL and
MILDRED REED HALL

*People communicate with more than just words. An important part
of every encounter are the messages we send with our bodies and
faces: the smile, the frown, the slouch of the shoulders, or the tightly
crossed legs are only a few gestures which add another dimension to
our verbal statements. These gestures as well as their social meaning
change from one culture to another. In this article, the Halls describe
and explain the function of nonverbal behavior in
social encounters.*

Bob leaves his apartment at 8:15 A.M. and stops at the corner drugstore
for breakfast. Before he can speak, the counterman says, "The usual?"
Bob nods yes. While he savors his Danish, a fat man pushes onto the
adjoining stool and overflows into his space. Bob scowls and the man
pulls himself in as much as he can. Bob has sent two messages without
speaking a syllable.

Henry has an appointment to meet Arthur at 11 o'clock; he arrives
at 11:30. Their conversation is friendly, but Arthur retains a lingering
hostility. Henry has unconsciously communicated that he doesn't think
the appointment is very important or that Arthur is a person who needs
to be treated with respect.

George is talking to Charley's wife at a party. Their conversation
is entirely trivial, yet Charley glares at them suspiciously. Their physical
proximity and the movements of their eyes reveal that they are powerfully attracted to each other.

José Ybarra and Sir Edmund Jones are at the same party and it is

Originally appeared in *Playboy* Magazine; copyright © 1971 by Edward T. Hall and Mildred
Reed Hall. Reprinted with permission of the authors.

important for them to establish a cordial relationship for business reasons. Each is trying to be warm and friendly, yet they will part with mutual distrust and their business transaction will probably fall through. José, in Latin fashion, moved closer and closer to Sir Edmund as they spoke, and this movement was miscommunicated as pushiness to Sir Edmund, who kept backing away from this intimacy, and this was miscommunicated to José as coldness. The silent languages of Latin and English cultures are more difficult to learn than their spoken languages.

In each of these cases, we see the subtle power of nonverbal communication. The only language used throughout most of the history of humanity (in evolutionary terms, vocal communication is relatively recent), it is the first form of communication you learn. You use this preverbal language, consciously and unconsciously, every day to tell other people how you feel about yourself and them. This language includes your posture, gestures, facial expressions, costume, the way you walk, even your treatment of time and space and material things. All people communicate on several different levels at the same time but are usually aware of only the verbal dialog and don't realize that they respond to nonverbal messages. But when a person says one thing and really believes something else, the discrepancy between the two can usually be sensed. Nonverbal-communication systems are much less subject to the conscious deception that often occurs in verbal systems. When we find ourselves thinking, "I don't know what it is about him, but he doesn't seem sincere," it's usually this lack of congruity between a person's words and his behavior that makes us anxious and uncomfortable.

Few of us realize how much we all depend on body movement in our conversation or are aware of the hidden rules that govern listening behavior. But we know instantly whether or not the person we're talking to is "tuned in" and we're very sensitive to any breach in listening etiquette. In white middle-class American culture, when someone wants to show he is listening to someone else, he looks either at the other person's face or, specifically, at his eyes, shifting his gaze from one eye to the other.

If you observe a person conversing, you'll notice that he indicates he's listening by nodding his head. He also makes little "Hmm" noises. If he agrees with what's being said, he may give a vigorous nod. To show pleasure or affirmation, he smiles; if he has some reservations, he looks skeptical by raising an eyebrow or pulling down the corners of his mouth. If a participant wants to terminate the conversation, he may start shifting his body position, stretching his legs, crossing or uncrossing them, bobbing his foot or diverting his gaze from the speaker. The more he fidgets, the more the speaker becomes aware that he has lost his audience. As a last measure, the listener may look at his watch to indicate the imminent end of the conversation.

Talking and listening are so intricately intertwined that a person cannot do one without the other. Even when one is alone and talking to oneself, there is part of the brain that speaks while another part listens. In all conversations, the listener is positively or negatively reinforcing the speaker all the time. He may even guide the conversation without knowing it, by laughing or frowning or dismissing the argument with a wave of his hand.

The language of the eyes — another age-old way of exchanging feelings — is both subtle and complex. Not only do men and women use their eyes differently but there are class, generation, regional, ethnic and national cultural differences. Americans often complain about the way foreigners stare at people or hold a glance too long. Most Americans look away from someone who is using his eyes in an unfamiliar way because it makes them self-conscious. If a man looks at another man's wife in a certain way, he's asking for trouble, as indicated earlier. But he might not be ill-mannered or seeking to challenge the husband. He might be a European in this country who hasn't learned our visual mores. Many American women visiting France or Italy are acutely embarrassed because, for the first time in their lives, men really look at them — their eyes, hair, nose, lips, breasts, hips, legs, thighs, knees, ankles, feet, clothes, hairdo, even their walk. These same women, once they have become used to being looked at, often return to the United States and are overcome with the feeling that "No one ever really looks at me anymore."

Analyzing the mass of data on the eyes, it is possible to sort out at least three ways in which the eyes are used to communicate: dominance vs. submission, involvement vs. detachment, and positive vs. negative attitude. In addition, there are three levels of consciousness and control, which can be categorized as follows: (1) conscious use of the eyes to communicate, such as the flirting blink and the intimate nose-wrinkling squint; (2) the very extensive category of unconscious but learned behavior governing where the eyes are directed and when (this unwritten set of rules dictates how and under what circumstances the sexes, as well as people of all status categories, look at each other); and (3) the response of the eye itself, which is completely outside both awareness and control — changes in the cast (the sparkle) of the eye and the pupillary reflex.

The eye is unlike any other organ of the body, for it is an extension of the brain. The unconscious pupillary reflex and the cast of the eye have been known by people of Middle Eastern origin for years — although most are unaware of their knowledge. Depending on the context, Arabs and others look either directly at the eyes or deeply *into* the eyes of their interlocutor. We became aware of this in the Middle East several years ago while looking at jewelry. The merchant suddenly started to push a particular bracelet at a customer and said, "You buy this one." What interested us was that the bracelet was not the one that had been consciously selected by the purchaser. But the merchant, watching the pupils of the eyes, knew what the purchaser really wanted to buy. Whether he specifically knew *how* he knew is debatable.

A psychologist at the University of Chicago, Eckhard Hess, was the first to conduct systematic studies of the pupillary reflex. His wife remarked one evening, while watching him reading in bed, that he must be very interested in the text because his pupils were dilated. Following up on this, Hess slipped some pictures of nudes into a stack of photographs that he gave to his male assistant. Not looking at the photographs but watching his assistant's pupils, Hess was able to tell precisely when the assistant came to the nudes. In further experiments, Hess retouched the eyes in a photograph of a woman. In one print, he made the pupils small, in another, large; nothing else was changed. Subjects who were given the photographs found the woman with the dilated pupils much more attractive. Any man who has had the experience of seeing a woman look at him as her pupils widen with reflex speed knows that she's flashing him a message.

The eye-sparkle phenomenon frequently turns up in our interviews of couples in love. It's apparently one of the first reliable clues in the other person that love is genuine. To date, there is no scientific data to explain eye sparkle; no investigation of the pupil, the cornea or even the white sclera of the eye shows how the sparkle originates. Yet we all know it when we see it.

One common situation for most people involves the use of the eyes in the street and in public. Although eye behavior follows a definite set of rules, the rules vary according to the place, the needs and feelings of the people, and their ethnic background. For urban whites, once they're within definite recognition distance (16–32 feet for people with average eyesight), there is mutual avoidance of eye contact — unless they want something specific: a pickup, a handout or information of some kind. In the West and in small towns generally, however, people are much more likely to look at and greet one another, even if they're strangers.

It's permissible to look at people if they're beyond recognition distance; but once inside this sacred zone, you can only steal a glance at strangers. You *must* greet friends, however; to fail to do so is insulting.

Yet, to stare too fixedly even at them is considered rude and hostile. Of course, all of these rules are variable.

A great many blacks, for example, greet each other in public even if they don't know each other. To blacks, most eye behavior of whites has the effect of giving the impression that they aren't there, but this is due to white avoidance of eye contact with *anyone* in the street.

Another very basic difference between people of different ethnic backgrounds is their sense of territoriality and how they handle space. This is the silent communication, or miscommunication, that caused friction between Mr. Ybarra and Sir Edmund Jones in our earlier example. We know from research that everyone has around himself an invisible bubble of space that contracts and expands depending on several factors: his emotional state, the activity he's performing at the time and his cultural background. This bubble is a kind of mobile territory that he will defend against intrusion. If he is accustomed to close personal distance between himself and others, his bubble will be smaller than that of someone who's accustomed to greater personal distance. People of North European heritage — English, Scandinavian, Swiss and German — tend to avoid contact. Those whose heritage is Italian, French, Spanish, Russian, Latin American or Middle Eastern like close personal contact.

People are very sensitive to any intrusion into their spatial bubble. If someone stands too close to you, your first instinct is to back up. If that's not possible, you lean away and pull yourself in, tensing your muscles. If the intruder doesn't respond to these body signals, you may then try to protect yourself, using a briefcase, umbrella or raincoat. Women — especially when traveling alone — often plant their pocketbook in such a way that no one can get very close to them. As a last resort, you may move to another spot and position yourself behind a desk or a chair that provides screening. Everyone tries to adjust the space around himself in a way that's comfortable for him; most often, he does this unconsciously.

Emotions also have a direct effect on the size of a person's territory. When you're angry or under stress, your bubble expands and you require more space. New York psychiatrist Augustus Kinzel found a difference in what he calls Body-Buffer Zones between violent and nonviolent prison inmates. Dr. Kinzel conducted experiments in which each prisoner was placed in the center of a small room and then Dr. Kinzel slowly walked toward him. Nonviolent prisoners allowed him to come quite close, while prisoners with a history of violent behavior couldn't tolerate his proximity and reacted with some vehemence.

Apparently, people under stress experience other people as looming larger and closer than they actually are. Studies of schizophrenic patients have indicated that they sometimes have a distorted perception of space, and several psychiatrists have reported patients who experience their body boundaries as filling up an entire room. For these patients, anyone who comes into the room is actually inside their body, and such an intrusion may trigger a violent outburst.

Unfortunately, there is little detailed information about normal people who live in highly congested urban areas. We do know, of course, that the noise, pollution, dirt, crowding and confusion of our cities induce feelings of stress in most of us, and stress leads to a need for greater space. The man who's packed into a subway, jostled in the street, crowded into an elevator and forced to work all day in a bull pen or in a small office without auditory or visual privacy is going to be very stressed at the end of his day. He needs places that provide relief from constant overstimulation of his nervous system. Stress from overcrowding is cumulative and people can tolerate more crowding early in the day than later; note the increased bad temper during the evening rush hour as compared with the morning melee. Certainly one factor in people's desire to commute by car is the need for privacy and relief from crowding (except, often, from other cars); it may be the only time of the day when nobody can intrude.

In crowded public places, we tense our muscles and hold ourselves stiff, and thereby communicate to others our desire not to intrude on their space and, above all, not to touch them. We also avoid eye contact, and the total effect is that of someone who has "tuned out." Walking along the street, our bubble expands slightly as we move in a stream of strangers, taking care not to bump into them. In the office, at meetings, in restaurants, our bubble keeps changing as it adjusts to the activity at hand.

Most white middle-class Americans use four main distances in their business and social relations: intimate, personal, social, and public. Each of these distances has a near and a far phase and is accompanied by changes in the volume of the voice. Intimate distance varies from direct physical contact with another person to a distance of six to eighteen inches and is used for our most private activities — caressing another person or making love. At this distance, you are overwhelmed by sensory inputs from the other person — heat from the body, tactile stimulation from the skin, the fragrance of perfume, even the sound of breathing — all of which literally envelop you. Even at the far phase, you're still within easy touching distance. In general, the use of intimate distance in public between adults is frowned on. It's also much too close for strangers, except under conditions of extreme crowding.

In the second zone — personal distance — the close phase is one and a half to two and a half feet; it's at this distance that wives usually stand from their husbands in public. If another woman moves into this zone, the wife will most likely be disturbed. The far phase — two and a half to four feet — is the distance used to "keep someone at arm's length" and is the most common spacing used by people in conversation.

The third zone — social distance — is employed during business transactions or exchanges with a clerk or repairman. People who work together tend to use close social distance — four to seven feet. This is also the distance for conversation at social gatherings. To stand at this distance from someone who is seated has a dominating effect (e.g., teacher to pupil, boss to secretary). The far phase of the third zone — seven to twelve feet — is where people stand when someone says, "Stand back so I can look at you." This distance lends a formal tone to business or social discourse. In an executive office, the desk serves to keep people at this distance.

The fourth zone — public distance — is used by teachers in classrooms or speakers at public gatherings. At its farthest phase — 25 feet and beyond — it is used for important public figures. Violations of this distance can lead to serious complications. During his 1970 U.S. visit, the president of France, Georges Pompidou, was harassed by pickets in Chicago, who were permitted to get within touching distance. Since pickets in France are kept behind barricades a block or more away, the president was outraged by this insult to his person, and President Nixon was obliged to communicate his concern as well as offer his personal apologies.

It is interesting to note how American pitchmen and panhandlers exploit the unwritten, unspoken conventions of eye and distance. Both take advantage of the fact that once explicit eye contact is established, it is rude to look away, because to do so means to brusquely dismiss the other person and his needs. Once having caught the eye of his mark, the panhandler then locks on, not letting go until he moves through the public zone, the social zone, the personal zone and, finally, into the intimate sphere, where people are most vulnerable.

Touch also is an important part of the constant stream of communication that takes place between people. A light touch, a firm touch, a blow, a caress are all communications. In an effort to break down barriers among people, there's been a recent upsurge in group-encounter activities, in which strangers are encouraged to touch one another. In special situations such as these, the rules for not touching are broken with group approval and people gradually lose some of their inhibitions.

Although most people don't realize it, space is perceived and distances are set not by vision alone but with all the senses. Auditory space is perceived with the ears, thermal space with the skin, kinesthetic space with the muscles of the body and olfactory space with the nose. And, once again, it's one's culture that determines how his senses are programmed — which sensory information ranks highest and lowest. The important thing to remember is that culture is very persistent. In this country, we've noted the existence of culture patterns that determine distance between people in the third and fourth generations of some families, despite their prolonged contact with people of very different cultural heritages.

Whenever there is great cultural distance between two people, there are bound to be problems arising from differences in behavior and expectations. An example is the American couple who consulted a psychiatrist about their marital problems. The husband was from New England and had been brought up by reserved parents who taught him to control his emotions and to respect the need for privacy. His wife was from an Italian family and had been brought up in close contact with all the members of her large family, who were extremely warm, volatile, and demonstrative.

When the husband came home after a hard day at the office, dragging his feet, and longing for peace and quiet, his wife would rush to him and smother him. Clasping his hands, rubbing his brow, crooning over his weary head, she never left him alone. But when the wife was upset or anxious about her day, the husband's response was to withdraw completely and leave her alone. No comforting, no affectionate embrace, no attention — just solitude. The woman became convinced her husband didn't love her and, in desperation, she consulted a psychiatrist. Their problem wasn't basically psychological but cultural.

Why has man developed all these different ways of communicating messages without words? One reason is that people don't like to spell out certain kinds of messages. We prefer to find other ways of showing our feelings. This is especially true in relationships as sensitive as courtship. Men don't like to be rejected and most women don't want to turn a man down bluntly. Instead, we work out subtle ways of encouraging or discouraging each other that save face and avoid confrontations.

How a person handles space in dating others is an obvious and very sensitive indicator of how he or she feels about the other person. On a first date, if a woman sits or stands so close to a man that he is acutely conscious of her physical presence — inside the intimate-distance zone — the man usually construes it to mean that she is encouraging him. However, before the man starts moving in on the woman, he should be sure what message she's really sending; otherwise, he risks bruising his ego. What is close to someone of North European background may be neutral or distant to someone of Italian heritage. Also, women sometimes use space as a way of misleading a man and there are few things that put men off more than women who communicate contradictory messages — such as women who cuddle up and then act insulted when a man takes the next step.

How does a woman communicate interest in a man? In addition to such familiar gambits as smiling at him, she may glance shyly at him, blush and then look away. Or she may give him a real come-on look and move in very close when he approaches. She may touch his arm and ask for a light. As she leans forward to light her cigarette, she may brush him lightly, enveloping him in her perfume. She'll probably continue to smile at him and she may use what ethologists call preening gestures — touching the back of her hair, thrusting her breasts forward, tilting her hips as she stands or crossing her legs if she's seated, perhaps even exposing one thigh or putting a hand on her thigh and stroking it. She may also stroke her wrists as she converses or show the palm of her hand as a way of gaining his attention. Her skin may be unusually flushed or quite pale, her eyes brighter, the pupils larger.

If a man sees a woman whom he wants to attract, he tries to present himself by his posture and stance as someone who is self-assured. He moves briskly and confidently. When he catches the eye of the woman, he may hold her glance a little longer than normal. If he gets an encouraging smile, he'll move in close and engage her in small talk. As they converse, his glance shifts over her face and body. He, too, may make preening gestures — straightening his tie, smoothing his hair, or shooting his cuffs.

How do people learn body language? The same way they learn spoken language — by observing and imitating people around them as they're growing up. Little girls imitate their mothers or an older female. Little boys imitate their fathers or a respected uncle or a character on television. In this way, they learn the gender signals appropriate for their sex. Regional, class, and ethnic patterns of body behavior are also learned in childhood and persist throughout life.

Such patterns of masculine and feminine body behavior vary widely from one culture to another. In America, for example, women stand with their thighs together. Many walk with their pelvis tipped slightly forward and their upper arms close to their body. When they sit, they cross their legs at the knee or, if they are well past middle age, they may cross their ankles. American men hold their arms away from their body, often swinging them as they walk. They stand with their legs apart (an extreme example is the cowboy, with legs apart and thumbs tucked into his belt). When they sit, they put their feet on the floor with legs apart and, in some parts of the country, they cross their legs by putting one ankle on the other knee.

Leg behavior indicates sex, status, and personality. It also indicates whether or not one is at ease or is showing respect or disrespect for the other person. Young Latin-American males avoid crossing their legs. In their world of *machismo*, the preferred position for young males when with one another (if there is no older dominant male present to whom they must show respect) is to sit on the base of their spine with their leg muscles relaxed and their feet wide apart. Their respect position is like our military equivalent; spine straight, heels and ankles together — almost identical to that displayed by properly brought up young women in New England in the early part of this century.

American women who sit with their legs spread apart in the presence of males are *not* normally signaling a come-on — they are simply (and often unconsciously) sitting like men. Middle-class women in the presence of other women to whom they are very close may on occasion throw themselves down on a soft chair or sofa and let themselves go. This is a signal that nothing serious will be taken up. Males, on the other hand, lean back and prop their legs up on the nearest object.

The way we walk, similarly, indicates status, respect, mood, and ethnic or cultural affiliation. The many variants of the female walk are too well known to go into here, except to say that a man would have to be blind not to be turned on by the way some women walk — a fact that made Mae West rich before scientists ever studied these matters. To white Americans, some French middle-class males walk in a way that is both humorous and suspect. There is a bounce and looseness to the French walk, as though the parts of the body were somehow unrelated. Jacques Tati, the French movie actor, walks this way; so does the great mime, Marcel Marceau.

Blacks and whites in America — with the exception of middle- and upper-middle-class professionals of both groups — move and walk very differently from each other. To the blacks, whites often seem incredibly stiff, almost mechanical in their movements. Black males, on the other hand, have a looseness and coordination that frequently makes whites a little uneasy; it's too different, too integrated, too alive, too male. Norman Mailer has said that squares walk from the shoulders, like bears, but blacks and hippies walk from the hips, like cats.

All over the world, people walk not only in their own characteristic way but have walks that communicate the nature of their involvement with whatever it is they're doing. The purposeful walk of North Europeans is an important component of proper behavior on the job. Any male who has been in the military knows how essential it is to walk properly (which makes for a continuing source of tension between blacks and whites in the Service). The quick shuffle of servants in the Far East in the old days was a show of respect. On the island of Truk, when we last visited, the inhabitants even had a name for the respectful walk that one used when in the presence of a chief or when walking past a chief's house. The term was *sufan*, which meant to be humble and respectful.

The notion that people communicate volumes by their gestures, facial expressions, posture and walk is not new; actors, dancers, writers, and psychiatrists have long been aware of it. Only in recent years, however, have scientists begun to make systematic observations of body motions. Ray L. Birdwhistell of the University of Pennsylvania is one of the pioneers in body-motion research and coined the term kinesics to describe this field. He developed an elaborate notation system to record both facial and body movements, using an approach similar to that of the linguist, who studies the basic elements of speech. Birdwhistell and other kinesicists such as Albert Sheflen, Adam Kendon, and William Condon take movies of people interacting. They run the film over and over again, often at reduced speed for frame-by-frame analysis, so that they can observe even the slightest body movements not perceptible at normal interaction speeds. These movements are then recorded in notebooks for later analysis.

To appreciate the importance of nonverbal-communication systems, consider the unskilled inner-city black looking for a job. His handling of time and space alone is sufficiently different from the white middle-class pattern to create great misunderstandings on both sides. The black is told to appear for a job interview at a certain time. He arrives late. The white interviewer concludes from his tardy arrival that the black is irresponsible and not really interested in the job. What the interviewer doesn't know is that the black time system (often referred to by blacks as C. P. T. — colored people's time) isn't the same as that of whites. In the words of a black student who had been told to make an appointment to see his professor: "Man, you *must* be putting me on. I never had an appointment in my life."

The black job applicant, having arrived late for his interview, may further antagonize the white interviewer by his posture and his eye behavior. Perhaps he slouches and avoids looking at the interviewer; to him, this is playing it cool. To the interviewer, however, he may well look shifty and sound uninterested. The interviewer has failed to notice the actual signs of interest and eagerness in the black's behavior, such as the subtle shift in the quality of the voice — a gentle and tentative excitement — an almost imperceptible change in the cast of the eyes and a relaxing of the jaw muscles.

Moreover, correct reading of black-white behavior is continually complicated by the fact that both groups are comprised of individuals — some of whom try to accommodate and some of whom make it a point of pride *not* to accommodate. At present, this means that many Americans, when thrown into contact with one another, are in the precarious position of not knowing which pattern applies. Once identified and analyzed, nonverbal-communications systems can be taught, like a foreign language. Without this training, we respond to nonverbal communications in terms of our own culture; we read everyone's behavior as if it were our own, and thus we often misunderstand it.

Several years ago in New York City, there was a program for sending children from predominantly black and Puerto Rican low-income neighborhoods to summer school in a white upper-class neighborhood on the East Side. One morning, a group of young black and Puerto Rican boys raced down the street, shouting and screaming and overturning garbage cans on their way to school. A doorman from an apartment building nearby chased them and cornered one of them inside a building. The boy drew a knife and attacked the doorman. This tragedy would not have occurred if the doorman had been familiar with the behavior of boys from low-income neighborhoods, where such antics are routine and socially acceptable and where pursuit would be expected to invite a violent response.

The language of behavior is extremely complex. Most of us are lucky to have under control one subcultural system — the one that reflects our sex, class, generation, and geographic region within the United States. Because of its complexity, efforts to isolate bits of nonverbal communication and generalize from them are in vain; you don't become an instant expert on people's behavior by watching them at cocktail parties. Body language isn't something that's independent of the person, something that can be donned and doffed like a suit of clothes.

Our research and that of our colleagues has shown that, far from being a superficial form of communication that can be consciously manipulated, nonverbal-communication systems are interwoven into the fabric of the personality and, as sociologist Erving Goffman has demonstrated, into society itself. They are the warp and woof of daily interactions with others and they influence how one expresses oneself, how one experiences oneself as a man or a woman.

Nonverbal communications signal to members of your own group what kind of person you are, how you feel about others, how you'll fit into and work in a group, whether you're assured or anxious, the degree to which you feel comfortable with the standards of your own culture, as well as deeply significant feelings about the self, including the state of your own psyche. For most of us, it's difficult to accept the reality of another's behavioral system. And, of course, none of us will ever become fully knowledgeable of the importance of every nonverbal signal. But as long as each of us realizes the power of these signals, this society's diversity can be a source of great strength rather than a further — and subtly powerful — source of division.

8

Cosmetics: The language of bodily adornment

TERENCE S. TURNER

Bodily adornment among the Tchikrin of Brazil includes elaborate painting, earplugs, lip plugs, and various styles of clothing. Terence Turner not only describes these practices, but deciphers their complex code to reveal their meaning. He suggests that body decorations have similar functions in all societies.

Something profound in the nature of man, in his role as a member of a society or culture, seems to be bound up with his universal urge to decorate or transform the surface of his body. We might well ask if the boundaries and appendages of the body carry some universal symbolic significance, and if so, whether their adornment is a way of focusing and expressing this symbolic meaning. In other words, bodily adornment may be a kind of symbolic language. But if it is, how can we decipher its "message"?

The Tchikrin, one of the least-known peoples of the central Brazilian wilderness (a region virtually unpenetrated by Brazilian settlers), are among the world's most exotic body adorners. Their elaborate body painting, their penis sheaths and earplugs, and their spectacular lip plugs raise the question of the symbolic significance of bodily adornment in a uniquely compelling way.

The Tchikrin are the northernmost group of the large Kayapo tribe, a member of the Ge-speaking linguistic family. Their villages are built in a circle around a large central plaza, each house the residence of an extended family. Throughout their lives the women remain in the house-

Originally published as "Tchikrin: A Central Brazilian Tribe and Its Language of Bodily Adornment." With permission from *Natural History*, Vol. 78, No. 8; Copyright the American Museum of Natural History, 1969.

holds of their birth. Men, however, leave their maternal houses at about the age of eight, when they move to the men's house, which is usually built in the center of the plaza. Only after consummating their marriages by fathering a child do men move into their wives' houses.

The pattern of a man's life cycle focuses on his movement from his maternal household, to the men's house, to his wife's household. Before, during, and after these moves, he is classified according to named age grades, each with its distinctive social properties, styles of body painting and hair cutting, and bodily ornaments. There is a separate and rather different system of age grades for women.

Newborn and nursing infants of both sexes are classified in a category whose name means "little ones." They are the most elaborately ornamented Tchikrin of any age. A few days after a baby's birth, its ear lobes — and if it is a boy, its lower lip — are pierced, usually by its father. Cigar-shaped earplugs of reddened wood are inserted in the ear lobes and replaced from time to time with larger ones until the holes in the lobes have become quite large. A narrow dowel or string of beads is also inserted in a boy's lower lip, but this ornament is not enlarged until much later in life. At the same time, the mother crochets cotton bands, reddens them with paint, and fastens them around the infant's wrists, ankles, and knees. When these grow too tight they are cut away and replaced with larger ones.

The cast-off arm and leg bands and the discarded sets of earplugs are saved by the mother in a special pouch, together with the baby's desiccated umbilical cord. The bands and plugs constitute a sort of record of the baby's growth — analogous, in a way, to a modern mother's "baby book." When the baby grows older the father takes its pouch and hangs it on, or buries it at the root of, a hardwood tree in the savanna. This gives the child a magical infusion of strength and well-being, symbolically neutralizing the weakness and vulnerability of its infancy, for hardwood trees are potent sources of strength, endurance, and health in Kayapo ritual symbolism. The red color of the earplugs and cotton bands serves much the same symbolic function — the fostering of growth and strength — for red is associated with health, energy, and vitality.

Body painting is an outstanding feature of the decoration of both male and female babies. Mothers, grandmothers, or other kinswomen, using a stylus made of the center rib of a leaf, draw complex linear patterns over the entire body of the child. Women also paint each other in this complex style, but except for rare ceremonial occasions, they are not allowed to paint men and older boys. Since only women use the stylus method, the men paint each other in a rougher, simpler pattern.

When a boy is weaned, learns to talk well, and can walk easily, which usually happens between the ages of three and four, he "graduates" from the age grade of little ones to that of "boys about to enter the men's house." This transition, like most changes from one major age category to the next, is accompanied by changes in bodily adornment and features of grooming such as hair style. The boy is now stripped of his infantile ornaments (earplugs and cotton arm and leg bands) and his hair is cut short. Boys of this age spend little time with their mothers and sisters; they already form a quasi-independent masculine play group, a precursor of the age sets and societies of the men's house. Their semi-independence of their maternal families and passage out of infancy are expressed not only by doffing their infantile ornaments and long hair but also by the infrequency with which their mothers paint them in the time-consuming linear "stylus" fashion. Boys of this age are far more apt to be painted with broad areas or bands of black and red, applied directly with the hand.

At about the age of eight (the Tchikrin do not reckon age by number of years, but by broad criteria of physical size and maturity) a decisive event occurs in a boy's life. In a brief but solemn ceremony, an unrelated man called a "substitute father" comes to the boy's maternal house, where he sits waiting silently with his wailing father and mother. The substitute father leads him out into the plaza and paints his body solid black. He then takes the boy by the hand into the men's house, which becomes his home.

He is now cut off from the world of family and blood relationships. The painting ritual thus marks the end of childhood for the boy and he enters a new age grade called "the painted ones." From this time on the boy will never again (except for rare ceremonial occasions) be painted by a woman. Henceforth, he will be painted only by other men, in the rough hand style or with a stamp made of a fruit rind that is cut in a simple pattern.

At puberty, boys go through a brief ceremony in which they are given penis sheaths to wear. After this they may replace their beaded lip ornaments with small versions of the mature men's lip plugs. They also let their hair grow long again, in the style of adult men and women.

Hair is associated with sexual powers. Long hair connotes full participation in sexually based relationships. However, since infants as well as mature adults have long hair, it is evident that the Kayapo notion of participation in sexual relations is considerably different and more complex than our own. For the Kayapo, there are two modes of sexual participation. One, like our own culture's conception, consists of the mature individual's active exercise of his sexual powers, above all in the relationship between husband and wife. The other, for which our culture has no counterpart, consists of the infant's passive biological (and social) dependence on the family, a dependence founded upon its parents' procreative sexual relationship. The Kayapo think of an infant before it is weaned more as an extension of its parents' biological being than as an independent individual. It is conceived as still participating in the biological communion with its parents that it enjoyed in the womb. This is understandable in view of the Kayapo notion of pregnancy — that the fetus grows by nursing inside the mother. Birth, therefore, does not fundamentally change the relationship between mother and infant; it merely transfers its locus from inside her body to outside. The father is also involved in this biological connection, for while the child is still in the womb, his semen — like the mother's milk — is thought to nourish the fetus. The birth of the baby terminates this direct physical link with the father, a rupture that renders the father's relation to his newborn child extremely delicate and fraught with danger. In order to minimize this danger, for several days the father abstains from physical exertions or "strong" and "dangerous" acts, such as killing animals, that might otherwise have a deleterious impact on the child's health.

Because weaning marks the end of full physical communion between mother and child, a child's hair is cut at this time. Short hair symbolizes the attenuation of his direct biological connection with others, a connection that is restored when the child grows to physical maturity and is ready to exercise his own sexual powers. The same principle underlies the custom of cutting the hair as a gesture of mourning for the death of a spouse, sibling, or child. The effect of such a kinsman's death is equivalent to weaning, since it suppresses ties, which the Kayapo conceive as based on an intimate biological bond, between the person who has died and the survivor.

A distinction is made between hair of the head and hair of the face and body. Facial hair is customarily plucked as a matter of ordinary grooming of both sexes and all ages. Here again, however, the sexual significance of hair emerges in one of the more stereotyped forms of Kayapo love-play — it is considered to impart a special *frisson* for lovers to pluck a stray eyebrow or eyelash from each other's faces with their teeth.

The Kayapo recognize, in ritual and other ways, the correlation between the development of sexual maturity and the weakening of family ties. They attempt to offset this tendency toward the isolation of the individual from social control by developing alternate forms of communal integration of the individual's developing sexual powers. Public recognition of the individual's steps toward sexual and social maturity is ritually associated with changes in his social status that move him inexorably toward marriage and the founding of his own family.

The penis sheath is the symbolic expression of the social control and regulation of mature male sexual powers. It is bestowed at puberty, and only after the sheath-bestowing ceremony is a youth's hair allowed to grow long again. Sheath and coiffure are thus complementary aspects of the public recognition of the growing boy's biological sexuality and, at the same time, of its integration into the social order.

Penis sheath, lip plug, and long hair symbolize the community's recognition of a boy's physical maturity, but they do not confer on him the right to put his newly recognized powers into practice. He only wins this right by going through the initiation ceremony, which is completely distinct from the penis-sheath rite and centers around the ceremonial "marriage," or betrothal, of the boy. This ritual marriage is not considered binding: it only establishes in principle the boy's ability to have sexual relations and marry any girl he chooses. Going through the initiation ceremony entitles a boy to move up into the age grade of "bachelor youths."

Bachelor youths eventually become engaged in earnest. Engagement, a private arrangement with a girl and her parents, culminates in the girl's pregnancy and the birth of a child. This event marks the climax of the youth's transition from boyhood to mature manhood, and he thereupon passes from the symbolic tutelage of his substitute father, who has presided over the successive stages of the long initiation process. Having founded his own family, he is definitively free of his lingering childhood bonds to his maternal family. He is entitled to move out of the men's house into his wife's house, and simultaneously to graduate to the age grade of mature men, significantly called "fathers." Fathers make up the membership of the men's societies, which meet (but do not reside) in the men's house and conduct the political affairs of the community.

These vital transitions in a man's life are expressed by a final transformation in bodily ornamentation — the replacement of the youth's small lip plug by a saucerlike plate, which may reach a diameter of four inches, or an alternative form, a long cylinder of rock crystal or wood. As an expression of mature manhood, this extraordinary ornament has a complex significance.

One aspect of its symbolism is implicit in the contrast between the lip plug and earplug. Both hearing and speaking have specific social associations for the Kayapo, and these associations relate to each other as complementary passive and active values. Hearing is a passive activity. The word *mari* "hearing" signifies understanding in the passive sense of knowing about something. Hearing in this sense is used in the common idiomatic expression of affirmation of specific relationships. If a man has good relations with his father's side of the family, for example, he says, "I hear them strongly" (*mari taytch*). Speaking, on the other hand, is perhaps the most fundamental social act of self-assertion, and its assertive connotations are highly elaborated and associated with mature masculinity. Flamboyant oratory is one of the major activities of Kayapo men.

The huge lip plugs of the father's age grade are consciously associated with this flamboyant oral assertiveness. The dynamism and oral aggressiveness of adult male public behavior rests on a foundation of sexual assertiveness: graduation to father status depends on a man's actually siring a child. The fulfillment of male sexual powers in paternity and the resulting integration of men in specific family units are, in other words, what earn men the right to aggressive, oral self-assertion in the men's house. The full-size lip plug, in its double character as the badge of paternity and the symbol of mature male oral aggressiveness, precisely embodies this relationship between the phallic and oral components of adult masculinity, and by the same token, of the family and communal levels of men's social relations.

If paternity is the criterion for communal recognition of male maturity, then infants assume a reciprocal importance as the "objective correlatives" of manhood in both its biological and social aspects (phallic power and family membership). Infants, then, are the passive extensions, or corroborations, of the father's sexual powers and social position as *paterfamilias*. The relation of the infant to its father is in fact analogous to that between hearing (in its Kayapo sense of passive affirmation of social relations) and speaking (considered as social self-assertion). The symbolic complementarity of infantile earplug and paternal lip plug neatly expresses this social complementarity, especially when the phallic connotations of the cigar-shaped earplugs are taken into account. The same considerations explain why women do not wear lip plugs and why neither adult men nor women wear earplugs.

In contrast to the man's pattern of life, for the Tchikrin woman there is no dramatic transformation in social relations involved in biological parenthood. The residence rule dictates that women spend their entire life cycle in the households into which they are born. The contrasts between female and male body decoration reflect the difference in social pattern.

Girls, like boys, dispense with their earplugs and have their hair cut upon weaning. They continue, however, to wear crocheted red cotton arm and leg bands — in recognition of their continuing membership in their parental families — until they are judged ready for childbearing.

At about the age of eight — the same age that a boy leaves home to enter the men's house — a girl is initiated into sexual relations under the aegis of a special ceremonial guardian. This event marks her graduation into the age grade of "given ones." In all probability the name indicates (the Kayapo have no explicit explanation for it) that girls of this age grade are considered to be "bestowed" upon the initiated men of the village for sexual purposes. Given ones are expected to take an active and enthusiastic part in communal dances; dancing in groups during communal rituals is, in fact, their chief collective activity.

The rite that recognizes that a girl has reached the stage of potential motherhood bears many resemblances to the boy's ceremony of induction into the men's house, and has the same purpose of formally dissolving the childhood bond to the parental family. In the girls' ceremony, a "substitute mother" paints the girls' thighs, breasts, and upper arms with broad black stripes, and cuts off their arm and leg bands (the symbols of parental ties). Henceforth, they are known as "black-thighed ones," and are considered ready to consummate their courtships with one of their suitors in marriage by giving birth to a child. Only this event differentiates women in a social sense from their parental families, since it enables them to set up distinct families of their own within the household they share with their parents. Independence from the parental family (established much earlier for boys by their move to the men's house) is the prerequisite for social recognition of their reproductive powers as fully developed, autonomous, and "adult." This recognition, as we have seen, is symbolized for both sexes by long hair. For this reason, a woman is allowed to wear her hair long only upon the birth of her first child.

After attaining black-thighed status, a girl is qualified to join one of the mature women's societies, whose members gather regularly, every few weeks or so, to paint each other. It is interesting that while adult women often use the hand technique of the mature men to paint each other, they may equally well employ the stylus method used by mothers to paint their infants. Men and boys are almost never painted in this style after they leave home for the men's house; the use of it by adult women is another mark of their greater continuity with the social circumstances of childhood.

The typical daily routine of a Tchikrin mother, however, has relatively little place for collective activities. She must nurse her baby and care for her younger children. One of the most frequent maternal chores is delousing, which, interestingly enough, conforms to a sexually asymmetrical pattern partially similar to that of body painting. Women delouse children, other women, and men (usually their husbands), but men do not delouse women.

A woman's day usually includes a trip to her garden or perhaps an expedition to gather firewood, normally cut by women. She is likely to return from either heavily burdened. She must cook for her husband and children (each nuclear family within the household gardens and cooks for itself). The Tchikrin, like other members of the Ge linguistic group, lack pottery. They cook by baking bundles of food wrapped in leaves, in a temporary earth "oven" composed of heated stones, leaves, and earth. At the end of the day a woman may get a little time to relax with her husband on the family bed, a mat-covered platform of split logs.

Lip plug, earplugs, penis sheath, hair style, cotton leg and arm bands, and body painting make up a symbolic language that expresses a wide range of information about social status, sex, and age. As a language, however, it does more than merely communicate this information from one individual to another: at a deeper level, it establishes a channel of communication *within* the individual between the social and biological aspects of his personality.

The social and psychological "message" of bodily adornment is coded and transmitted on an even more basic level by the colors used in body painting, and the symbolic associations of the parts of the body to which each color is applied. The colors of Tchikrin body painting are red (made from the seeds of the urucú plant), black (made from the juice of the genipa fruit), and, rarely, white (made from white clay), and these are used in determinate ways. Red is always applied on the extremities of the body — the forearms and hands, lower legs and feet, and the face. Black is always used on the trunk and upper parts of the limbs, as well as for the square cheek patches and borders along the shaved area of the forehead. The black face paintings, executed with painstaking care, are often covered immediately after they are finished with a heavy coat of red, which renders them almost invisible. The explanation for this peculiar practice lies in the symbolic values of the colors involved.

Red always connotes energy, health, and "quickness," both in the sense of swiftness and of heightened sensitivity (which the Kayapo conceive of as "quickness" or "lightness" of skin). Black, on the other hand, is associated with transitions between clearly defined states or categories, with "borderline" conditions or regions where normal clear-cut structures of ideas and rules of behavior are "blacked out."

It is interesting that the word for black, *tuk*, also means "dead," and is the adjective used for the zone of land just outside the village, which separates it from the completely wild forest and savanna country. The graveyard and the secluded camps used by groups going through "transitional" rites, such as initiation, are located in this interstitial area. Death itself is conceived of by the Tchikrin as a transitional phase between life and total extinction. The ghosts of the dead live on for one generation in the village of the dead, after which they "die" once more, this time passing into total oblivion.

White, which occurs only in relatively infrequent ceremonial decorations, is associated less with transition than with the pure, "terminal" state of complete transcendence of the normal social world. It is, for example, the color of ghosts. White clay is the food of ghosts, and the villages of the ghosts are always located near outcroppings of white clay or rocks.

Body painting for both ordinary social and ritual occasions seems to be a means of expressing heightened integration and participation in the social order as well as a means of heightening individual biological and psychological powers. Red is applied on the parts of the body most immediately associated with swiftness, agility, and sensory contact with the outside world (feet, hands, and face). This seems logical enough from what we have seen of the symbolic values of the color red. Black is used for the parts of the body most intimately associated with the individual's biological being, his inner self as contrasted with his faculties of relating to the world (the trunk, upper parts of the limbs, and certain areas of the head).

Why should black, which symbolizes the marginal, transitional, or imperfectly integrated aspects of the social order, be thus associated with the individual's presocial (biological) being in those situations where integration into society is being dramatized and reaffirmed?

To answer this question adequately we must start from an understanding of the symbolic significance of the skin in Kayapo culture. The skin, for the Kayapo, is the boundary of the individual on several levels of meaning. In the obvious physical sense, it separates the individual from the external environment, which includes other people. But in a more subtle sense, the skin symbolizes the boundary between two levels of the human personality: the lower level, based on presocial drives emanating from the individual's biological constitution, and the higher level of moral conscience and intellectual consciousness based on cultural principles derived from social sources outside the individual. More simply, this inner, psychological boundary corresponds to the boundary between the physical individual and his society.

The proper balance of relations between the levels of the individual's personality, like proper relations between individuals in society, depends in Kayapo thought on the right sort of communication taking place across these two correlated boundaries. They must be crossed in both directions, for society needs the biological energies of individuals, but it also needs to control them to prevent disruption and chaos. The individual subsists through his biological energies, but he needs the steadying influence of social values, cognitive categories, and moral principles or he will "go berserk" (a recognized condition in Kayapo, known as *aybanh*). Disease, death, the breaking of certain taboos, and going berserk are all conceived as improper forms of eruption of the biological level of existence into the social, orderly level.

The interesting point for our purposes is that all of these "eruptions" are associated with disorders or treatments of the skin: sick people are painted red, dead people either red or black, taboo-breakers get hives or other skin diseases, the skin of berserks becomes alternately overheated and then cold and insensitive, etc. When black, the color associated with transition between the social and asocial worlds, is painted on the skin of the central parts of the body, it expresses the transcendence of the boundary between individual and society and thus reaffirms the mutual integration of the biological individual and the "body social."

It becomes easy to understand, then, why the Tchikrin paint over the black designs of the face with red: They are concerned not so much with esthetic results as with a symbolic statement, in which both colors have complementary "messages" to transmit. The overpainting with red serves to energize, to charge with biological and psychic life-force, the sensory and intelligent part of the person whose socialization has been asserted by the black designs below.

Body painting at this general level of meaning really amounts to the imposition of a second, social "skin" on the naked biological skin of the individual. This second skin of culturally standardized patterns symbolically expresses the "socialization" of the human body — the subordination of the physical aspects of individual existence to common social values and behavior.

It would be misleading to lay too much emphasis on the superficial differences between Tchikrin body adornment and our own culture's elaborate array of clothing and hair styles, makeup, and jewelry. Among the Tchikrin, as among ourselves, the decoration of the surface of the body serves as a symbolic link between the "inner man" and some of his society's most important values.

IV

Kinship and family

Social life is essential to human existence. We remain in the company of other people from the day we are born to the time of our death. People teach us to speak. They show us how to relate to our surroundings. They give us the help and the support we need to achieve personal security and mental well-being. Alone, we are relatively frail, defenseless primates; in groups we are astonishingly adaptive and powerful. Yet despite these advantages, well-organized human societies are difficult to achieve. Some species manage to produce social organization genetically. But people are not like bees or ants. We lack the genetically coded directions for behavior that make these insects successful social animals. Although we seem to inherit a general need for social approval, we also harbor individual interests and ambitions that can block or destroy close social ties. To overcome these divisive tendencies, human groups organize around several principles designed to foster cooperation and group loyalty. Kinship is among the strongest of these.

What underlies the strength of kinship bonds? The answer appears to lie in the strong emotional content of the relationships established by birth and marriage, for these associations are the building blocks of kinship. The birth of a child sets up a particularly durable social bond.

A child's appearance is announced by an increasingly uncomfortable pregnancy and is accompanied by danger and pain during birth. A mother already feels close to someone she has worked so hard to produce. The helpless infant draws strong feelings of support from its parents and others who happen to be near. As a child grows to adulthood, it may receive more or less support from its parents, depending on the child-training customs of the society into which it is born. In every society, however, children tend to be loyal to their parents, and parents feel responsibility and love for their children. The relationship automatically creates the beginning of a kinship system.

Marriage is neither as durable or intense an association as the bond between parent and child. But it is nonetheless a universal feature of social organization and a basic relationship capable of generating strong loyalty. Mating is an intimate feature of the tie as is coparenthood and often, economic cooperation. Marriage links lines of blood-related relatives together and permits the birth of legitimate children.

Based on birth and marriage, kinship systems may include hundreds of relatives in various kinds of groups. Although distantly related people may feel less loyalty and obligation toward each other, large kinship systems work remarkably well as the primary basis of organization in many societies.

Whether large or small, kinship systems always include families. Usually these consist of at least an adult couple and their children. This nuclear family, as it is called, is characteristic of American society, and it lasts only as long as its members continue to remain at home. In a great many societies the ideal family size is much larger than this. The Chinese family described by Margery Wolf often consists of a couple, their sons and their sons' wives, and their grandchildren and any other unattached children. Extended families of this sort provide a very different style of life than do our small families. As we see in the following selections, kinship is different from one society to the next and for different family members within the same household. And larger kinship systems are easier to understand once we see how people use them.

9

Matrilineal kinship:
Coming home to Bokelab

MICHAEL A. RYNKIEWICH

*A kinship system is much more than a set of formal rules defining
identities, roles, and groups. It is a personal guide used by
individuals to meet their own needs and aspirations.
Michael Rynkiewich uses this theme to show how a Marshallese Is-
lander, Benjinij, uses his knowledge of kinship to reestablish himself
on Bojalablab Atoll. Arriving in ignorance after a prolonged absence,
Benjinij learns to identify his kinsmen, treat them properly, and use
his relationships with them to secure land, a household,
and power.*

One of the most important ways people all over the world are alike is
the fundamental basis on which they organize their social lives. To relate
effectively to each other, people must identify themselves and those
around them, behave according to roles composed of specific rules for
action, and participate in clearly defined groups. Although all of us use
information about identity, role, and groups to guide our daily social
behavior, the specific knowledge used by different peoples to accomplish
this end varies. For example, if you were to live with the people of a
Highland New Guinea community, you would quickly discover that
their social organization was so different from yours that you would
have to learn about a new set of identities, system of roles, and collection
of groups. Only after gathering such information would you be able to

This article was written especially for this book. Copyright © 1974 by Little, Brown and
Company (Inc.). The research on which it is based was carried out in the Marshall Islands
between June 1969 and December 1970. Bojalablab Atoll and the people in the story are
fictional, but the account is an accurate recording of form, meaning, and functions of
Marshallese kinship.

get along properly with the members of the community in the context of their social system. Even in our own society many small groups have such different organizations that a new language of social behavior must be learned to fit acceptably within them.

Take a football team, for example. Suppose that you were pulled from the stands by a coach at a professional football game, dressed in a uniform, and sent on the field. As you run toward the players whose uniforms are the same color as yours, the coach yells these instructions: "Tell the quarterback to run a sixty series option down, out and down, to the split end." Unless you had played football before, you might not even realize that the term *quarterback* labels a kind of identity for one player. Even if you did understand what a quarterback was, you might not know about any of his identifying attributes, for example, that he wears a number between 10 and 19 on his back. You might also miss the fact that you are the split end (your number is 88, a sign of your position), that you should talk to the quarterback outside the huddle, and that you should line up ten to fifteen yards from the tackle on the line of scrimmage. In addition, you would not understand the instructions for action contained in the phrase "sixty series option" so you would have little idea about what your teammates planned to do or how your opponents might react. Without such information about identities, expectations for behavior, and group composition, you could not begin to play football in a socially organized manner as part of a team. The same principles govern people's behavior in every social situation.

Social organization can be achieved in several basic ways. The structure of the football team, for example, reflects a need to meet particular characteristics inherent in the game itself. As a consequence, the team has a limited and specialized social organization. On the other hand, most societies use a more general approach to achieve systematic social interaction. Instead of the exigencies of a particular game, they face such wider needs as sustenance and defense that must be met if the members of the group are to survive. Thus, their organization is often based on more general human characteristics such as age, sex, and rank. Of these, however, by far the most common and important is kinship.

Kinship provides a way of defining identities, roles, and groups for people everywhere. In many societies kinship is the dominant principle for social organization. The term *kinship* is not as simple as it sounds. Americans tend to think of kinsmen as blood relatives, but in many parts of the world this definition is too limited. In such cases kinship is a complex language of social relationships that includes not only those who are related genealogically through blood and marriage, but also people who share no blood connection but who somehow come to be identified as kinsmen. This extension of the system is possible because individuals determine the identity of kinsmen not only by genealogical linkage, but by behavior as well. Thus, when someone acts like a kinsman, he is often treated as one. Conversely, some people may not be called relatives although they are related by blood ties. They simply do not behave as kinsmen should.

This emphasis on the importance of social organization and the stress on identity, role, and group should not be allowed to obscure the place of the individual in social interaction. People do use kinship rules to structure and interpret behavior, but they also manipulate their knowledge of kinship to serve their own interests. Just as a quarterback uses his knowledge of football and the many plays and options open to him to move his offense and win the game, so the individual uses his understanding of his kinship system to meet his own requirements and aspirations. Like every set of cultural rules, kinship is a flexible and ever-changing system.

To better understand the importance and the meaning of kinship, it is useful to look at a society — Bokelab islet of Bojalablab Atoll in the Marshall Islands — in which it plays a dominant role. By taking the perspective of one man, Benjinij, from this society, we can consider some of the problems he solves by the judicious use of his knowledge about kinship. Benjinij is returning to Bojalablab after a long absence. To reestablish himself there among his kinsmen, he must identify and relate to his relatives and demonstrate and manipulate his membership rights in a landholding kinship group.

GOING HOME

Benjinij steadied himself at the bow as the ship left the calm lagoon water and met the jolting ocean waves. His mind was not on the trade goods in the ship's hold nor on the copra the ship would buy. He was a passenger getting off at the first stop, Bokelab islet. He could not see it yet, but it was just over the horizon and his mind dwelt on his situation.

Benjinij's mother had been born on Bojalablab Atoll, the ship's destination. His father was from another atoll, and his mother had gone with her husband to live there. When Benjinij was quite young, the Japanese had sent his father to Palau island for training as a carpenter. Benjinij and his mother went along. However, both of Benjinij's parents were killed in air raids during World War II. When peace returned, the now mature Benjinij became a sailor, and at age 30, ten years after the conflict had ended, he was coming to live with his mother's people.

Bojalablab Atoll stood against the red of the late afternoon sky, like a pencil line marked on the horizon. As the ship drew nearer, the line differentiated into beach, brush, and coconut trees. Benjinij watched the waves, hypnotized by their motion. As he watched, a wave rose to four feet at the edge of the reef, then flattened as it raced over the barrier, its surface reflecting the vivid colors of the coral below. Then the wave's leading edge, white with foam, flung itself on the beach.

The ship slowed and the noise of its small boat being raised from the deck brought Benjinij back from his reverie. When the ship had anchored, Benjinij climbed in the small boat so that he could be first ashore. The steersman caught a wave, then alternately throttled and accelerated the boat's engine to keep just behind the crest. Just as it seemed that it would be smashed on the shore, the boat swerved sharply to the left in response to the steersman's hand and settled down in the lee of the wave, coming gently to rest on the sandy beach. Benjinij walked onto Bokelab islet, home at last.

As he stood on the beach of his mother's home for the first time, Benjinij's thoughts turned to the problems that confronted him. He could see several people coming toward the shore and others standing near bags of dried coconut meat. Many of them were his kinsmen whom he would eventually have to identify by determining their relationship to him. Only then would he know how to behave toward them and what to expect they would do in return. His parents had taught him what every Marshallese child should know about kinsmen, but he was not very practiced in relating to these particular kin nor did he know their particular histories or the instances of cooperation and conflict. In addition, he did not know to which groups he or they belonged. He had much to learn to establish himself here, to be socially, economically, and politically successful. His key to the network of relationships on Bokelab islet was something his mother had told him years earlier, that her brother's name was Tibnil and if he ever returned to Bokelab he should depend on him for help.

Benjinij asked for directions to Tibnil's household, and started off down the road that ran parallel to the lagoon. He found Tibnil sitting in his cookhouse talking with two younger men of the household as they waited for the women to finish baking the breadfruit and fish collected that afternoon. They exchanged greetings and Benjinij was enjoined to come in the cookhouse and sit. Though Tibnil would not have recognized him, an old man on the ship had sent word that Benjinij was coming. Consequently, as is the custom, no questions were asked about the other's name. Tibnil did speak at length about his joy at Benjinij's arrival, lamenting the death of his sister and brother-in-law. Benjinij would eat, sleep, and work within this household because he had the kinship right to stay with his mother's brother as long as he liked. Thus, a bond was renewed and through Tibnil, Benjinij began to find his way into the complex network formed by kinsmen.

KINDS OF KIN

The few basic terms Benjinij used to identify his kinsmen are presented in Figure I. He calls everyone in his grandfather's generation either *jimau* (male) or *jibu* (female); as he grows old, all kin of his grandchildren's generation he will term *jibu* for either sex. (This differs from our own system in which we mark off grandfather from great-uncle and first cousin twice-removed, and grandson from grand-nephew and first cousin twice-removed.)

In general, Benjinij calls everyone of his father's generation *jinu* (female) or *jema* (male), and everyone in his children's generation, *neju* (either sex). Two exceptions are his mother's brothers, only Tibnil in this case, whom he calls *uleba*, and his sister's sons, whom he would call *mangeru*.

In Benjinij's own generation, he refers to anyone born before him as *jeu* (either sex) and everyone born later *jetu* (either sex). Again, this includes kinsmen we would call brother, sister, first cousin, second cousin, and so on. These ten basic terms, though they can be modified somewhat, enable him to identify all his relatives except his brothers-in-law.

All these terms are used to address kinsmen. However, Benjinij must make one other distinction, though it is usually not used in address, but only to refer to a particular group of relatives. In Benjinij's own generation, female parallel cousins and female cross-cousins differ. The children of Benjinij's father's brother and his mother's sister are called parallel cousins because the sex of the two connecting relatives is the same: mother and her sister, father and his brother. Female parallel cousins are classed with Benjinij's own sister and are referred to by a combination of terms; *jeu jinu* if older than Benjinij and *jetu jinu* if younger. On the other hand, cross-cousins, the children of Benjinij's father's sister and his mother's brother, are referred to as *jeu reliku* if older and *jetu reliku* if younger. The significance of this distinction will become clear in the discussion of proper kinship behavior.

Knowing possible classes of kinsmen did not tell Benjinij which kin fit into each category. To make this discovery, he had to depend partly on genealogical information. For example, his mother had told him that Tibnil was her brother, so he was to be called *uleba*. But the genealogical links for many people he met were never entirely clear to him. To place them, he listened to what Tibnil and other known relatives called such kin. For example, when Benjinij arrived at Tibnil's house he was greeted by two pretty girls and some other children. Benjinij did not know who they were, but during his first few days there he heard what they called Tibnil. When one of the girls, LiNana, called Tibnil "father," Benjinij knew that she stood in the relationship of younger

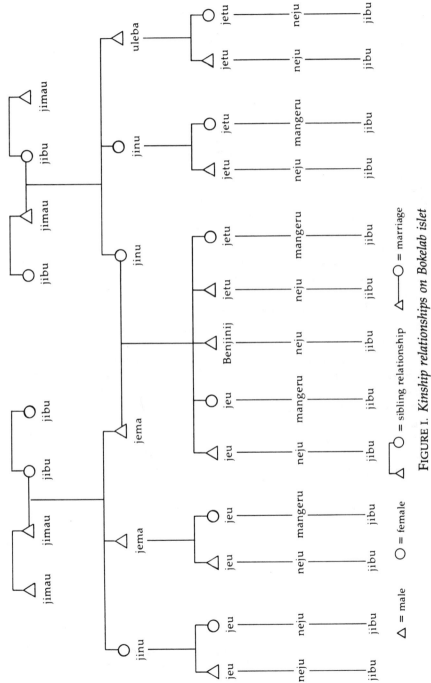

FIGURE I. *Kinship relationships on Bokelab islet*

△ = male   ○ = female   △—○ = marriage   △ = sibling relationship

cross-cousin to him because she was female, younger than him, and a child of his mother's brother.

When the other girl called Tibnil "mother's brother," Benjinij knew that she was an elder sister and parallel cousin. Benjinij quickly figured out the kinship identities of most people on the islet, and from this knowledge he was able to behave in a proper way toward them.

KINSHIP ROLES

To produce such behavior Benjinij needed to know what to call his kinsmen. He would not, for example, act the same way toward Tibnil, his mother's brother, as he would toward a man he called "father." The former relationship involves both authority and some degree of permitted disrespect. Marshallese sayings give the expectation that the mother's brother will be a hard taskmaster while the sister's son is often mischievous. On the other hand, the relationship between father and child has little authority but a lot of respect, so that a child would never be mischievous with his father.

Although each kinsman requires special forms of behavior, with little exception all may be classified into two groups based on opposite forms of action. One kind of relationship can be called reserved. In the context of Marshallese culture, in the presence of certain kinsmen Benjinij cannot refer to such bodily functions as defecation, urination, bathing, and sexual intercourse. The relationship implies respect and some degree of social distance.

As illustrated in Table I, the most reserved relationship exists between Benjinij and anyone he calls sister and parallel cousin. He is careful never to be alone with such kinswomen for fear of fostering the idea that a sexual interest exists between them. These kinswomen often make requests of Benjinij and he does all he can to meet such demands. Moreover, he is careful that no one else should behave improperly when he is in their presence. Once Benjinij and a "sister," a parallel cousin, sat with a group of young people by the road. A boy began to tell about

TABLE I. *Basic Marshallese kinship roles*

Reserved behavior	Joking behavior
Sister (parallel cousin)	Cross-cousin
Mother	Grandmother
Father	Grandfather
Child	Grandchild
Mother's brother or sister's child	

a fight in which one man was kicked in the groin. Benjinij quickly disappeared. The next day he took the young storyteller aside and told him in annoyed tones to be more careful about ascertaining the relationship of those in his audience before he started talking about such private matters. Relatives called mother, father, and child must also be treated with respect (Table I).

The other major relationship is marked by joking. In many ways, it is the opposite of the reserved relationship because any kind of joking is permitted with no hint of respect or authority. People in these relationships need not hide from each other knowledge of when and where they perform bodily functions. Sexual intercourse between such relatives is permitted, except in the case of genealogical grandparents and grandchildren. The joking relationship provides some of the most interesting and humorous exchanges between kinsmen, often taking the form of a game with one relative trying to outdo another in the grossness of his references to sexual parts and functions.

For example, Benjinij might be expected to engage in such a discussion of private parts with his cross-cousin, LiNana, if he met her on the road. First, he would likely pretend not to notice her and walk by without a greeting. But she would not allow such a challenge to go unmet, and might open with a comment like, "Your penis!" He could reply, "You have no pubic hair!" to which she might respond, "The hair of your anus!" The conversation would likely escalate with such assertions and retorts as, "Nothing is larger than the lips of your vagina." "Your little penis is half-baked." "Why is there mud in your vagina?" (implying promiscuity in the sense that she will lie anywhere, even in the mud), and the parting and winning shout, "Go masturbate yourself!" Such joking behavior is also enjoyed with kin called grandfather, grandmother, and grandchild. Thus, by knowing kinship terms, Benjinij can identify people and use appropriate behavior with them. In only a few months, Benjinij had become part of an ongoing social system which gave him support for his new life on Bokelab.

DESCENT GROUPS

Although Benjinij had managed to establish himself in the islet's social network of kinsmen, he also wanted a household of his own, a place to work, a family, and the respect of the community. To acquire these things he needed land. The place he had in mind was a plot located near the middle of the islet rising quickly from the lagoon shore to 10 feet above high tide, then dropping off to a densely wooded interior with several taro pits before ending on the side facing the ocean. The strip was only three quarters of a mile long, but like most plots of land, it touched both shores to give the people access to the whole range of the islet's micro-environments. Benjinij suspected that he might have some claim to the land because Tibnil had often sent him there to work. He determined to see if he could get permission to live there.

Benjinij sat with Tibnil one evening, intent on asking him about the land, but he avoided doing so directly. Instead, he asked about Marshallese custom with respect to group membership and inheritance. He knew that both Americans and Japanese placed great importance on their fathers, even taking the paternal name as their own. He also knew from such sayings as "the children of women are most important" that the Marshallese way was different. When he asked about the meaning of that saying, Tibnil replied with this story:

> An old woman, Likatunger, promised the chieftainship to whichever of her sons would win a canoe race. As each of them departed she entreated him to take her along. But when she cried, "*Ekatuke iu!*" each son from the eldest on down replied, "*Kattar wut jetu*" (wait for my younger brother). Only her youngest son, Jabrau, stopped long enough to take her on board. She then gave him the paraphernalia with which to sail and Jabrau easily overtook his brothers. As he broke into the lead his eldest brother asked permission to ride along. Jabrau took him on board, but he knew his brother intended to jump off the canoe first when it reached shore and claim the chieftainship. Therefore, on the last tack, Jabrau allowed the boom to swing, knocking his brother overboard and breaking his back in the process. Jabrau won the chieftainship *kinke e jela kataike ngan jinen* (because he knew how to submit to his mother).

Tibnil stressed that land and authority came through mothers, not fathers. Benjinij had suspected as much and asked Tibnil where the latter got his authority to manage the land. Tibnil said the rights were not his alone, that they were passed down over many generations. Then he began to list all those people who had had a right in the land he controlled, beginning with the name of the oldest woman he could remember, and then her brother. He named her children, both male and female, her daughter's male and female children, and her daughter's daughter's male and female children. On and on he went, naming only the children of women, finally arriving at Benjinij's mother, and then Benjinij himself (their genealogical positions are shown in Figure II).

Benjinij now knew he was on the right track. The group whose members Tibnil had named is called *bwij* or matrilineage. Matrilineages are formed by the descent ideology that "the children of women are most important," their new members including only the children of each group's female members. The matrilineage is the major landholding unit on Bojalablab atoll and like corporations, no one of its members may dispose of any matrilineage land rights or be denied the use of matri-

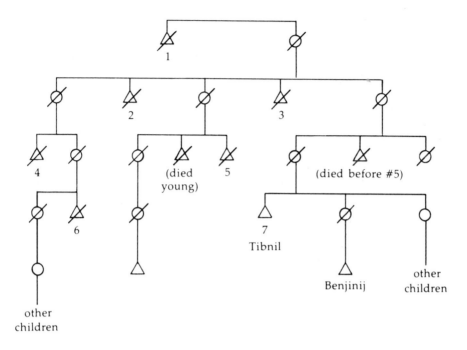

Lineage heads are numbered in succession.
Deceased relatives are shown with a diagonal line through them.

FIGURE II. *Begjinij's matrilineage*

lineage land, except when he has gravely insulted his fellow lineage mates. A matrilineage does have a leader called an *alab*, meaning land manager or lineage head. He handles lineage affairs and represents the kin group in its dealings with other members of the community. He does not own the land; no individual does. Rather, it belongs to the whole group, including the dead and those not yet born. However, the lineage head can allocate specific pieces of land to lineage members and sometimes others, for their own temporary use.

To affirm the source of his rights as lineage head, Tibnil recited the order of succession. He went from the brother of the oldest woman, to his sister's son, and on through brothers and cousins, skipping only those who had died before their chance for succession came (marked on Figure II by numbers). When he had finished, Benjinij knew he had come to the right place. His mother's words, "Go to my brother and he will take care of you," came back to him. He asked for and received permission to build a house on the land he wanted.

ESTABLISHING A HOUSEHOLD

Planning the house and organizing the work was left to Tibnil, who told the women of his own and other households of the lineage to begin collecting pandanus leaves to make thatch and mats. The men of the lineage and other male members of their households cut down pandanus trees and sawed them up to make posts and rafters. Benjinij worked for cash to buy plywood for the walls and, although normally he had to give Tibnil a small percentage of the profits from the sale of any coconut meat derived from lineage land, Tibnil helped Benjinij by not requiring this share. The land was cleared, coral pebbles brought for the floor and yard, walls erected, and roof thatched in about three weeks.

When the house was finished, Benjinij moved in, but not by himself. For several months he had been keeping company in secret with his cross-cousin, LiNana. They had decided to live together for a while, and her father, Tibnil, had agreed. She was pregnant so one of her younger sisters came along to help keep their house. Benjinij had land to work and a household to support.

GAINING POWER

Benjinij had successfully achieved his initial goals because he became adept at manipulating the systems of kinship and descent. However, a year after he moved into his new house, he faced a problem that he could not have envisioned on his arrival. He had to struggle against his kinsmen to protect his position in the matrilineage and the community.

The problem started when Tibnil became ill and died and his sister asserted that she would succeed him as lineage head. Her claim was based on the rule that says the successor should come from the senior generation of the lineage, and she was the only living member of that generation. Benjinij was close to her and knew he would enjoy her favor if she were the leader. However, two others were contending for the position. An old woman of another branch of the lineage claimed that she should become Tibnil's successor, although she was part of the next lower generation. She cited another rule of succession to back her claim, that lineage heads should come from the oldest branch of the lineage, the one to which she belonged. A man from the middle branch of the lineage also claimed Tibnil's position. Although he was in a generation junior to Tibnil's sister and in a lineage branch less old than that of the second claimant, he was a male and entitled to hold power over women. Each contender had a valid claim to leadership, but the rules were contradictory. Naturally, each cited only those rules which demonstrated the priority of his or her claim.

Benjinij vociferously defended the right of Tibnil's sister to succeed. The second woman had the support of her children, and to Benjinij's surprise, the man from the middle branch of the lineage was supported by his sons. True, he was the only living member of the middle branch and had no other supporters, but his sons did not even belong to the lineage, holding membership in their mother's group instead. Benjinij asked Tibnil's sister why these sons would dare argue their father's case. She explained:

> You know that the branches of a matrilineage sometimes split away from each other. Each one takes some of the lineage land and selects its own lineage head. Each branch then becomes a separate matrilineage. Look at our matrilineage. We own three pieces of land, and we have three branches. Many generations have gone by since we were all real siblings. His sons want him to be lineage head in the hope that as the leader he will force our matrilineage to split into three separate ones. If that happened, their father would be the sole member of his matrilineage, and the sole owner of one of the pieces of land. Then, because he is the last of his branch, his sons would inherit his land when he died. That is why we must oppose him, because our land could be stolen away by people who are not in our lineage.

Benjinij had learned a lesson: kinsmen not only cooperate on matters, but they also dispute over the rights they share. If he did not resist the claims of the old man, his plot of land might be taken from the lineage. After this talk, Benjinij argued more earnestly than ever for the succession of Tibnil's sister.

The sons of the old man talked against Benjinij, but their father did not cooperate. Less than a year after the dispute began, he died. A short time later the woman from the oldest branch of the lineage also died and Tibnil's sister was left as undisputed leader of the lineage.

With Tibnil's sister in firm control, Benjinij was assured of control over his own affairs within the framework of the lineage, for he was its oldest living male. Tibnil's sister, embarrassed to go to the islet's council because of her sex, sent Benjinij in her stead. Though she kept the title, he did the work and gained experience representing his lineage to the community. Years later, when Tibnil's sister died, Benjinij's succession as lineage head was not disputed.

THE MEANING OF KINSHIP

When Benjinij stepped ashore on Bokelab islet, he had to establish himself in an ongoing, socially organized community. The cultural knowledge he used to enter the social network is different from the information we would use if we moved to a different town in the United

States. Although he had to refine this knowledge by attempting to apply it in many new social situations, Benjinij succeeded because he understood the basic features of the Marshallese kinship and descent systems. Because he knew the proper kinship terms and the appropriate ways to behave, he became part of a household and a member of the community. He was able to claim his position as a member of a landholding group and eventually gain an allocation of land because he understood the principles of matrilineal descent. Through the complexities and conflicts of a dispute among lineage members, Benjinij emerged in a strong position because he had backed a winner. In sum, Benjinij's basic needs — food, sex, shelter, power, and meaning — were at least partially satisfied through the Marshallese systems of kinship and descent.

10

Uterine families
and the women's community

MARGERY WOLF

*Is the meaning of the family the same for men and women? Margery
Wolf answers "no" in this article based on fieldwork in a rural
Taiwanese village. For men living in the community, the patrilineal
family extends in an unbroken line of ancestors and descendants.
Membership is permanent; loyalty assured. For women, the
patrilineal family is temporary. Born into one family and married into
another, women discover that their happiness and interests depend on
their membership in an informal uterine family that grows up inside
the household. Family relationships can only be understood if we take
the women's as well as the men's views into account.*

Few women in China experience the continuity that is typical of the
lives of the menfolk. A woman can and, if she is ever to have any
economic security, must provide the links in the male chain of descent,
but she will never appear in anyone's genealogy as that all-important
name connecting the past to the future. If she dies before she is married,
her tablet will not appear on her father's altar; although she was a
temporary member of his household, she was not a member of his
family. A man is born into his family and remains a member of it throughout his life and even after his death. He is identified with the family
from birth, and every action concerning him, up to and including his
death, is in the context of that group. Whatever other uncertainties may
trouble his life, his place in the line of ancestors provides a permanent
setting. There is no such secure setting for a woman. She will abruptly

leave the household into which she is born, either as an infant or as an adult bride, and enter another whose members treat her with suspicion or even hostility.

A man defines his family as a large group that includes the dead, the not-yet-born, and the living members of his household. But how does a woman define her family? This is not a question that China specialists often consider, but from their treatment of the family in general, it would seem that a woman's family is identical with that of the senior male in the household in which she lives. Although I have never asked, I imagine a Taiwanese man would define a woman's family in very much those same terms. Women, I think, would give quite a different answer. They do not have an unchanging place, assigned at birth, in any group, and their view of the family reflects this.

When she is a child, a woman's family is defined for her by her mother and to some extent by her grandmother. No matter how fond of his daughter the father may be, she is only a temporary member of his household and useless to his family — he cannot even marry her to one of his sons as he could an adopted daughter. Her irrelevance to her father's family in turn affects the daughter's attitude toward it. It is of no particular interest to her, and the need to maintain its continuity has little meaning for her beyond the fact that this continuity matters a great deal to some of the people she loves. As a child she probably accepts to some degree her grandmother's orientation toward the family: the household, i.e., those people who live together and eat together, including perhaps one or more of her father's married brothers and their children. But the group that has the most meaning for her and with which she will have the most lasting ties is the smaller, more cohesive unit centering on her mother, i.e., the uterine family — her mother and her mother's children. Father is important to the group, just as grandmother is important to some of the children, but he is not quite a member of it, and for some uterine families he may even be "the enemy." As the girl grows up and her grandmother dies and a brother or two marries, she discovers that her mother's definition of the family is becoming less exclusive and may even include such outsiders as her brother's new wife. Without knowing precisely when it happened, she finds that her brother's interests and goals have shifted in a direction she cannot follow. Her mother does not push her aside, but when the mother speaks of the future, she speaks in terms of her son's future. Although the mother sees her uterine family as adding new members and another generation, her daughter sees it as dissolving, leaving her with strong particular relationships, but with no group to which she has permanent loyalties and obligations.

When a young woman marries, her formal ties with the household of her father are severed. In one of the rituals of the wedding ceremony the bride's father or brothers symbolically inform her by means of spilt water that she, like the water, may never return, and when her wedding sedan chair passes over the threshold of her father's house, the doors are slammed shut behind her. If she is ill-treated by her husband's family, her father's family may intervene, but unless her parents are willing to bring her home and support her for the rest of her life (and most parents are not), there is little they can do beyond shaming the other family. This is usually enough.

As long as her mother is alive, the daughter will continue her contacts with her father's household by as many visits as her new situation allows. If she lives nearby she may visit every few days, and no matter where she lives she must at least be allowed to return at New Year. After her mother dies her visits may become perfunctory, but her relations with at least one member of her uterine family, the group that centered on her mother, remain strong. Her brother plays an important ritual role throughout her life. She may gradually lose contact with her sisters as she and they become more involved with their own children, but her relations with her brother continue. When her sons marry, he is the guest of honor at the wedding feasts, and when her daughters marry he must give a small banquet in their honor. If her sons wish to divide their father's estate, it is their mother's brother who is called on to supervise. And when she dies, the coffin cannot be closed until her brother determines to his own satisfaction that she died a natural death and that her husband's family did everything possible to prevent it.

With the ritual slam of her father's door on her wedding day, a young woman finds herself quite literally without a family. She enters the household of her husband — a man who in an earlier time, say fifty years ago, she would never have met and who even today, in modern rural Taiwan, she is unlikely to know very well. She is an outsider, and for Chinese an outsider is always an object of deep suspicion. Her husband and her father-in-law do not see her as a member of their family. But they do see her as essential to it; they have gone to great expense to bring her into their household for the purpose of bearing a new generation for their family. Her mother-in-law, who was mainly responsible for negotiating the terms of her entry, may harbor some resentment over the hard bargaining, but she is nonetheless eager to see another generation added to *her* uterine family. A mother-in-law often has the same kind of ambivalence toward her daughter-in-law as she has toward her husband — the younger woman seems a member of her family at times and merely a member of the household at others. The new bride may find that her husband's sister is hostile or at best condescending, both attitudes reflecting the daughter's distress at an outsider who seems to be making her way right into the heart of the family.

Chinese children are taught by proverb, by example, and by experience that the family is the source of their security, and relatives the only people who can be depended on. Ostracism from the family is one of the harshest sanctions that can be imposed on erring youth. One of the reasons mainlanders as individuals are considered so untrustworthy on Taiwan is the fact that they are not subject to the controls of (and therefore have no fear of ostracism from) their families. If a timid new bride is considered an object of suspicion and potentially dangerous because she is a stranger, think how uneasy her own first few months must be surrounded by strangers. Her irrelevance to her father's family may result in her having little reverence for descent lines, but she has warm memories of the security of the family her mother created. If she is ever to return to this certainty and sense of belonging, a woman must create her own uterine family by bearing children, a goal that happily corresponds to the goals of the family into which she has married. She may gradually create a tolerable niche for herself in the household of her mother-in-law, but her family will not be formed until she herself forms it of her own children and grandchildren. In most cases, by the time she adds grandchildren, the uterine family and the household will almost completely overlap, and there will be another daughter-in-law struggling with loneliness and beginning a new uterine family.

The ambiguity of a man's position in relation to the uterine families accounts for much of the hostility between mother-in-law and daughter-in-law. There is no question in the mind of the older woman but that her son *is* her family. The daughter-in-law might be content with this situation once her sons are old enough to represent her interests in the household and in areas strictly under men's control, but until then, she is dependent on her husband. If she were to be completely absorbed into her mother-in-law's family — a rare occurrence unless she is a *sim-pua* — there would be little or no conflict; but under most circumstances she must rely on her husband, her mother-in-law's son, as her spokesman, and here is where the trouble begins. Since it is usually events within the household that she wishes to affect, and the household more or less overlaps with her mother-in-law's uterine family, even a minor foray by the younger woman suggests to the older one an all-out attack on everything she has worked so hard to build in the years of her own loneliness and insecurity. The birth of grandchildren further complicates their relations, for the one sees them as new members for her family and the other as desperately needed recruits to her own small circle of security.

In summary, my thesis contends . . . that because we have heretofore focused on men when examining the Chinese family — a reasonable approach to a patrilineal system — we have missed not only some of the system's subtleties but also its near-fatal weaknesses. With a male focus we see the Chinese family as a line of descent, bulging to encompass all the members of a man's household and spreading out through his descendants. With a female focus, however, we see the Chinese family not as a continuous line stretching between the vague horizons of past and future, but as a contemporary group that comes into existence out of one woman's need and is held together insofar as she has the strength to do so, or, for that matter, the need to do so. After her death the uterine family survives only in the mind of her son and is symbolized by the special attention he gives her earthly remains and her ancestral tablet. The rites themselves are demanded by the ideology of the patriliny, but the meaning they hold for most sons is formed in the uterine family. The uterine family has no ideology, no formal structure, and no public existence. It is built out of sentiments and loyalties that die with its members, but it is no less real for all that. The descent lines of men are born and nourished in the uterine families of women, and it is here that a male ideology that excludes women makes its accommodations with reality.

Women in rural Taiwan do not live their lives in the walled courtyards of their husbands' households. If they did, they might be as powerless as their stereotype. It is in their relations in the outside world (and for women in rural Taiwan that world consists almost entirely of the village) that women develop sufficient backing to maintain some independence under their powerful mothers-in-law and even occasionally to bring the men's world to terms. A successful venture into the men's world is no small feat when one recalls that the men of a village were born there and are often related to one another, whereas the women are unlikely to have either the ties of childhood or the ties of kinship to unite them. All the same, the needs, shared interests, and common problems of women are reflected in every village in a loosely knit society that can when needed be called on to exercise considerable influence.

Women carry on as many of their activities as possible outside the house. They wash clothes on the riverbank, clean and pare vegetables at a communal pump, mend under a tree that is a known meetingplace, and stop to rest on a bench or group of stones with other women. There is a continual moving back and forth between kitchens, and conversations are carried on from open doorways through the long, hot afternoons of summer. The shy young girl who enters the village as a bride is examined as frankly and suspiciously by the women as an animal that is up for sale. If she is deferential to her elders, does not criticize or compare her new world unfavorably with the one she has left, the older

residents will gradually accept her presence on the edge of their conversations and stop changing the topic to general subjects when she
brings the family laundry to scrub on the rocks near them. As the young
bride meets other girls in her position, she makes allies for the future,
but she must also develop relationships with the older women. She
learns to use considerable discretion in making and receiving confi-
dences, for a girl who gossips freely about the affairs of her husband's
household may find herself labeled a troublemaker. On the other hand,
a girl who is too reticent may find herself always on the outside of the
group, or worse yet, accused of snobbery. I described in *The House of
Lim* the plight of Lim Chui-ieng, who had little village backing in her
troubles with her husband and his family as the result of her arrogance
toward the women's community. In Peihotien the young wife of the
storekeeper's son suffered a similar lack of support. Warned by her
husband's parents not to be too "easy" with the other villagers lest they
try to buy things on credit, she obeyed to the point of being considered
unfriendly by the women of the village. When she began to have serious
troubles with her husband and eventually his family, there was no one
in the village she could turn to for solace, advice, and most important,
peacemaking.

Once a young bride has established herself as a member of the
women's community, she has also established for herself a certain amount
of protection. If the members of her husband's family step beyond the
limits of propriety in their treatment of her — such as refusing to allow
her to return to her natal home for her brother's wedding or beating her
without serious justification — she can complain to a woman friend,
preferably older, while they are washing vegetables at the communal
pump. The story will quickly spread to the other women, and one of
them will take it on herself to check the facts with another member of
the girl's household. For a few days the matter will be thoroughly discussed whenever a few women gather. In a young wife's first few years
in the community, she can expect to have her mother-in-law's side of
any disagreement given fuller weight than her own — her mother-in-
law has, after all, been a part of the community a lot longer. However,
the discussion itself will serve to curb many offenses. Even if the older
woman knows that public opinion is falling to her side, she will still be
somewhat more judicious about refusing her daughter-in-law's next request. Still, the daughter-in-law who hopes to make use of the village
forum to depose her mother-in-law or at least gain herself special privilege will discover just how important the prerogatives of age and length
of residence are. Although the women can serve as a powerful protective
force for their defenseless younger members, they are also a very conservative force in the village.

Taiwanese women can and do make use of their collective power to lose face for their menfolk in order to influence decisions that are ostensibly not theirs to make. Although young women may have little or no influence over their husbands and would not dare express an unsolicited opinion (and perhaps not even a solicited one) to their fathers-in-law, older women who have raised their sons properly retain considerable influence over their sons' actions, even in activities exclusive to men. Further, older women who have displayed years of good judgment are regularly consulted by their husbands about major as well as minor economic and social projects. But even men who think themselves free to ignore the opinions of their women are never free of their own concept, face. It is much easier to lose face than to have face. We once asked a male friend in Peihotien just what "having face" amounted to. He replied, "When no one is talking about a family, you can say it has face." This is precisely where women wield their power. When a man behaves in a way that they consider wrong, they talk about him — not only among themselves, but to their sons and husbands. No one "tells him how to mind his own business," but it becomes abundantly clear that he is losing face and by continuing in this manner may bring shame to the family of his ancestors and descendants. Few men will risk that.

The rules that a Taiwanese man must learn and obey to be a successful member of his society are well developed, clear, and relatively easy to stay within. A Taiwanese woman must also learn the rules, but if she is to be a successful woman, she must learn not to stay within them, but to *appear* to stay within them; to manipulate them, but not to appear to be manipulating them; to teach them to her children, but not to depend on her children for her protection. A truly successful Taiwanese woman is a rugged individualist who has learned to depend largely on herself while appearing to lean on her father, her husband, and her son. The contrast between the terrified young bride and the loud, confident, often lewd old woman who has outlived her mother-in-law and her husband reflects the tests met and passed by not strictly following the rules and by making purposeful use of those who must. The Chinese male's conception of women as "narrow-hearted" and socially inept may well be his vague recognition of this facet of women's power and technique.

The women's subculture in rural Taiwan is, I believe, below the level of consciousness. Mothers do not tell their about-to-be-married daughters how to establish themselves in village society so that they may have some protection from an oppressive family situation, nor do they warn them to gather their children into an exclusive circle under their own control. But girls grow up in village society and see their mothers and sisters-in-law settling their differences to keep them from a public airing or presenting them for the women's community to judge. Their mothers have created around them the meaningful unit in their fathers' households, and when they are desperately lonely and unhappy in the households of their husbands, what they long for is what they have lost. . . . [Some] areas in the subculture of women . . . mesh perfectly into the main culture of the society. The two cultures are not symbiotic because they are not sufficiently independent of one another, but neither do they share identical goals or necessarily use the same means to reach the goals they do share. Outside the village the women's subculture seems not to exist. The uterine family also has no public existence, and appears almost as a response to the traditional family organized in terms of a male ideology.

11

The marriage contract: Bridewealth in Lebanon

PAUL D. STARR and
NURA S. ALAMUDDIN

Marriage does not automatically represent a stable, satisfying relationship. Conflict may stem from a variety of sources, threatening the union and making life unpleasant for both husband and wife. To deal with this problem, it is common for people living in the Middle East to negotiate marriage contracts that, among other things, determine the amount of bridewealth that the groom must eventually pay the bride. In this article, Paul Starr and Nura Alamuddin describe how the Druse of Lebanon set the amount of the mahr *(bridewealth), basing their decision on such factors as physical condition, social standing, political alliance, endogamy, and age. Like the marriage contracts that are beginning to appear in the United States,* mahr *is designed to yield a longer lasting, more emotionally satisfying marriage relationship.*

With the women's liberation movement in the Western nations has come the proposal that couples entering into marriage negotiate an extensive contract that specifies the nature of their relationship. These agreements may include any of the financial or personal aspects of a marriage — the wife's use of her maiden name, birth control methods, whether or not to have children (and if so, the number), residence patterns, the division of household labor, the use of income, sexual rights and freedom, relationships with in-laws, and the distribution of property should

Originally published as "Marriage: Lebanese Style." With permission from *Natural History*, Vol. 90, No. 4; Copyright the American Museum of Natural History, 1981.

the marriage end. All such provisions may not be legally binding but they can, it is argued, help us to examine the incomplete assumptions we hold about our intimate relationships and make them more equitable, satisfying, and enduring.

Marriage contracts in the industrialized West have been negotiated by a relatively few avant-garde couples, and their use strikes many as a passing fashion brought on by the push for sexual equality. But in the Middle East and other parts of the world, marriage contracts have been used by many people for hundreds, even thousands, of years.

In spite of the continuing reliance on marriage contracts throughout the Middle East, few analyses of what these agreements mean to those who use them have been possible. . . . [H]owever, we were able to examine a large sample (3,398) of the marriage contracts negotiated by members of the Druse sect in that country from 1931 through 1974.

One of Lebanon's numerous religious sects, the Druse are also an important Arab minority group in neighboring Syria and Israel. They have continually played an important role in the history of the Levant and from the sixteenth through the eighteenth century were one of the most powerful groups in the region. Originally emerging from the sectarian turmoil of eleventh-century Cairo, the theology of the Druse includes many features that distinguish it from the mainstream of Islam. Aside from the monogamous marriage practices of the Druse, however, their contemporary way of life reflects the traditional values found among most other Arab Islamic groups in the Middle East. In fact, although polygamy is permissible in other Islamic groups in the region, fewer than 3 percent of the husbands who can legally have more than one wife at the same time do so. In most respects, then, Druse marriage patterns reflect values that commonly prevail among Moslems in the Levant.

The marriage contract plays a fundamental part in the institution of marriage among the Druse. Legalizing the union, and giving it a religious sanction, a contract is usually the product of lengthy and elaborate negotiations on the part of a couple's senior kin. Some of its provisions involve only the initial establishment of the union, while others serve to help perpetuate the union or cope with its termination. The standard contract form that has been used in recent decades by the Central Druse Religious Court in Beirut includes the names, birthplaces, birth dates, and home villages of the bride and groom; the names of their fathers, deputies, and witnesses; and a place for seals and signatures. It also specifies the physical status of the bride and whether she is a virgin, a widow, or a divorcée. (Given the very strict puritanical code of the Druse, it is unthinkable that a woman could be listed as a nonvirgin and not have been previously married.) The most important part of the contract deals with the *mahr*, a payment made by the husband to the bride or her kin. There are two types of *mahr*. The first, or immediate, type is to be given before, during, or shortly after the contract-signing ceremony, and usually includes some money and such gifts as jewelry, furniture, and a sewing machine. The second, or deferred, *mahr* is a cash amount that the groom and his family agree to pay the bride in the event that he divorces her or dies before she does. Should a woman initiate a divorce, she would commonly forfeit the deferred sum.

Mahr can serve different purposes. Some regard it as purchase money, while others view it as a symbol, a ritualistic demonstration of the groom's esteem for the bride. Clearly, immediate *mahr* in the form of furniture, clothing, a sewing machine, or other goods is helpful in establishing the couple's household. The deferred *mahr* can be regarded as a kind of insurance policy to help protect the wife from the economic deprivation that she would be likely to suffer through the loss of her husband by either divorce or death. Deferred *mahr* can also reflect the degree of the husband's commitment to his spouse. Even though it is legally relatively easy for a man to obtain a divorce in the Middle East, this course of action becomes less likely, especially among rural peasants, if a husband is required to pay a large lump sum as compensation. As with so many other social inventions, the reasons for the existence of *mahr* can be as varied as the uses to which it can be put.

Given the significant role *mahr* plays during negotiations preceding a match, as well as throughout a marriage, we chose to focus our inquiry on how various characteristics of the couple influenced the amount of deferred *mahr* agreed upon.

We looked initially at how the "physical status" of the bride affected her position in the "marketplace." Virgins were seen worthy of a much higher *mahr* than either widows, divorcées, or those described as *thayyib* (literally, "nonvirgins," also referring to widows and divorcées). The inferiority of previously divorced brides, as reported to us by various Druse informants, was apparent. Their *mahr* was less than a tenth of that for virgin brides, and less than half of that for either widows or *thayyib* women.

We looked next into the effect that the social standing of the couple's families had on *mahr*. Traditionally, Druse families are either of the sheikly class or are commoners. This distinction, based on the historic exploits of ancient nobles and warriors, is commonly known and accepted within the sect. The great majority of Druse marry within their class, with sheikly unions specifying a higher *mahr* than those between commoners. If a man of high status marries a commoner, however, he pays much less than he would for a bride from his class. Most interesting is the very high *mahr* a commoner agrees to pay for a sheikly bride. In the few instances in which a commoner has gained the hand of a sheikly bride, he has paid a high price for the status that his partner brings to the marriage. When a high-status groom has a commoner bride, however, the status he confers upon her is presumed to be an ample reward. He agrees to pay a little more than half the *mahr* given a sheikly bride.

Status is not the only social boundary that influences marriages among the Druse. As with many other Middle Eastern groups, their families have historically belonged to larger political factions. The Druse have two basic factions, the Yazbaki and the Jumblati, with a small minority of families maintaining an affiliation with both. These groups have historically been at odds over issues within the community and have often been in opposition on the larger national scene. Each has been allied with opposing coalitions made up of other Lebanese Christian and Moslem groups. Reflecting the increased liability that cross-factional marriage entails, the average *mahr* for such a match is significantly higher than a marriage within either the Yazbaki or the Jumblati faction. The lowest *mahr* was found in marriages between families that had ties to both political factions, presumably because these marriages should be less affected by internal political turmoil.

Endogamy, the custom of marrying within a particular group, is a basic feature of Middle Eastern marriages, with the strongest preference for unions between a man and his father's brother's daughter. If the most desired form is not possible, the preference is for matches within the same clan. To determine how the satisfaction of these preferences might affect the amount of *mahr* agreed upon, we examined how it was influenced by the couples being related and by their residing in the same area.

We found that marriages within the same clan had the lowest *mahr*, suggesting that the perceived liability for such matches was also low. Surprisingly, however, closeness in terms of the physical proximity of two families resulted in a lower *mahr* than did closeness in terms of kinship. For example, when the couple's families were related but separated by long distances, as in the case of a wedding between one branch of a clan that lived in Syria and another branch that lived near Beirut, the average *mahr* was much higher than when the families were unrelated but living in the same village. The conclusion that physical proximity is more desirable than closeness in terms of kinship and may promote a better marriage was also shown in other situations. Among the highest average *mahr* were those that involved the greatest physical separation of the bride from her family, as in the case of women going to marry Lebanese immigrants living in Australia or the United States. Obviously, the greater the distance a bride is from her family, the less they are able to aid her. To compensate for this disadvantage and to increase her protection, a larger *mahr* is sought.

Observations and discussions with Druse of a variety of backgrounds indicated that personal characteristics of the potential mates, as well as those of their respective families, also produced variations in *mahr*. It is common for undesirable suitors to be turned down in a diplomatic way by demanding an exceptionally high *mahr*. If a suitor is seen as "too old" for a woman, is divorced, or has a reputation for being unstable or unreliable in some respect, a woman's parents will usually seek a very high *mahr*, to get him either to withdraw or to provide a considerable amount of "insurance" for their daughter. The general physical attractiveness, intelligence, education, and personality of those involved are also important. A highly desirable match from the point of view of the couple and families involved is seldom lost because of a lack of agreement about the *mahr*.

The contracts had no details about most of the personal characteristics of those married but did include their ages. This enabled us to see how differences in the ages of the bride and the groom affected the amount set. Conventionally, Druse men marry women who are about seven years younger than themselves. We anticipated that significant departures from this norm would result in a higher *mahr*. The actual situation turned out to be different. From no age difference to a difference of nineteen years, the less the age difference, the less the *mahr* specified. Clearly, the perceived liability steadily increased as the difference in age between a younger bride and an older groom became greater. But at a difference of more than nineteen years the level of *mahr* decreased significantly and then leveled off. Seeking an explanation for this phenomenon, we realized that most of these matches were what the Druse term "nurse-bride" marriages. In these unions an older man, often a widower, takes a younger bride to help cook, manage the household, and care for any infirmities he may have. A lower *mahr* is set because the wife can expect a reasonable inheritance upon the death of her aged spouse and may also anticipate marrying again. In those rare marriages in which an older woman took a younger husband, there was no clear pattern.

Because we had data covering a 44-year period, we were also able to assess the effect that tremendous economic and social changes have had upon Druse marriage patterns. Reflecting the great economic growth of Lebanon since the early 1930s, the typical *mahr* has increased sharply. During the 1930s, the average *mahr* was 220 LL (Lebanese pounds). In the early 1970s, it was 11,461 LL, an increase of more than 5,200 percent. In other respects, however, Druse marriage patterns have changed very little. Marriages between families of different social strata (sheiks and commoners) continued to be unusual, making up less than 2 percent of the total. Unions between those belonging to different political factions are more common, but the proportion — about one in four marriages — has changed little since the 1930s. Similarly, about one-third of all marriages continue to occur within a single clan, a stable proportion. Surprisingly, and in contrast to so many other groups in the modernizing societies of the Middle East, even the Druse age at first marriage has remained fairly constant during the last four decades, averaging about twenty-one for brides and twenty-eight for grooms. In spite of the many changes that have taken place in Lebanon during the last few decades, the basic structural features of Druse society have remained amazingly resilient and express little change. During the same period the frequency of divorce also remained low, affecting an estimated less than one in ten couples.

Initially, the use of the marriage contract among the Druse would appear to be much different from that envisioned by its proponents in the West. In the Middle East, it is a long-established safeguard for women, who occupy an unquestionably inferior position in relation to their husbands. It establishes a penalty the husband must pay should he divorce his wife and helps perpetuate the marriage in spite of the wife's subservient position. It also at least partly compensates widows for the economic and personal loss incurred by the death of a spouse. On the other hand, advocates of the use of the contract in the West see it as an innovation to help couples overcome the traditional subordination of women within a marriage relationship by achieving an acceptable consensus about important individual concerns.

A closer look reveals, however, that both approaches actually seek the same end — the cultivation between men and women of enduring, emotionally satisfying relationships that create a buffer against life's stresses. That a mechanism like the marriage contract has emerged from two very different cultures suggests that it may indeed be a useful tool. In our society, where the persistent quest for "something better" often results in personal relationships that are numerous, brief, and unsatisfying, no workable alternative should be overlooked.

12

Sororities and the husband game

JOHN FINLEY SCOTT

*Every society has norms governing marriage. In American society, as
in many others, class differences are maintained by our marriage
rules. The structure and function of the university sorority as they
existed in the 1960s are analyzed by John Finley Scott for their effect
upon class structure.*

> Marriages, like births, deaths, or initiations at puberty, are rearrangements
> of structure that are constantly recurring in any society; they are moments
> of the continuing social process regulated by custom; there are institu-
> tionalized ways of dealing with such events. — A. R. Radcliffe-Brown,
> *African Systems of Kinship and Marriage.*

In many simple societies, the institutionalized ways of controlling marriage run to diverse schemes and devices. Often they include special
living quarters designed to make it easy for marriageable girls to attract
a husband: the Bontok people of the Philippines keep their girls in a
special house, called the *olag*, where lovers call, sex play is free, and
marriage is supposed to result. The Ekoi of Nigeria, who like their women
fat, send them away to be specially fattened for marriage. Other peoples,
such as the Yao of central Africa and the aborigines of the Canary Islands,
send their daughters away to "convents" where old women teach them
the special skills and mysteries that a young wife needs to know.

Accounts of such practices have long been a standard topic of
anthropology lectures in universities, for their exotic appeal keeps the
students, large numbers of whom are sorority girls, interested and alert.
The control of marriage in simple societies strikes these girls as quite
different from the freedom that they believe prevails in America. This

is ironic, for the American college sorority is a pretty good counterpart in complex societies of the fatting houses and convents of the primitives.

Whatever system they use, parents in all societies have more in mind than just getting their daughters married; they want them married to the *right* man. The criteria for defining the right man vary tremendously, but virtually all parents view some potential mates with approval, some with disapproval, and some with downright horror. Many ethnic groups, including many in America, are *endogamous*, that is, they desire marriage of their young only to those within the group. In *shtetl* society, the Jewish villages of eastern Europe, marriages were arranged by a *shatchen*, a matchmaker, who paired off the girls and boys with due regard to the status, family connections, wealth, and personal attractions of the participants. But this society was strictly endogamous — only marriage within the group was allowed. Another rule of endogamy relates to social rank or class, for most parents are anxious that their children marry at least at the same level as themselves. Often they hope the children, and especially the daughters, will marry at a higher level. Parents of the *shtetl*, for example, valued *hypergamy* — the marriage of daughters to a man of higher status — and a father who could afford it would offer substantial sums to acquire a scholarly husband (the most highly prized kind) for his daughter.

The marriage problem, from the point of view of parents and of various ethnic groups and social classes, is always one of making sure that girls are available for marriage with the right man while at the same time guarding against marriage with the wrong man.

THE UNIVERSITY CONVENT

The American middle class has a particular place where it sends its daughters so they will be easily accessible to the boys — the college campus. Even for the families who worry about the bad habits a nice girl can pick up at college, it has become so much a symbol of middle-class status that the risk must be taken, the girl must be sent. American middle-class society has created an institution on the campus that, like the fatting house, makes the girls more attractive; like the Canary Island convent, teaches skills that middle-class wives need to know; like the *shtetl*, provides matchmakers; and without going so far as to buy husbands of high rank, manages to dissuade the girl from making alliances with lower-class boys. That institution is the college sorority.

A sorority is a private association which provides separate dormitory facilities with a distinctive Greek letter name for selected female college students. Membership is by invitation only, and requires recommendation by former members. Sororities are not simply the feminine counterpart of the college fraternity. They differ from fraternities because marriage is a more important determinant of social position for women than for men in American society, and because standards of conduct associated with marriage correspondingly bear stronger sanctions for women than for men. Sororities have much more "alumnae" involvement than fraternities, and fraternities adapt to local conditions and different living arrangements better than sororities. The college-age sorority "actives" decide only the minor details involved in recruitment, membership, and activities; parent-age alumnae control the important choices. The prototypical sorority is not the servant of youthful interests; on the contrary, it is an organized agency for controlling those interests. Through the sorority, the elders of family, class, ethnic, and religious communities can continue to exert remote control over the marital arrangements of their young girls.

The need for remote control arises from the nature of the educational system in an industrial society. In simple societies, where children are taught the culture at home, the family controls the socialization of children almost completely. In more complex societies, education becomes the province of special agents and competes with the family. The conflict between the family and outside agencies increases as children move through the educational system and is sharpest when the children reach college age. College curricula are even more challenging to family value systems than high school courses, and children frequently go away to college, out of reach of direct family influence. Sometimes a family can find a college that does not challenge family values in any way: devout Catholic parents can send their daughters to Catholic colleges; parents who want to be sure that daughter meets only "Ivy League" men can send her to one of the "Seven Sisters" — the women's equivalent of the Ivy League, made up of Radcliffe, Barnard, Smith, Vassar, Wellesley, Mt. Holyoke, and Bryn Mawr — if she can get in.

The solution of controlled admissions is applicable only to a small proportion of college-age girls, however. There are nowhere near the number of separate, sectarian colleges in the country that would be needed to segregate all the college-age girls safely, each with her own kind. Private colleges catering mostly to a specific class can still preserve a girl from meeting her social or economic inferiors, but the fees at such places are steep. It costs more to maintain a girl in the Vassar dormitories than to pay her sorority bills at a land-grant school. And even if her family is willing to pay the fees, the academic pace at the elite schools is much too fast for most girls. Most college girls attend large, tax-supported universities where the tuition is relatively low and where admissions policies let in students from many strata and diverse ethnic backgrounds. It is on the campuses of the free, open, and competitive state universities of the country that the sorority system flourishes.

When a family lets its daughter loose on a large campus with a heterogenous population, there are opportunities to be met and dangers to guard against. The great opportunity is to meet a good man to marry, at the age when the girls are most attractive and the men most amenable. For the girls, the pressure of time is urgent; though they are often told otherwise, their attractions are in fact primarily physical, and they fade with time. One need only compare the relative handicaps in the marital sweepstakes of a thirty-eight-year-old single male lawyer and a single, female teacher of the same age to realize the urgency of the quest.

The great danger of the public campus is that young girls, however properly reared, are likely to fall in love, and — in our middle-class society at least — love leads to marriage. Love is a potentially random factor, with no regard for class boundaries. There seems to be no good way of preventing young girls from falling in love. The only practical way to control love is to control the type of men the girl is likely to encounter; she cannot fall dangerously in love with a man she has never met. Since kinship groups are unable to keep "undesirable" boys off the public campus entirely, they have to settle for control of counter-institutions within the university. An effective counter-institution will protect a girl from the corroding influences of the university environment.

There are roughly three basic functions which a sorority can perform in the interest of kinship groups:

It can ward off the wrong kind of men.
It can facilitate moving-up for middle-status girls.
It can solve the "Brahmin problem" — the difficulty of proper marriage that afflicts high-status girls.

Kinship groups define the "wrong kind of man" in a variety of ways. Those who use an ethnic definition support sororities that draw an ethnic membership line; the best examples are the Jewish sororities, because among all the ethnic groups with endogamous standards (in America at any rate), only the Jews so far have sent large numbers of daughters away to college. But endogamy along class lines is even more pervasive. It is the most basic mission of the sorority to prevent a girl from marrying out of her group (exogamy) or beneath her class (hypogamy). As one of the founders of a national sorority artlessly put it in an essay titled "The Mission of the Sorority":

There is a danger, and a very grave danger, that four years' residence in a dormitory will tend to destroy right ideals of home life and substitute in their stead a belief in the freedom that comes from community living . . . culture, broad, liberalizing, humanizing culture, we cannot get too much of, unless while acquiring it we are weaned from home and friends, from ties of blood and kindred.

A sorority discourages this dangerous weaning process by introducing the sisters only to selected boys; each sorority, for example, has dating relations with one or more fraternities, matched rather nicely to the sorority on the basis of ethnicity and/or class. (A particular sorority, for example, will have dating arrangements not with all the fraternities on campus, but only with those whose brothers are a class-match for their sisters.) The sorority's frantically busy schedule of parties, teas, meetings, skits, and exchanges keep the sisters so occupied that they have neither time nor opportunity to meet men outside the channels the sorority provides.

MARRYING UP

The second sorority function, that of facilitating hypergamy, is probably even more of an attraction to parents than the simpler preservation of endogamy. American society is not so much oriented to the preservation of the *status quo* as to the pursuit of upward mobility.

In industrial societies, children are taught that if they study hard they can get the kind of job that entitles them to a place in the higher ranks. This incentive actually is appropriate only for boys, but the emphasis on using the most efficient available means to enter the higher levels will not be lost on the girls. And the most efficient means for a girl — marriage — is particularly attractive because it requires so much less effort than the mobility through hard work that is open to boys. To the extent that we do socialize the sexes in different ways, we are more likely to train daughters in the ways of attracting men than to motivate them to do hard, competitive work. The difference in motivation holds even if the girls have the intelligence and talent required for status climbing on their own. For lower-class girls on the make, membership in a sorority can greatly improve the chances of meeting (and subsequently marrying) higher-status boys.

Now we come to the third function of the sorority — solving the Brahmin problem. The fact that hypergamy is encouraged in our society creates difficulties for girls whose parents are already in the upper strata. In a hypergamous system, high-status *men* have a strong advantage; they can offer their status to a prospective bride as part of the marriage bargain, and the advantages of high status are often sufficient to offset many personal drawbacks. But a *woman's* high status has very little exchange value because she does not confer it on her husband.

This difficulty of high-status women in a hypergamous society we may call the Brahmin problem. Girls of Brahmin caste in India and

Southern white women of good family have the problem in common. In order to avoid the horrors of hypogamy, high-status women must compete for high-status men against women from all classes. Furthermore, high-status women are handicapped in their battle by a certain type of vanity engendered by their class. They expect their wooers to court them in the style to which their fathers have accustomed them; this usually involves more formal dating, gift-giving, escorting, taxiing, etc., than many college swains can afford. If upper-stratum men are allowed to find out that the favors of lower-class women are available for a much smaller investment of time, money, and emotion, they may well refuse to court upper-status girls.

In theory, there are all kinds of ways for upper-stratum families to deal with surplus daughters. They can strangle them at birth (female infanticide); they can marry several to each available male (polygyny); they can offer money to any suitable male willing to take one off their hands (dowries, groom-service fees). All these solutions have in fact been used in one society or another, but for various reasons none is acceptable in our society. Spinsterhood still works, but marriage is so popular and so well rewarded that everybody hopes to avoid staying single.

The industrial solution to the Brahmin problem is to corner the market, or more specifically to shunt the eligible bachelors into a special marriage market where the upper-stratum women are in complete control of the bride-supply. The best place to set up this protected marriage-market is where many suitable men can be found at the age when they are most willing to marry — in short, the college campus. The kind of male collegians who can be shunted more readily into the specialized marriage-market that sororities run, are those who are somewhat uncertain of their own status and who aspire to move into higher strata. These boys are anxious to bolster a shaky self-image by dating obviously high-class sorority girls. The fraternities are full of them.

How does a sorority go about fulfilling its three functions? The first item of business is making sure that the girls join. This is not as simple as it seems, because the values that sororities maintain are more important to the older generation than to the college-age girls. Although the sorority image is one of membership denied to the "wrong kind" of girls, it is also true that sororities have quite a problem recruiting the "right kind." Some are pressured into pledging by their parents. Many are recruited straight out of high school, before they know much about what really goes on at college. High school recruiters present sorority life to potential rushees as one of unending gaiety; life outside the sorority is painted as bleak and dateless.

A membership composed of the "right kind" of girls is produced by the requirement that each pledge must have the recommendation of, in most cases, two or more alumnae of the sorority. Membership is often passed on from mother to daughter — this is the "legacy," whom sorority actives have to invite whether they like her or not. The sort of headstrong, innovative, or "sassy" girl who is likely to organize a campaign inside the sorority against prevailing standards is unlikely to receive alumnae recommendations. This is why sorority girls are so complacent about alumnae dominance, and why professors find them so bland and uninteresting as students. Alumnae dominance extends beyond recruitment, into the daily life of the house. Rules, regulations, and policy explanations come to the house from the national association. National headquarters is given to explaining unpopular policy by an available stratagem; a favorite device (not limited to the sorority) is to interpret all nonconformity as sexual, so that the girl who rebels against wearing girdle, high heels, and stockings to dinner two or three times a week stands implicitly accused of promiscuity. This sort of argument, based on the shrewdness of many generations, shames into conformity many a girl who otherwise might rebel against the code imposed by her elders. The actives in positions of control (house manager, pledge trainer, or captain) are themselves closely supervised by alumnae. Once the right girls are initiated, the organization has mechanisms that make it very difficult for a girl to withdraw. Withdrawal can mean difficulty in finding alternative living quarters, loss of prepaid room-and-board fees, and stigmatization.

Sororities keep their members, and particularly their flighty pledges, in line primarily by filling up all their time with house activities. Pledges are required to study at the house, and they build the big papier-mâché floats (in collaboration with selected fraternity boys) that are a traditional display of "Greek Row" for the homecoming game. Time is encompassed completely; activities are planned long in advance, and there is almost no energy or time available for meeting inappropriate men.

The girls are taught — if they do not already know — the behavior appropriate to the upper strata. They learn how to dress with expensive restraint, how to make appropriate conversation, how to drink like a lady. There is some variety here among sororities of different rank; members of sororities at the bottom of the social ladder prove their gentility by rigid conformity in dress and manner to the stereotype of the sorority girl, while members of top houses feel socially secure even when casually dressed. If you are born rich you can afford to wear Levi's and sweatshirts.

PRELIMINARY EVENTS

The sorority facilitates dating mainly by exchanging parties, picnics, and other frolics with the fraternities in its set. But to augment this the "fixer-uppers" (the American counterpart of the *shatchen*) arrange dates with selected boys; their efforts raise the sorority dating rate above the independent level by removing most of the inconvenience and anxiety from the contracting of dates.

Dating, in itself, is not sufficient to accomplish the sorority's purposes. Dating must lead to pinning, pinning to engagement, engagement to marriage. In sorority culture, all dating is viewed as a movement toward marriage. Casual, spontaneous dating is frowned upon; formal courtship is still encouraged. Sorority ritual reinforces the progression from dating to marriage. At the vital point in the process, where dating must be turned into engagement, the sorority shores up the structure by the pinning ritual, performed after dinner in the presence of all the sorority sisters (who are required to stay for the ceremony) and attended, in its classic form, by a choir of fraternity boys singing outside. The commitment is so public that it is difficult for either partner to withdraw. Since engagement is already heavily reinforced outside the sorority, pinning ceremonies are more elaborate than engagements.

The social columns of college newspapers faithfully record the successes of the sorority system as it stands today. Sorority girls get engaged faster than "independents," and they appear to be marrying more highly ranked men. But what predictions can we make about the system's future?

All social institutions change from time to time, in response to changing conditions. In the mountain villages of the Philippines, the steady attacks of school and mission on the immorality of the *olag* have almost demolished it. Sororities, too, are affected by changes in the surrounding environment. Originally they were places where the few female college students took refuge from the jeers and catcalls of men who thought that nice girls didn't belong on campus. They assumed their present, endogamy-conserving form with the flourishing of the great land-grant universities in the first half of this century.

ON THE BRINK

The question about the future of the sorority system is whether it can adapt to the most recent changes in the forms of higher education. At present, neither fraternities nor sororities are in the pink of health. On some campuses there are chapter houses which have been reduced to taking in nonaffiliated boarders to pay the costs of running the property. New sorority chapters are formed, for the most part, on new or low-prestige campuses (where status-anxiety is rife); at schools of high prestige fewer girls rush each year and the weaker houses are disbanding.

University administrations are no longer as hospitable to the Greeks as they once were. Most are building extensive dormitories that compete effectively with the housing offered by sororities; many have adopted regulations intended to minimize the influence of the Greeks on campus activities. The campus environment is changing rapidly: academic standards are rising, admission is increasingly competitive and both male and female students are more interested in academic achievement; the proportion of graduate students seriously training for a profession is increasing; campus culture is often so obviously pluralist that the Greek claim to monopolize social activity is unconvincing.

The sorority as it currently stands is ill-adapted to cope with the new surroundings. Sorority houses were built to provide a setting for lawn parties, dances, and dress-up occasions, and not to facilitate study; crowding and noise are severe, and most forms of privacy do not exist. The sorority songs that have to be gone through at rushing and chapter meetings today all seem to have been written in 1915 and are mortifying to sing today. The arcane rituals, so fascinating to high school girls, grow tedious and sophomoric to college seniors.

But the worst blow of all to the sorority system comes from the effect of increased academic pressure on the dating habits of college men. A student competing for grades in a professional school, or even in a difficult undergraduate major, simply has not the time (as he might have had in, say, 1925) to get involved in the sorority forms of courtship. Since these days almost all the "right kind" of men *are* involved in demanding training, the traditions of the sorority are becoming actually inimical to hypergamous marriage. Increasingly, then, sororities do not solve the Brahmin problem but make it worse.

One can imagine a sorority designed to facilitate marriage to men who have no time for elaborate courtship. In such a sorority, the girls — to start with small matters — would improve their telephone arrangements, for the fraternity boy in quest of a date today must call several times to get through the busy signals, interminable paging, and lost messages to the girl he wants. They might arrange a private line with prompt answering and faithfully recorded messages, with an unlisted number given only to busy male students with a promising future. They would even accept dates for the same night as the invitation, rather than, as at present, necessarily five to ten days in advance, for the only thing a first-year law student can schedule that far ahead nowadays is his studies. Emphasis on fraternity boys would have to go, for living in a fraternity and pursuing a promising (and therefore competitive) major field of study are rapidly becoming mutually exclusive. The big formal dances would go (the fraternity boys dislike them now); the football floats would go; the pushcart races would go. The girls would reach the hearts of their men not through helping them wash their sports cars but through typing their term papers.

But it is inconceivable that the proud traditions of the sororities that compose the National Panhellenic Council could ever be bent to fit the new design. Their structure is too fixed to fit the changing college and their function is rapidly being lost. The sorority cannot sustain itself on students alone. When parents learn that membership does not benefit their daughters, the sorority as we know it will pass into history.

V

Sex roles

For most people, social interaction is unconscious and automatic. We associate with other people from the time we are born. Of course we experience moments when we feel socially awkward and out of place, but generally we learn to act toward others with confidence. Yet our unconscious ease masks an enormously complex process. When we enter a social situation, how do we know what to do? What should we say? How are we supposed to act? Are we dressed appropriately? Are we talking to the right person? Without knowing it, we have learned a complex set of cultural categories for social interaction that enable us to estimate the social situation, identify the people in it, act appropriately, and recognize larger groups of people.

Status and role are basic to social intercourse. Status refers to the cultural knowledge necessary for categorizing different kinds of interacting people. The old saying, "You can't tell the players without a program," goes for our daily associations as well. Instead of a program, however, we identify the actors by a range of signs from the way they dress to the claims they make about themselves. Most statuses are stated, so we may be heard to say things like, "That's President Davis," or "She's a lawyer," when we explain social situations to others. This identification of actors is a prerequisite for appropriate social interaction.

Social roles are the rules for action associated with particular identities. We use them to interpret and generate social behavior. For example, a professor plays a role in the classroom. Although unaware of
this role, the professor will stand, use the blackboard, look at notes,
and speak with a slightly more formal air than usual. The professor does
not wear blue jeans and a T-shirt, chew gum, sit cross-legged on the
podium, or sing. These actions might be appropriate for this person
when assuming the identity of "friend" at a party, but they are out of
place in the classroom.

Anthropologists regularly describe statuses and roles in the course
of their fieldwork. Kinship roles, as we saw in the last section, are
especially important in the social organization of many societies. So are
roles associated with economic, political, legal, and religious systems as
we shall see later. In this section we focus on one important aspect of
roles, the degree to which sex determines their assignment and content.
How are female and male roles different? What accounts for relative
variations in equality and inequality between the sexes from one society
to the next? The following selections focus especially on women's roles
in different societies. They explore the reasons for female inequality and
some of the strategies women use to adapt to male dominated worlds.

13

Society and sex roles

ERNESTINE FRIEDL

Many anthropologists claim that males hold formal authority over females in every society. Although the degree of masculine authority may vary from one group to the next, males always have more power. For some researchers, this unequal male-female relationship is the result of biological inheritance. As with other primates, they argue, male humans are naturally more aggressive, females more docile. Ernestine Friedl challenges this explanation in this selection. Comparing a variety of hunting and gathering groups, she concludes that relations between men and women are shaped by a culturally defined division of labor based on sex, not by inherited predisposition. Given access to resources that circulate publicly, women can attain equal or dominant status in any society, including our own.

"Women must respond quickly to the demands of their husbands," says anthropologist Napoleon Chagnon describing the horticultural Yanomamö Indians of Venezuela. When a man returns from a hunting trip, "the woman, no matter what she is doing, hurries home and quietly but rapidly prepares a meal for her husband. Should the wife be slow in doing this, the husband is within his rights to beat her. Most reprimands . . . take the form of blows with the hand or with a piece of firewood. . . . Some of them chop their wives with the sharp edge of a machete or axe, or shoot them with a barbed arrow in some nonvital area, such as the buttocks or leg."

Among the Semai agriculturalists of central Malaya, when one person refuses the request of another, the offended party suffers *punan*, a mixture of emotional pain and frustration. "Enduring *punan* is com-

From *Human Nature*, April 1978. Copyright © 1978 by Human Nature, Inc. Reprinted by permission of the publisher.

monest when a girl has refused the victim her sexual favors," reports Robert Dentan. "The jilted man's 'heart becomes sad.' He loses his energy and his appetite. Much of the time he sleeps, dreaming of his lost love. In this state he is in fact very likely to injure himself 'accidentally.' " The Semai are afraid of violence; a man would never strike a woman.

The social relationship between men and women has emerged as one of the principal disputes occupying the attention of scholars and the public in recent years. Although the discord is sharpest in the United States, the controversy has spread throughout the world. Numerous national and international conferences, including one in Mexico sponsored by the United Nations, have drawn together delegates from all walks of life to discuss such questions as the social and political rights of each sex, and even the basic nature of males and females.

Whatever their position, partisans often invoke examples from other cultures to support their ideas about the proper role of each sex. Because women are clearly subservient to men in many societies, like the Yanomamö, some experts conclude that the natural pattern is for men to dominate. But among the Semai no one has the right to command others, and in West Africa women are often chiefs. The place of women in these societies supports the argument of those who believe that sex roles are not fixed, that if there is a natural order, it allows for many different arrangements.

The argument will never be settled as long as the opposing sides toss examples from the world's cultures at each other like intellectual stones. But the effect of biological differences on male and female behavior can be clarified by looking at known examples of the earliest forms of human society and examining the relationship between technology, social organization, environment, and sex roles. The problem is to determine the conditions in which different degrees of male dominance are found, to try to discover the social and cultural arrangements that give rise to equality or inequality between the sexes, and to attempt to apply this knowledge to our understanding of the changes taking place in modern industrial society.

As Western history and the anthropological record have told us, equality between the sexes is rare; in most known societies females are subordinate. Male dominance is so widespread that it is virtually a human universal; societies in which women are consistently dominant do not exist and have never existed.

Evidence of a society in which women control all strategic resources like food and water, and in which women's activities are the most prestigious has never been found. The Iroquois of North America and the Lovedu of Africa came closest. Among the Iroquois, women raised food, controlled its distribution, and helped to choose male political leaders. Lovedu women ruled as queens, exchanged valuable cattle, led ceremonies, and controlled their own sex lives. But among both the Iroquois and the Lovedu, men owned the land and held other positions of power and prestige. Women were equal to men; they did not have ultimate authority over them. Neither culture was a true matriarchy.

Patriarchies are prevalent, and they appear to be strongest in societies in which men control significant goods that are exchanged with people outside the family. Regardless of who produces food, the person who gives it to others creates the obligations and alliances that are at the center of all political relations. The greater the male monopoly on the distribution of scarce items, the stronger their control of women seems to be. This is most obvious in relatively simple hunter-gatherer societies.

Hunter-gatherers, or foragers, subsist on wild plants, small land animals, and small river or sea creatures gathered by hand; large land animals and sea mammals hunted with spears, bows and arrows, and blow guns; and fish caught with hooks and nets. The 300,000 hunter-gatherers alive in the world today include the Eskimos, the Australian aborigines, and the Pygmies of Central Africa.

Foraging has endured for two million years and was replaced by farming and animal husbandry only 10,000 years ago; it covers more than 99 percent of human history. Our foraging ancestry is not far behind us and provides a clue to our understanding of the human condition.

Hunter-gatherers are people whose ways of life are technologically simple and socially and politically egalitarian. They live in small groups of 50 to 200 and have neither kings, nor priests, nor social classes. These conditions permit anthropologists to observe the essential bases for inequalities between the sexes without the distortions induced by the complexities of contemporary industrial society.

The source of male power among hunter-gatherers lies in their control of a scarce, hard to acquire, but necessary nutrient — animal protein. When men in a hunter-gatherer society return to camp with game, they divide the meat in some customary way. Among the !Kung San of Africa, certain parts of the animal are given to the owner of the arrow that killed the beast, to the first hunter to sight the game, to the one who threw the first spear, and to all men in the hunting party. After the meat has been divided, each hunter distributes his share to his blood relatives and his in-laws, who in turn share it with others. If an animal is large enough, every member of the band will receive some meat.

Vegetable foods, in contrast, are not distributed beyond the immediate household. Women give food to their children, to their husbands, to other members of the household, and rarely, to the occasional visitor. No one outside the family regularly eats any of the wild fruits and vegetables that are gathered by the women.

The meat distributed by the men is a public gift. Its source is widely known, and the donor expects a reciprocal gift when other men return from a successful hunt. He gains honor as a supplier of a scarce item and simultaneously obligates others to him.

These obligations constitute a form of power or control over others, both men and women. The opinions of hunters play an important part in decisions to move the village; good hunters attract the most desirable women; people in other groups join camps with good hunters; and hunters, because they already participate in an internal system of exchange, control exchange with other groups for flint, salt, and steel axes. The male monopoly on hunting unites men in a system of exchange and gives them power; gathering vegetable food does not give women equal power even among foragers who live in the tropics, where the food collected by women provides more than half the hunter-gatherer diet.

If dominance arises from a monopoly on big-game hunting, why has the male monopoly remained unchallenged? Some women are strong enough to participate in the hunt and their endurance is certainly equal to that of men. Dobe San women of the Kalahari Desert in Africa walk an average of 10 miles a day carrying from 15 to 33 pounds of food plus a baby.

Women do not hunt, I believe, because of four interrelated factors: variability in the supply of game; the different skills required for hunting and gathering; the incompatibility between carrying burdens and hunting; and the small size of seminomadic foraging populations.

Because the meat supply is unstable, foragers must make frequent expeditions to provide the band with gathered food. Environmental factors such as seasonal and annual variation in rainfall often affect the size of the wildlife population. Hunters cannot always find game, and when they do encounter animals, they are not always successful in killing their prey. In northern latitudes, where meat is the primary food, periods of starvation are known in every generation. The irregularity of the game supply leads hunter-gatherers in areas where plant foods are available to depend on these predictable foods a good part of the time. Someone must gather the fruits, nuts, and roots and carry them back to camp to feed unsuccessful hunters, children, the elderly, and anyone who might not have gone foraging that day.

Foraging falls to the women because hunting and gathering cannot be combined on the same expedition. Although gatherers sometimes notice signs of game as they work, the skills required to track game are not the same as those required to find edible roots or plants. Hunters scan the horizon and the land for traces of large game; gatherers keep their eyes to the ground, studying the distribution of plants and the texture of the soil for hidden roots and animal holes. Even if a woman who was collecting plants came across the track of an antelope, she could not follow it; it is impossible to carry a load and hunt at the same time. Running with a heavy load is difficult, and should the animal be sighted, the hunter would be off balance and could neither shoot an arrow nor throw a spear accurately.

Pregnancy and child care would also present difficulties for a hunter. An unborn child affects a woman's body balance, as does a child in her arms, on her back, or slung at her side. Until they are two years old, many hunter-gatherer children are carried at all times, and until they are four, they are carried some of the time.

An observer might wonder why young women do not hunt until they become pregnant, or why mature women and men do not hunt and gather on alternate days, with some women staying in camp to act as wet nurses for the young. Apart from the effects hunting might have on a mother's milk production, there are two reasons. First, young girls begin to bear children as soon as they are physically mature and strong enough to hunt, and second, hunter-gatherer bands are so small that there are unlikely to be enough lactating women to serve as wet nurses. No hunter-gatherer group could afford to maintain a specialized female hunting force.

Because game is not always available, because hunting and gathering are specialized skills, because women carrying heavy loads cannot hunt, and because women in hunter-gatherer societies are usually either pregnant or caring for young children, for most of the last two million years of human history men have hunted and women have gathered.

If male dominance depends on controlling the supply of meat, then the degree of male dominance in a society should vary with the amount of meat available and the amount supplied by the men. Some regions, like the East African grasslands and the North American woodlands, abounded with species of large mammals; other zones, like tropical forests and semideserts, are thinly populated with prey. Many elements affect the supply of game, but theoretically, the less meat provided exclusively by the men, the more egalitarian the society.

All known hunter-gatherer societies fit into four basic types: those in which men and women work together in communal hunts and as teams gathering edible plants, as did the Washo Indians of North America; those in which men and women each collect their own plant foods although the men supply some meat to the group, as do the Hadza of Tanzania; those in which male hunters and female gatherers work apart but return to camp each evening to share their acquisitions, as do the

Tiwi of North Australia; and those in which the men provide all the food by hunting large game, as do the Eskimo. In each case the extent of male dominance increases directly with the proportion of meat supplied by individual men and small hunting parties.

Among the most egalitarian of hunter-gatherer societies are the Washo Indians, who inhabited the valleys of the Sierra Nevada in what is now southern California and Nevada. In the spring they moved north to Lake Tahoe for the large fish runs of sucker and native trout. Everyone — men, women, and children — participated in the fishing. Women spent the summer gathering edible berries and seeds while the men continued to fish. In the fall some men hunted deer but the most important source of animal protein was the jackrabbit, which was captured in communal hunts. Men and women together drove the rabbits into nets tied end to end. To provide food for the winter, husbands and wives worked as teams in the late fall to collect pine nuts.

Since everyone participated in most food-gathering activities, there were no individual distributors of food and relatively little difference in male and female rights. Men and women were not segregated from each other in daily activities; both were free to take lovers after marriage; both had the right to separate whenever they chose; menstruating women were not isolated from the rest of the group; and one of the two major Washo rituals celebrated hunting while the other celebrated gathering. Men were accorded more prestige if they had killed a deer, and men directed decisions about the seasonal movement of the group. But if no male leader stepped forward, women were permitted to lead. The distinctive feature of groups such as the Washo is the relative equality of the sexes.

The sexes are also relatively equal among the Hadza of Tanzania but this near-equality arises because men and women tend to work alone to feed themselves. They exchange little food. The Hadza lead a leisurely life in the seemingly barren environment of the East African Rift Gorge that is, in fact, rich in edible berries, roots, and small game. As a result of this abundance, from the time they are 10 years old, Hadza men and women gather much of their own food. Women take their young children with them into the bush, eating as they forage, and collect only enough food for a light family meal in the evening. The men eat berries and roots as they hunt for small game, and should they bring down a rabbit or a hyrax, they eat the meat on the spot. Meat is carried back to the camp and shared with the rest of the group only on those rare occasions when a poisoned arrow brings down a large animal — an impala, a zebra, an eland, or a giraffe.

Because Hadza men distribute little meat, their status is only slightly higher than that of the women. People flock to the camp of a good hunter and the camp might take on his name because of his popularity, but he is in no sense a leader of the group. A Hadza man and a woman have an equal right to divorce and each can repudiate a marriage simply by living apart for a few weeks. Couples tend to live in the same camp as the wife's mother but they sometimes make long visits to the camp of the husband's mother. Although a man may take more than one wife, most Hadza males cannot afford to indulge in this luxury. In order to maintain a marriage, a man must supply both his wife and his mother-in-law with some meat and trade goods, such as beads and cloth, and the Hadza economy gives few men the wealth to provide for more than one wife and mother-in-law. Washo equality is based on cooperation; Hadza equality is based on independence.

In contrast to both these groups, among the Tiwi of Melville and Bathurst Islands off the northern coast of Australia, male hunters dominate female gatherers. The Tiwi are representative of the most common form of foraging society, in which the men supply large quantities of meat, although less than half the food consumed by the group. Each morning Tiwi women, most with babies on their backs, scatter in different directions in search of vegetables, grubs, worms, and small game such as bandicoots, lizards, and opossums. To track the game, they use hunting dogs. On most days women return to camp with some meat and with baskets full of *korka*, the nut of a native palm, which is soaked and mashed to make a porridge-like dish. The Tiwi men do not hunt small game and do not hunt every day, but when they do they often return with kangaroo, large lizards, fish, and game birds.

The porridge is cooked separately by each household and rarely shared outside the family, but the meat is prepared by a volunteer cook, who can be male or female. After the cook takes one of the parts of the animal traditionally reserved for him or her, the animal's "boss," the one who caught it, distributes the rest to all near kin and then to all others residing with the band. Although the small game supplied by the women is distributed in the same way as the big game supplied by the men, Tiwi men are dominant because the game they kill provides most of the meat.

The power of Tiwi men is clearest in their betrothal practices. Among the Tiwi, a woman must always be married. To ensure this, female infants are betrothed at birth and widows are remarried at the gravesides of their late husbands. Men form alliances by exchanging daughters, sisters, and mothers in marriage and some collect as many as 25 wives. Tiwi men value the quantity and quality of the food many wives can collect and the many children they can produce.

The dominance of the men is offset somewhat by the influence of adult women in selecting their next husbands. Many women are active strategists in the political careers of their male relatives, but to the exasperation of some sons attempting to promote their own futures, widowed mothers sometimes insist on selecting their own partners. Women also influence the marriages of their daughters and granddaughters, especially when the selected husband dies before the bestowed child moves to his camp.

Among the Eskimo, representative of the rarest type of forager society, inequality between the sexes is matched by inequality in supplying the group with food. Inland Eskimo men hunt caribou throughout the year to provision the entire society, and maritime Eskimo men depend on whaling, fishing, and some hunting to feed their extended families. The women process the carcasses, cut and sew skins to make clothing, cook, and care for the young; but they collect no food of their own and depend on the men to supply all the raw materials for their work. Since men provide all the meat, they also control the trade in hides, whale oil, seal oil, and other items that move between the maritime and inland Eskimos.

Eskimo women are treated almost exclusively as objects to be used, abused, and traded by men. After puberty all Eskimo girls are fair game for any interested male. A man shows his intentions by grabbing the belt of a woman and if she protests, he cuts off her trousers and forces himself upon her. These encounters are considered unimportant by the rest of the group. Men offer their wives' sexual services to establish alliances with trading partners and members of hunting and whaling parties.

Despite the consistent pattern of some degree of male dominance among foragers, most of these societies are egalitarian compared with agricultural and industrial societies. No forager has any significant opportunity for political leadership. Foragers, as a rule, do not like to give or take orders, and assume leadership only with reluctance. Shamans (those who are thought to be possessed by spirits) may be either male or female. Public rituals conducted by women in order to celebrate the first menstruation of girls are common, and the symbolism in these rituals is similar to that in the ceremonies that follow a boy's first kill.

In any society, status goes to those who control the distribution of valued goods and services outside the family. Equality arises when both sexes work side by side in food production, as do the Washo, and the products are simply distributed among the workers. In such circumstances, no person or sex has greater access to valued items than do others. But when women make no contribution to the food supply, as in the case of the Eskimo, they are completely subordinate.

When we attempt to apply these generalizations to contemporary industrial society, we can predict that as long as women spend their discretionary income from jobs on domestic needs, they will gain little social recognition and power. To be an effective source of power, money must be exchanged in ways that require returns and create obligations. In other words, it must be invested.

Jobs that do not give women control over valued resources will do little to advance their general status. Only as managers, executives, and professionals are women in a position to trade goods and services, to do others favors, and therefore to obligate others to them. Only as controllers of valued resources can women achieve prestige, power, and equality.

Within the household, women who bring in income from jobs are able to function on a more nearly equal basis with their husbands. Women who contribute services to their husbands and children without pay, as do some middle-class Western housewives, are especially vulnerable to dominance. Like Eskimo women, as long as their services are limited to domestic distribution they have little power relative to their husbands and none with respect to the outside world.

As for the limits imposed on women by their procreative functions in hunter-gatherer societies, childbearing and child care are organized around work as much as work is organized around reproduction. Some foraging groups space their children three to four years apart and have an average of only four to six children, far fewer than many women in other cultures. Hunter-gatherers nurse their infants for extended periods, sometimes for as long as four years. This custom suppresses ovulation and limits the size of their families. Sometimes, although rarely, they practice infanticide. By limiting reproduction, a woman who is gathering food has only one child to carry.

Different societies can and do adjust the frequency of birth and the care of children to accommodate whatever productive activities women customarily engage in. In horticultural societies, where women work long hours in gardens that may be far from home, infants get food to supplement their mothers' milk, older children take care of younger children, and pregnancies are widely spaced. Throughout the world, if a society requires a woman's labor, it finds ways to care for her children.

In the United States, as in some other industrial societies, the accelerated entry of women with preschool children into the labor force has resulted in the development of a variety of child-care arrangements. Individual women have called on friends, relatives, and neighbors. Public and private child-care centers are growing. We should realize that the declining birth rate, the increasing acceptance of childless or single-child families, and a de-emphasis on motherhood are adaptations to a sexual division of labor reminiscent of the system of production found in hunter-gatherer societies.

In many countries where women no longer devote most of their productive years to childbearing, they are beginning to demand a change in the social relationship of the sexes. As women gain access to positions that control the exchange of resources, male dominance may become archaic, and industrial societies may one day become as egalitarian as the Washo.

14

Male and female: The doctor-nurse game

LEONARD I. STEIN

The characteristics of sex and occupational role are related in this article to inequality. Leonard Stein describes the game played between doctor and nurse in American hospitals, the object of which is for the nurse to transmit recommendations for the treatment of patients to the doctor without appearing to challenge his authority as a male and a physician. Using rules of behavior defined for this purpose in American culture, the nurse must be indirect and deferential as she advises on treatment, while the doctor must be positive and accepting. If either breaks the rules, interaction becomes strained, and effective working relations in the hospital break down.

The relationship between the doctor and the nurse is a very special one. There are few professions where the degree of mutual respect and co-operation between co-workers is as intense as that between the doctor and nurse. Superficially, the stereotype of this relationship has been dramatized in many novels and television serials. When, however, it is observed carefully in an interactional framework, the relationship takes on a new dimension and has a special quality which fits a game model. The underlying attitudes which demand that this game be played are unfortunate. These attitudes create serious obstacles in the path of meaningful communications between physicians and nonmedical professional groups.

The physician traditionally and appropriately has total responsibility for making the decisions regarding the management of his patients' treatment. To guide his decisions he considers data gleaned from several sources. He acquires a complete medical history, performs a thorough

From "The Doctor-Nurse Game," *Archives of General Psychiatry* 16 (June 1967): 699–703. Copyright 1967, American Medical Association. Reprinted by permission of the author and the publisher.

physical examination, interprets laboratory findings, and at times, obtains recommendations from physician-consultants. Another important factor in his decision making is the recommendations he receives from the nurse. The interaction between doctor and nurse through which these recommendations are communicated and received is unique and interesting.

THE GAME

One rarely hears a nurse say, "Doctor, I would recommend that you order a retention enema for Mrs. Brown." A physician, upon hearing a recommendation of that nature, would gape in amazement at the effrontery of the nurse. The nurse, upon hearing the statement, would look over her shoulder to see who said it, hardly believing the words actually came from her own mouth. Nevertheless, if one observes closely, nurses make recommendations of more import every hour and physicians willingly and respectfully consider them. If the nurse is to make a suggestion without appearing insolent and the doctor is to seriously consider that suggestion, their interaction must not violate the rules of the game.

Object of the game. The object of the game is as follows: the nurse is to be bold, have initiative, and be responsible for making significant recommendations, while at the same time she must appear passive. This must be done in such a manner so as to make her recommendations appear to be initiated by the physician.

Both participants must be acutely sensitive to each other's nonverbal and cryptic verbal communications. A slight lowering of the head, a minor shifting of position in the chair, or a seemingly nonrelevant comment concerning an event which occurred eight months ago must be interpreted as a powerful message. The game requires the nimbleness of a high wire acrobat, and if either participant slips the game can be shattered; the penalties for frequent failure are apt to be severe.

Rules of the game. The cardinal rule of the game is that open disagreement between the players must be avoided at all costs. Thus, the nurse must communicate her recommendations without appearing to be making a recommendation statement. The physician, in requesting a recommendation from a nurse, must do so without appearing to be asking for it. Utilization of this technique keeps anyone from committing themselves to a position before a sub rosa agreement on that position has already been established. In that way open disagreement is avoided. The greater the significance of the recommendation, the more subtly the game must be played.

To convey a subtle example of the game with all its nuances would require the talents of a literary artist. Lacking these talents, let me give you the following example which is unsubtle, but happens frequently. The medical resident on hospital call is awakened by telephone at 1:00 A.M. because a patient on a ward, not his own, has not been able to fall asleep. Dr. Jones answers the telephone and the dialogue goes like this:

> This is Dr. Jones.
> (An open and direct communication.)
> Dr. Jones, this is Miss Smith on 2W — Mrs. Brown, who learned today of her father's death, is unable to fall asleep.
> (This message has two levels. Openly, it describes a set of circumstances, a woman who is unable to sleep and who that morning received word of her father's death. Less openly, but just as directly, it is a diagnostic and recommendation statement; i.e., Mrs. Brown is unable to sleep because of her grief, and she should be given a sedative. Dr. Jones, accepting the diagnostic statement and replying to the recommendation statement, answers.)
> What sleeping medication has been helpful to Mrs. Brown in the past?
> (Dr. Jones, not knowing the patient, is asking for a recommendation from the nurse, who does know the patient, about what sleeping medication should be prescribed. Note, however, his question does not appear to be asking her for a recommendation. Miss Smith replies.)
> Pentobarbital mg 100 was quite effective night before last.
> (A disguised recommendation statement. Dr. Jones replies with a note of authority in his voice.)
> Pentobarbital mg 100 before bedtime as needed for sleep; got it?
> (Miss Smith ends the conversation with the tone of a grateful supplicant.)
> Yes, I have, and thank you very much, doctor.

The above is an example of a successfully played doctor-nurse game. The nurse made appropriate recommendations which were accepted by the physician and were helpful to the patient. The game was successful because the cardinal rule was not violated. The nurse was able to make her recommendation without appearing to, and the physician was able to ask for recommendations without conspicuously asking for them.

The scoring system. Inherent in any game are penalties and rewards for the players. In game theory, the doctor-nurse game fits the nonzero sum game model. It is not like chess, where the players compete with each other and whatever one player loses the other wins. Rather, it is the kind of game in which the rewards and punishments are shared by both players. If they play the game successfully they both win rewards, and if they are unskilled and the game is played badly, they both suffer the penalty.

The most obvious reward from the well-played game is a doctor-nurse team that operates efficiently. The physician is able to utilize the nurse as a valuable consultant, and the nurse gains self-esteem and professional satisfaction from her job. The less obvious rewards are no less important. A successful game creates a doctor-nurse alliance; through this alliance the physician gains the respect and admiration of the nursing service. He can be confident that his nursing staff will smooth the path for getting his work done. His charts will be organized and waiting for him when he arrives, the ruffled feathers of patients and relatives will have been smoothed down, and his pet routines will be happily followed, and he will be helped in a thousand and one other ways.

The doctor-nurse alliance sheds its light on the nurse as well. She gains a reputation for being a "damn good nurse." She is respected by everyone and appropriately enjoys her position. When physicians discuss the nursing staff it would not be unusual for her name to be mentioned with respect and admiration. Their esteem for a good nurse is no less than their esteem for a good doctor.

The penalties for a game failure, on the other hand, can be severe. The physician who is an unskilled gamesman and fails to recognize the nurses' subtle recommendation messages is tolerated as a "clod." If, however, he interprets these messages as insolence and strongly indicates he does not wish to tolerate suggestions from nurses, he creates a rocky path for his travels. The old truism "If the nurse is your ally you've got it made, and if she has it in for you, be prepared for misery" takes on life-sized proportions. He receives three times as many phone calls after midnight as his colleagues. Nurses will not accept his telephone orders because "telephone orders are against the rules." Somehow, this rule gets suspended for the skilled players. Soon he becomes like Joe Bfstplk in the "Li'l Abner" comic strip. No matter where he goes, a black cloud constantly hovers over his head.

The unskilled gamesman nurse also pays heavily. The nurse who does not view her role as that of consultant, and therefore does not attempt to communicate recommendations, is perceived as a dullard and is mercifully allowed to fade into the woodwork.

The nurse who does see herself as a consultant but refuses to follow the rules of the game in making her recommendations has hell to pay. The outspoken nurse is labeled a "bitch" by the surgeon. The psychiatrist describes her as unconsciously suffering from penis envy and her behavior is the acting out of her hostility towards men. Loosely translated, the psychiatrist is saying she is a bitch. The employment of the unbright outspoken nurse is soon terminated. The outspoken bright nurse whose recommendations are worthwhile remains employed. She is, however, constantly reminded in a hundred ways that she is not loved.

To understand how the game evolved, we must comprehend the nature of the doctors' and nurses' training which shaped the attitudes necessary for the game.

Medical student training. The medical student in his freshman year studies as if possessed. In the anatomy class he learns every groove and prominence on the bones of the skeleton as if life depended on it. As a matter of fact, he literally believes just that. He not infrequently says, "I've got to learn it exactly; a life may depend on me knowing that." A consequence of this attitude, which is carefully nurtured throughout medical school, is the development of a phobia: the over-determined fear of making a mistake. The development of this fear is quite understandable. The burden the physician must carry is at times almost unbearable. He feels responsible in a very personal way for the lives of his patients. When a man dies leaving young children and a widow, the doctor carries some of her grief and despair inside himself; and when a child dies, some of him dies too. He sees himself as a warrior against death and disease. When he loses a battle, through no fault of his own, he nevertheless feels pangs of guilt, and he relentlessly searches himself to see if there might have been a way to alter the outcome. For the physician a mistake leading to a serious consequence is intolerable, and any mistake reminds him of his vulnerability. There is little wonder that he becomes phobic. The classical way in which phobias are managed is to avoid the source of the fear. Since it is impossible to avoid making some mistakes in an active practice of medicine, a substitute defensive maneuver is employed. The physician develops the belief that he is omnipotent and omniscient, and therefore incapable of making mistakes. This belief allows the phobic physician to actively engage in his practice rather than avoid it. The fear of committing an error in a critical field like medicine is unavoidable and appropriately realistic. The physician, however, must learn to live with the fear rather than handle it defensively through a posture of omnipotence. This defense markedly interferes with his interpersonal professional relationships.

Physicians, of course, deny feelings of omnipotence. The evidence, however, renders their denials to whispers in the wind. The slightest mistake inflicts a large narcissistic wound. Depending on his underlying personality structure the physician may be obsessed for days about it, quickly rationalize it away, or deny it. The guilt produced is unusually exaggerated and the incident is handled defensively. The ways in which physicians enhance and support each other's defenses when an error is made could be the topic of another paper. The feeling of omnipotence becomes generalized to other areas of his life. A report of the Federal

Aviation Agency (FAA), as quoted in *Time Magazine* (August 5, 1966), states that in 1964 and 1965 physicians had a fatal-accident rate four times as high as the average for all other private pilots. Major causes of the high death rate were risk-taking attitudes and judgments. Almost all of the accidents occurred on pleasure trips, and were therefore not necessary risks to get to a patient needing emergency care. The trouble, suggested an FAA official, is that too many doctors fly with "the feeling that they are omnipotent." Thus, the extremes to which the physician may go in preserving his self-concept of omnipotence may threaten his own life. This overdetermined preservation of omnipotence is indicative of its brittleness and its underlying foundation of fear of failure.

The physician finds himself trapped in a paradox. He fervently wants to give his patient the best possible medical care, and being open to the nurses' recommendations helps him accomplish this. On the other hand, accepting advice from nonphysicians is highly threatening to his omnipotence. The solution for the paradox is to receive sub rosa recommendations and make them appear to be initiated by himself. In short, he must learn to play the doctor-nurse game.

Some physicians never learn to play the game. Most learn in their internship, and a perceptive few learn during their clerkships in medical school. Medical students frequently complain that the nursing staff treats them as if they had just completed a junior Red Cross first-aid class instead of two years of intensive medical training. Interviewing nurses in a training hospital sheds considerable light on this phenomenon. In their words they said,

> A few students just seem to be with it, they are able to understand what you are trying to tell them, and they are a pleasure to work with; most, however, pretend to know everything and refuse to listen to anything we have to say and I guess we do give them a rough time.

In essence, they are saying that those students who quickly learn the game are rewarded, and those that do not are punished.

Most physicians learn to play the game after they have weathered a few experiences like the one described below. On the first day of his internship, the physician and nurse were making rounds. They stopped at the bed of a fifty-two-year-old woman who, after complimenting the young doctor on his appearance, complained to him of her problem with constipation. After several minutes of listening to her detailed description of peculiar diets, family home remedies, and special exercises that have helped her constipation in the past, the nurse politely interrupted the patient. She told her the doctor would take care of the problem and that he had to move on because there were other patients waiting to see him. The young doctor gave the nurse a stern look, turned toward the patient, and kindly told her he would order an enema for her that very afternoon. As they left the bedside, the nurse told him the patient has had a normal bowel movement every day for the past week and that in the twenty-three days the patient has been in the hospital she has never once passed up an opportunity to complain of her constipation. She quickly added that *if* the doctor wanted to order an enema, the patient would certainly receive one. After hearing this report the intern's mouth fell open and the wheels began turning in his head. He remembered the nurse's comment to the patient that "the doctor had to move on," and it occurred to him that perhaps she was really giving him a message. This experience and a few more like it, and the young doctor learns to listen for the subtle recommendations the nurses make.

Nursing student training. Unlike the medical student who usually learns to play the game after he finishes medical school, the nursing student begins to learn it early in her training. Throughout her education she is trained to play the doctor-nurse game.

Student nurses are taught how to relate to physicians. They are told he has infinitely more knowledge than they, and thus he should be shown the utmost respect. In addition, it was not many years ago when nurses were instructed to stand whenever a physician entered a room. When he would come in for a conference the nurse was expected to offer him her chair, and when both entered a room the nurse would open the door for him and allow him to enter first. Although these practices are no longer rigidly adhered to, the premise upon which they were based is still promulgated. One nurse described that premise as, "He's God almighty and your job is to wait on him."

To inculcate subservience and inhibit deviancy, nursing schools, for the most part, are tightly run, disciplined institutions. Certainly there is great variation among nursing schools, and there is little question that the trend is toward giving students more autonomy. However, in too many schools this trend has not gone far enough, and the climate remains restrictive. The student's schedule is firmly controlled and there is very little free time. Classroom hours, study hours, mealtime, and bedtime with lights out are rigidly enforced. In some schools meaningless chores are assigned, such as cleaning bedsprings with cotton applicators. The relationship between student and instructor continues this military flavor. Often their relationship is more like that between recruit and drill sergeant than between student and teacher. Open dialogue is inhibited by attitudes of strict black and white, with few, if any, shades of gray. Straying from the rigidly outlined path is sure to result in disciplinary action.

The inevitable result of these practices is to instill in the student nurse a fear of independent action. This inhibition of independent action is most marked when relating to physicians. One of the students' greatest fears is making a blunder while assisting a physician and being publicly ridiculed by him. This is really more a reflection of the nature of their training than the prevalence of abusive physicians. The fear of being humiliated for a blunder while assisting in a procedure is generalized to the fear of humiliation for making any independent act in relating to a physician, especially the act of making a direct recommendation. Every nurse interviewed felt that making a suggestion to a physician was equivalent to insulting and belittling him. It was tantamount to questioning his medical knowledge and insinuating he did not know his business. In light of her image of the physician as an omniscient and punitive figure, the questioning of his knowledge would be unthinkable.

The student, however, is also given messages quite contrary to the ones described above. She is continually told that she is an invaluable aid to the physician in the treatment of the patient. She is told that she must help him in every way possible, and she is imbued with a strong sense of responsibility for the care of her patient. Thus she, like the physician, is caught in a paradox. The first set of messages implies that the physician is omniscient and that any recommendation she might make would be insulting to him and leave her open to ridicule. The second set of messages implies that she is an important asset to him, has much to contribute, and is duty-bound to make those contributions. Thus, when her good sense tells her a recommendation would be helpful to him she is not allowed to communicate it directly, nor is she allowed not to communicate it. The way out of the bind is to use the doctor-nurse game and communicate the recommendation without appearing to do so.

FORCES PRESERVING THE GAME

Upon observing the indirect interactional system which is the heart of the doctor-nurse game, one must ask the question, "Why does this inefficient mode of communication continue to exist?" The forces mitigating against change are powerful.

Rewards and punishments. The doctor-nurse game has a powerful innate self-perpetuating force — its system of rewards and punishments. One potent method of shaping behavior is to reward one set of behavioral patterns and to punish patterns which deviate from it. As described earlier, the rewards given for a well-played game and the punishments meted out to unskilled players are impressive. This system alone would be sufficient to keep the game flourishing. The game, however, has additional forces.

The strength of the set. It is well recognized that sets are hard to break. A powerful attitudinal set is the nurse's perception that making a suggestion to a physician is equivalent to insulting and belittling him. An example of where attempts are regularly made to break this set is seen on psychiatric treatment wards operating on a therapeutic community model. This model requires open and direct communication between members of the team. Psychiatrists working in these settings expend a great deal of energy in urging for and rewarding openness before direct patterns of communication become established. The rigidity of the resistance to break this set is impressive. If the physician himself is a prisoner of a set and therefore does not actively try to destroy it, change is near impossible.

The need for leadership. Lack of leadership and structure in any organization produces anxiety in its members. As the importance of the organization's mission increases, the demand by its members for leadership commensurately increases. In our culture human life is near the top of our hierarchy of values, and organizations which deal with human lives, such as law and medicine, are very rigidly structured. Certainly some of this is necessary for the systematic management of the task. The excessive degree of rigidity, however, is demanded by its members for their own psychic comfort rather than for its utility in efficiently carrying out its mission. The game lends support to this thesis. Indirect communication is an inefficient mode of transmitting information. However, it effectively supports and protects a rigid organizational structure with the physician in clear authority. Maintaining an omnipotent leader provides the other members with a great sense of security.

Sexual roles. Another influence perpetuating the doctor-nurse game is the sexual identity of the players. Doctors are predominately men and nurses are almost exclusively women. There are elements of the game which reinforce the stereotyped roles of male dominance and female passivity. Some nursing instructors explicitly tell their students that their femininity is an important asset to be used when relating to physicians.

THE COMMUNITY

The doctor and nurse have a shared history and thus have been able to work out their game so that it operates more efficiently than one would expect in an indirect system. Major difficulty arises, however, when the physician works closely with other disciplines which are not normally considered part of the medical sphere. With expanding medical horizons encompassing cooperation with sociologists, engineers, anthropologists, computer analysts, etc., continued expectation of a doctor-nurselike interaction by the physician is disastrous. The sociologist, for example, is not willing to play that kind of game. When his direct communications are rebuffed the relationship breaks down.

The major disadvantage of a doctor-nurselike game is its inhibitory effect on open dialogue which is stifling and anti-intellectual. The game is basically a transactional neurosis, and both professions would enhance themselves by taking steps to change the attitudes which breed the game. . . .

15

Men's clubs:
No girls allowed

THOMAS GREGOR

*Men set themselves apart from women in many societies. In Africa,
the males of Mbuti Pygmy society reserve most of the sacred* molimo
*ritual, held in honor of the forest, to themselves. Rural Greek men
regularly drink together without the presence of women. In this
article, Thomas Gregor explores the phenomenon of the men's club.
He notes that the prestigious Bohemian club, an all-men's
organization of San Francisco, in many ways resembles the men's
house among the tribal Mehinaku of South America. Men's clubs
everywhere, he argues, tend to serve as a place for men to relax, joke
about women, drop formal rules, guard sacred knowledge and
rituals, and display the feminine side of their personalities without
fear of outside reproach.*

In October of 1980 the California Department of Housing and Fair Employment, an irresistible force in state sex discrimination cases, took aim at an immovable object: the exclusive "men only" Bohemian Club of San Francisco. The club, it was charged, employed 300 men at its Sonoma County Retreat but not one woman. The resulting litigation would have attracted little attention were it not for the prominence of the membership. President Ronald Reagan, Vice-President George Bush, Secretary of Defense Caspar Weinberger, and Attorney General William French Smith are only a few of the better known members.

In the course of the California discrimination proceedings, members of the club explained that having women about spoiled the fun.

Originally published as "No Girls Allowed," *Science 82*, Vol. 3, No. 8, pp. 26–31. Reprinted by permission of *Science 84* Magazine, Copyright 1982 the American Association for the Advancement of Science.

"When women are around," pointed out former California Governor Edmund G. Brown, "any man is more genteel and careful of his words." He would be embarrassed to tell sexual jokes, he said, or to participate in the off-color theatrical revues staged by the members. Not that any of the members dislike women. Far from it. As columnist William Buckley quipped at the same hearing, "I have nothing against E flat, but if I were writing a symphony in D, I would try to do without it."

The Bohemians are an unusually swank and powerful bunch, but they are not the first to try to do without women. Exclusive men's clubs are found in many societies throughout the world among people of all cultural levels. While by no means universal, these clubs are often associated with strongly patriarchal societies.

My own anthropological introduction to a men's club occurred in 1967 among the Mehinaku Indians of central Brazil, a setting far less posh than the one provided by the San Francisco Bohemians. Shortly after I arrived in the Mehinaku village, one of the men took me by the arm and led me to a small house in the center of the community. Inside, the men worked on crafts and oiled and painted each others' bodies with a waxy, red pigment. The mood was loud and boisterous. A shouted remark set off a chorus of laughter, and then a whoop of appreciation from everyone present. Suddenly, one of the men stood up in front of the others and began to address me in a way that claimed everyone's attention. Not understanding a word or knowing how to respond, I glanced at the other men beside me. For the most part they were serious and attentive. After several minutes, the lecture was over. I turned to one of the men who had some knowledge of Portuguese. He explained: "You are in the house of the spirit Kowka. This house is only for men. Women may not see anything in here. If a woman comes in, then all the men take her into the woods and she is raped. It has always been that way."

I had been introduced to a key institution in Mehinaku life. A man's place, when he is not out fishing or working in his garden, is with his comrades in the men's house. A man who spends too much time in his house with his wife and family is called a trash-yard person, a star (because he only comes out to join his comrades at night), or a woman.

Within the men's house, there is an atmosphere of easy informality. "There is no shame in the men's house," say the villagers, meaning that the respect and deference owed in-laws and older kin is suspended in favor of masculine comradeliness. Above all, the men's house is a setting for jokes and laughter. As is true of our own fraternity and locker room comics, the Mehinaku pranksters specialize in sexual and scatological jokes.

Yuma has just entered the men's house. "Yuma," calls one of the men, "how is your 'forest' growing?" (Yuma, unlike most of the Mehinaku, has relatively abundant body hair.) "Any monkeys swinging about in the trees?" shouts another humorist from the opposite end of the house. Soon all the men are in on the joke, speculating on the nature of the dangerous game lurking in poor Yuma's "forest."

But the men's house is not all fun and games. It also serves as an information and labor exchange. A man who has found a good location for fishing generously informs his comrades in the men's house. Here, too, the men organize collective fishing expeditions, house-raisings, and harvests. Less formally, anyone in the men's retreat is fair game for a villager in search of an extra hand. Only an incorrigibly lazy or "tired" man would try to slip away on some pretended errand.

The men's house is a sacred place as well as a social club. It is "the place of spirits." From the rafters hang masks, bullroarers, musical instruments, and costumes crucial to the propitiation of the spirits that live within. The "Chief of the Spirits" is Kowka, the spirit of the sacred flutes. Kowka can take away a person's soul and thus make him seriously ill. To propitiate Kowka and restrain his anger, the men play the flutes several times a week. The main musician, "the master of the songs," carries the melody, while two others, "those who play on the side," accompany him. The songs have names: "Demon Woman," "Sadness," "Evening Song." The flutes have a deep, bassoonlike tone, and the melodies are hauntingly beautiful.

In the family houses, the women may listen to "Kowka's speech," but they never see his flutes or the men who impersonate him. One of the village elders explains: "Look, the men's house now has two sets of Kowka's flutes. The women will not come inside. They are afraid of Kowka. If a woman does come in, someone will say, 'Ah, that one saw Kowka!' Then at night she will be taken, and Kowka will have sex with her. . . . That is the way it has always been, since our grandfathers' day." In fact, no one has been raped since a woman accidentally saw the flutes as they were played on the plaza more than 35 years ago. But the women remember what occurred and know the men are prepared to do it again.

Gang rape is the most dramatic of a much larger set of sanctions and rules that separate men and women among the Mehinaku. These include a nearly ironclad division of labor preventing men and women from doing the same work. Fishing and hunting are men's specializations, while harvesting and processing manioc (the tapioca plant) is woman's work. Crafts also fall on either side of the sexual divide, so that men make baskets and arrows and carve wooden benches, while women weave hammocks.

Although separation in work does not imply inequality, Mehinaku culture is uncompromisingly patriarchal. Fish is said to be the best food above all others, while the woman's manioc is "tasteless." Ritual is largely men's ritual, and politics is a man's game. The women, the men claim, are empty-headed and prone to gossip. They cannot recall the myths that make up the villagers' oral tradition, for the words "will not stay in their stomachs." A gossip (male or female) is called a woman mouth.

The men's opinion of femininity is partly shared by women themselves, who are in awe of the men. "I am frightened by the men," explains Kaiyalu, a young woman. "They are fearful. I would not speak on the plaza. I could not go fishing. The line would cut my hands. I am afraid of big animals. We women have no strength, we have no anger. The men are worthy of respect."

The Mehinaku pattern is very similar to other tribal societies scattered throughout South America, Oceania, and Africa. Like the Mehinaku, they have clubhouses that are forbidden to the women. Within are stored sacred instruments: flutes, trumpets, and bells that the women see at pain of gang rape or death. Typically, the atmosphere within the men's club is rowdy and informal, but once outside, the mood changes, and the women are ruled with a firm hand.

The list of similarities extends beyond the general structure of men's organizations to include some of their ritual details. These include the use of the bullroarer and a recurrent myth that ascribes the origin of the men's club to women. Among the Mehinaku the bullroarer is also sacred and a woman's hair will fall out, according to myth, if she should see one. The Mehinaku believe that long ago the women held power and controlled the sacred flutes. A male mutiny chased the women into hiding, and since that time men have ruled life and flutes.

So compelling are the parallels in many tribal men's organizations that they may well have common historical roots whose antiquity goes back to an epoch prior to settlement of the New World. A study of a small tribal group like the Mehinaku thereby reflects on the broader nature of masculine sexual politics and casts a new light on our own society with its fraternities and men's clubs.

Like the Mehinaku, America is a patriarchy. For many, this is an unpalatable conclusion, but a look at the economy and politics of our society shows that it is true. Women make 59 cents for every dollar earned by their male coworkers. A woman with a college degree brings home the salary of a man with a high school education. To a large extent, this economic inequality is explained by occupational segregation. One-fourth of all female workers are found in five relatively underpaid occupations: elementary school teacher, secretary, bookkeeper, waitress, and household worker. In contrast, men permeate and control all sectors of the economy.

In politics, the pattern is just as clear. The higher the political office, the less likely a woman is to fill it. Women are the mayors of only four percent of American cities, and despite affirmative action programs, women make up only two percent of the administrators identified as policy makers within the federal government. In the House of Representatives, they have historically held three percent of the seats and none of the chairmanships of important committees. There have never been more than two female senators in any recent Congress, nor have any of the major parties ever nominated a woman for the office of president or vice-president.

One of the barriers to women's participation in politics and economics is the "old boy network." Men socialize with one another, exchange information, conduct business deals, and recommend their protégés (seldom women) for advancement. American men's houses facilitate this process even though few of them are overtly concerned with money and power. "Weaving spiders, come not here" is the motto of the Bohemian Club. This line from Shakespeare's *A Midsummer Night's Dream* enjoins the members from serious discussions of politics and commerce. But a look at the roster of Bohemians turns up more than a few prodigious weavers. The membership list is a web of America's highly placed and well-connected power elite, according to sociologist G. William Domhoff. The chairmen of America's largest corporations, federal judges, and the founder of Common Cause have all rubbed shoulders in clubby good fellowship at the Bohemian. But do they do business? A congressman told columnist Jack Anderson, "If I were to run for the Senate, I can think of no place where I could spend time more productively."

In the less powerful men's clubs, be they volunteer fire departments or fraternities, observers find the same hidden agenda of exchange of information and influence. In the midst of the high jinks, as the curtains are drawn on the last stag movie, while the trenchermen tuck away the last morsels at the Annual Bull's Balls Lunch — the members are cementing business relationships and angling for position.

The parallels between tribal men's societies and our own clubs include a show of sexual aggression. The hostility toward women found in some tribal men's houses is less overt in American clubs, but it is visible in informal banter. According to a study by William Fry, all-male settings foster highly patterned jokes about women that characterize them as sexually insatiable "dumb blondes," greedy and unfeeling. Beyond this hostility, it is clear that although women are absent from both tribal and American men's clubs they are not forgotten. In many tribal societies, the men's house is strategically located in the center of the community so that the women form an audience (admittedly in distant seats) to the men's aggressive horseplay. In our society the clubs are farther from home, but women remain uppermost in the men's minds. Among the Bohemians, notes Domhoff, "the topic is out-ranked as a subject for light conversation only by remarks about drinking enormous quantities of alcohol and urinating on redwoods."

There is much that is suspect about the exaggeratedly masculine conduct in men's institutions: the hostile perceptions of women, the sexual bravado, and the need to have a secure retreat. The data from tribal societies are especially telling in this regard, since the men are openly fearful of women. Like the Mehinaku, they may believe that sexual relations and other contact with women cause disease, stunt growth, weaken wrestlers, and profane sacred rituals. Moreover, despite the hostility and anxiety, some of the men's behavior hints that deep down the masculine personality is alloyed with a feminine identity. Intermixed with the boisterousness of the Mehinaku men's house are rituals in which the men address each other as "husband" and "wife" and scarify their bodies to shed what is regarded as menstrual blood. Rituals of this kind are not rare in societies with men's organizations and have been reported in South America, Melanesia, and elsewhere.

When considered alongside the pattern of aggression and anxiety, these rituals imply that the men are insecure in their masculine roles and frightened by the feminine component of their own personalities. In the arena of ritual, and with the support of their fellows, they can safely express the female side of their male selves. In everyday life, however, this femininity is shouted down by rowdy jokes and masculine camaraderie.

Can the same conclusion be drawn about American men's clubs? Testifying in favor of the Bohemian Club at the California sex discrimination hearings, former Governor Edmund Brown argued that the presence of women would irretrievably alter the character of this organization. Not only would the men feel inhibited from telling off-color jokes, but they would no longer be willing to cross-dress for the comic transvestite revues staged by the members.

Although it stretches the imagination to picture the well-heeled Bohemians in high heels, comic and often hostile stage characterizations of women are typical of many American men's clubs. It is difficult to generalize about the inner motives of individual participants. Some are in the chorus line simply because it is politic to please a boss who may be directing the show. For others, however, the appeal is the same as it is for many of the Mehinaku. What the tribal men's clubs state in ritual, we Americans often express in comedy: the feminine component of a somewhat insecure masculine identity.

The similarity of men's organizations in several geographically and culturally distant patriarchal societies is evidence of a commonality to the male experience. Even though our college fraternities and volunteer fire departments may not be the lineal descendants of tribal institutions, we recreate within them the same masculine ethos. There is one language for the expression of masculinity, and it is voiced as clearly in American men's houses as it is in those of tribal peoples.

As for the future of our men's clubs, the political and psychological needs they fill make them compellingly attractive and resistant to change. Occasionally, however, even Bohemians must squirm a bit. In 1981 the California Department of Housing and Fair Employment chose to rule against the club despite a judge's recommendation that female staff would "alter the behavior of the members." The case was appealed, however, and the State Superior Court plans to review it. . . . Even if the Bohemians lose, the state will have chipped away only at the edges of female exclusion. The club may hire more women, but the membership will remain all male. The courts cannot yet touch the blackball that is the heart of the institution: No Girls Allowed.

16

Rape-free or rape-prone

BERYL LIEFF BENDERLY

Some Americans view the high incidence of rape as an inevitable feature of relations between the sexes. Others see it as proof of a weakening national moral fiber. In this study, Beryl Lieff Benderly reports on a cross-cultural study of rape conducted by anthropologist Peggy Sanday, which argues that rape is culturally conditioned. Sanday discovered that rape is present in only about half of the 156 societies she reviewed, and that in such societies, rape was culturally conditioned. Rape-prone societies, on the one hand, regularly teach aggressive behavior, competitiveness, and the notion that men must overcome women. Such societies seem to be less stable, to face uncertainties that thrust men into the forefront. Rape-free societies, on the other hand, value feminine qualities and enjoy a stability that nullifies the necessity for male physical prowess.

The typical American rapist is not, as many people assume, sexually deprived. Rather he is a hostile, aggressive man who likes to do violence to women. Not until the women's movement, when victims became more willing to report rapes, did social scientists discover that rape is not so much a sexual act as a violent crime with profoundly damaging effects. Furthermore, scientists say it is far more pervasive than they had thought.

One highly significant observation, however, went along unnoticed: Rape is not an unavoidable fact of human nature. There are cultures in the world where it is virtually unknown. American women are several hundred times as likely to be raped as are women in certain other cultures. But there also are extremely violent societies where women

From *Science 82*, Vol. 3, No. 8, pp. 40–43. Copyright © 1982 by Beryl Lieff Benderly. Reprinted by permission of the Virginia Barber Literary Agency.

are three times more likely to be attacked than they are in the United States.

New research suggests that the incidence of rape depends in particular on cultural factors: the status of women, the values that govern the relations between the sexes, and the attitudes taught to boys. Although the findings are tentative, they contradict the widely publicized feminist hypothesis that rape is inherent to the relations between men and women, an idea that received considerable attention in Susan Brownmiller's book, *Against Our Will*, published in 1975.

Now comes Peggy Reeves Sanday, a University of Pennsylvania anthropologist who has compared data from scores of cultures to find that rape is anything but universal. It does not stem from a biological drive, she believes, but is rather a conditioned response to the way certain kinds of societies are organized. Sexual violence is no more inherent to masculinity than football. Many American men may express their masculinity by making bone-jarring tackles or watching others do so, but that is because this culture encourages them to perform these strange rituals, not because their inherent nature demands linebacker blitzes or quarterback sneaks. Likewise, Sanday believes, "Human sexual behavior, though based on a biological need, is expressed in cultural terms." Human violence takes many forms, and rape is but one of them.

But what predisposes a culture toward or against rape? To find out, Sanday consulted a cross-cultural sample of 156 societies published in 1969 by George Peter Murdock and Douglas R. White. This sample, while accepted by many anthropologists as a standard basis for cross-cultural comparison, has its drawbacks as a research tool. The societies she referred to were studied at different times by different anthropologists interested in different aspects of each culture. Sensitive information, such as that on rape, might not have been disclosed to a visiting stranger who was not deliberately trying to find out about it. Nevertheless, Sanday found information on rape that she believes to be reliable for 95 of these societies.

Almost half of the reports (47 percent) Sanday studied were rape-free societies with sexual assault "absent or . . . rare." Less than a quarter (17 percent) proved to be "unambiguously rape-prone," displaying "the social use of rape to threaten or punish women or the presence of a high incidence of rape of their own or other women." Reports of rape exist for the remaining 36 percent, but the incidence is not known. Although some of these societies may actually have little rape, Sanday added them to the rape-prone to form the category "rape-present." Thus the split between sample societies that have rape and those that do not is close to even.

A model rape-free society, according to Sanday, is the Ashanti of

West Africa. Their principal ethnographer, R. S. Rattray, mentions only a single incidence of rape, although he does not ignore other sexual offenses such as incest and adultery. Ashanti women are respected and influential members of the community. The Ashanti religion emphasizes women's contribution to the general well-being. The main female deity, the Earth Goddess, is believed to be the creator of past and future generations as well as the source of food and water. Women participate fully in religious life, taking as important a ritual role as men.

The Mbuti Pygmies, extensively described by anthropologist Colin Turnbull, present another aspect of rape-free social life. They hunt with nets in the jungle of central Africa and live harmoniously with the forest, which provides all their needs — food, clothing, shelter. The Mbuti believe that the forest takes offense at anger and discord. The people live in cooperative small bands, men and women sharing both work and decisions. No Mbuti attempts to dominate another, nor does the group as a whole seek to dominate nature. Indeed, they refer to the forest in terms of endearment, as they would a parent or lover. Here again women play important symbolic and political roles. The feminine qualities of nurturance and fertility rank among the culture's most valued traits.

Very different traits stand out in rape-prone societies such as the Gusii of Kenya. Anthropologist Robert LeVine reports that judicial authorities counted 47.2 rapes per 100,000 population in a year when the U.S. rate, one of the highest in the industrial world, was 13.85 per 100,000. "Normal heterosexual intercourse between Gusii males and females is conceived as an act in which a man overcomes the resistance of a woman and causes her pain," writes Sanday. It's customary for respectable old ladies to taunt the young bridegroom about his inadequate sexual equipment on the way to his wedding. He retaliates and asserts his manhood by bragging to his friends that he reduced his bride to tears on their wedding night, that she remained in pain the next morning. No wife respects a husband who fails to take her by force.

The degree of tension pervading the Gusii battle of the sexes may be unusual, but the use of rape to conquer unwilling brides or to keep women under tight control is not. Men of certain Plains Indian tribes once invited groups of friends to gang-rape unfaithful wives. Mundurucu men of the Amazon threaten to rape any woman approaching the sacred trumpets, which embody supernatural tribal power and are safeguarded in a special men's house.

As Sanday suspected, she found patterns of behavior common to rape-prone societies, and they differed markedly from traits of rape-free peoples. Societies with a high incidence of rape, she discovered, tolerate violence and encourage men and boys to be tough, aggressive, and competitive. Men in such cultures generally have special, politically important gathering spots off limits to women, whether they be in the Mundurucu men's club or the corner tavern. Women take little or no part in public decision making or religious rituals; men mock or scorn women's practical judgment. They also demean what they consider women's work and remain aloof from childbearing and rearing. These groups usually trace their beginnings to a male supreme being.

Men in such societies, Sanday says, often "perceive themselves as civilized animals." Indeed, the word *macho*, now slang for that attitude, is the Spanish for "male of an animal species," a significant qualification in a language that distinguishes, more carefully than English, the properties of beasts from those of humans.

In short, Sanday concludes, "Rape is not inherent in men's nature but results from their image of that nature." It is a product of a certain set of beliefs, which in turn derive from particular social circumstances. Male dominance, Sanday believes, serves its purpose. Rape-prone societies often have histories of unstable food supplies, warfare, or migration. Such rigors force men to the forefront to repel attackers and compete with others for scarce resources and land. A belief system that glorifies masculine violence, that teaches men to regard strength and physical force as the finest expression of their nature, reconciles them to the necessity of fighting and dying in society's interest. Unstable or threatened societies — gin-ridden, trigger-happy American frontiersmen, Southern planters outnumbered by their restive slaves, children of Israel approaching Canaan, the Azande conquerors of neighboring African tribes — depended for their survival on the physical prowess of their men. Danger brings soldiers and fighters to the front line and encourages the development of male-dominated social structures. And these often include concepts of men as bestial creatures and women as property. It is interesting that a number of rape-prone societies provide restitution to the rape victim's husband rather than to the victim herself.

On the other hand, stable cultures that face no danger from predatory enemies and that harmoniously occupy ancestral surroundings neither need nor condone such violence. Their food supplies usually fluctuate little from season to season or year to year, so they face neither the threat of starvation nor the need to compete with neighbors for resources. Women and men share power and authority because both contribute equally to society's welfare, and fighters are not necessary. Rape-free societies glorify the female traits of nurturance and fertility. Many such peoples believe that they are the offspring of a male and female deity or that they descended from a universal womb.

Although data on hundreds of societies have been available to anthropologists for generations, Sanday is one of the first to dig out broad patterns of behavior relating to rape. Just as the general society paid little attention to rape until Brownmiller's book made the front pages, rape has also been a "nonsubject" in anthropology. But not, anthropologists hope, for long.

The way society trains its boys and girls to think about themselves and each other determines to a large extent how rape-prone or rape-free that society will be. Sanday believes we can mitigate the damage our unconscious biases do by raising boys, for example, with more reverence for nurturance and less for violence. We can encourage women to resist assault. "One must be careful," Sanday says, "in blaming men alone or women alone for the high incidence of rape in our society. In a way we all conspire to perpetuate it. We expect men to attack, just as we expect women to submit."

But we can do something about such patterns of thought. Rape is not inevitable.

VI

Cultural ecology

Ecology refers to the relationship of an organism to other elements within its environmental sphere. Every species, no matter how simple or complex, fits into a larger complex ecological system; all are adapted to their ecological niches unless rapid environmental alterations outstrip the organism's ability and potential to adapt successfully. An important aim of ecological studies is to show how organisms fit within particular environments. Such studies also look at the effect environments have on the shape and behavior of life forms.

Every species, including our own, has adapted biologically, through a process of genetically produced variation and natural selection. For example, we walk upright instead of on all fours like most other primates because our ancestors moved from a forest to a terrestrial habitat. But bipedal locomotion, as our two-legged gait is called, is not only a genetic response to life on the ground. Our upright stance is also a response to an early human predisposition, sharing. By sharing, our ancestors could maintain more permanent camps and devise a division of labor based on sex. But to share, people had to be able to carry things back to camp. Walking on two feet instead of four made such carrying possible.

Biological processes have led to another important characteristic,

181

the development of a large and complex brain. The human brain is capable of holding an enormous inventory of information. With it, we can classify the parts of our environment and retain instructions for complex ways to deal with the things in our world. Because we can communicate our knowledge symbolically through language, we are able to teach one another. Instead of a genetic code that directs behavior automatically, we operate with a learned cultural code. Culture gives us the ability to behave in a much wider variety of ways, and to change rapidly to new situations. With culture, people have been able to live successfully in almost every part of the world. It is partly due to this variety of natural habitats that the study of cultural ecology, or the way we culturally adapt to our environments, is so interesting.

We may look at cultural ecology in at least two way. First, we can view how particular human technologies affect the worlds in which people live. We could, for example, try to assess the impact that a nuclear power plant has on its environment through waste, heat, and radiation.

Second, we can look at the impact a particular environment has on human culture, on the technologies a group must develop, and on other culturally defined aspects of life such as social structure. For example, we might attempt to discover how life in a bleak, cold, arctic environment affects Eskimo technology and social organization.

The articles in this section reflect a range of interests in cultural ecology, from the relationship between food production and population growth to the ways hunters and gatherers survive on wild foods.

17

The hunters:
Scarce resources in the Kalahari

RICHARD BORSHAY LEE

*Peoples who hunt and gather wild foods experience an intimate
relationship with their natural environments. A band's size and
structure, the breadth of its territory, and the frequency and pattern
of its movement depend on the abundance of vegetable foods, game,
and water. For many Western anthropologists, the life of hunter-
gatherers seems precarious and fraught with hardship. Yet, according
to Richard B. Lee, this picture is largely inaccurate. In this article he
points out that the !Kung Bushmen who live in the Kalahari Desert
of South Africa survive well in what Westerners would consider a
marginal habitat. Depending, like most hunter-gatherers, on
vegetable foods for their sustenance, the !Kung actually spend little
time at food collecting, yet they live long and fruitful lives in their
desert home.*

The current anthropological view of hunter-gatherer subsistence rests
on two questionable assumptions. First is the notion that these people
are primarily dependent on the hunting of game animals, and second
is the assumption that their way of life is generally a precarious and
arduous struggle for existence.

Recent data on living hunter-gatherers show a radically different
picture. We have learned that in many societies, plant and marine resources are far more important than are game animals in the diet. More
important, it is becoming clear that, with a few conspicuous exceptions,
the hunter-gatherer subsistence base is at least routine and reliable and

Reprinted by permission from Richard Lee and Irvin DeVore, editors, *Man the Hunter*
(Hawthorne, NY: Aldine Publishing Company); copyright © 1968 Wenner-Gren Foundation for Anthropological Research, Inc.

at best surprisingly abundant. Anthropologists have consistently tended to underestimate the viability of even those "marginal isolates" of hunting peoples that have been available to ethnographers.

The purpose of this paper is to analyze the food getting activities of one such "marginal" people, the !Kung Bushmen of the Kalahari Desert. Three related questions are posed: How do the Bushmen make a living? How easy or difficult is it for them to do this? What kinds of evidence are necessary to measure and evaluate the precariousness or security of a way of life? And after the relevant data are presented, two further questions are asked: What makes this security of life possible? To what extent are the Bushmen typical of hunter-gatherers in general?

BUSHMAN SUBSISTENCE

The !Kung Bushmen of Botswana are an apt case for analysis. They inhabit the semi-arid northwest region of the Kalahari Desert. With only six to nine inches of rainfall per year, this is, by any account, a marginal environment for human habitation. In fact, it is precisely the unattractiveness of their homeland that has kept the !Kung isolated from extensive contact with their agricultural and pastoral neighbors.

Field work was carried out in the Dobe area, a line of eight permanent waterholes near the South-West Africa border and 125 miles south of the Okavango River. The population of the Dobe area consists of 466 Bushmen, including 379 permanent residents living in independent camps or associated with Bantu cattle posts, as well as 87 seasonal visitors. The Bushmen share the area with some 340 Bantu pastoralists largely of the Herero and Tswana tribes. The ethnographic present refers to the period of field work: October, 1963–January, 1965.

The Bushmen living in independent camps lack firearms, livestock, and agriculture. Apart from occasional visits to the Herero for milk, these !Kung are entirely dependent upon hunting and gathering for their subsistence. Politically they are under the nominal authority of the Tswana headman, although they pay no taxes and receive very few government services. European presence amounts to one overnight government patrol every six to eight weeks. Although Dobe-area !Kung have had some contact with outsiders since the 1880's, the majority of them continue to hunt and gather because there is no viable alternative locally available to them.

Each of the fourteen independent camps is associated with one of the permanent waterholes. During the dry season (May-October) the entire population is clustered around these wells. Table I shows the numbers at each well at the end of the 1964 dry season. Two wells had no camp resident and one large well supported five camps. The number of camps at each well and the size of each camp changed frequently

TABLE I. *Numbers and distribution of resident Bushmen and Bantu by waterhole**

Name of waterhole	No. of camps	Population of camps	Other Bushmen	Total Bushmen	Bantu
Dobe	2	37	—	37	—
!angwa	1	16	23	39	84
Bate	2	30	12	42	21
!ubi	1	19	—	19	65
!gose	3	52	9	61	18
/ai/ai	5	94	13	107	67
!xabe	—	—	8	8	12
Mahopa	—	—	23	23	73
Total	14	248	88	336	340

*Figures do not include 130 Bushmen outside area on the date of census.

during the course of the year. The "camp" is an open aggregate of cooperating persons which changes in size and composition from day to day. Therefore, I have avoided the term "band" in describing the !Kung Bushman living groups.

Each waterhole has a hinterland lying within a six-mile radius which is regularly exploited for vegetable and animal foods. These areas are not territories in the zoological sense, since they are not defended against outsiders. Rather they constitute the resources that lie within a convenient walking distance of a waterhole. The camp is a self-sufficient subsistence unit. The members move out each day to hunt and gather, and return in the evening to pool the collected foods in such a way that every person present receives an equitable share. Trade in foodstuffs between camps is minimal; personnel do move freely from camp to camp, however. The net effect is of a population constantly in motion. On the average, an individual spends a third of his time living only with close relatives, a third visiting other camps, and a third entertaining visitors from other camps.

Because of the strong emphasis on sharing, and the frequency of movement, surplus accumulation of storable plant foods and dried meat is kept to a minimum. There is rarely more than two or three days' supply of food on hand in a camp at any time. The result of this lack of surplus is that a constant subsistence effort must be maintained throughout the year. Unlike agriculturalists who work hard during the planting and harvesting seasons and undergo "seasonal unemployment" for several months, the Bushmen hunter-gatherers collect food every third or fourth day throughout the year.

Vegetable foods comprise from 60–80 per cent of the total diet by weight, and collecting involves two or three days of work per woman per week. The men also collect plants and small animals but their major contribution to the diet is the hunting of medium and large game. The men are conscientious but not particularly successful hunters; although men's and women's work input is roughly equivalent in terms of man-day of effort, the women provide two to three times as much food by weight as the men.

Table II summarizes the seasonal activity cycle observed among the Dobe-area !Kung in 1964. For the greater part of the year, food is locally abundant and easily collected. It is only during the end of the dry season in September and October, when desirable foods have been eaten out in the immediate vicinity of the waterholes that the people have to plan longer hikes of 10–15 miles and carry their own water to those areas where the mongongo nut is still available. The important point is that food is a constant, but distance required to reach food is a variable; it is short in the summer, fall, and early winter, and reaches its maximum in the spring.

This analysis attempts to provide quantitative measures of sub-sistence status including data on the following topics: abundance and variety of resources, diet selectivity, range size and population density, the composition of the work force, the ratio of work to leisure time, and the caloric and protein levels in the diet. The value of quantitative data is that they can be used comparatively and also may be useful in ar-cheological reconstruction. In addition, one can avoid the pitfalls of subjective and qualitative impressions; for example, statements about food "anxiety" have proven to be difficult to generalize across cultures.

Abundance and variety of resources. It is impossible to define "abun-dance" of resources absolutely. However, one index of *relative* abun-dance is whether or not a population exhausts all the food available from a given area. By this criterion, the habitat of the Dobe-area Bushmen is abundant in naturally occurring foods. By far the most important food is the mongongo (mangetti) nut (*Ricinodendron rautanenii* Schinz). Al-though tens of thousands of pounds of these nuts are harvested and eaten each year, thousands more rot on the ground each year for want of picking.

The mongongo nut, because of its abundance and reliability, alone accounts for 50 per cent of the vegetable diet by weight. In this respect it resembles a cultivated staple crop such as maize or rice. Nutritionally it is even more remarkable, for it contains five times the calories and ten times the proteins per cooked unit of the cereal crops. The average daily per-capita consumption of 300 nuts yields about 1,260 calories and 56 grams of protein. This modest portion, weighing only about 7.5 ounces,

TABLE II. *The Bushman annual round*

Season	Jan.	Feb. Summer Rains	Mar.	April Autumn Dry	May	June	July Winter Dry	Aug.	Sept.	Oct. Spring Dry	Nov.	Dec. First Rains
Availability of water	Temporary summer pools everywhere			Large summer pools				Permanent waterholes only				Summer pools developing
Group moves	Widely dispersed at summer pools			At large summer pools				All population restricted to permanent waterholes				Moving out to summer pools
Men's subsistence activities	1. Hunting with bow, arrows, and dogs (year-round)											
	2. Running down immatures						Trapping small game in snares				Running down newborn animals	
	3. Some gathering (year-round)											
Women's subsistence activities	1. Gathering of mongongo nuts (year-round)											
	2. Fruits, berries, melons						Roots, bulbs, resins				Roots, leafy greens	
Ritual activities	Dancing, trance performances, and ritual curing (year-round)					Boys' initiation*						†
Relative subsistence hardship			Water-food distance minimal				Increasing distance from water to food				Water-food distance minimal	

*Held once every five years; none in 1963-64.

† New Year's: Bushmen join the celebrations of their missionized Bantu neighbors.

contains the caloric equivalent of 2.5 pounds of cooked rice and the protein equivalent of 14 ounces of lean beef.

Furthermore the mongongo nut is drought resistant and it will still be abundant in the dry years when cultivated crops may fail. The extremely hard outer shell protects the inner kernel from rot and allows the nuts to be harvested for up to twelve months after they have fallen to the ground. A diet based on mongongo nuts is in fact more reliable than one based on cultivated foods, and it is not surprising, therefore, that when a Bushman was asked why he hadn't taken to agriculture he replied: "Why should we plant, when there are so many mongongo nuts in the world?"

Apart from the mongongo, the Bushmen have available 84 other species of edible food plants, including 29 species of fruits, berries, and melons and 30 species of roots and bulbs. The existence of this variety allows for a wide range of alternatives in subsistence strategy. During the summer months the Bushmen have no problem other than to choose among the tastiest and most easily collected foods. Many species, which are quite edible but less attractive, are bypassed, so that gathering never exhausts *all* the available plant foods of an area. During the dry season the diet becomes much more eclectic and the many species of roots, bulbs, and edible resins make an important contribution. It is this broad base that provides an essential margin of safety during the end of the dry season when the mongongo nut forests are difficult to reach. In addition, it is likely that these rarely utilized species provide important nutritional and mineral trace elements that may be lacking in the more popular foods.

Diet selectivity. If the Bushmen were living close to the "starvation" level, then one would expect them to exploit every available source of nutrition. That their life is well above this level is indicated by the data in Table III. Here all the edible plant species are arranged in classes according to the frequency with which they were observed to be eaten. It should be noted, that although there are some 85 species available, about 90 per cent of the vegetable diet by weight is drawn from only 23 species. In other words, 75 percent of the listed species provide only 10 per cent of the food value.

In their meat-eating habits, the Bushmen show a similar selectivity. Of the 223 local species of animals known and named by the Bushmen, 54 species are classified as edible, and of these only 17 species were hunted on a regular basis. Only a handful of the dozens of edible species of small mammals, birds, reptiles, and insects that occur locally are regarded as food. Such animals as rodents, snakes, lizards, termites, and grasshoppers, which in the literature are included in the Bushman dietary, are despised by the Bushmen of the Dobe area.

Range size and population density. The necessity to travel long distances, the high frequency of moves, and the maintenance of populations at low densities are also features commonly associated with the hunting and gathering way of life. Density estimates for hunters in western North America and Australia have ranged from 3 persons/square mile to as low as 1 person/100 square miles. In 1963–65, the resident and visiting Bushmen were observed to utilize an area of about 1,000 square miles during the course of the annual round for an effective population density of 41 persons/100 square miles. Within this area, however, the amount of ground covered by members of an individual camp was surprisingly small. A day's round-trip of twelve miles serves to define a "core" area six miles in radius surrounding each water point. By fanning out in all directions from their well, the members of a camp can gain access to the food resources of well over 100 square miles of territory within a two-hour hike. Except for a few weeks each year, areas lying beyond this six-mile radius are rarely utilized, even though they are no less rich in plants and game than are the core areas.

Although the Bushmen move their camps frequently (five or six times a year) they do not move them very far. A rainy season camp in the nut forests is rarely more than ten or twelve miles from the home waterhole, and often new campsites are occupied only a few hundred yards away from the previous one. By these criteria, the Bushmen do not lead a free-ranging nomadic way of life. For example, they do not undertake long marches of 30 to 100 miles to get food, since this task can be readily fulfilled within a day's walk of home base. When such long marches do occur they are invariably for visiting, trading, and marriage arrangements, and should not be confused with the normal routine of subsistence.

Demographic factors. Another indicator of the harshness of a way of life is the age at which people die. Ever since Hobbes characterized life in the state of nature as "nasty, brutish and short," the assumption has been that hunting and gathering is so rigorous that members of such societies are rapidly worn out and meet an early death. Silberbauer, for example, says of the Gwi Bushmen of the central Kalahari that "life expectancy . . . is difficult to calculate, but I do not believe that many live beyond 45." And Coon has said of hunters in general:

> The practice of abandoning the hopelessly ill and aged has been observed in many parts of the world. It is always done by people living in poor environments where it is necessary to move about frequently to obtain food, where food is scarce, and transportation difficult. . . . Among peoples who are forced to live in this way the oldest generation, the generation of individuals who have passed their physical peak is reduced in numbers and influence. There is no body of elders to hand on tradition

TABLE III. !Kung Bushman plant foods

Food class	Part eaten								Totals (percentages)		
	Fruit and nut	Bean and root	Fruit and stalk	Root, bulb	Fruit, berry, melon	Resin	Leaves	Seed, bean	Total number of species in class	Estimated contribution by weight to vegetable diet	Estimated contribution of each species
I. Primary Eaten daily throughout year (mongongo nut)	1	—	—	—	—	—	—	—	1	c. 50	c. 50*
II. Major Eaten daily in season	1	1	1	1	4	—	—	—	8	c. 25	c. 3
III. Minor Eaten several times per week in season	—	—	—	7	3	2	2	—	14	c. 15	c. 1

IV. Supplementary Eaten when classes I–III locally unavailable	—	—	9	12	10	1	—	32	c. 7	c. 0.2
V. Rare Eaten several times per year	—	—	9	4	—	—	—	13	c. 3	c. 0.1
VI. Problematic Edible but not observed to be eaten	—	—	4	6	4	1	2	17	nil	nil
Total Species	2	1	30	29	16	4	2	85	100	—

* 1 species constitutes 50 per cent of the vegetable diet by weight.
† 23 species constitute 90 per cent of the vegetable diet by weight.
‡ 62 species constitute the remaining 10 per cent of the diet.

and control the affairs of younger men and women, and no formal system of age grading.

The !Kung Bushmen of the Dobe area flatly contradict this view. In a total population of 466, no fewer than 46 individuals (17 men and 29 women) were determined to be over 60 years of age, a proportion that compares favorably to the percentage of elderly in industrialized populations.

The aged hold a respected position in Bushman society and are the effective leaders of the camps. Senilicide is extremely rare. Long after their productive years have passed, the old people are fed and cared for by their children and grandchildren. The blind, the senile, and the crippled are respected for the special ritual and technical skills they possess. For instance, the four elders at !gose waterhole were totally or partially blind, but this handicap did not prevent their active participation in decision-making and ritual curing.

Another significant feature of the composition of the work force is the late assumption of adult responsibility by the adolescents. Young people are not expected to provide food regularly until they are married. Girls typically marry between the ages of 15 and 20, and boys about five years later, so that it is not unusual to find healthy, active teenagers visiting from camp to camp while their older relatives provide food for them.

As a result, the people in the age group 20–60 support a surprisingly large percentage of non-productive young and old people. About 40 per cent of the population in camps contribute little to the food supplies. This allocation of work to young and middle-aged adults allows for a relatively carefree childhood and adolescence and a relatively unstrenuous old age.

Leisure and work. Another important index of ease or difficulty of subsistence is the amount of time devoted to the food quest. Hunting has usually been regarded by social scientists as a way of life in which merely keeping alive is so formidable a task that members of such societies lack the leisure time necessary to "build culture." The !Kung Bushmen would appear to conform to the rule, for as Lorna Marshall says:

> It is vividly apparent that among the !Kung Bushmen, ethos, or "the spirit which actuates manners and customs," is survival. Their time and energies are almost wholly given to this task, for life in their environment requires that they spend their days mainly in procuring food.

It is certainly true that getting food is the most important single activity in Bushman life. However, this statement would apply equally well to small-scale agricultural and pastoral societies too. How much time is *actually* devoted to the food quest is fortunately an empirical question. And an analysis of the work effort of the Dobe Bushmen shows some unexpected results. From July 6 to August 2, 1964, I recorded all the daily activities of the Bushmen living at the Dobe waterhole. Because of the coming and going of visitors, the camp population fluctuated in size day by day, from a low of 23 to a high of 40, with a mean of 31.8 persons. Each day some of the adult members of the camp went out to hunt and/or gather while others stayed home or went visiting. The daily recording of all personnel on hand made it possible to calculate the number of man-days of work as a percentage of total number of man-days of consumption.

Although the Bushmen do not organize their activities on the basis of a seven-day week, I have divided the data this way to make them more intelligible. The work-week was calculated to show how many days out of seven each adult spent in subsistence activities (Table IV, Column 7). Week II has been eliminated from the totals since the investigator contributed food. In week I, the people spent an average of 2.3 days in subsistence activities, in week III, 1.9 days, and in week IV, 3.2 days. In all, the adults of the Dobe camp worked about two and a half days a week. Since the average working day was about six hours long, the fact emerges that !Kung Bushmen of Dobe, despite their harsh environment, devote from twelve to nineteen hours a week to getting food. Even the hardest working individual in the camp, a man named ≠oma who went out hunting on sixteen of the 28 days, spent a maximum of 32 hours a week in the food quest.

Because the Bushmen do not amass a surplus of foods, there are no seasons of exceptionally intensive activities such as planting and harvesting, and no seasons of unemployment. The level of work observed is an accurate reflection of the effort required to meet the immediate caloric needs of the group. This work diary covers the midwinter dry season, a period when food is neither at its most plentiful nor at its scarcest levels, and the diary documents the transition from better to worse conditions (see Table II). During the fourth week the gatherers were making overnight trips to camps in the mongongo nut forests seven to ten miles distant from the waterhole. These longer trips account for the rise in the level of work, from twelve or thirteen to nineteen hours per week.

If food getting occupies such a small proportion of a Bushman's waking hours, then how *do* people allocate their time? A woman gathers on one day enough food to feed her family for three days, and spends the rest of her time resting in camp, doing embroidery, visiting other camps, or entertaining visitors from other camps. For each day at home,

TABLE IV. *Summary of Dobe work diary*

Week	(1) Mean group size	(2) Adult-days	(3) Child-days	(4) Total man-days of consumption	(5) Man-days of work	(6) Meat (lbs.)	(7) Average work-week/ adult	(8) Index of sub- sistence effort
I (July 6–12)	25.6 (23–29)	114	65	179	37	104	2.3	.21
II (July 13–19)	28.3 (23–27)	125	73	198	22	80	1.2	.11
III (July 20–26)	34.3 (29–40)	156	84	240	42	177	1.9	.18
IV (July 27–Aug.2)	35.6 (32–40)	167	82	249	77	129	3.2	.31
4-wk. total	30.9	562	304	866	178	490	2.2	.21
Adjusted total*	31.8	437	231	668	156	410	2.5	.23

* See text.

Key: Column 1: Mean group size = $\dfrac{\text{total man-days of consumption}}{7}$.

Column 7: Work-week = the number of work days per adult per week.

Column 8: Index of subsistence effort = $\dfrac{\text{man-days of work}}{\text{man-days of consumption}}$ (e.g., in Week I, the value of "S" = .21, i.e., 21 days of work/100 days of consumption or 1 work day produces food for 5 consumption days).

kitchen routines, such as cooking, nut cracking, collecting firewood, and fetching water, occupy one to three hours of her time. This rhythm of steady work and steady leisure is maintained throughout the year.

The hunters tend to work more frequently than the women, but their schedule is uneven. It is not unusual for a man to hunt avidly for a week and then do nothing at all for two or three weeks. Since hunting is an unpredictable business and subject to magical control, hunters sometimes experience a run of bad luck and stop hunting for a month or longer. During these periods, visiting, entertaining, and especially dancing are the primary activities of men. (Unlike the Hadza, gambling is only a minor leisure activity.)

The trance-dance is the focus of Bushman ritual life; over 50 per cent of the men have trained as trance-performers and regularly enter trance during the course of the all-night dances. At some camps, trance-dances occur as frequently as two or three times a week and those who have entered trances the night before rarely go out hunting the following day. . . . In a camp with five or more hunters, there are usually two or three who are actively hunting and several others who are inactive. The net effect is to phase the hunting and non-hunting so that a fairly steady supply of meat is brought into camp.

Caloric returns. Is the modest work effort of the Bushmen sufficient to provide the calories necessary to maintain the health of the population? Or have the !Kung, in common with some agricultural peoples, adjusted to a permanently substandard nutritional level?

During my field work I did not encounter any cases of kwashiorkor, the most common nutritional disease in the children of African agricultural societies. However, without medical examinations, it is impossible to exclude the possibility that subclinical signs of malnutrition existed.

Another measure of nutritional adequacy is the average consumption of calories and proteins per person per day. The estimate for the Bushmen is based on observations of the weights of foods of known composition that were brought into Dobe camp on each day of the study period. The per-capita figure is obtained by dividing the total weight of foodstuffs by the total number of persons in the camp. These results are set out in detail elsewhere and can only be summarized here. During the study period 410 pounds of meat were brought in by the hunters of the Dobe camp, for a daily share of nine ounces of meat per person. About 700 pounds of vegetables were gathered and consumed during the same period. Table V sets out the calories and proteins available per capita in the !Kung Bushman dietary from meat, mongongo nuts, and other vegetable sources.

This output of 2,140 calories and 93.1 grams of protein per person per day may be compared with the Recommended Daily Allowances

TABLE V. *Caloric and protein levels in the !Kung Bushman dietary, July–August, 1964*

Class of food	Percentage contribution to diet by weight	Per capita consumption			Percentage caloric contribution of meat and vegetables
		Weight in grams	Protein in grams	Calories per person per day	
Meat	37	230	34.5	690	33
Mongongo nuts	33	210	56.7	1,260	
Other vegetable foods	30	190	1.9	190	67
Total all sources	100	630	93.1	2,140	100

(RDA) for persons of the small size and stature but vigorous activity regime of the !Kung Bushmen. The RDA for Bushmen can be estimated at 1,975 calories and 60 grams of protein per person per day. Thus it is apparent that food output exceeds energy requirements by 165 calories and 33 grams of protein. One can tentatively conclude that even a modest subsistence effort of two or three days work per week is enough to provide an adequate diet for the !Kung Bushmen.

THE SECURITY OF BUSHMAN LIFE

I have attempted to evaluate the subsistence base of one contemporary hunter-gatherer society living in a marginal environment. The !Kung Bushmen have available to them some relatively abundant high-quality foods, and they do not have to walk very far or work very hard to get them. Furthermore this modest work effort provides sufficient calories to support not only active adults, but also a large number of middle-aged and elderly people. The Bushmen do not have to press their youngsters into the service of the food quest, nor do they have to dispose of the oldsters after they have ceased to be productive.

The evidence presented assumes an added significance because this security of life was observed during the third year of one of the most severe droughts in South Africa's history. Most of the 576,000 people of Botswana are pastoralists and agriculturalists. After the crops had failed three years in succession and over 100,000 head of cattle had died on the range for lack of water, the World Food Program of the

United Nations instituted a famine relief program which has grown to include 180,000 people, over 30 per cent of the population. This program did not touch the Dobe area in the isolated northwest corner of the country and the Herero and Tswana women there were able to feed their families only by joining the Bushman women to forage for wild foods. Thus the natural plant resources of the Dobe area were carrying a higher proportion of population than would be the case in years when the Bantu harvested crops. Yet this added pressure on the land did not seem to adversely affect the Bushmen.

It one sense it was unfortunate that the period of my field work happened to coincide with the drought, since I was unable to witness a "typical" annual subsistence cycle. However, in another sense, the coincidence was a lucky one, for the drought put the Bushmen and their subsistence system to the acid test and, in terms of adaptation to scarce resources, they passed with flying colors. One can postulate that their subsistence base would be even more substantial during years of higher rainfall.

What are the crucial factors that make this way of life possible? I suggest that the primary factor is the Bushmen's strong emphasis on vegetable food sources. Although hunting involves a great deal of effort and prestige, plant foods provide from 60–80 per cent of the annual diet by weight. Meat has come to be regarded as a special treat; when available, it is welcomed as a break from the routine of vegetable foods, but it is never depended upon as a staple. No one ever goes hungry when hunting fails.

The reason for this emphasis is not hard to find. Vegetable foods are abundant, sedentary, and predictable. They grow in the same place year after year, and the gatherer is guaranteed a day's return of food for a day's expenditure of energy. Game animals, by contrast, are scarce, mobile, unpredictable, and difficult to catch. A hunter has no guarantee of success and may in fact go for days or weeks without killing a large mammal. During the study period, there were eleven men in the Dobe camp, of whom four did no hunting at all. The seven active men spent a total of 78 man-days hunting, and this work input yielded eighteen animals killed, or one kill for every four man-days of hunting. The probability of any one hunter making a kill on a given day was 0.23. By contrast, the probability of a woman finding plant food on a given day was 1.00. In other words, hunting and gathering are not equally felicitous subsistence alternatives.

Consider the productivity per man-hour of the two kinds of subsistence activities. One man-hour of hunting produces about 100 edible calories, and of gathering, 240 calories. Gathering is thus seen to be 2.4

times more productive than hunting. In short, hunting is a *high-risk, low-return* subsistence activity, while gathering is a *low-risk, high-return* subsistence activity.

It is not at all contradictory that the hunting complex holds a central place in the Bushmen ethos and that meat is valued more highly than vegetable foods. Analogously, steak is valued more highly than potatoes in the food preferences of our own society. In both situations the meat is more "costly" than the vegetable food. In the Bushman case, the cost of food can be measured in terms of time and energy expended. By this standard, 1,000 calories of meat "costs" ten man-hours, while the "cost" of 1,000 calories of vegetable foods is only four man-hours. Further, it is to be expected that the less predictable, more expensive food source would have a greater accretion of myth and ritual built up around it than would the routine staples of life, which rarely if ever fail.

CONCLUSIONS

Three points ought to be stressed. First, life in the state of nature is not necessarily nasty, brutish, and short. The Dobe-area Bushmen live well today on wild plants and meat, in spite of the fact that they are confined to the least productive portion of the range in which Bushman peoples were formerly found. It is likely that an even more substantial subsistence would have been characteristic of these hunters and gatherers in the past, when they had the pick of African habitats to choose from.

Second, the basis of Bushman diet is derived from sources other than meat. This emphasis makes good ecological sense to the !Kung Bushmen and appears to be a common feature among hunters and gatherers in general. Since a 30 to 40 per cent input of meat is such a consistent target for modern hunters in a variety of habitats, is it not reasonable to postulate a similar percentage for prehistoric hunters? Certainly the absence of plant remains on archeological sites is by itself not sufficient evidence for the absence of gathering. Recently-abandoned Bushman campsites show a similar absence of vegetable remains, although this paper has clearly shown that plant foods comprise over 60 per cent of the actual diet.

Finally, one gets the impression that hunting societies have been chosen by ethnologists to illustrate a dominant theme, such as the extreme importance of environment in the molding of certain cultures. Such a theme can best be exemplified by cases in which the technology is simple and/or the environment is harsh. This emphasis on the dramatic may have been pedagogically useful, but unfortunately it has led to the assumption that a precarious hunting subsistence base was characteristic of all cultures in the Pleistocene. This view of both modern and ancient hunters ought to be reconsidered. Specifically I am suggesting a shift in focus away from the dramatic and unusual cases, and toward a consideration of hunting and gathering as a persistent and well-adapted way of life.

18

India's sacred cow

MARVIN HARRIS

Other people's religious practices and beliefs may often appear to be
wasteful. They seem to involve a large expenditure of scarce resources
on ritual; they contain taboos that restrict the use of apparently
useful materials. Their existence seems irrational in the face of
ecological needs. One example that many cite in support of this
viewpoint is the religious proscription on the slaughter of cattle in
India. How can people permit millions of cattle to roam about eating,
but uneaten, in a land so continuously threatened by food shortages
and starvation? In this article, Marvin Harris challenges the view
that religious value is ecologically irrational. Dealing with the Indian
case, he argues that Indian cattle, far from being useless, are an
essential part of India's productive base. Religious restrictions on
killing cattle are ecologically sensible; they have developed and
persisted to insure a continuous supply of these valuable animals.

News photographs that came out of India during the famine of the late
1960s showed starving people stretching out bony hands to beg for food
while sacred cattle strolled behind them undisturbed. The Hindu, it
seems, would rather starve to death than eat his cow or even deprive
it of food. The cattle appear to browse unhindered through urban markets eating an orange here, a mango there, competing with people for
meager supplies of food.

By Western standards, spiritual values seem more important to
Indians than life itself. Specialists in food habits around the world like
Fred Simoons at the University of California at Davis consider Hinduism
an irrational ideology that compels people to overlook abundant, nu-
tritious foods for scarcer, less healthful foods.

From *Human Nature*, February 1978. Copyright © 1978 by Human Nature, Inc. Reprinted
by permission of the publisher.

What seems to be an absurd devotion to the mother cow pervades Indian life. Indian wall calendars portray beautiful young women with bodies of fat white cows, often with milk jetting from their teats into sacred shrines.

Cow worship even carries over into politics. In 1966 a crowd of 120,000 people, led by holy men, demonstrated in front of the Indian House of Parliament in support of the All-Party Cow Protection Campaign Committee. In Nepal, the only contemporary Hindu kingdom, cow slaughter is severely punished. As one story goes, the car driven by an official of a United States agency struck and killed a cow. In order to avoid the international incident that would have occurred when the official was arrested for murder, the Nepalese magistrate concluded that the cow had committed suicide.

Many Indians agree with Western assessments of the Hindu reverence for their cattle, the zebu, or *Bos indicus,* a large-humped species prevalent in Asia and Africa. M. N. Srinivas, an Indian anthropologist states: "Orthodox Hindu opinion regards the killing of cattle with abhorrence, even though the refusal to kill the vast number of useless cattle which exists in India today is detrimental to the nation." Even the Indian Ministry of Information formerly maintained that "the large animal population is more a liability than an asset in view of our land resources." Accounts from many different sources point to the same conclusion: India, one of the world's great civilizations, is being strangled by its love for the cow.

The easy explanation for India's devotion to the cow, the one most Westerners and Indians would offer, is that cow worship is an integral part of Hinduism. Religion is somehow good for the soul, even if it sometimes fails the body. Religion orders the cosmos and explains our place in the universe. Religious beliefs, many would claim, have existed for thousands of years and have a life of their own. They are not understandable in scientific terms.

But all this ignores history. There is more to be said for cow worship than is immediately apparent. The earliest Vedas, the Hindu sacred texts from the Second Millennium B.C., do not prohibit the slaughter of cattle. Instead, they ordain it as a part of sacrificial rites. The early Hindus did not avoid the flesh of cows and bulls; they ate it at ceremonial feasts presided over by Brahman priests. Cow worship is a relatively recent development in India; it evolved as the Hindu religion developed and changed.

This evolution is recorded in royal edicts and religious texts written during the last 3,000 years of Indian history. The Vedas from the First Millennium B.C. contain contradictory passages, some referring to ritual slaughter and others to a strict taboo on beef consumption. A. N. Bose, in *Social and Rural Economy of Northern India, 600 B.C.–200 A.D.*, concludes that many of the sacred-cow passages were incorporated into the texts by priests of a later period.

By 200 A.D. the status of Indian cattle had undergone a spiritual transformation. The Brahman priesthood exhorted the population to venerate the cow and forbade them to abuse it or to feed on it. Religious feasts involving the ritual slaughter and consumption of livestock were eliminated and meat eating was restricted to the nobility.

By 1000 A.D., all Hindus were forbidden to eat beef. Ahimsa, the Hindu belief in the unity of all life, was the spiritual justification for this restriction. But it is difficult to ascertain exactly when this change occurred. An important event that helped to shape the modern complex was the Islamic invasion, which took place in the Eighth Century A.D. Hindus may have found it politically expedient to set themselves off from the invaders, who were beefeaters, by emphasizing the need to prevent the slaughter of their sacred animals. Thereafter, the cow taboo assumed its modern form and began to function much as it does today.

The place of the cow in modern India is every place — on posters, in the movies, in brass figures, in stone and wood carvings, on the streets, in the fields. The cow is a symbol of health and abundance. It provides the milk that Indians consume in the form of yogurt and ghee (clarified butter), which contribute subtle flavors to much spicy Indian food.

This, perhaps, is the practical role of the cow, but cows provide less than half the milk produced in India. Most cows in India are not dairy breeds. In most regions, when an Indian farmer wants a steady, high-quality source of milk he usually invests in a female water buffalo. In India the water buffalo is the specialized dairy breed because its milk has a higher butterfat content than zebu milk. Although the farmer milks his zebu cows, the milk is merely a by-product.

More vital than zebu milk to South Asian farmers are zebu calves. Male calves are especially valued because from bulls come oxen, which are the mainstay of the Indian agricultural system.

Small, fast oxen drag wooden plows through late-spring fields when monsoons have dampened the dry, cracked earth. After harvest, the oxen break the grain from the stalk by stomping through mounds of cut wheat and rice. For rice cultivation in irrigated fields, the male water buffalo is preferred (it pulls better in deep mud), but for most other crops, including rainfall rice, wheat, sorghum, and millet, and for transporting goods and people to and from town, a team of oxen is preferred. The ox is the Indian peasant's tractor, thresher and family car combined; the cow is the factory that produces the ox.

If draft animals instead of cows are counted, India appears to have too few domesticated ruminants, not too many. Since each of the 70 million farms in India requires a draft team, it follows that Indian peasants should use 140 million animals in the fields. But there are only 83 million oxen and male water buffalo on the subcontinent, a shortage of 30 million draft teams.

In other regions of the world, joint ownership of draft animals might overcome a shortage, but Indian agriculture is closely tied to the monsoon rains of late spring and summer. Field preparation and planting must coincide with the rain, and a farmer must have his animals ready to plow when the weather is right. When the farmer without a draft team needs bullocks most, his neighbors are all using theirs. Any delay in turning the soil drastically lowers production.

Because of this dependence on draft animals, loss of the family oxen is devastating. If a beast dies, the farmer must borrow money to buy or rent an ox at interest rates so high that he ultimately loses his land. Every year foreclosures force thousands of poverty-stricken peasants to abandon the countryside for the overcrowded cities.

If a family is fortunate enough to own a fertile cow, it will be able to rear replacements for a lost team and thus survive until life returns to normal. If, as sometimes happens, famine leads a family to sell its cow and ox team, all ties to agriculture are cut. Even if the family survives, it has no way to farm the land, no oxen to work the land, and no cows to produce oxen.

The prohibition against eating meat applies to the flesh of cows, bulls, and oxen, but the cow is the most sacred because it can produce the other two. The peasant whose cow dies is not only crying over a spiritual loss but over the loss of his farm as well.

Religious laws that forbid the slaughter of cattle promote the recovery of the agricultural system from the dry Indian winter and from periods of drought. The monsoon, on which all agriculture depends, is erratic. Sometimes it arrives early, sometimes late, sometimes not at all. Drought has struck large portions of India time and again in this century, and Indian farmers and the zebus are accustomed to these natural disasters. Zebus can pass weeks on end with little or no food and water. Like camels, they store both in their humps and recuperate quickly with only a little nourishment.

During droughts the cows often stop lactating and become barren. In some cases the condition is permanent but often it is only temporary. If barren animals were summarily eliminated, as Western experts in animal husbandry have suggested, cows capable of recovery would be lost along with those entirely debilitated. By keeping alive the cows that can later produce oxen, religious laws against cow slaughter assure the recovery of the agricultural system from the greatest challenge it faces — the failure of the monsoon.

The local Indian governments aid the process of recovery by maintaining homes for barren cows. Farmers reclaim any animal that calves or begins to lactate. One police station in Madras collects strays and pastures them in a field adjacent to the station. After a small fine is paid, a cow is returned to its rightful owner when the owner thinks the cow shows signs of being able to reproduce.

During the hot, dry spring months most of India is like a desert. Indian farmers often complain they cannot feed their livestock during this period. They maintain the cattle by letting them scavenge on the sparse grass along the roads. In the cities cattle are encouraged to scavenge near food stalls to supplement their scant diet. These are the wandering cattle tourists report seeing throughout India.

Westerners expect shopkeepers to respond to these intrusions with the deference due a sacred animal; instead, their response is a string of curses and the crack of a long bamboo pole across the beast's back or a poke at its genitals. Mahatma Gandhi was well aware of the treatment sacred cows (and bulls and oxen) received in India. "How we bleed her to take the last drop of milk from her. How we starve her to emaciation, how we ill-treat the calves, how we deprive them of their portion of milk, how cruelly we treat the oxen, how we castrate them, how we beat them, how we overload them."

Oxen generally receive better treatment than cows. When food is in short supply, thrifty Indian peasants feed their working bullocks and ignore their cows, but rarely do they abandon the cows to die. When cows are sick, farmers worry over them as they would over members of the family and nurse them as if they were children. When the rains return and when the fields are harvested, the farmers again feed their cows regularly and reclaim their abandoned animals. The prohibition against beef consumption is a form of disaster insurance for all India.

Western agronomists and economists are quick to protest that all the functions of the zebu cattle can be improved with organized breeding programs, cultivated pastures, and silage. Because stronger oxen would pull the plow faster, they could work multiple plots of land, allowing farmers to share their animals. Fewer healthy, well-fed cows could provide Indians with more milk. But pastures and silage require arable land, land needed to produce wheat and rice.

A look at Western cattle farming makes plain the cost of adopting advanced technology in Indian agriculture. In a study of livestock production in the United States, David Pimentel of the College of Agriculture and Life Sciences at Cornell University found that 91 percent of the cereal, legume, and vegetable protein suitable for human consumption is consumed by livestock. Approximately three quarters of the arable land in the United States is devoted to growing food for livestock. In the production of meat and milk, American ranchers use enough fossil fuel to equal more than 82 million barrels of oil annually. (See Figure I.)

Indian cattle do not drain the system in the same way. In a 1971 study of livestock in West Bengal, Stewart Odend'hal of the University of Missouri found that Bengalese cattle ate only the inedible remains of subsistence crops — rice straw, rice hulls, the tops of sugar cane, and mustard-oil cake. Cattle graze in the fields after harvest and eat the remains of crops left on the ground; they forage for grass and weeds on the roadsides. The food for zebu cattle costs the human population virtually nothing. "Basically," Odend'hal says, "the cattle convert items of little direct human value into products of immediate utility." (See Figure II.)

In addition to plowing the fields and producing milk, the zebus produce dung, which fires the hearths and fertilizes the fields of India. Much of the estimated 800 million tons of manure produced annually is collected by the farmers' children as they follow the family cows and bullocks from place to place. And when the children see the droppings of another farmer's cattle along the road, they pick those up also. Odend'hal reports that the system operates with such high efficiency that the children of West Bengal recover nearly 100 percent of the dung produced by their livestock.

From 40 to 70 percent of all manure produced by Indian cattle is used as fuel for cooking; the rest is returned to the fields as fertilizer. Dried dung burns slowly, cleanly, and with low heat — characteristics that satisfy the household needs of Indian women. Staples like curry and rice can simmer for hours. While the meal slowly cooks over an unattended fire, the women of the household can do other chores. Cow chips, unlike firewood, do not scorch as they burn.

It is estimated that the dung used for cooking fuel provides the energy-equivalent of 43 million tons of coal. At current prices, it would cost India an extra 1.5 billion dollars in foreign exchange to replace the dung with coal. And if the 350 million tons of manure that are being used as fertilizer were replaced with commercial fertilizers, the expense would be even greater. Roger Revelle of the University of California at San Diego has calculated that 89 percent of the energy used in Indian agriculture (the equivalent of about 140 million tons of coal) is provided by local sources. Even if foreign loans were to provide the money, the capital outlay necessary to replace the Indian cow with tractors and fertilizers for the fields, coal for the fires, and transportation for the family would probably warp international financial institutions for years.

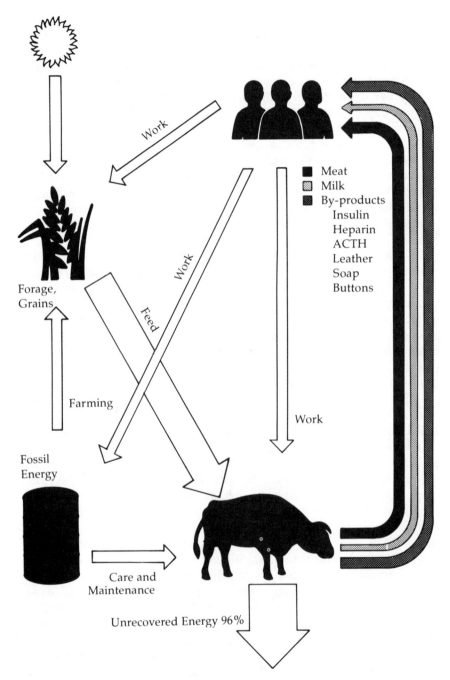

Forage,
Grains

Fossil
Energy

Work

Feed

Farming

Work

Work

Care and
Maintenance

Meat
Milk
By-products
Insulin
Heparin
ACTH
Leather
Soap
Buttons

Unrecovered Energy 96%

FIGURE I. *American cattle: Energy consumption and production*

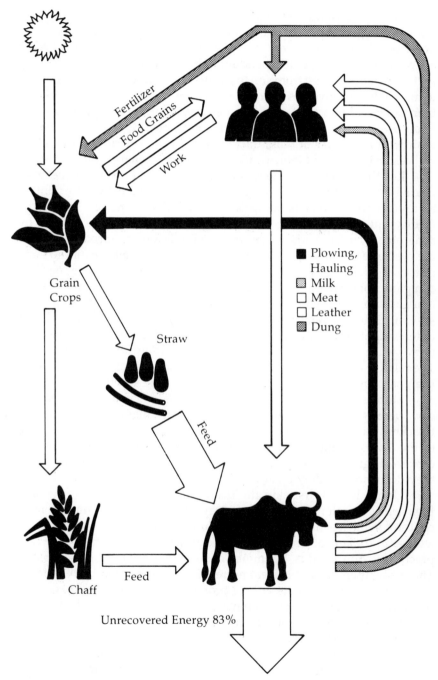

FIGURE II. *Indian cattle: Energy consumption and production*

Instead of asking the Indians to learn from the American model of industrial agriculture, American farmers might learn energy conservation from the Indians. Every step in an energy cycle results in a loss of energy to the system. Like a pendulum that slows a bit with each swing, each transfer of energy from sun to plants, plants to animals, and animals to human beings involves energy losses. Some systems are more efficient than others; they provide a higher percentage of the energy inputs in a final, useful form. Seventeen percent of all energy zebus consume is returned in the form of milk, traction and dung. American cattle raised on Western range land return only 4 percent of the energy they consume.

But the American system is improving. Based on techniques pioneered by Indian scientists, at least one commercial firm in the United States is reported to be building plants that will turn manure from cattle feedlots into combustible gas. When organic matter is broken down by anaerobic bacteria, methane gas and carbon dioxide are produced. After the methane is cleansed of the carbon dioxide, it is available for the same purposes as natural gas — cooking, heating, electricity generation. The company constructing the biogasification plant plans to sell its product to a gas-supply company, to be piped through the existing distribution system. Schemes similar to this one could make cattle ranches almost independent of utility and gasoline companies, for methane can be used to run trucks, tractors, and cars as well as to supply heat and electricity. The relative energy self-sufficiency that the Indian peasant has achieved is a goal American farmers and industry are now striving for.

Studies like Odend'hal's understate the efficiency of the Indian cow, because dead cows are used for purposes that Hindus prefer not to acknowledge. When a cow dies, an Untouchable, a member of one of the lowest ranking castes in India, is summoned to haul away the carcass. Higher castes consider the body of the dead cow polluting; if they do handle it, they must go through a rite of purification.

Untouchables first skin the dead animal and either tan the skin themselves or sell it to a leather factory. In the privacy of their homes, contrary to the teachings of Hinduism, untouchable castes cook the meat and eat it. Indians of all castes rarely acknowledge the existence of these practices to non-Hindus, but more are aware that beefeating takes place. The prohibition against beefeating restricts consumption by the higher castes and helps distribute animal protein to the poorest sectors of the population that otherwise would have no source of these vital nutrients.

Untouchables are not the only Indians who consume beef. Indian Muslims and Christians are under no restriction that forbids them beef, and its consumption is legal in many places. The Indian ban on cow slaughter is state, not national, law and not all states restrict it. In many cities, such as New Delhi, Calcutta, and Bombay, legal slaughterhouses sell beef to retail customers and to the restaurants that serve steak.

If the caloric value of beef and the energy costs involved in the manufacture of synthetic leather were included in the estimates of energy, the calculated efficiency of Indian livestock would rise considerably.

As well as the system works, experts often claim that its efficiency can be further improved. Alan Heston, an economist at the University of Pennsylvania, believes that Indians suffer from an overabundance of cows simply because they refuse to slaughter the excess cattle. India could produce at least the same number of oxen and the same quantities of milk and manure with 30 million fewer cows. Heston calculates that only 40 cows are necessary to maintain a population of 100 bulls and oxen. Since India averages 70 cows for every 100 bullocks, the difference, 30 million cows, is expendable.

What Heston fails to note is that sex ratios among cattle in different regions of India vary tremendously, indicating that adjustments in the cow population do take place. Along the Ganges River, one of the holiest shrines of Hinduism, the ratio drops to 47 cows for every 100 male animals. This ratio reflects the preference for dairy buffalo in the irrigated sectors of the Gangetic Plains. In nearby Pakistan, in contrast, where cow slaughter is permitted, the sex ratio is 60 cows to 100 oxen.

Since the sex ratios among cattle differ greatly from region to region and do not even approximate the balance that would be expected if no females were killed, we can assume that some culling of herds does take place; Indians do adjust their religious restrictions to accommodate ecological realities.

They cannot kill a cow but they can tether an old or unhealthy animal until it has starved to death. They cannot slaughter a calf but they can yoke it with a large wooden triangle so that when it nurses it irritates the mother's udder and gets kicked to death. They cannot ship their animals to the slaughterhouse but they can sell them to Muslims, closing their eyes to the fact that the Muslims will take the cattle to the slaughterhouse.

These violations of the prohibition against cattle slaughter strengthen the premise that cow worship is a vital part of Indian culture. The practice arose to prevent the population from consuming the animal on which Indian agriculture depends. During the First Millennium B.C., the Ganges Valley became one of the most densely populated regions of the world.

Where previously there had been only scattered villages, many towns and cities arose and peasants farmed every available acre of land. Kingsley Davis, a population expert at the University of California at

Berkeley, estimates that by 300 B.C. between 50 million and 100 million people were living in India. The forested Ganges Valley became a windswept semidesert and signs of ecological collapse appeared; droughts and floods became commonplace, erosion took away the rich topsoil, farms shrank as population increased, and domesticated animals became harder and harder to maintain.

It is probable that the elimination of meat eating came about in a slow, practical manner. The farmers who decided not to eat their cows, who saved them for procreation to produce oxen, were the ones who survived the natural disasters. Those who ate beef lost the tools with which to farm. Over a period of centuries, more and more farmers probably avoided beef until an unwritten taboo came into existence.

Only later was the practice codified by the priesthood. While Indian peasants were probably aware of the role of cattle in their society, strong sanctions were necessary to protect zebus from a population faced with starvation. To remove temptation, the flesh of cattle became taboo and the cow became sacred.

The sacredness of the cow is not just an ignorant belief that stands in the way of progress. Like all concepts of the sacred and the profane, this one affects the physical world; it defines the relationships that are important for the maintenance of Indian society.

Indians have the sacred cow; we have the "sacred" car and the "sacred" dog. It would not occur to us to propose the elimination of automobiles and dogs from our society without carefully considering the consequences, and we should not propose the elimination of zebu cattle without first understanding their place in the social order of India.

Human society is neither random nor capricious. The regularities of thought and behavior called culture are the principal mechanisms by which we human beings adapt to the world around us. Practices and beliefs can be rational or irrational, but a society that fails to adapt to its environment is doomed to extinction. Only those societies that draw the necessities of life from their surroundings, without destroying those surroundings, inherit the earth. The West has much to learn from the great antiquity of Indian civilization, and the sacred cow is an important part of that lesson.

19

The food connection

PETER FARB and
GEORGE ARMELAGOS

*The spread of food crops from one continent to another and changes
in food technology have had a profound impact on the size of world
populations and the efficiency of food production, according to Peter
Farb and George Armelagos in this selection. They challenge the
usual argument that industrialization and the development of
Western medicine largely explains population growth. Instead, they
argue, the spread of plants from the Americas, such as maize,
potatoes, and peanuts, has permitted greater agricultural yields
within a broader range of soils and climates. With increased food
supply has come larger populations, better nutrition, and greater
resistence to disease. Food-producing efficiency, initially low among
hunters and gatherers, horticulturists, and pastoralists, reaches its
peak with intensive agriculture, particularly agriculture
involving irrigation, and actually declines with
modern mechanized farming.*

The modern cultural adaptation that emerged first in Britain, then in
Western Europe and North America, is now spreading rapidly around
the globe — and even penetrating into the lands of remote pastoralists,
horticulturists, and hunter-gatherers. Often regarded as synonymous
with the Industrial Revolution — which began almost exactly two hundred
years ago with James Watt's improved version of the steam engine —
modernization entails much more than the replacement of human mus-

cle by energy from machines. It involves developments in the structure of the family, the division of labor, the growth of population, and the environment, as well as diet.

The Industrial Revolution could not have taken place without the agricultural revolution that preceded it and that was based on an increase in production due both to new crops from the Americas and to new methods of farming. Yields of food were increased substantially by such simple techniques as the rotation of crops — a sequence from year to year, for example, of barley, clover, wheat, and turnips, instead of leaving the field fallow when its fertility had been depleted. The selective breeding of cattle also greatly increased the yields of meat and milk. In such ways, what had been an inefficient system of agriculture was eventually replaced by large-scale mechanized farming that took on the character of modern industry. Oliver Goldsmith in his poem *The Deserted Village* — published in 1770, five years before Watt's improved steam engine first came into use — described how the mechanization of agriculture had already forced many farmers to abandon their small holdings and migrate to the cities. This considerable portion of the British population provided the labor for an industrialization that would otherwise have been impossible.

One phenomenon of modernization has been an increasingly rapid rise in population. In 1750 the total population of the world was probably about 750 million, by 1830 it had increased to a billion, by 1930 it was two billion, and by 1975 four billion. In other words, the human species needed millions of years to reach a population of a billion, but thereafter the second billion was added in only a hundred years, the third in thirty years, and the fourth in a mere fifteen years. This growth was long attributed to a drop in the death rate that stemmed from advances in medicine, but some demographers now question whether medicine had much of an effect. Tuberculosis, for example, was the largest single cause of death in Britain in the last century, yet in the fifty years previous to 1882 — when the tubercle baccillus was first identified by Robert Koch — deaths caused by it had already declined by about half. Pneumonia, influenza, infectious bronchitis, and other diseases also began significant declines early in the nineteenth century, years before immunization and potent new drugs could have had any effect.

If not medical advances, then what can explain the change in the response to infection by people living in modern societies? The answer seems to be the profound effect of improved nutrition on the body's response to microorganisms. The decline in the death rate that occurred in Europe and in North America during the last century is being witnessed today in developing nations, and has the same probable cause. Well-nourished people have a much lower rate of infection and, even if infected, are much more likely to recover as compared to poorly nourished people. Before the widespread use of the measles vaccine, practically every child in every country caught measles, but three hundred times more deaths occurred in the poorer countries than in the richer ones. The reason was not that the virus was somehow more potent in poor countries or that these lacked medical services, but that in poorly nourished countries the virus attacked children who, because of chronic malnutrition, were less able to resist it.

Along with an improved agriculture came the introduction into Europe of new crops from the Americas, notably white potatoes into northern Europe and maize into southern Europe. In both Spain and Italy, where the cultivation of maize was widespread, populations soared — nearly doubling in Spain and increasing from eleven to eighteen million in Italy between the beginning and the end of the eighteenth century. The potato was not accepted so readily in Europe, even though it had been cultivated in the Andean highlands of Peru for about 2,500 years. It was at first regarded with suspicion, in part because it was grown from a tuber rather than from seeds, as were all other edible plants in Europe up to that time. But by the beginning of the eighteenth century, the potato had become a common food for peasants, who found in it the perfect crop for small parcels of arable land. Just one acre planted to potatoes could feed a family of five or six, plus a cow or pig, for most of a year. The plant could grow in a wide variety of soils, and it required no tools other than a spade and a hoe. It matured within three or four months, as compared to the well over half a year required for grain crops, and it had the advantage of a high nutritional value.

The most dramatic effect of the potato's introduction into Europe was seen in Ireland. By the middle of the eighteenth century, most of the Irish population was subsisting almost exclusively on potatoes, and Ireland's perennially recurring famines appeared at last to be ended. Potatoes do not have aphrodisiac powers, as was once believed, but they did contribute to the sudden increase in the Irish population, making large families possible because they provided a maximum of sustenance with a minimum of labor. The population of Ireland grew from just above three million in 1754 to more than eight million in 1845. Then a blight struck, bringing about the Great Potato Famine that was to last four years.

An increase in population as a result of new foods rather than of industrialization and medical advances also took place in China. The sweet potato, long grown by South American Indians, was early imported as a crop into China and was established by 1594, when it provided sustenance at a time when the native grains were succumbing to drought. An eighteenth-century agricultural commentary extolled sweet potatoes as a versatile crop that could be boiled, ground, or fermented; could be fed to animals, as well as to humans; and could grow in sandy, mountainous, and salty soils where grains did not survive. By that century, other New World crops were being widely grown: maize was allowing people from the crowded Yangtze region to migrate inland and farm drier lands; the white potato made it possible to bring into production lands that were too impoverished even for growing maize; and peanuts could be grown in the previously useless soils along river and streams. The new crops allowed a Chinese population that had reached the limits of its previous resources to begin a new spurt in growth. The numbers expanded from about 150 million people in the early 1700s to about 450 million only a century and a half later. The worldwide growth in population over the past several centuries is similar to what occurred in China, and can be assumed to have occurred for similar reasons. As soon as food resources could be moved from continent to continent because of the invention of long-distance transportation, a surge in population took place, one that had little to do with industrialization, shorter work hours, or advances in the practice of medicine.

People in modern societies usually assume that their own kind of mechanized agriculture is the most efficient known. But if the question is asked whether mechanized producers are really extracting from the soil a greater number of calories of food in proportion to the calories of energy they expend, the answer is no. In fact, they are very inefficient in this regard when compared with other adaptations — as is shown by a simple equation developed by anthropologist Marvin Harris that makes it possible to analyze the efficiency of any system for providing food energy:

$$\frac{E}{m \times t \times r} = e$$

That is, a society's annual production of food energy, E (as expressed in thousands of calories, or kilocalories), divided by the number of food producers (m), times the hours each works at food production during the year (t), times the calories expended per producer each hour in doing the work (r) equals e, that society's techno-environmental efficiency (in other words, the calories produced for each calorie of energy expended). Obviously, e must be greater than one because no society can survive for very long unless it produces more energy than it expends; actually, the value of e must be substantially higher than one to provide for such nonproducing activities as toolmaking, ceremonials, and recreation, among other things, and also to support the young, the elderly, the sick, and other nonproducers in the society. The larger e becomes, therefore, the greater is the society's techno-environmental efficiency in producing food energy above the amount it expends.

In a hunting-gathering society, such as the San, or Bushmen, of the Kalahari Desert, the equation is applied by Marvin Harris (using data collected by Richard Lee) as follows: A camp of twenty adults (m), each working 805 hours a year (t) and expending 150 calories per hour (r), to produce 23,000,000 kilocalories annually (E), has an efficiency of 9.5 (e) — which means that the San are producing between nine and ten calories for each calorie of energy expended.

This low efficiency does not allow much of a margin of safety and is insufficient to provide food for full-time specialists such as wood-carvers or priests. But the San cannot increase their efficiency because the average expenditure per producer of 150 calories an hour cannot be raised substantially; the human body simply cannot withstand long periods of being overheated or out of breath (which is why the average value for r of 150 remains the same in all of the adaptations to be discussed here). For each adult in the camp to work more than 805 hours a year (an average of a mere two hours or so a day) would not solve the problem because the San can neither transport nor store a surplus, and any increased effort would quickly deplete the food resources around the camp. They might try to enlarge the population of their camp to increase the number of producers, but the food supply in the Kalahari Desert is insufficient to support dense populations that lack the knowledge and tools to build irrigation dams. So long as the San follow their traditional ways, they obviously can do almost nothing to increase their techno-environmental efficiency.

Nor would it be possible for the San to switch to horticulture, given both the harsh environment and their limited technology for overcoming it. Even if they could, Marvin Harris has shown, using energy data from a horticultural village in Gambia, West Africa, how little would be gained. Instead of the 20 food producers in the San camp, this Gambian village had 334, as well as a better climate for plant growth and a more complex technology. Yet the application of the equation shows an efficiency only slightly above that of the San. For an annual production of 460,000,000 kilocalories, 334 persons, each working 820 hours annually and expending 150 calories an hour, produce a little over 11 calories for each calorie of expended energy.

The main advantage of horticulture over hunting-gathering is not its much greater efficiency but rather that people can live together in larger and more permanent settlements. The denser population of a sedentary village allows for protection against enemies and gives greater opportunity for cultural interaction.

Detailed energy data do not exist for pastoral peoples, but their efficiency is believed to be no greater than for hunter-gatherers and horticulturists. It may indeed be less, since to allow domesticated animals to eat plant foods and then to eat the animal or its milk and blood takes the process of production through an extra step, with a loss of calories along the way. This assumption seems supported by the few studies that have been made. For one tribe of southern Tunisia that herds sheep and goats and also practices a little horticulture, anthropologist William Bedoian has calculated a techno-environmental efficiency of about six; for some Indians in the Andes of South America who are almost exclusively pastoralists, R. Brooke Thomas has determined the figure to be a little more than two.

Figures on efficiency under other adaptations do not increase by much until the complex level of irrigation agriculture is reached. This adaptation can feed more people on less land than any other, including mechanized agriculture. Over the millenniums, it has developed most notably in eastern Asia because of particular conditions prevailing there: many people to provide the labor for building and maintaining irrigation works, abundant water, and a shortage of arable land. As the irrigation system develops and production is intensified, more and more people are fed from the same amount of land — although at the price of increasing the amount of labor per unit of land, which means that the land must be worked ever more intensively by more people. Given this cycle, no one can become richer by working harder because the payments allocated to labor must be divided among a larger and larger force. And since such systems can develop only in the presence of an autocratic government, any economic growth that occurs is inevitably siphoned off by the bureaucratic elite that exists outside of the energy system.

A detailed study of labor inputs and food yields for an irrigation village in Yunnan Province, China, before the fall of the Nationalist government shows a greatly increased techno-environmental efficiency over hunting-gathering, horticulture, and pastoralism. Four hundred eighteen persons, each working 1,129 hours annually, produced 3,788,000,000 kilocalories, resulting in between 53 and 54 calories produced for each calorie of energy expended. A higher efficiency, it should be noted, does not produce an increase in leisure, as is often supposed. Rather, each producer must work harder — in fact, some 35 percent more labor was performed by each of these Chinese than by each of the San.

Of the nearly four billion kilocalories produced annually by this Chinese village, the villagers were estimated to need no more than a sixth of that amount. What happened, then, to the more than three billion kilocalories they produced each year over what they consumed?

The surplus was used to feed the scores of millions in Chinese towns and cities who did not participate directly in food production, was sent to market and exchanged for manufactured goods, or was taken away in the form of taxes levied by the local, provincial, and national governments and in the form of rent payments to large landowners.

Modern societies are too complex to be analyzed by the equation employed here, but a few generalizations can be made. Once again, it is a mistake to suppose that modern societies allow people to work less hard for their daily bread. Out of the 1,129 hours worked by one Chinese irrigation farmer in a year, only 122 were needed to grow enough food to sustain that farmer. A blue-collar worker in the United States, on the other hand, spends 180 hours earning enough money to purchase a year's supply of food. Notwithstanding Western notions of the Chinese peasants' incessant labor, it is plain that they actually need to work less by a third than North Americans or Europeans to keep themselves supplied with food. Moreover, although a mechanized farmer in the American Midwest need put in an annual total of only nine hours of work for each acre to achieve an astounding 6,000 calories for each calorie of effort, that figure ignores the enormous amounts of human labor that go into manufacturing and transporting the trucks, tractors, combines, fuel, fertilizer, pesticides, fence wire, and everything else used by the farmer, not to mention transporting the food itself. For every person who actually works on a Midwestern farm, the labor of at least two others off the farm is needed to supply equipment and services directly to the farmer — aside from the very many more whose labors contribute indirectly to the final product. Altogether, a total of 2,790 calories of energy must be expended to produce and deliver to a consumer in the United States just one can of corn providing a total of 270 calories. The production of meat entails an even greater deficit: an expenditure of 22,000 calories is needed to produce the somewhat less than four ounces of beefsteak that also provides 270 calories.

In short, present-day agriculture is much less efficient than traditional irrigation methods that have been used by Asians, among others, in this century and by Mayas, Mesopotamians, Egyptians, and Chinese in antiquity. The primary advantage of mechanized agriculture is that it requires the participation of fewer farmers, but for that, the price paid in machines, fossil fuels, and other expenditures of energy is enormous. A severe price is also paid in human labor. Once the expensive machines have been manufactured and deployed on the farms, they are economically efficient only if operated throughout the daylight hours, and indeed farmers in the United States often labor for sixteen hours a day. The boast of industrialized societies that they have decreased the workload is valid only in comparison with the exploitation of labor that existed in the early decades of the Industrial Revolution. If the prevailing forty-hour work week of North America and Europe were proposed to the San, whoever did so would be considered to be exploitive, inhuman, or plain mad.

VII

Economic systems

People everywhere must obtain material things and the help of others if they are to meet their biological and social needs. We use clothing and shelter to maintain our body temperature at about 98.6 degrees. We need vegetable and animal products in order to sustain ourselves. We require the services of other people when we are helpless children or oldsters unable to fend for ourselves. Cultural preferences may determine the kind of clothes we wear and the foods we eat, but all people must meet these needs to survive. Similarly, people everywhere have social needs. Human beings are social animals. They associate with each other in complex networks; they assume various identities and play many different roles. Once again, culture dictates a variety of ways for people to conduct their social lives, but in every society interaction requires the use of material goods and the exchange of services. Providing goods and services people require to meet their biological and social wants is the task of economic systems.

Production is a most important function of any economic system. Production provides people with needed raw materials and allows them to manufacture the many items they require. But production is no simple matter. It demands special units of production, the groups of people who work together. Some productive groups are based on family and kinship; others are specially organized groups like the factory crews of industrialized nations. Production also involves a technology, i.e., the knowledge people employ to make and use tools and extract and refine raw materials. It is easy to underestimate the technological sophistication of nonidustrialized peoples like the hunter-gatherer !Kung Bushmen of Africa. But it is wise to note that people's technology generally works for them, permitting adaptation to an incredible variety of natural environments. From the viewpoint of particular individuals, few technologies are simple. An engineer working in an American steel plant operates using an extremely complex repertoire of technological knowledge. But so does the !Kung hunter as he reads the faint signs left behind by the antelope he is tracking.

Perhaps the largest difference between the !Kung and our own economies lies in the distribution of goods and services. The !Kung exchange things and help each other because they are obliged to do so. They live in a world of relatives, friends, and associates with whom the exchange of goods and assistance is a normal part of interaction. Exchanges associated with role obligation are usually referred to as reciprocal. Reciprocal exchange exists in American society too, for we employ it when we work together in our families, exchange Christmas gifts, or tip waitresses. But we are more reliant on market exchange, which depends more on our present needs and desires, our resources, and the cost of the things we want. Market exchange is characteristic of complex societies where people must seek fulfillment of their economic needs from strangers. Whether exchange is reciprocal or market, no matter how production is organized and technology developed, all human beings rely on an economy to survive and to live a satisfying life.

20

The impact of money
on an African subsistence economy

PAUL J. BOHANNAN

*In this article Paul Bohannan describes the early colonial economy of
the Tiv of Nigeria and shows that it contained three spheres of
exchange. These spheres — subsistence, prestige, and women in
marriage — were separated by the rule that goods from one could not
be used to purchase goods in another without loss of prestige to one
party in the exchange. When general-purpose money was introduced
from the West, it became possible to equate the values of each sphere,
and radical change took place. The author discusses in detail the
changes resulting from the introduction of money.*

It has often been claimed that money was to be found in much of the
African continent before the impact of the European world and the
extension of trade made coinage general. When we examine these claims,
however, they tend to evaporate or to emerge as tricks of definition. It
is an astounding fact that economists have, for decades, been assigning
three or four qualities to money when they discuss it with reference to
our own society or to those of the medieval and modern world, yet the
moment they have gone to ancient history or to the societies and economies studied by anthropologists they have sought the "real" nature of
money by allowing only one of these defining characteristics to dominate
their definitions.

All economists learned as students that money serves at least three
purposes. It is a means of exchange, it is a mode of payment, it is a
standard of value. Depending on the vintage and persuasion of the

From "The Impact of Money on an African Subsistence Economy," *The Journal of Economic
History 19* (December 1959) : 491–503. Reprinted by permission of the publisher and the
author. Some footnotes, the bibliographic citations, and the bibliography are omitted.

author of the book one consults, one may find another money use — storage of wealth. In newer books, money is defined as merely the means of unitizing purchasing power, yet behind that definition still lie the standard, the payment, and the exchange uses of money.

It is interesting that on the fairly rare occasions that economists discuss primitive money at all — or at least when they discuss it with any empirical referent — they have discarded one or more of the money uses in framing their definitions. Paul Einzig,[1] to take one example from many, first makes a plea for "elastic definitions," and goes on to point out that different economists have utilized different criteria in their definitions; he then falls into the trap he has been exposing: he excoriates Menger for utilizing only the "medium of exchange" criterion and then himself omits it, utilizing only the standard and payment criteria, thus taking sides in an argument in which there was no real issue.

The answer to these difficulties should be apparent. If we take no more than the three major money uses — payment, standard, and means of exchange — we will find that in many primitive societies as well as some of the ancient empires, one object may serve one money use while quite another object serves another money use. In order to deal with this situation, and to avoid the trap of choosing one of these uses to define "real" money, Karl Polanyi[2] and his associates have labeled as "general-purpose money" any item which serves all three of these primary money uses, while an item which serves only one or two is "special-purpose money." With this distinction in mind, we can see that special-purpose money was very common in pre-contact Africa, but that general-purpose money was rare.

This paper is a brief analysis of the impact of general-purpose money and increase in trade in an African economy which had known only local trade and had used only special-purpose money.

The Tiv are a people, still largely pagan, who live in the Benue Valley in Central Nigeria, among whom I had the good fortune to live and work for well over two years. They are prosperous subsistence farmers and have a highly developed indigenous market in which they exchanged their produce and handicrafts, and through which they carried on local trade. The most distinctive feature about the economy of the Tiv — and it is a feature they share with many, perhaps most, of the pre-monetary peoples — is what can be called a multi-centric economy. Briefly, a multi-centric economy is an economy in which a society's

---

[1] Paul Einzig, *Primitive Money in Its Ethnological, Historical and Economic Aspects* (London: Eyre and Spottiswoode, 1949), pp. 319–26.

[2] Karl Polanyi, "The Economy as Instituted Process," in Karl Polanyi, Conrad M. Arensberg, and Harry W. Pearson, eds., *Trade and Market in the Early Empires* (Glencoe, Ill.: The Free Press and The Falcon's Wing Press, 1957), pp. 264–66.

exchangeable goods fall into two or more mutually exclusive spheres, each marked by different institutionalization and different moral values. In some multi-centric economies these spheres remain distinct, though in most there are more or less institutionalized means of converting wealth from one into wealth in another.

Indigenously there were three spheres in the multi-centric economy of the Tiv. The first of these spheres is that associated with subsistence, which the Tiv called *yiagh*. The commodities in it include all locally produced foodstuffs: the staple yams and cereals, plus all the condiments, vegetable side-dishes, and seasonings, as well as small livestock — chickens, goats, and sheep. It also includes household utensils (mortars, grindstones, calabashes, baskets, and pots), some tools (particularly those used in agriculture), and raw materials for producing any items in the category.

Within this sphere, goods are distributed either by gift giving or through marketing. Traditionally, there was no money of any sort in this sphere — all goods changed hands by barter. There was a highly developed market organization at which people exchanged their produce for their requirements, and in which today traders buy produce in cheap markets and transport it to sell in dearer markets. The morality of this sphere of the economy is the morality of the free and uncontrolled market.

The second sphere of the Tiv economy is one which is in no way associated with markets. The category of goods within this sphere is slaves, cattle, ritual "offices" purchased from the Jukun, that type of large white cloth known as *tugudu*, medicines and magic, and metal rods. One is still entitled to use the present tense in this case, for ideally the category still exists in spite of the fact that metal rods are today very rare, that slavery has been abolished, that European "offices" have replaced Jukun offices and cannot be bought, and that much European medicine has been accepted. Tiv still quote prices of slaves in cows and brass rods, and of cattle in brass rods and *tugudu* cloth. The price of magical rites, as it has been described in the literature, was in terms of *tugudu* cloth or brass rods (though payment might be made in other items); payment for Jukun titles was in cows and slaves, *tugudu* cloths and metal rods.[3]

None of these goods ever entered the market as it was institutionalized in Tivland, even though it might be possible for an economist to find the principle of supply and demand at work in the exchanges which characterized it. The actual shifts of goods took place at ceremonies, at more or less ritualized wealth displays, and on occasions when "doctors"

[3] B. Akiga Sai, *Akiga's Story* (London: International Institute of African Languages and Cultures, 1939), p. 382 and passim.

performed rites and prescribed medicines. Tiv refer to the items and the activities within this sphere by the word *shagba*, which can be roughly translated as prestige.

Within the prestige sphere there was one item which took on all of the money uses and hence can be called a general-purpose currency, though it must be remembered that it was of only a *very limited range*. Brass rods were used as means of exchange *within the sphere*; they also served as a standard of value within it (though not the only one), and as a means of payment. However, this sphere of the economy was tightly sealed off from the subsistence goods and its market. After European contact, brass rods occasionally entered the market, but they did so only as means of payment, not as medium of exchange or as standard of valuation. Because of the complex institutionalization and morality, no one ever sold a slave for food; no one, save in the depths of extremity, ever paid brass rods for domestic goods.

The supreme and unique sphere of exchangeable values for the Tiv contains a single item: rights in human beings other than slaves, particularly rights in women. Even twenty-five years after official abolition of exchange marriage, it is the category of exchange in which Tiv are emotionally most entangled. All exchanges within this category are exchanges of rights in human beings, usually dependent women and children. Its value are expressed in terms of kinship and marriage.

Tiv marriage is an extremely complex subject. Again, economists might find supply and demand principles at work, but Tiv adamantly separate marriage and market. Before the coming of the Europeans all "real" marriages were exchange marriages. In its simplest form, an exchange marriage involves two men exchanging sisters. Actually, this simple form seldom or never occurred. In order for every man to have a ward (*ingol*) to exchange for a wife, small localized agnatic lineages formed ward-sharing groups ("those who eat one Ingol" — *mbaye ingol i mom*). There was an initial "exchange" — or at least, distribution — of wards among the men of this group, so that each man became the guardian (*tien*) of one or more wards. The guardian, then, saw to the marriage of his ward, exchanging her with outsiders for another woman (her "partner" or *ikyar*) who becomes the bride of the guardian or one of his close agnatic kinsmen, or — in some situations — becomes a ward in the ward-sharing group and is exchanged for yet another woman who becomes a wife.

Tiv are, however, extremely practical and sensible people, and they know that successful marriages cannot be made if women are not consulted and if they are not happy. Elopements occurred, and sometimes a woman in exchange was not forthcoming. Therefore, a debt existed from the ward-sharing group of the husband to that of the guardian.

These debts sometimes lagged two or even three generations behind actual exchanges. The simplest way of paying them off was for the eldest daughter of the marriage to return to the ward-sharing group of her mother, as ward, thus cancelling the debt.

Because of its many impracticalities, the system had to be buttressed in several ways in order to work: one way was a provision for "earnest" during the time of the lag, another was to recognize other types of marriage as binding to limited extents. These two elements are somewhat confused with one another, because of the fact that right up until the abolition of exchange marriage in 1927, the inclination was always to treat all non-exchange marriages as if they were "lags" in the completion of exchange marriages.

When lags in exchange occurred, they were usually filled with "earnests" of brass rods, or occasionally, it would seem, of cattle. The brass rods or cattle in such situations were *never* exchange equivalents (*ishe*) for the woman. The only "price" of one woman is another woman.

Although Tiv decline to grant it antiquity, another type of marriage occurred at the time Europeans first met them — it was called "accumulating a woman/wife" (*kem kwase*). It is difficult to tell today just exactly what it consisted in, because the terminology of this union has been adapted to describe the bridewealth marriage that was declared by an administrative fiat of 1927 to be the only legal form.

Kem marriage consisted in acquisition of sexual, domestic and economic rights in a woman — but not the rights to filiate her children to the social group of the husband. Put in another way, in exchange marriage, both rights *in genetricem* (rights to filiate a woman's children) and rights *in uxorem* (sexual, domestic and economic rights in a woman) automatically were acquired by husbands and their lineages. In *kem* marriage, only rights *in uxorem* were acquired. In order to affiliate the *kem* wife's children, additional payments had to be made to the woman's guardians. These payments were for the children, not for the rights *in genetricem* in their mother, which could be acquired only by exchange of equivalent rights in another woman. *Kem* payments were paid in brass rods. However, rights in women had no equivalent or "price" in brass rods or in any other item — save, of course, identical rights in another woman. *Kem* marriage was similar to but showed important differences from bridewealth marriage as it is known in South and East Africa. There rights in women and rights in cattle form a single economic sphere, and could be exchanged directly for one another. Among Tiv, however, conveyance of rights in women necessarily involved direct exchange of another woman. The Tiv custom that approached bridewealth was not an exchange of equivalents, but payment in a medium that was specifically not equivalent.

Thus, within the sphere of exchange marriage there was no item that fulfilled any of the uses of money; when second-best types of marriage were made, payment was in an item which was specifically not used as a standard of value.

That Tiv do conceptualize exchange articles as belonging to different categories, and that they rank the categories on a moral basis, and that most but not all exchanges are limited to one sphere, gives rise to the fact that two different kinds of exchanges may be recognized: exchange of items contained within a single category, and exchanges of items belonging to different categories. For Tiv, these two different types of exchange are marked by separate and distinct moral attitudes.

To maintain this distinction between the two types of exchanges which Tiv mark by different behavior and different values, I shall use separate words. I shall call those exchanges of items within a single category "conveyances" and those exchanges of items from one category to another "conversions." Roughly, conveyances are morally neutral; conversions have a strong moral quality in their rationalization.

Exchanges within a category — particularly that of subsistence, the only one intact today — excite no moral judgments. Exchanges between categories, however, do excite a moral reaction: the man who exchanges lower category goods for higher category goods does not brag about his market luck but about his "strong heart" and his success in life. The man who exchanges high category goods for lower rationalizes his action in terms of high-valued motivation (most often the needs of his kinsmen).

The two institutions most intimately connected with conveyance are markets and marriage. Conveyance in the prestige sphere seems (to the latter-day investigator, at least) to have been less highly institutionalized. It centered on slave dealing, on curing, and on the acquisition of status.

Conversion is a much more complex matter. Conversion depends on the fact that some items of every sphere could, on certain occasions, be used in exchanges in which the return was *not* considered equivalent (*ishe*). Obviously, given the moral ranking of the spheres, such a situation leaves one party to the exchange in a good position, and the other in a bad one. Tiv says that it is "good" to trade food for brass rods, but that it is "bad" to trade brass rods for food, that it is good to trade your cows or brass rods for a wife, but very bad to trade your marriage ward for cows or brass rods.

Seen from the individual's point of view, it is profitable and possible to invest one's wealth if one converts it into a morally superior category: to convert subsistence wealth into prestige wealth and both into women is the aim of the economic endeavor of individual Tiv.

To put it into economists' terms: conversion is the ultimate type of maximization.

We have already examined the marriage system by which a man can convert his brass rods to a wife: he could get a *kem* wife and *kem* her children as they were born. Her daughters, then, could be used as wards in his exchange marriages. It is the desire of every Tiv to "acquire a woman" (*ngoho kwase*) either as wife or ward in some way other than sharing in the ward-sharing group. A wife whom one acquires in any other way is not the concern of one's marriage-ward sharing group because the woman or other property exchanged for her did not belong to the marriage-ward group. The daughters of such a wife are not divided among the members of a man's marriage-ward group, but only among his sons. Such a wife is not only indicative of a man's ability and success financially and personally, but rights in her are the only form of property which is not ethically subject to the demands of his kinsmen.

Conversion from the prestige sphere to the kinship sphere was, thus, fairly common; it consisted in all the forms of marriage save exchange marriage, usually in terms of brass rods.

Conversion from the subsistence sphere to the prestige sphere was also usually in terms of metal rods. They, on occasion, entered the market place as payment. If the owner of the brass rods required an unusually large amount of staples to give a feast, making too heavy a drain on his wives' food supplies, he might buy it with brass rods.

However, brass rods could not possibly have been a general currency. They were not divisible. One could not receive "change" from a brass rod. Moreover, a single rod was worth much more than the usual market purchases for any given day of most Tiv subsistence traders. Although it might be possible to buy chickens with brass rods, one would have to have bought a very large quantity of yams to equal one rod, and to buy an item like pepper with rods would be laughable.

Brass rods, thus, overlapped from the prestige to the subsistence sphere on some occasions, but only on special occasions and for large purchases.

Not only is conversion possible, but it is encouraged — it is, in fact, the behavior which proves a man's worth. Tiv are scornful of a man who is merely rich in subsistence goods (or, today, in money). If, having adequate subsistence, he does not seek prestige in accordance with the old counters, or if he does not strive for more wives, and hence more children, the fault must be personal inadequacy. They also note that they all try to keep a man from making conversions; jealous kinsmen of a rich man will bewitch him and his people by fetishes, in order to make him expend his wealth on sacrifices to repair the fetishes, thus maintaining economic equality. However, once a conversion has been made, demands of kinsmen are not effective — at least, they take a new form.

Therefore, the man who successfully converts his wealth into higher categories is successful — he has a "strong heart." He is both feared and respected.

In this entire process, metal rods hold a pivotal position, and it is not surprising that early administrators considered them money. Originally imported from Europe, they were used as "currency" in some part of southern Nigeria in the slave trade. They are dowels about a quarter of an inch in diameter and some three feet long; they can be made into jewelry, and were used as a source of metal for castings.

Whatever their use elsewhere, brass rods in Tivland had some but not all of the attributes of money. Within the prestige sphere, they were used as a standard of equivalence, and they were a medium of exchange; they were also a mode for storage of wealth, and were used as payment. In short, brass rods were a general-purpose currency *within the prestige sphere*. However, outside of the prestige sphere — markets and marriage were the most active institutions of exchange outside it — brass rods fulfilled only one of these functions of money: payment. We have examined in detail the reasons why equivalency could not exist between brass rods and rights in women, between brass rods and food.

We have, thus, in Tivland, a multi-centric economy of three spheres, and we have a sort of money which was general-purpose money within the limited range of the prestige sphere, and a special-purpose money in the special transactions in which the other spheres overlapped it.

The next question is: what happened to this multi-centric economy and to the morality accompanying it when it felt the impact of the expanding European economy in the nineteenth and early twentieth centuries, and when an all-purpose money of very much greater range was introduced?

The Western impact is not, of course, limited to economic institutions. Administrative organizations, missions and others have been as effective instruments of change as any other.

One of the most startling innovations of the British administration was a general peace. Before the arrival of the British, one did not venture far beyond the area of one's kinsmen or special friends. To do so was to court death or enslavement.

With government police systems and safety, road-building was also begun. Moving about the country has been made both safe and comparatively easy. Peace and the new road network led to both increased trade and a greater number of markets.

Not only has the internal marketing system been perturbed by the introduction of alien institutions, but the economic institutions of the Tiv have in fact been put into touch with world economy. Northern Nigeria, like much of the rest of the colonial world, was originally taken over by trading companies with governing powers. The close linkage of government and trade was evident when taxation was introduced into Tivland. Tax was originally paid in produce, which was transported and sold through Hausa traders, who were government contractors. A few years later, coinage was introduced; taxes were demanded in that medium. It became necessary for Tiv to go into trade or to make their own contract with foreign traders in order to get cash. The trading companies, which had had "canteens" on the Benue for some decades, were quick to cooperate with the government in introducing a "cash crop" which could be bought by the traders in return for cash to pay taxes, and incidentally to buy imported goods. The crop which proved best adapted for this purpose in Tivland was beniseed (*sesamum indicum,*) a crop Tiv already grew in small quantities. Acreage need only be increased and facilities for sale established.

There is still another way in which Tiv economy is linked, through the trading companies, to the economy of the outside world. Not only do the companies buy their cash crops, they also "stake" African traders with imported goods. There is, on the part both of the companies and the government, a desire to build up "native entrepreneurial classes." Imported cloth, enamelware, and ironmongery are generally sold through a network of dependent African traders. Thus, African traders are linked to the companies, and hence into international trade.

Probably no single factor has been so important, however, as the introduction of all-purpose money. Neither introduction of cash crops and taxes nor extended trading has affected the basic congruence between Tiv ideas and their institutionalization to the same extent as has money. With the introduction of money the indigenous ideas of maximization — that is, conversion of all forms of wealth into women and children — no longer leads to the result it once did.

General-purpose money provides a common denominator among all the spheres, thus making the commodities within each expressible in terms of a single standard and hence immediately exchangeable. This new money is misunderstood by Tiv. They use it as a standard of value in the subsistence category, even when — as is often the case — the exchange is direct barter. They use it as a means of payment of bridewealth under the new system, but still refuse to admit that a woman has a "price" or can be valued in the same terms as food. At the same time, it has become something formerly lacking in all save the prestige sphere of Tiv economy — a means of exchange. Tiv have tried to categorize money with the other new imported goods and place them all in a fourth economic sphere, to be ranked morally below subsistence. They have, of course, not been successful in so doing.

What in fact happened was that general-purpose money was introduced to Tivland, where fomerly only special-purpose money had been known.

It is in the nature of a general-purpose money that it standardizes the exchangeability value of every item to a common scale. It is precisely this function which brass rods, a "limited-purpose money" in the old system, did not perform. As we have seen, brass rods were used as a standard in some situations of conveyance in the intermediate or "prestige" category. They were also used as a means of payment (but specifically not as a standard) in some instances of conversion.

In this situation, the early Administrative officers interpreted brass rods as "money," by which they meant a general-purpose money. It became a fairly easy process, in their view, to establish by fiat an exchange rate between brass rods and a new coinage, "withdraw" the rods, and hence "replace" one currency with another. The actual effect, as we have seen, was to introduce a general-purpose currency in place of a limited-purpose money. Today all conversions and most conveyances are made in terms of coinage. Yet Tiv constantly express their distrust of money. This fact, and another — that a single means of exchange has entered all the economic spheres — has broken down the major distinctions among the spheres. Money has created in Tivland a uni-centric economy. Not only is the money a general-purpose money, but it applies to the full range of exchangeable goods.

Thus, when semi-professional traders, using money, began trading in the foodstuffs marketed by women and formerly solely the province of women, the range of the market was very greatly increased and hence the price in Tiv markets is determined by supply and demand far distant from the local producer and consumer. Tiv react to this situation by saying that foreign traders "spoil" their markets. The overlap of marketing and men's long-distance trade in staples also results in truckload after truckload of foodstuffs exported from major Tiv markets every day they meet. Tiv say that food is less plentiful today than it was in the past, though more land is being farmed. Tiv elders deplore this situation and know what is happening, but they do not know just where to fix the blame. In attempts to do something about it, they sometimes announce that no women are to sell any food at all. But when their wives disobey them men do not really feel that they were wrong to have done so. Tiv sometimes discriminate against non-Tiv traders in attempts to stop export of food. In their condemnation of the situation which is depriving them of their food faster than they are able to increase production, Tiv elders always curse money itself. It is money which, as the instrument for selling one's life subsistence, is responsible for the worsened situation — money and the Europeans who brought it.

Of even greater concern to Tiv is the influence money has had on marriage institutions. Today every woman's guardian, in accepting money as bridewealth, feels that he is converting down. Although attempts are made to spend money which is received in bridewealth to acquire brides for one's self and one's sons, it is in the nature of money, Tiv insist, that it is most difficult to accomplish. The good man still spends his bridewealth receipts for brides — but good men are not so numerous as would be desirable. Tiv deplore the fact that they are required to "sell" (*te*) their daughters and "buy" (*yam*) wives. There is no dignity in it since the possibility of making a bridewealth marriage into an exchange marriage has been removed.

With money, thus, the institutionalization of Tiv economy has become uni-centric, even though Tiv still see it with multi-centric values. The single sphere takes many of its characterisitics from the market, so that the new situation can be considered a spread of the market. But throughout these changes in institutionalization, the basic Tiv value of maximization — converting one's wealth into the highest category, women and children — has remained. And in this discrepancy between values and institutions, Tiv have come upon what is to them a paradox, for all that Westerners understand it and are familiar with it. Today it is easy to sell subsistence goods for money to buy prestige articles and women, thereby aggrandizing oneself at a rapid rate. The food so sold is exported, decreasing the amount of subsistence goods available for consumption. On the other hand, the number of women is limited. The result is that bridewealth gets higher: rights in women have entered the market, and since the supply is fixed, the price of women has become inflated.

The frame of reference given me by the organizer of this symposium asked for comments on the effects of increased monetization on trade, on the distribution of wealth and indebtedness. To sum up the situation in these terms, trade has vastly increased with the introduction of general-purpose money but also with the other factors brought by a colonial form of government. At the same time, the market has expanded its range of applicability in the society. The Tiv are, indigenously, a people who valued egalitarian distribution of wealth to the extent that they believe they bewitched one another to whittle down the wealth of one man to the size of that of another. With money, the degree and extent of differentiation by wealth has greatly increased and will probably continue to increase. Finally, money has brought a new form of indebtedness — one which we know, only too well. In the indigenous system, debt took either the form of owing marriage wards and was hence congruent with the kinship system, or else took the form of decreased prestige. There was no debt in the sphere of subsistence because there was no credit there save among kinsmen and neighbors whose activities were aspects of family status, not acts of money-lenders. The introduction of general-purpose money and the concomitant spread of the market has divorced debt from kinship and status and has created the notion of debt in the subsistence sphere divorced from the activities of kinsmen and neighbors.

In short, because of the spread of the market and the introduction of general-purpose money, Tiv economy has become a part of the world economy. It has brought about profound changes in the institutionalization of Tiv society. Money is one of the shatteringly simplifying ideas of all time, and like any other new and compelling idea, it creates its own revolution. The monetary revolution, at least in this part of Africa, is the turn away from the multi-centric economy. Its course may be painful, but there is very little doubt about its outcome.

21

The shrink-wrap solution: Anthropology in business

DAVID W. McCURDY and DONNA F. CARLSON

Americans rarely think of cultural anthropology as a training ground for jobs in business and corporations. They would be surprised to learn that the discipline has been successfully used by corporate managers. In this article, David McCurdy and Donna Carlson describe a case in which a manager, partly trained in ethnographic field methods, used her skills to solve a set of persistent problems that afflicted the company for which she works. The key to her success lay in her use of the concept of culture and the notion of microculture, and in her ability to see her employees' worlds through their eyes.

"But what can I do with anthropology?" a college sophomore asks her advisor. Like a number of other students, she finds anthropology interesting but hard to justify as a major. She wishes to continue taking anthropology courses, but they seem remote from the practical world. Anthropology is concerned with a variety of fascinating peoples, but many of these groups live in distant places and in ways that seem to have little bearing on life in modern America. How can her growing knowledge about them help her get a job?

In addition, her parents would question her judgment if she declares an anthropology major. They didn't take anthropology when they went to college and they still think that members of the discipline dig up bones and ancient temples, or live with curious remote primitive tribes. After all, wouldn't a major in computer science, economics, political science, biology, or journalism make more sense? Despite their feelings, she wonders if anthropology might not have some practical application.

There have always been jobs in anthropology, but most of them were found traditionally in academic settings. Before World War II there were few anthropologists and very few anthropology departments in institutions of higher learning. The small number of students who persisted in the discipline occasionally found jobs in colleges and universities, museums, or government service where their specialized knowledge about particular cultures and peoples was put to use.

World War II changed this picture to some extent in the United States. For the first time, anthropologists — most of them employed in colleges and universities — were drafted into government service. They were asked to write down what they knew about the cultures of other peoples and nations with whom the United States was at war or in whose territories fighting would take place. Their work was to be used to train the troops destined to enter these lands.

This first burst of applied anthropology was followed closely by a second, which was brought about by growing tensions between the United States and Russia. This cold war gave a significant boost to both applied and academic anthropology as international concerns grew and the U.S. government attempted to help so-called underdeveloped nations: it was anthropologists who could find out more about the people the government wished to influence. Hundreds of colleges and universities added anthropology programs and hired anthropologists for the first time. Interest in the discipline soared, and undergraduate majors in the 1950s and 60s could look forward with confidence to academic careers following graduate training.

But the picture changed after the Vietnam War. The country turned away from internationalism as Americans recoiled from the conflict. The American economy slowed; recession struck seriously at least twice. Anthropology suddenly found itself with a host of new graduate schools turning out large numbers of trained anthropologists. Now, however, just as more graduates appeared, academic jobs disappeared. Some anthropologists dropped out of the discipline to work in unrelated fields; others, however, went into the marketplace and, with some improvisation, managed to introduce anthropology into new work settings. Hundreds became consultants. Others found work in medicine and health care, government, and a variety of service organizations. And surprisingly, a growing number found a home in business, in a corporate world that just a few years earlier would have held little attraction for them. It is their ability to show that cultural anthropology has business application that is beginning to open up a potential source of employment for larger numbers of anthropology graduates.

But what does anthropology have to do with the business world? The answer lies not so much in the special knowledge of particular societies and cultures that many anthropologists possess, but in the way anthropologists conduct research and analysis. Whereas other social sciences moved toward *quantitative* methods of research (testing theory by using survey questionnaires and repetitive observations), anthropologists most often conducted *qualitative* research. Called "the ethnographic approach," this method yields a highly detailed account of the culture of a particular group. Its primary purpose is the discovery of what is really going on, not the testing of theory, although ethnographic data can be used for that too. It is this qualitative approach that has turned out to be most valuable in the world of business and industry. In the pages that follow, we shall illustrate this point by looking at a case where a corporate manager, trained as a cultural anthropologist and ethnographer when she was an undergraduate, used her ethnographic ability to solve a persistent problem that had plagued a division of the company in which she worked. As we shall see, the key to the solution lay in her knowledge about culture, microculture, ethnography, and systems analysis.

THE PROBLEM

The manager, whom we will name Susan, works for a large multinational corporation called UTC (not the company's real name). UTC is divided into a number of parts, including divisions, subdivisions, departments, and other units designed to facilitate its highly varied business enterprises. The company is well diversified, engaging in research, manufacturing, and customer services. In addition to serving a wide cross section of public and private customers, it also works on a variety of government contracts for both military and nonmilitary agencies.

One of its divisions is educational. UTC has established a large number of customer outlets in cities throughout the United States, forming what it calls its "customer outlet network." They are staffed by educational personnel who are trained to offer a variety of special courses and enrichment programs. These courses and programs are marketed mainly to other businesses or to individuals who desire special training or practical information. For example, a small company might have UTC provide its employees with computer training, including instruction on hardware, programming, computer languages, and computer program applications. Another company might ask for instruction on effective management or accounting procedures. The outlets' courses for individuals include such topics as "how to get a job," "writing a resume," or "enlarging your own business."

To organize and manage its customer outlet network, UTC has created a special division. The division office is located at the corporate headquarters and is responsible for developing new courses, improving old ones, training customer outlet personnel, and marketing customer outlet courses, or "products" as they are called inside the company. The division also has departments that develop, produce, and distribute the special learning materials used in customer outlet courses. These include books, pamphlets, video- and audiotapes and -cassettes, slides, overlays, and films. These materials are stored in a warehouse and are shipped, as they are ordered, to customer outlets around the country.

It is with this division that Susan first worked as a manager. She had started her career with the company in a small section of the division that designed various program materials. She had worked her way into management, holding a series of increasingly important positions. She was then asked to take over the management of a part of the division that had the manufacture, storage, and shipment of learning materials as one of its responsibilities.

But there was a catch. She was given this new management position with instructions to solve a persistent, although vaguely defined, problem. "Improve the service," they had told her, and "get control of the warehouse inventory." In this case, "service" meant the process of filling orders sent in by customer outlets for various materials stored in the warehouse. The admonition to improve the service seemed to indicate that service was poor, but all she was told about the situation was that customer outlet personnel complained about the service; she did not know exactly why or what "poor" meant.

In addition, inventory was "out of control." Later she was to discover the extent of the difficulty.

> We had a problem with inventory. The computer would say we had two hundred of some kind of book in stock, yet it was back ordered because there was nothing on the shelf. We were supposed to have the book but physically there was nothing there. I'm going, "Uh, we have a small problem. The computer never lies, like your bank statement, so why don't we have the books?"

If inventory was difficult to manage, so were the warehouse employees. They were described by another manager as "a bunch of knuckle draggers. All they care about is getting their money. They are lazy and don't last long at the job." Strangely, the company did not view the actions of the warehouse workers as a major problem. Only later did Susan tie in poor morale in the warehouse with the other problems she had been given to solve.

MANAGEMENT BY DEFENSE

Although Susan would take the ethnographic approach to management problems, that was not what many other managers did. They took a defensive stance, a position opposite to the discovery procedures of ethnography. Their major concern — like that of many people in positions of leadership and responsibility — was to protect their authority and their ability to manage and to get things done. Indeed, Susan also shared this need. But their solution to maintaining their position was different from hers. For them, claiming ignorance and asking questions — the hallmark of the ethnographic approach — is a sign of weakness. Instead of discovering what is going on when they take on a new management assignment, they often impose new work rules and procedures. Employees learn to fear the arrival of new managers because their appearance usually means a host of new, unrealistic demands. They respond by hiding what they actually do, withholding information that would be useful to the manager. Usually, everyone's performance suffers.

Poor performance leads to elaborate excuses as managers attempt to blame the troubles on others. Susan described this tendency.

> When I came into the new job, this other manager said, "Guess what? You have got a warehouse. You are now the proud owner of a forklift and a bunch of knuckle draggers." And I thought, management's perception of those people is very low. They are treating them as dispensable, that you can't do anything with them. They say the workers don't have any career motives. They don't care if they do a good job. You have to force them to do anything. You can't motivate them. It's only a warehouse, other managers were saying. You can't really do that much about the problems there so why don't you just sort of try to keep it under control.

Other managers diminished the importance of the problem itself. It was not "poor service" that was the trouble. The warehouse was doing the best it could with what it had. It was just that the customers — the staff at the customer outlets — were complainers. As Susan noted:

> The people providing the service thought that outlet staff were complainers. They said, "Staff complain about everything. But it can't be that way. We have checked it all out and it isn't that bad."

Making excuses and blaming others leads to low morale and a depressed self-image. Problems essentially are pushed aside in favor of a "let's just get by" philosophy.

ETHNOGRAPHIC MANAGEMENT

By contrast, managers take the offensive when they use ethnographic techniques. That is what Susan did when she assumed her new managerial assignment over the learning materials manufacturing and distribution system. To understand what the ethnographic approach means, however, we must first look briefly at what anthropologists do when they conduct ethnographic field research. Our discussion necessarily involves a look at the concepts of culture and microculture as well as ethnography. For as we will shortly point out, companies have cultures of their own, a point that has recently received national attention; but more importantly for the problem we are describing here, companies are normally divided into subgroups, each with its own microculture. It is these cultures and microcultures that anthropologically trained managers can study ethnographically, just as fieldworkers might investigate the culture of a !Kung band living in the Kalahari Desert of West Africa or the Gypsies living in San Francisco.

Ethnography refers to the process of discovering and describing culture, so it is important to discuss this general and often elusive concept. There are numerous definitions of culture, each stressing particular sets of attributes. The definition we employ here is especially appropriate for ethnographic field work. We may define culture as the acquired knowledge that people use to generate behavior and interpret experience. In growing up, one learns a system of cultural knowledge appropriate to the group. For example, an American child learns to chew with a closed mouth because that is the cultural rule. The child's parents interpret open-mouthed chewing as an infraction and tell the child to chew "properly." A person uses such cultural knowledge throughout life to guide actions and to give meaning to surroundings.

Because culture is learned, and because people can easily generate new cultural knowledge as they adapt to other people and things, human behavior and perceptions can vary dramatically from one group to another. In India, for example, children learn to chew "properly" with their mouths open. Their cultural worlds are quite different from the ones found in the United States.

Cultures are associated with groups of people. Traditionally, anthropologists associated culture with relatively distinctive ethnic groups. Culture referred to the whole life-way of a society and particular cultures could be named. Anthropologists talked of German culture, Ibo culture, and Bhil culture. Culture was everything that was distinctive about the group.

Culture is still applied in this manner today, but with the advent of complex societies and a growing interest among anthropologists in understanding them, the culture concept has also been used in a more limited way. Complex societies such as our own are composed of thousands of groups. Members of these groups usually share the national culture, including a language and a huge inventory of knowledge for doing things, but the groups themselves have specific cultures of their own. For example, if you were to walk into the regional office of a stock brokerage firm, you would hear the people there talking an apparently foreign language. You might stand in the "bull pen," listen to brokers make "cold calls," "sell short," "negotiate a waffle," or get ready to go to a "dog and pony show." The fact that events such as this feel strange when you first encounter them is strong evidence to support the notion that you don't yet know the culture that organizes them. We call such specialized groups "microcultures."

We are surrounded by microcultures, participating in a few, encountering many others. Our family has a microculture. So may our neighborhood, our college, and even our dormitory floor. The waitress who serves us lunch at the corner restaurant shares a culture with her coworkers. So do bank tellers at our local savings and loan. Kin, occupational groups, and recreational associations each tend to display special microcultures. Such cultures can be, and now often are, studied by anthropologists interested in understanding life in complex American society.

The concept of microculture is essential to Susan as she begins to attack management problems at UTC because she assumes that conflict between different microcultural groups is most likely at the bottom of the difficulty. One microculture she could focus on is UTC company culture. She knows, for example, that there are a variety of rules and expectations — written and unwritten — for how things should be done at the company. She must dress in her "corporates," for example, consisting of a neutral colored suit, bow tie, stockings, and conservative shoes. UTC also espouses values about the way employees should be treated, how people are supposed to feel about company products, and a variety of other things that set that particular organization apart from other businesses.

But the specific problems that afflicted the departments under Susan's jurisdiction had little to do with UTC's corporate culture. They seemed rather to be the result of misunderstanding and misconnection between two units, the warehouse and the customer outlets. Each had its own microculture. Each could be investigated to discover any information that might lead to a solution of the problems she had been given.

Such investigation would depend on the extent of Susan's ethnographic training. As an undergraduate in college, she had learned how to conduct ethnographic interviews, observe behavior, and analyze and interpret data. She was not a professional anthropologist, but she felt she was a good enough ethnographer to discover some relevant aspects of microcultures at UTC.

Ethnography is the process of discovering and describing a culture. For example, an anthropologist who travels to India to conduct a study of village culture will use ethnographic techniques. The anthropologist will move into a community, occupy a house, watch people's daily routines, attend rituals, and spend hours interviewing informants. The goal is to discover a detailed picture of what is going on by seeing village culture through the eyes of informants. The anthropologist wants the insider's perspective. Villagers become teachers, patiently explaining different aspects of their culture, praising the anthropologist for acting correctly and appearing to understand, laughing when the anthropologist makes mistakes or seems confused. When the anthropologist knows what to do and can explain in local terms what is going on or what is likely to happen, real progress has been made. The clearest evidence of such progress is if informants say, "You are almost human now," or "You are beginning to talk just like us."

The greatest enemy of good ethnography is the preconceived notion. Anthropologists do not conduct ethnographic research by telling informants what they are like based on earlier views of them. They teach the anthropologist how to see their world: the anthropologist does not tell them what their world should really be like. All too often in business, a new manager will take over a department and begin to impose changes on its personnel to fit a preconceived perception of them. The fact that the manager's efforts are likely to fail makes sense in light of this ignorance. The manager doesn't know their microculture. Nor have they been asked about it.

But can a corporate manager really do ethnography? After all, managers have positions of authority to maintain, as we noted earlier. It is all right for professional anthropologists to enter the field and act ignorant; they don't have a position to maintain and they don't have to continue to live with their informants. The key to the problem appears to be the "grace period." Most managers are given one by their employees when they are new on the job. A new manager cannot be expected to know everything. It is permissible to ask basic questions. The grace period may last only a month or two, but it is usually long enough to find out valuable information.

This is the opportunity that Susan saw as she assumed direction of the warehouse distribution system. As she described it:

> I could use the first month, actually the first six weeks, to find out what was going on, to act dumb and find out what people actually did and why. I talked to end customers. I talked to salespeople, people who were

trying to sell things to help customer outlets with their needs. I talked to coordinators at headquarters staff who were trying to help all these customer outlets do their jobs and listened to what kinds of complaints they had heard. I talked to the customer outlet people and the guys in the warehouse. I had this six-week grace period where I could go in and say, "I don't know anything about this. If you were in my position, what would you do, or what would make the biggest difference, and why would it make a difference?" You want to find out what the world they are operating in is like. What do they value. And people were excited because I was asking and listening and, by God, intending to do something about it instead of just disappearing again.

As we shall see shortly, Susan's approach to the problem worked. But it also resulted in an unexpected bonus. Her ethnographic approach symbolized unexpected interest and concern to her employees. That, combined with realistic management, gave her a position of respect and authority. Their feelings for her were expressed by one warehouse worker when he said:

When she [Susan] was going to be transferred to another job, we gave her a party. We took her to this country-and-western place and we all got to dance with the boss. We told her that she was the first manager who ever tried to understand what it was like to work in the warehouse. We thought she would come in like the other managers and make a lot of changes that didn't make sense. But she didn't. She made it work better for us.

PROBLEMS AND CAUSES

An immediate benefit of her ethnographic enquiry was a much clearer view of what poor service meant to customer outlet personnel. Susan discovered that learning materials, such as books and cassettes, took too long to arrive after they were ordered. Worse, material did not arrive in the correct quantities. Sometimes there would be too many items, but more often there were too few, a particularly galling discrepancy since customer outlets were charged for what they ordered, not what they received. Books also arrived in poor condition, their covers ripped or scratched, edges frayed, and ends gouged and dented. This, too, bothered customer outlet staff because they were often visited by potential customers who were not impressed by the poor condition of their supplies. Shortages and scruffy books did nothing to retain regular customers either.

The causes of these problems and the difficulties with warehouse inventory also emerged from ethnographic enquiry. Susan discovered, for example, that most customer outlets operated in large cities, where often they were housed in tall buildings. Materials shipped to their office address often ended up sitting in ground-level lobbies, because few of the buildings had receiving docks or facilities. Books and other items also arrived in large boxes, weighing up to 100 pounds. Outlet staff, most of whom were women, had to go down to the lobby, open those boxes that were too heavy for them to carry, and haul armloads of supplies up the elevator to the office. Not only was this time-consuming, but customer outlet staff felt it was beneath their dignity to do such work. They were educated specialists, after all.

The poor condition of the books was also readily explained. By packing items loosely in such large boxes, warehouse workers ensured trouble in transit. Books rattled around with ease, smashing into each other and the side of the box, resulting in torn covers and frayed edges. Clearly no one had designed the packing and shipping process with customer outlet staff in mind.

The process, of course, originated in the central warehouse, and here as well, ethnographic data yielded interesting information about the causes of the problem. Susan learned, for example, how materials were stored in loose stacks on the warehouse shelves. When orders, usually sent through the mail, arrived at the warehouse, they were placed in a pile and filled in turn (although there were times when special preference was given to some customer outlets). A warehouse employee filled an order by first checking it against the stock recorded by the computer, then by going to the appropriate shelves and picking the items by hand. Items were packed in the large boxes and addressed to customer outlets. With the order complete, the employee was supposed to enter the number of items picked and shipped in the computer so that inventory would be up to date.

But, Susan discovered, workers in the warehouse were under pressure to work quickly. They often fell behind because materials the computer said were in stock were not there, and because picking by hand took so long. Their solution to the problem of speed resulted in a procedure that even further confused company records.

> Most of the people in the warehouse didn't try to count well. People were looking at the books on the shelves and were going, "Eh, that looks like about the right number. You want ten? Gee, that looks like about ten." Most of the time the numbers they shipped were wrong.

The causes of inaccurate amounts in shipping were thus revealed. Later, Susan discovered that books also disappeared in customer outlet building lobbies. While staff members carried some of the materials upstairs, people passing by the open boxes helped themselves.

Other problems with inventory also became clear. UTC employees, who sometimes walked through the warehouse, would often pick up interesting materials from the loosely stacked shelves. More importantly, rushed workers often neglected to update records in the computer.

THE SHRINK-WRAP SOLUTION

The detailed discovery of the nature and causes of service and inventory problems suggested a relatively painless solution to Susan. If she had taken a defensive management position and failed to learn the insider's points of view, she might have resorted to more usual remedies that were impractical and unworkable. Worker retraining is a common answer to corporate difficulties, but it is difficult to accomplish and often fails. Pay incentives, punishments, and motivation enhancements such as prizes and quotas are also frequently tried. But they tend not to work because they don't address fundamental causes.

Shrink-wrapping books and other materials did. Shrink-wraping is a packaging device that emerged a few years ago. Clear plastic sheeting is placed around items to be packaged, then through a rapid heating and cooling process, shrunk into a tight covering. The plastic molds itself like a tight skin around the things it contains, preventing any internal movement or external contamination. Susan described her decision.

> I decided to have the books shrink-wrapped. For a few cents more, before the books ever arrived in the warehouse, I had them shrink-wrapped in quantities of five and ten. I made it part of the contract with the people who produced the books for us.

On the first day that shrink-wrapped books arrived at the warehouse, Susan discovered that they were immediately unwrapped by workers who thought a new impediment had been placed in their way. Told to stack them in wrapped bundles, the positive effect of shrink-wrapping soon became apparent. For example, most customer outlets ordered books in units of fives and tens. Warehouse personnel could now easily count out orders in fives and tens, instead of having to count each book or estimate numbers in piles. Suddenly, orders filled at the warehouse contained the correct number of items.

Employees were also able to work more quickly, since they no longer had to count each book. Orders were filled faster, pleasing customer outlet staff, and warehouse employees no longer felt the pressure of time so intensely. Shrink-wrapped materials also travelled more securely. Books, protected by their plastic covering, arrived in good condition, again delighting the personnel at customer outlets.

Susan also changed the way materials were shipped, based on what she had learned from talking to employees. She limited the maximum size of shipments to 25 pounds by using smaller boxes. She also had packages marked "inside delivery" so that deliverymen would carry the materials directly to the customer outlet offices. If they failed to do so, boxes were light enough to carry upstairs. No longer would items be lost in skyscraper lobbies.

Inventory control became more effective. Because they could package and ship materials more quickly, the workers in the warehouse had enough time to enter the size and nature of shipments in the computer. Other UTC employees no longer walked off with books from the warehouse, because the shrink-wrapped bundles were larger and more conspicuous, and because taking five or ten books is more like stealing than "borrowing" one.

Finally, the improved service dramatically changed morale in the division. Customer outlet staff members, with their new and improved service, felt that finally someone had cared about them. They were more positive and they let people at corporate headquarters know about their feelings. "What's happening down there?" they asked. "The guys in the warehouse must be taking vitamins."

Morale soared in the warehouse. For the first time, other people liked the service workers there provided. Turnover decreased as pride in their work rose. They began to care more about the job, working faster with greater care. Managers who had previously given up on the "knuckle draggers" now asked openly about what had gotten into them.

Interestingly, Susan's superiors didn't really understand how she had worked this miracle. They simply know that what she did worked.

Susan believes the ethnographic approach is the key. She has managers who work for her read anthropology, especially books on ethnography, and she insists that they "find out what is going on."

Conclusion

We have suggested that studying anthropology gives students a special skill — an ethnographic perspective marked by an ability to observe and listen that we believe is especially useful for managers. We feel that anthropological training, with exposure to the full range of human variation and often with ethnographic field experience, enables students to see behavior from its actors' point of view. This is the ability that managers can apply to problems encountered in large, multicultural groups. In short, specific knowledge of particular peoples and cultures will not usually lead anthropology students to find jobs; it is the basic way of seeing and finding out about people that counts. This view of education can be extended to other disciplines as well. Although some students find jobs that require them to know and use the specific content of their course work, few find work closely related to the detailed subject matter of their major discipline. We know of a historian who is a bank president, a geologist who is a buildings and grounds supervisor, and an engineer who is a professional musician. Also, for thousands upon thousands of occupations no direct academic training is offered at all. The basic skills learned during the college career are a key to finding and holding such jobs.

A special problem for those who take anthropology is public ignorance. Certainly most people expect anthropology students to have some experience reading, writing, and analyzing data, all important skills for later life. But many can't imagine that studying diverse cultures gives anthropologists a special ethnographic perspective distinguishing them from graduates in other fields. Times are changing, though. More and more people have taken anthropology courses and recognize the discipline's utility: more professional anthropologists are finding work outside academia, and businesses have discovered the concept of culture and recognize their growing need for qualitative information. Above all, their ability to discover culture and conduct qualitative research will make anthropologists attractive to corporations and other complex groups in the future.

22

Young traders of northern Nigeria
ENID SCHILDKROUT

Economic systems shape family relations in every society. Among the Bhils of India, for example, entire families share agricultural work and other activities such as herding and the collection of forest produce. The result is a large, cooperative domestic unit. In the United States, on the other hand, people usually work at separate jobs for cash. The result is smaller, more easily fractured family units. In this article, Enid Schildkrout describes an unusual situation in which the household structure of the Hausa living in northern Nigeria partly depends on the economic activities of children. Because they are Muslims and constrained by the immobility of purdah, Hausa women can only take an active commercial role through the efforts of their children. Children can travel freely where women cannot, trading goods made by their female relatives and running errands for food and raw materials. This system may break down, however, if newly built Western-style schools rob women of their young helpers.

Thirty years ago, Erik Erikson wrote that "the fashionable insistence on dramatizing the dependence of children on adults often blinds us to the dependence of the older generation on the younger one." As a psychoanalyst, Erikson was referring mainly to the emotional bonds between parents and children, but his observation is a reminder that in many parts of the world, adults depend on children in quite concrete ways. In northern Nigeria, children with trays balanced on their heads, carrying and selling a variety of goods for their mothers or themselves, are a common sight in villages and towns. Among the Muslim Hausa, aside from being a useful educational experience, this children's trade,

With permission from *Natural History*, Vol. 90, No. 6; Copyright the American Museum of Natural History, 1981.

as well as children's performance of household chores and errands, complements the activity of adults and is socially and economically significant.

Children's services are especially important to married Hausa women, who, in accordance with Islamic practices, live in purdah, or seclusion. In Nigeria, purdah is represented not so much by the wearing of the veil but by the mud-brick walls surrounding every house or compound and by the absence of women in the markets and the streets. Women could not carry out their domestic responsibilities, not to mention their many income-earning enterprises, without the help of children, who are free from the rigid sexual segregation that so restricts adults. Except for elderly women, only children can move in and out of their own and other people's houses without violating the rules of purdah. Even children under three years of age are sent on short errands, for example, to buy things for their mothers.

Hausa-speaking people are found throughout West Africa and constitute the largest ethnic group in northern Nigeria, where they number over eighteen million. Their adherence to Islam is a legacy of the centuries during which Arabs came from the north to trade goods of North African and European manufacture. The majority of the Hausa are farmers, but markets and large commercial cities have existed in northern Nigeria since long before the period of British colonial rule. The city of Kano, for example, which was a major emporium for the trans-Saharan caravan trade, dates back to the eighth century. Today it has a population of about one million.

Binta is an eleven-year-old girl who lives in Kano, in a mud-brick house that has piped water, but no electricity. The household includes her father and mother, her three brothers, her father's second wife and her three children, and a foster child, who is the daughter of one of Binta's cousins. By Kano standards, it is a middle-income family. Binta's father sells shoes, and her mother cooks and sells bean cakes and *tuwo*, the stiff porridge made of guinea corn (*Sorghum vulgare*), which is the Hausa staple. Binta described for me one day's round of activities, which began very early when she arose to start trading.

"After I woke up, I said my prayers and ate breakfast. Then I went outside the house to sell the bean cakes my mother makes every morning. Soon my mother called me in and asked me to take more bean cakes around town to sell; she spoke to me about making an effort to sell as much as I usually do. I sold forty-eight bean cakes at one kobo each [one kobo is worth one and a half cents]. After I returned home, some people came to buy more cakes from me. Then I went out for a second round of trading before setting out for Arabic school. I study the Koran there every morning from eight to nine.

"When school was over, I washed and prepared to sell *tuwo*. First my mother sent me to another neighborhood to gather the customers' empty bowls. I also collected the money from our regular customers. My mother put the *tuwo* in the bowls and told me the amount of money to collect for each. Then I delivered them to the customers.

"On my way home, a man in the street, whom I know, sent me on an errand to buy him fifteen kobo worth of food; he gave me a reward of one kobo. I then sold some more *tuwo* outside our house by standing there and shouting for customers. When the *tuwo* was finished, I was sent to another house to buy some guinea corn, and one of the women there asked me to bring her one of my mother's big pots. The pot was too heavy for me to carry, but finally one of my brothers helped me take it to her.

"When I returned, my mother was busy pounding some grain, and she sent me out to have some locust bean seeds pounded. She then sent me to pick up three bowls of pounded guinea corn, and she gave me money to take to the woman who had pounded it. The woman told me to remind my mother that she still owed money from the day before.

"When I came home I was sent out to trade again, this time with salt, bouillon cubes, and laundry detergent in small packets. Afterward I prepared some pancakes using ingredients I bought myself — ten kobo worth of flour, one kobo worth of salt, five kobo worth of palm oil, and ten kobo worth of firewood. I took this food outside to sell it to children.

"My mother then gave me a calabash of guinea corn to take for grinding; my younger sister also gave me two calabashes of corn to take. The man who ran the grinding machine advised me that I should not carry such a large load, so I made two trips on the way back. He gave me and my younger brothers, who accompanied me, one kobo each.

"I was then told to take a bath, which I did. After that I was sent to visit a sick relative who was in the hospital. On the way I met a friend, and we took the bus together. I also bought some cheese at the market for five kobo. I met another friend on the way home, and she bought some fish near the market for ten kobo and gave me some. I played on the way to the hospital. When I got home, I found the women of the house preparing a meal. One of them was already eating, and I was invited to eat with her.

"After nightfall, I was sent to take some spices for pounding, and I wasted a lot of time there. The other children and I went to a place where some fruits and vegetables are sold along the street. We bought vegetables for soup for fifty kobo, as my mother had asked me to do. By the time I got home it was late, so I went to sleep."

Binta's many responsibilities are typical for a girl her age. Like many women, Binta's mother relies upon her children in carrying out an occupation at home. Although purdah implies that a woman will be supported by her husband and need not work, most Hausa women do work, keeping their incomes distinct from the household budget. Women usually cook one main meal a day and purchase their other meals from other women. In this way they are able to use their time earning a living instead of performing only unpaid domestic labor.

Among the Hausa, men and women spend relatively little time together, eating separately and, except in certain ritual contexts, rarely doing the same things. Differences in gender are not as important among children, however. In fact, it is precisely because children's activities are not rigidly defined by sex that they are able to move between the world of women, centered in the inner courtyard of the house, and the world of men, whose activities take place mainly outside the home. Children of both sexes care for younger children, go to the market, and help their mothers cook.

Both boys and girls do trading, although it is more common for girls. From the age of about five until marriage, which is very often at about age twelve for girls, many children like Binta spend part of every day selling such things as fruits, vegetables, and nuts; bouillon cubes, bread, and small packages of detergent, sugar, or salt; and bowls of steaming rice or *tuwo*. If a woman embroiders, children buy the thread and later take the finished product to the client or to an agent who sells it.

Women in purdah frequently change their occupations depending on the availability of child helpers. In Kano, women often trade in commodities that can be sold in small quantities, such as various kinds of cooked food. Sewing, embroidery, mat weaving, and other craft activities (including, until recently, spinning) are less remunerative occupations, and women pursue them when they have fewer children around to help. Unlike the situation common in the United States, where children tend to hamper a woman's ability to earn money, the Hausa woman finds it difficult to earn income without children's help. Often, if a woman has no children of her own, a relative's child will come to live with her.

Child care is another service children perform that benefits women. It enables mothers to devote themselves to their young infants, whom they carry on their backs until the age of weaning, between one and two. Even though women are always at home, they specifically delegate the care of young children to older ones. The toddler moves from the mother's back into a group of older children, who take the responsibility very seriously. Until they are old enough, children do not pick up infants or very young children, but by the age of nine, both boys and girls bathe

young children, play with them, and take them on errands. The older
children do a great deal of direct and indirect teaching of younger ones.
As soon as they can walk, younger children accompany their older
siblings to Arabic school. There the children sit with their agemates, and
the teacher gives them lessons according to their ability.

Much of a child's activity is directed toward helping his or her
parents, but other relatives — grandparents, aunts, uncles, and step-
mothers — and adults living in the same house as servants or tenants
may call on a child for limited tasks without asking permission of the
parents. Like other Muslims, Hausa men may have up to four wives,
and these women freely call on each other's children to perform household chores. Even strangers in the street sometimes ask a child to do
an errand, such as delivering a message, particularly if the chore requires
entering a house to which the adult does not have access. The child will
be rewarded with a small amount of money or food.

Adults other than parents also reprimand children, who are taught
very early to obey the orders of grownups. Without ever directly refusing
to obey a command, however, children do devise numerous strategies
of noncompliance, such as claiming that another adult has already co-
opted their time or simply leaving the scene and ignoring the command.
Given children's greater mobility, there is little an adult can do to enforce
compliance.

Besides working on behalf of adults, children also participate in a
"children's economy." Children have their own money — from school
allowances given to them daily for the purchase of snacks, from gifts,
from work they may have done, and even from their own investments.
For example, boys make toys for sale, and they rent out valued property,
such as slide viewers or bicycles. Just as women distinguish their own
enterprises from the labor they do as wives, children regard the work
they do for themselves differently from the work they do on behalf of
their mothers. When Binta cooks food for sale, using materials she has
purchased with her own money, the profits are entirely her own, although she may hand the money over to her mother for safekeeping.

Many girls begin to practice cooking by the age of ten. They do
not actually prepare the family meals, for this heavy and tedious work
is primarily the wives' responsibility. But they do carry out related chores,
such as taking vegetables out for grinding, sifting flour, and washing
bowls. Many also cook food for sale on their own. With initial help from
their mothers or other adult female relatives, who may give them a
cooking pot, charcoal, or a small stove, children purchase small amounts
of ingredients and prepare various snacks. Since they sell their products
for less than the adult women do, and since the quantities are very

small, their customers are mainly children. Child entrepreneurs even extend credit to other children.

Aisha is a ten-year-old girl who was notoriously unsuccessful as a trader. She disliked trading and regularly lost her mother's investment. Disgusted, her mother finally gave her a bit of charcoal, some flour and oil, and a small pot. Aisha set up a little stove outside her house and began making small pancakes, which she sold to very young children. In three months she managed to make enough to buy a new dress, and in a year she bought a pair of shoes. She had clearly chosen her occupation after some unhappy trials at street trading.

In the poorest families, as in Aisha's, the profit from children's work goes toward living expenses. This may occur in households that are headed by divorced or widowed women. It is also true for the *al-majirai*, or Arabic students, who often live with their teachers. The proceeds of most children's economic activity, however, go to the expenses of marriage. The income contributes to a girl's dowry and to a boy's bridewealth, both of which are considerable investments.

The girl's dowry includes many brightly painted enamel, brass, and glass bowls, collected years before marriage. These utensils are known as *kayan daki*, or "things of the room." After the wedding they are stacked in a large cupboard beside the girl's bed. Very few of them are used, but they are always proudly displayed, except during the mourning period if the husband dies. *Kayan daki* are not simply for conspicuous display, however. They remain the property of the woman unless she sells them or gives them away. In the case of divorce or financial need, they can provide her most important and immediate source of economic security.

Kayan daki traditionally consisted of brass bowls and beautifully carved calabashes. Today the most common form is painted enamel bowls manufactured in Nigeria or abroad. The styles and designs change frequently, and the cost is continually rising. Among the wealthier urban women and the Western-educated women, other forms of modern household equipment, including electric appliances and china tea sets, are becoming part of the dowry.

The money a young girl earns on her own, as well as the profits she brings home through her trading, are invested by her mother or guardian in *kayan daki* in anticipation of her marriage. Most women put the major part of their income into their daughters' *kayan daki*, as well as helping their sons with marriage expenses. When a woman has many children, the burden can be considerable.

For girls, marriage, which ideally coincides with puberty, marks the transition to adult status. If a girl marries as early as age ten, she does not cook for her husband or have sexual relations with him for some time, but she enters purdah and loses the freedom of childhood. Most girls are married by age fifteen, and for many the transition is a difficult one.

Boys usually do not marry until they are over twenty and are able to support a family. They also need to have raised most of the money to cover the cost of getting married. Between the ages of eight and ten, however, they gradually begin to move away from the confines of the house and to regard it as a female domain. They begin taking their food outside and eating it with friends, and they roam much farther than girls in their play activities. By the onset of puberty, boys have begun to observe the rules of purdah by refraining from entering the houses of all but their closest relatives. In general, especially if they have sisters, older boys spend less time than girls doing chores and errands and more time playing and, in recent years, going to school. Traditionally, many boys left home to live and study with an Arabic teacher. Today many also pursue Western education, sometimes in boarding school. Although the transition to adulthood is less abrupt for boys, childhood for both sexes ends by age twelve to fourteen.

As each generation assumes the responsibilities of adulthood and the restrictions of sexual separation, it must rely on the younger members of society who can work around the purdah system. Recently, however, the introduction of Western education has begun to threaten this traditional arrangement, in part just by altering the pattern of children's lives.

The Nigerian government is now engaged in a massive program to provide Western education to all school-age children. This program has been undertaken for sound economic and political reasons. During the colonial period, which ended in the early 1960s, the British had a "hands-off" policy regarding education in northern Nigeria. They ruled through the Islamic political and judicial hierarchy and supported the many Arabic schools, where the Koran and Islamic law, history, and religion were taught. The British discouraged the introduction of Christian mission schools in the north and spent little on government schools.

The pattern in the rest of Nigeria was very different. In the non-Muslim areas of the country, mission and government schools grew rapidly during the colonial period. The result of this differential policy was the development of vast regional imbalances in the extent and level of Western education in the country. This affected the types of occupational choices open to Nigerians from different regions. Despite a longer tradition of literacy in Arabic in the north, few northerners were eligible for those civil service jobs that required literacy in English, the language of government business. This was one of many issues in the tragic civil war that tore Nigeria apart in the 1960s. The current goal of enrolling all northern children in public schools, which offer training in English and secular subjects, has, therefore, a strong and valid political rationale.

Western education has met a mixed reception in northern Nigeria. While it has been increasingly accepted for boys — as an addition to, not a substitute for, Islamic education — many parents are reluctant to enroll their daughters in primary school. Nevertheless, there are already many more children waiting to get into school than there are classrooms and teachers to accommodate them. If the trend continues, it will almost certainly have important, if unintended, consequences for purdah and the system of child enterprise that supports it.

Children who attend Western school continue to attend Arabic school, and thus are removed from the household for much of the day. For many women this causes considerable difficulty in doing daily housework. It means increased isolation and a curtailment of income-producing activity. It creates a new concern about where to obtain the income for children's marriages. As a result of these practical pressures, the institution of purdah will inevitably be challenged. Also, the school-girl of today may develop new skills and new expectations of her role as a woman that conflict with the traditional ways. As Western education takes hold, today's young traders may witness a dramatic change in Hausa family life — for themselves as adults and for their children.

VIII

Law and politics

Every society faces the problem of controlling the behavior of its individual members. This task is accomplished in part by enculturation. As each individual learns the culture into which he or she is born, individual behavior conforms more and more closely to acceptable patterns. But no society has a perfect record of conformity. People do violate the rules of their culture, and choose to go against accepted ways of behavior. No culture can solve all conflicts of interest. Differences of opinion about the allocation of scarce resources arise and must be settled. Disputes break out and must be settled. It is for these reasons that law and politics are required by all societies.

Politics refers to the cultural processes used for making decisions that affect public policy. A band of hunters and gatherers must decide where to make camp for the night — a public policy decision. Citizens of a large city must decide where a new highway will be constructed — a public policy decision. The decisions differ and the political processes in which decisions are made also differ. But in each case politics is involved. Politics always involves power. Once a public policy decision, such as where to camp for the night, has been made, someone or some group has the power to enforce the decision. If a highway is to run through a residential section of a city and if a legitimate decision has been made, someone has the power to destroy or move the houses in the highway's path. In the selections that follow we see different ways that political power is exercised in widely variant cultures.

When disputes occur between individuals or groups within a society, law is needed. Law refers to processes — whether formal or informal — used for settling disputes. Every culture has means of settling disputes and of getting the people to accept the settlement. The legal and political systems cannot be thought of as separate parts of any culture, except for analytical purposes. In practice, both are backed by legitimate power and authority, and in many instances the two systems operate together. As the following selections will demonstrate, politics and law, while having similar functions from one society to the next, appear in a great variety of forms.

23

Beating the drunk charge

JAMES P. SPRADLEY

*In the urban American court studied in the following article, nearly
12,000 men are charged each year with public drunkenness. Though
many post bail and go free, most of the poor appear in court and
place themselves at the mercy of the judge. They are not entirely des-
titute, however, and have an elaborate set of strategies for "beating
the drunk charge." James Spradley analyzes these strategies, shows
their differential effectiveness, and demonstrates how they reflect specific values of American culture.*

It could be Miami, New York, Chicago, Minneapolis, Denver, Los An-
geles, Seattle, or any other American city. The criminal court may be in
the basement of a massive public building constructed at the turn of the
century, or high above the city in a modern skyscraper. The judges who
hear the never-ending list of cases may be veterans of the bench or men
whose memories of law school are fresh and clear. But one scene does
not change. Each weekday morning a group of unshaven men file into
court with crestfallen faces, wrinkled clothing, and bloodshot eyes. They
stand before the prosecuting attorney and hear him say, "You have been
charged with public drunkenness, how do you plead?"

The most staggering problem of law and order in America today
is public drunkenness. In 1968 the F.B.I. reported that one and a half
million arrests for this crime made up nearly one third of all arrests.
This means that every twenty seconds another person is arrested and
charged with being drunk in public. During 1967, in Seattle, Washington, 51 percent of all arrests and 65 percent of all cases that appeared
in the criminal court were for intoxication. In that same year the chief

of police stated, "As a public official I have no choice. Whether alcoholism is a disease or not would not affect my official position. Drunkenness is a crime. So we must enforce the law by arresting people. We
know in the Police Department that probably right at this moment there
are more than two hundred men in the city jail serving sentences for
drunkenness who have never posed any threat to the community in any
fashion at all."

Who are these men that are repeatedly arrested for drunkenness?
Who are the ones who spend much of their lives in jail for their public
behavior? The first task in this study was to discover how these men
identified themselves. This was necessary because the police, courts,
social scientists, and most citizens see them as criminals, homeless men,
derelicts, and bums who have lost the ability to organize their behavior
in the pursuit of goals. The word these men used to identify their subcultural membership was the term *tramp*. There were several different
kinds of tramps recognized by informants; for example, a "mission stiff"
is a tramp who frequents the skid-road missions, while a "rubber tramp"
travels about in his own car. This category system constitutes one of the
major social identity domains in the subculture.

Tramps have other ways to conceptualize their identity when they
"make the bucket," or are incarcerated. As an inmate in jail one is either
a *drunk*, a *trusty*, a *lockup*, a *kickout*, or a *rabbit*. In the particular jail
studied there are over sixty different kinds of trusties. This fact led some
tramps to believe they were arrested to provide cheap labor for the police
department. In their capacity as trusties, nearly 125 men provide jani-
torial service for the city hall, outlying police precincts, and the jail. They
assist in the preparation of food, maintain the firing range, care for police
vehicles, and do numerous other tasks. Most men soon learn that doing
time on a drunk charge is not a desirable occupation, so they use many
strategies to escape the confines of the jail or to reduce the length of
their sentence. When a man is arrested he is placed in the drunk tank
where he awaits his arraignment in court. Those sentenced to do time
will spend it in close association with other tramps. If a man is not
experienced in the ways of this culture, he will learn them while he is
in jail, for it is a veritable storehouse of invaluable information for those
who are repeatedly arrested for public intoxication. He will learn to think
of himself as a tramp and to survive on the street by employing more
than a dozen "ways of making it." More important, as he discovers that
the jailhouse has a revolving door for drunks, he will do his best to
"beat the drunk charge." The casual observer in court may find the
arraignment and sentencing of drunk cases to be a cut-and-dried process.
From the perspective of these men, however, it is more like a game of
skill and chance being played by the tramp and law-enforcement agen-

cies. In this article we shall examine the rules of this game, the strategies employed by tramps, and the underlying American cultural values that make it intelligible to the outsider.

PLANS FOR BEATING THE DRUNK CHARGE

Every culture contains one type of shared knowledge called *plans*. These are related to the achievement of goals. A plan is a set of rules that specifies a goal, conditions under which the goal will be chosen, techniques for the attainment of the goal, and conditions under which a particular technique will be used to attain the goal. The methods of ethnoscience are designed to map culturally shared systems of knowledge, and were used in this study to discover the plans tramps employ in their relationship to law-enforcement agencies.

The goal: Maximize freedom — minimize incarceration. There are many goals which tramps pursue. Most aims are referred to in a specific manner, such as "making a flop," "making a jug," "getting a dime," or "bailing out." Freedom is a general objective that includes such specific goals as rabbiting from jail, concealing one's identity, making a pay-off to a bull, leaving town, avoiding the police, and beating a drunk charge. Men do not always select one of these goals in order to maximize freedom — they sometimes even choose paths leading to *incarceration*. In a sample of a hundred men, 10 percent reported they had gone to jail and asked to be locked up in order to stop drinking. At other times a tramp will go to jail on his own to request a place to sleep or something to eat. Such cases are rare, and most tramps abhor imprisonment because they have learned a life style of mobility and the restrictions in the bucket lead to intense frustration. A testimonial to the fact that men do not seek imprisonment, as some outsiders believe, is the large number of strategies this culture has for avoiding incarceration. Almost every experience in the tramp world is defined, in part, by noting the degree of risk it entails for being jailed.

Techniques for the attainment of the goal. Because of the public nature of their life style, sooner or later most of these men end up in jail. Their specific objective at that time is to "beat the drunk charge." If successful, this could mean freedom in a few hours or at least a sentence of shorter duration than they would otherwise have received. The techniques for reaching this goal were discovered during interviews in which informants were asked: "Are there different ways to beat a drunk charge?" They responded with many specific instances in which they had taken action to beat the charge. These were classified as follows:

1. Bail out.
2. Bond out.

3. Request a continuance.
4. Have a good record.
5. Use an alias.
6. Plead guilty.
7. Hire a defense attorney.
8. Plead not guilty.
9. Submit a writ of habeas corpus.
10. Make a statement:
    a. Talk of family ties.
    b. Talk of present job.
    c. Talk of intent to work.
    d. Tell of extenuating circumstances.
    e. Offer to leave town.
11. Request the treatment center (alcoholic).

Each of these techniques labels a *category* of many different acts that are considered equivalent. For example, a man may bail out by using money he had with him when arrested, by borrowing from another man in jail, by contacting an employer who loans or gives him the money, and so on. There are several ways to "have a good record": a man must stay out of jail for at least six months for his record to begin to affect the length of his jail sentence. In order to do this a man may travel, quit drinking, stay off skid road, or go to an alcoholism treatment center for a long stay. Each kind of statement includes specific instances, varying from one man to another and from one time to the next. This category system is extremely important to tramps. Once they have learned these techniques, they practice them until their skill increases. Judges may consider an old-time tramp as a "con artist," but in this culture he is a man with expertise in carrying out these culturally shared techniques.

Conditions influencing selection. When a man is arrested he must process a great deal of information before he makes a decision to employ one or more of these techniques. He must assess his own resources, the probabilities of success, the risk of doing more time, etc. He needs to know the sentencing practices of the judge, the population of the jail, and the weather conditions. The most important factors that influence his decision are shown in Table I.

AMERICAN CULTURAL VALUES

Every society is based upon shared values — conceptions of the desirable in human experience. They are the basis for rewards and punishments. It is not surprising to most Americans that our culture, like most others, has rules about the undesirability of certain behavior *in*

TABLE I. *Conditions influencing selection of a way to beat a drunk charge*

Strategy	Risk of outcome?	Risk offending bulls?	Risk getting more time?	Risk doing dead time?	Money needed?
Bail out	No	No	No	No	$20
Bond out	No	No	No	No	$20+
Request a continuance	Yes	Yes	No	Yes	Yes
Have a good record	No	No	No	No	No
Use an alias	Yes	Yes	Yes	No	No
Plead guilty	Yes	No	No	No	No
Hire a defense attorney	Yes	Yes	No	Yes	Yes
Plead not guilty	Yes	Yes	Yes	Yes	No
Submit a writ of habeas corpus	Yes	Yes	Yes	Yes	No
Make a statement	Yes	No	Yes	No	No
Request a treatment center	Yes	Yes	Yes	Yes	No

public. We have outlawed nudity, begging, drinking, elimination of wastes, and intoxication in public places. We are offended by many other acts — if they occur in public. Tramps are booked for public intoxication, but they are often arrested because they urinate, sleep, or drink in some public place. Poverty has made it impossible for them to conceal their behavior behind the walls of a home. The extent of these restrictions upon *public* acts are in contrast to many non-Western societies where there is a wider range of acceptable public behavior. Because public drunkenness, which covers a multitude of other public sins, involves more arrests each year than any other crime, we may conclude that *privacy* is an important value in our culture.

Above the judge's bench in the criminal court where this study took place, there is a large wooden plaque inscribed "Equal Justice for All Under the Law." Given the laws prohibiting public behavior of various kinds, we might still expect that the punishment for violation would be distributed *equally.* Thus, if two men with the same criminal record are found guilty of the same crime, they should receive the same punishment. If two men are found drunk in public for the first time, it would be unfair to fine one a few dollars and require the other to pay several hundred dollars. Upon examining the penalties given for public drunkenness, we discover a rather startling fact: *the less a man conforms to other*

American values, the more severe his punishment — not because he violates other laws, but because he does not conform to the values of *materialism, moralism,* and *work.* These values are the basis for a set of implicit "punishment rules." Although they are unwritten, those who administer justice in our society have learned to punish the drunk offender on the basis of these rules.

Rule 1: *When guilty of public drunkenness, a man deserves greater punishment if he is poor.* In every society, when individuals violate legal norms they are punished. Physical torture, public humiliation, incarceration, and banishment from the society are some of the forms this punishment takes. It is not surprising that in our society, with its emphasis upon the value of material goods, violators are punished by making them give up some form of property. An individual may be fined after he has been convicted of public drunkenness. Most offenders pay money in the form of a "bail" prior to conviction. A few hours after being arrested, most men are able to be released from jail in a sober condition. They are still innocent before the law and an arraignment is scheduled at which time they may plead guilty or not guilty. If they enter the latter plea, they must appear in court at another time for a trial. In order to insure that a man returns for his arraignment he is asked to deposit bail money with the court, which will be returned to him when he is sentenced or acquitted. In most courts a man may choose to ignore the arraignment and thereby "forfeit" his bail. It is still within the power of the court to issue a warrant for his arrest in this case and compel him to appear in court, but this is seldom done. Instead, much like bail for a traffic violation, forfeiture of the drunk bail is considered as a just recompense to society for appearing drunk in public.

When arrested, tramps are eager to post bail since it means an immediate release from jail. They do not need to wait for the arraignment which may not occur for several days. The bail is $20 and is almost always forfeited. This system of punishment treats offenders equally — *unless a man does not have $20.*

Those who are caught in the grip of poverty are usually convicted, and their punishment is "doing time" instead of "paying money." In America, the rich have money, the poor have time. It might be possible to punish men equitably using these two different commodities but such is not the case. If a man is poor he must be unwilling to expend his energies in the pursuit of materialism, and therefore his punishment should be more severe than that given to those with money. How does this occur? Each time a man is arrested his bail is always twenty dollars, but if he is indigent, his sentences become longer with each conviction. A man can be arrested hundreds of times and bail out for only twenty dollars, but not if he is poor. Consider the case of one man who was arrested in Seattle over one hundred times during a twenty-one-year period. On many arrests he bailed out, but for about seventy convictions he was sentenced to jail, and gradually his sentences grew to the maximum of six months for a single arrest. During this period he was sentenced to nearly fourteen years in jail — a punishment he could have avoided for only a hundred dollars for each of those years. This man was given a life sentence on the installment plan, not for being drunk but for being poor. There are many cases where a rich man and a poor man are arrested and booked for drunkenness on the same night. The rich man is released in a few hours because he had twenty dollars. The poor man is released in a few months because he did not have twenty dollars. One way then to beat a drunk charge is to bail out. If you do not have money, it is still possible to use this strategy by bonding out or asking for a continuance. A bond requires some collateral or assurance that the twenty dollars *plus* a fee to the bondsman will be paid. A continuance enables you to wait a few more days before being sentenced, and during that time, it may be possible to get money from a friend or an employer. Whether he can use these ways to beat a drunk charge or not, the tramp who is repeatedly arrested soon learns he is being punished because he does not conform to the value of materialism.

Rule 2: *When guilty of public drunkenness, a man deserves greater punishment if he has a bad reputation.* Most cultures have a moralistic quality that often leads to stereotyping and generalizing about the quality of a man's character. In our society once a person has been convicted of a crime, he is viewed by others with suspicion. He may never violate legal norms again, but for all practical purposes he is morally reprehensible. Since judges increase the length of a man's sentence with each arrest, he must engage in behavior designed to give him a "good record" if he is to beat the drunk charge. One way to do this is by travelling. For example, if a man stayed out of jail in Seattle for six months, subsequent convictions would begin again with short sentences; thus, when arrested several times, he often decided it would be better if he went to another town. When his arrest record began to grow in this new place, he would move on; after a period of time he would return to Seattle. Men learn to calculate the number of "days hanging" for each city where they are arrested, and their mobility is determined by the magnitude of the next sentence. Some men use an alias when arrested in an attempt to obscure the fact that they have a long record. If this ploy is successful, a man who, because of his record, deserves a sentence of six months, may only be given two or three days. Another way to beat a drunk charge is to volunteer to go to an alcoholism treatment center. A man may not believe that he is an alcoholic or even that he has a "drinking problem," but if he will agree with society's judgment — that his long record of arrests shows he is morally debased — and ask to be helped, his incarceration will be reduced. But not all men are candidates for treatment. Those with the worst records are rejected and must do their time in jail. A man with a bad reputation thus will be given a more severe punishment for the same crime than one with a good reputation.

Rule 3: *When guilty of public drunkenness, a man deserves greater punishment if he does not have a steady job.* American culture places great value on work as an end in itself. Resistance to hippies and welfare programs alike is based, in part, on the value of work. Tramps know that judges punish more severely those who do not have steady employment. If a man cannot beat a drunk charge in some other way, he will make a statement telling the judge that he will find a job, return to a former job, or provide evidence that he is currently employed in a respectable occupation. Tramps often earn a living by "junking" to find things to sell, "spot jobbing," or "panhandling" (begging on the street) — but all these "occupations" are not admired in our society and cannot be used as evidence that one is conforming to the value of work. When a man appears in court with evidence that he is working, the judge will often suspend or shorten his sentence.

Tramps who have been unable to beat the drunk charge before being sentenced may capitalize on this value in another way. One man reported that he had written a letter to himself while in jail. The letter appeared to have been written by an employer in another city offering the man a steady job. The inmate asked another man who was being released from jail to carry the letter to that city and mail it from there. When it arrived, he used it to convince the judge that he should receive an early release in order to accept steady employment. Another inmate, when released from jail, went personally to the judge and pretended to be a contractor; he told him that a man who had worked for him was in jail and he would employ him if he were released. The judge complied with the request, and the two tramps left town together — proud of their achievement, surer than ever that one of the best ways to beat a drunk charge was to understand the value of work in American culture.

The values our culture places upon privacy, materialism, moralism, and work are not the only ones affecting the lives of tramps. These are men who live in a society that holds no place for them. Their life style is offensive to most Americans, and for this reason they are arrested, jailed, and punished by standards that do not apply to the rest of society. In response to these practices they have learned a culture with well-developed plans for survival. They have adopted a nomadic style of life — moving from one urban center to another to maximize their freedom. In spite of their efforts, sooner or later, most tramps find themselves arrested, and it is then that the techniques for beating a drunk charge will be found most useful.

24

Yanomamö: The fierce people

NAPOLEON A. CHAGNON

*Every society provides a basis for authority and ways to gain support
for such authority. In this article, Napoleon Chagnon describes the
Yanomamö, a group which bases its authority structure on a
continuum of violence and on claims to fierceness or willingness to
do violence.*

The Yanomamö Indians are a tribe in Venezuela and Brazil who practice
a slash-and-burn way of horticultural life. Traditionally, they have been
an inland "foot" tribe, avoiding larger rivers and settling deep in the
tropical jungle. Until about 1950 they had no sustained contact with
other peoples except, to a minor extent, with another tribe, the Carib-
speaking Makiritaris to the northeast.

I recently lived with the Yanomamö for more than a year, doing
research sponsored by the U.S. Public Health Service, with the cooperation of the Venezuela Institute for Scientific Research. My purpose
was to study Yanomamö social organization, language, sex practices,
and forms of violence, ranging from treacherous raids to chest-pounding
duels.

Those Yanomamö who have been encouraged to live on the larger
rivers (Orinoco, Mavaca, Ocamo, and Padamo) are slowly beginning to
realize that they are not the only people in the world; there is also a
place called Caraca-tedi (Caracas), from whence come foreigners of an
entirely new order. These foreigners speak an incomprehensible language, probably a degenerate form of Yanomamö. They bring malaria
pills, machetes, axes, cooking pots, and *copetas* ("guns"), have curious
ideas about indecency, and speak of a new "spirit."

However, the Yanomamö remain a people relatively unadulterated
by outside contacts. They are also fairly numerous. Their population is

With permission from *Natural History*, Vol. 66, No. 1; Copyright the American Museum
of Natural History, 1967.

roughly 10,000, the larger portion of them distributed throughout southern Venezuela. Here, in basins of the upper Orinoco and all its tribu-
taries, they dwell in some 75 scattered villages, each of which contains
from 40 to 300 individuals.

The largest, most all-embracing human reality to these people is
humanity itself; Yanomamö means true human beings. Their conception
of themselves as the only true "domestic" beings (those that dwell in
houses) is demonstrated by the comtempt with which they treat non-
Yanomamö, who, in their language, are "wild." For instance, when
referring to themselves, they use an honorific pronoun otherwise reserved for important spirits and headmen; when discussing nabäs ("non-
Yanomamö"), an ordinary pronoun is enough. Again, in one of the
myths about their origin, the first people to be created were the Yanomamö. All others developed by a process of degeneration and are, therefore, not quite on a par with the Yanomamö.

In addition to meaning "people," Yanomamö also refers to the
language. Their tribal name does not designate a politically organized
entity but is more or less equivalent to our concept of humanity. (This,
of course, makes their most outstanding characteristic — chronic warfare, of which I shall speak in detail — seem rather an anomaly.) Sub-
Yanomamö groupings are based on language differences, historical separation, and geographical location.

For instance, two distinguishable groups, Waika (from waikaö —
"to kill off") and Shamatari, speak nearly identical dialects; they are
differentiated mostly on the basis of a specific event that led to their
separation. The Shamatari, the group I know best, occupy the area south
of the Orinoco to, and including portions of, northern Brazil. Their
differentiation from the Waika probably occurred in the past 75 years.

According to the Indians, there was a large village on a northern
tributary of the upper Orinoco River, close to its headwaters. The village
had several factions, one of which was led by a man called Kayabawä
(big tree). A notably corpulent man, he also had the name Shamatari,
derived from shama, the "tapir," a robust ungulate found throughout
tropical South America. As the story goes, Shamatari's faction got into
a fight with the rest of the village over the possession of a woman, and
the community split into two warring halves. Gradually the fighting
involved more villages, and Shamatari led his faction south, crossed the
Orinoco, and settled there. He was followed by members of other villages that had taken his part in the fight.

Those who moved to the south side of the Orinoco came to be
called Shamataris by those living on the north side, and the term is now
applied to any village in this area, whether or not it can trace its origin
to the first supporters of Shamatari.

For the Yanomamö, the village is the maximum political unit and the maximum sovereign body, and it is linked to other villages by ephemeral alliances, visiting and trade relationships, and intermarriages. In essence, the village is a building — a continuous, open-roofed lean-to built on a circular plan and surrounded by a protective palisade of split palm logs. The roof starts at or near ground level, ascends at an angle of about 45 degrees, and reaches a height of some 20 to 25 feet. Individual segments under the continuous roof are not partitioned; from a hammock hung anywhere beneath it one can see (and hear, thanks to the band shell nature of the structure) all that goes on within the village.

The palisade, about three to six feet behind the base of the roof, is some ten feet high and is usually in various stages of disrepair, depending on the current warfare situation. The limited number of entrances are covered with dry palm leaves in the evening; if these are moved even slightly, the sound precipitates the barking of a horde of ill-tempered, underfed dogs, whose bad manners preadapt the stranger to what lies beyond the entrance.

A typical "house" (a segment under the continuous roof) shelters a man, his wife or wives, their children, perhaps one or both of the man's parents, and, farther down, the man's brothers and their families. The roof is alive with cockroaches, scorpions, and spiders, and the ground is littered with the debris of numerous repasts — bird, fish, and animal bones; bits of fur; skulls of monkeys and other animals; banana and plantain peelings; feathers; and the seeds of palm fruits. Bows and arrows stand against housepoles all over the village, baskets hang from roof rafters, and firewood is stacked under the lower part of the roof where it slopes to the ground. Some men will be whittling arrow points with agouti-tooth knives or tying feathers to arrow shafts. Some women will be spinning cotton, weaving baskets, or making hammocks or cotton waistbands. The children, gathered in the center of the village clearing, frequently tie a string to a lizard and entertain themselves by shooting the animal full of tiny arrows. And, of course, many people will be outside the compound, working in their gardens, fishing, or collecting palm fruits in the jungle.

If it is a typical late afternoon, most of the older men are gathered in one part of the village, blowing one of their hallucinatory drugs (*ebene*) up each other's nostrils by means of a hollow tube and chanting to the forest demons (*hekuras*) as the drug takes effect. Other men may be curing a sick person by sucking, massaging, and exhorting the evil spirit from him. Everybody in the village is swatting vigorously at the voracious biting gnats, and here and there groups of people delouse each other's heads and eat the vermin.

In composition, the village consists of one or more groups of patrilineally related kinsmen (*mashis*), but it also contains other categories, including people who have come from other villages seeking spouses. All villages try to increase their size and consider it desirable for both the young men and young women to remain at home after marriage. Since one must marry out of his *mashi*, villages with only one patrilineage frequently lose their young men to other villages; they must go to another village to *siohamou* (to "son-in-law") if they want wives. The parents of the bride-to-be, of course, want the young man to remain in their village to help support them in their old age, particularly if they have few or no sons. They will frequently promise a young man one or more of the sisters of his wife in order to make his stay more attractive.

He, on the other hand, would rather return to his home village to be with his own kinsmen, and the tendency is for postmarital residence to be patrilocal (with the father of the groom). If a village is rich in axes and machetes, it can and does coerce its poorer trading partners into permitting their young women to live permanently with the richer village. The latter thus obtains more women, while the poorer village gains some security in the trading network. The poor village then coerces other villages even poorer, or they raid them and steal their women.

The patrilineages that maintain the composition of the villages, rich or poor, include a man and his brothers and sisters, his children and his brothers' children, and the children of his sons and brothers' sons. The ideal marriage pattern is for a group of brothers to exchange sisters with another group of brothers. Furthermore, it is both permissible and desirable for a man to marry his mother's brother's daughter (his matrilateral cross-cousin) and/or his father's sister's daughter (his patrilateral cross-cousin) and, as we have seen earlier, to remain in his parents' village. Hence, the "ideal" village would have at least two patrilineages that exchanged marriageable people.

There is a considerable amount of adherence to these rules, and both brother-sister exchange and cross-cousin marriage are common. However, there are also a substantial number of people in each village who are not related in these ways. For the most part they are women and their children who have been stolen from other villages, segments of lineages that have fled from their own village because of fights, and individuals — mostly young men — who have moved in and attached themselves to the household of one of the lineage (*mashi*) leaders.

Even if the sex ratio is balanced, there is a chronic shortage of women. A pregnant woman or one who is still nursing her children must not have sexual relationships. This means that for as many as three years, even allowing for violations of the taboos, a woman is asexual as far as the men are concerned. Hence, men with pregnant wives, and bachelors too, are potentially disruptive in every village because they constantly seek liaisons with the wives of other men. Eventually such relationships are discovered and violence ensues.

The woman, even if merely suspected of having affairs with other men, is beaten with a club; burned with a glowing brand; shot with a barbed arrow in a non-vital area, such as the buttocks, so that removal of the barb is both difficult and painful; or chopped on the arms or legs with a machete or ax. Most women over thirty carry numerous scars inflicted on them by their enraged husbands. My study of genealogies also indicates that not a few women have been killed outright by their husbands. The woman's punishment for infidelity depends on the number of brothers she has in the village, for if her husband is too brutal, her brothers may club him or take her away and give her to someone else.

The guilty man, on the other hand, is challenged to a fight with clubs. This duel is rarely confined to the two parties involved, for their brothers and supporters join the battle. If nobody is seriously injured, the matter may be forgotten. But if the incidents are frequent, the two patrilineages may decide to split while they are still on relatively "peaceable" terms with each other and form two independent villages. They will still be able to reunite when threatened by raid from a larger village.

This is only one aspect of the chronic warfare of the Yanomamö — warfare that has a basic effect on settlement pattern and demography, intervillage political relationships, leadership, and social organization. The collective aggressive behavior is caused by the desire to accent "sovereignty" — the capacity to initiate fighting and to demonstrate this capacity to others.

Although the Yanomamö are habitually armed with lethal bows and arrows, they have a graded system of violence within which they can express their *waiteri*, or "fierceness." The form of violence is determined by the nature of the affront or wrong to be challenged. The most benign form is a duel between two groups, in which an individual from each group stands (or kneels) with his chest stuck out, head up in the air, and arms held back and receives a hard blow to the chest. His opponent literally winds up and delivers a close-fist blow from the ground, striking the man on the left pectoral muscle just above the heart. The impact frequently drops the man to his knees, and participants may cough up blood for several days after such a contest. After receiving several such blows, the man then has his turn to strike his opponent, while the respective supporters of each antagonist gather around and frenziedly urge their champion on.

All men in the two villages are obliged to participate as village representatives, and on one occasion I saw some individuals take as many as three or four turns of four blows each. Duels of this type usually result from minor wrongs, such as a village being guilty of spreading bad rumors about another village, questioning its generosity or fierceness, or accusing it of gluttony at a feast. A variant of this form of duel is side slapping, in which an open-handed blow is delivered across the flank just above the pelvis.

More serious are the club fights. Although these almost invariably result from cases in which a wife has been caught in an affair with another man, some fights follow the theft of food within the village. The usual procedure calls for a representative from each belligerent group. One man holds a ten-foot club upright, braces himself by leaning on the club and spreading his feet, then holds his head out for his opponent to strike. Following this comes his turn to do likewise to his adversary. These duels, more often than not, end in a free-for-all in which everybody clubs everybody else on whatever spot he can hit. Such brawls occasionally result in fatalities. However, since headmen of the respective groups stand by with bows drawn, no one dares deliver an intentionally killing blow, for if he does, he will be shot. The scalps of the older men are almost incredible to behold, covered as they are by as many as a dozen ugly welts. Yet, most of them proudly shave the top of their heads to display their scars.

Also precipitated by feuds over women are spear fights, which are even more serious than club fights. Members of a village will warn those of the offending village that they are coming to fight with spears. They specify that they are not planning to shoot arrows unless the others shoot first. On the day of the fight, the attackers enter the other village, armed with five or six sharpened clubs or slender shafts some eight feet long and attempt to drive the defenders out. If successful, the invaders steal all the valuable possessions — hammocks, cooking pots, and machetes — and retreat. In the spear fight that occurred while I was studying the tribe, the attackers were successful, but they wounded several individuals so badly that one of them died. The fighting then escalated to a raid, the penultimate form of violence.

Such raids may be precipitated by woman stealing or the killing of a visitor (visitors are sometimes slain because they are suspected of having practiced harmful magic that has led to a death in the host's village). Raids also occur if a man kills his wife in a fit of anger; her natal village is then obliged to avenge the death. Most raids, however, are in revenge for deaths that occurred in previous raids, and once the vendetta gets started, it is not likely to end for a long time. Something else may trigger a raid. Occasionally an ambitious headman wearies of peaceful times — a rarity, certainly — and deliberately creates a situation that will demonstrate his leadership.

A revenge raid is preceded by a feast in which the ground bones of the person to be avenged are mixed in a soup of boiled, ripe plantains (the mainstay of Yanomamö diet) and swallowed. Yanomamö are endo-cannibals, which means they consume the remains of members of their own group. This ceremony puts the raiders in the appropriate state of frenzy for the business of warfare. A mock raid — rather like a dress rehearsal — is conducted in their own village on the afternoon before the day of the raid, and a life-size effigy of an enemy, constructed of leaves or a log, is slain. That evening all the participants march, one at a time, to the center of the village clearing, while clacking their bows and arrows and screaming their versions of the calls of carnivorous birds, mammals, and even insects.

When all have lined up facing the direction of the enemy village, they sing their war song, "I am a meat-hungry buzzard," and shout several times in unison until they hear the echo return from the jungle. They then disperse to their individual sections of the village to vomit the symbolic rotten flesh of the enemy that they, as symbolic carnivorous vultures and wasps, partook of in the lineup. The same thing, with the exception of the song, is repeated at dawn the following morning. Then the raiders, covered with black paint made of chewed charcoal, march out of the village in single file and collect the hammocks and plantains that their women have previously set outside the village for them. On each night they spend en route to the enemy they fire arrows at a dummy in a mock raid. They approach the enemy village itself under cover of darkness, ambush the first person they catch, and retreat as rapidly as possible. If they catch a man and his family, they will shoot the man and steal the woman and her children. At a safe distance from her village, each of the raiders rapes the woman, and when they reach their own village, every man in the village may, if he wishes, do likewise before she is given to one of the men as a wife. Ordinarily she attempts to escape, but if caught, she may be killed. So constant is the threat of raids that every woman leaves her village in the knowledge that she may be stolen.

The supreme form of violence is the *nomohoni* — the "trick." During the dry season, the Yanomamö do a great deal of visiting. An entire village will go to another village for a ceremony that involves feasting, dancing, chanting, curing, trading, and just plain gossiping. Shortly after arrival, the visitors are invited to recline in the hammocks of the hosts. By custom they lie motionless to display their fine decorations

while the hosts prepare food for them. But now suppose that a village
has a grudge to settle with another, such as deaths to avenge. It enlists
the support of a third village to act as accomplice. This third village,
which must be on friendly terms with the intended victims, will invite
them to a feast. While the guests recline defenseless in the hammocks,
the hosts descend on them with axes and sharpened poles, treacherously
killing as many as they can. Those that manage to escape the slaughter
inside the village are shot outside the palisade by the village that insti-
gated the *nomohoni*. The women and children will be shared between
the two accomplices.

Throughout all this ferocity there are two organizational aspects of
violence. One concerns leadership: A man must be able to demonstrate
his fierceness if he is to be a true leader. It is equally important, however,
that he have a large natural following — that is, he must have many
male kinsmen to support his position and a quantity of daughters and
sisters to distribute to other men. Lineage leaders cannot accurately be
described as unilateral initiators of activities; rather, they are the vehicles
through which the group's will is expressed. For example, when a certain
palm fruit is ripe and is particularly abundant in an area some distance
from the village, everybody knows that the whole village will pack its
belongings and erect a temporary camp at that spot to collect the fruit.
The headman does little more than set the date. When his kinsmen see
him packing, they know that the time has come to leave for the collecting
trip. True, the headman does have some initiative in raiding, but not
even this is completely independent of the attitudes of his followers,
which dictate that a death must be avenged. However, when the purpose
of a raid is to steal women, the headman does have some freedom to
act on his own initiative.

As a general rule, the smaller his natural following, the more he
is obliged to demonstrate his personal qualities of fierceness and leadership. Padudiwä, the headman of one of the lineages in Bisaasi-tedi,
took pains to demonstrate his personal qualities whenever he could; he
had only two living brothers and four living sisters in his group. Most
of his demonstrations of ferocity were cruel beatings he administered
to his four wives, none of whom had brothers in the village to take their
part. Several young men who attached themselves to his household
admired him for this.

Padudiwä was also responsible for organizing several raids while
I lived with the villagers of Bisaasi-tedi. Every one of them was against
Patanowä-tedi, a village that was being raided regularly by some seven
or eight other villages, so that the danger of being raided in return was
correspondingly reduced. On one occasion, when three young men from

Patanowä-tedi arrived as emissaries of peace, Padudiwä wanted to kill them, although he had lived with them at one time and they were fairly close relatives. The murder was prevented by the headman of the other — and larger — lineage in the village, who warned that if an attempt were made on the lives of the visitors he himself would kill Padudiwä.

Obviously then, Padudiwä's reputation was built largely on calculated acts of fierceness, which carefully reduced the possibility of personal danger to himself and his followers, and on cunning and cruelty. To some extent he was obliged by the smallness of his gathering to behave in such a way, but he was certainly a man to treat with caution.

Despite their extreme aggressiveness, the Yanomamö have at least two qualities I admired. They are kind and indulgent with children and can quickly forget personal angers. (A few even treated me almost as an equal — in their culture this was a considerable concession.) But to portray them as "noble savages" would be misleading. Many of them are delightful and charming people when confronted alone and on a personal basis, but the greater number of them are much like Padudiwä — or strive to be that way. As they frequently told me, *Yanomamö täbä waiteri!* — "Yanomamö are fierce!"

25

Poor man, rich man, big-man, chief

MARSHALL D. SAHLINS

*Melanesia and Polynesia provide an interesting contrast in political
complexity, as Marshall Sahlins describes in the following article.
The Melanesian "big-man" is the self-made leader of his small
localized kinship group, whereas the Polynesian chief is a "born"
leader. The Polynesian system, which depends upon the ascribed
right of its chief to lead, attains far larger proportions than the
Melanesian structure, which depends on the ability of certain
individuals to influence others.*

With an eye to their own life goals, the native peoples of Pacific Islands
unwittingly present to anthropologists a generous scientific gift: an extended series of experiments in cultural adaptation and evolutionary
development. They have compressed their institutions within the confines of infertile coral atolls, expanded them on volcanic islands, created
with the means history gave them cultures adapted to the deserts of
Australia, the mountains and warm coasts of New Guinea, the rain
forests of the Solomon Islands. From the Australian Aborigines, whose
hunting and gathering existence duplicates in outline the cultural life of
the later Paleolithic, to the great chiefdoms of Hawaii, where society
approached the formative levels of the old Fertile Crescent civilizations,
almost every general phase in the progress of primitive culture is
exemplified.

Where culture so experiments, anthropology finds its laboratories — makes its comparisons.

In the southern and eastern Pacific two contrasting cultural prov-

From "Poor Man, Rich Man, Big-Man, Chief: Political Types in Melanesia and Polynesia,"
Comparative Studies in Society and History, Vol. 5, No. 3, pp. 285–303. Reprinted by permission of Cambridge University Press. Many footnotes, the bibliographic citations, and
the bibliography are omitted.

inces have long evoked anthropological interest: *Melanesia*, including New Guinea, the Bismarcks, Solomons, and island groups east to Fiji; and *Polynesia*, consisting in its main portion of the triangular constellation of lands between New Zealand, Easter Island, and the Hawaiian Islands. In and around Fiji, Melanesia and Polynesia intergrade culturally, but west and east of their intersection the two provinces pose broad contrasts in several sectors: in religion, art, kinship groupings, economics, political organization. The differences are the more notable for the underlying similarities from which they emerge. Melanesia and Polynesia are both agricultural regions in which many of the same crops — such as yams, taro, breadfruit, bananas, and coconuts — have long been cultivated by many similar techniques. Some recently presented linguistic and archaeological studies indeed suggest that Polynesian cultures originated from an eastern Melanesian hearth during the first millennium B.C. Yet in anthropological annals the Polynesians were to become famous for elaborate forms of rank and chieftainship, whereas most Melanesian societies broke off advance on this front at more rudimentary levels.

It is obviously imprecise, however, to make out the political contrast in broad culture-area terms. Within Polynesia, certain of the islands, such as Hawaii, the Society Islands and Tonga, developed unparalleled political momentum. And not all Melanesian polities, on the other side, were constrained and truncated in their evolution. In New Guinea and nearby areas of western Melanesia, small and loosely ordered political groupings are numerous, but in eastern Melanesia, New Caledonia and Fiji for example, political approximations of the Polynesian condition become common. There is more of an upward west to east slope in political development in the southern Pacific than a step-like, quantum progression. It is quite revealing, however, to compare the extremes of this continuum, the western Melanesian underdevelopment against the greater Polynesian chiefdoms. While such comparison does not exhaust the evolutionary variations, it fairly establishes the scope of overall political achievement in this Pacific phylum of cultures.

Measurable along several dimensions, the contrast between developed Polynesian and underdeveloped Melanesian polities is immediately striking for differences in scale. H. Ian Hogbin and Camilla Wedgwood concluded from a survey of Melanesian (most western Melanesian) societies that ordered, independent political bodies in the region typically include seventy to three hundred persons; more recent work in the New Guinea Highlands suggests political groupings of up to a thousand, occasionally a few thousand, people.[1] But in Polynesia

[1] H. Ian Hogbin and Camilla H. Wedgwood, "Local Groupings in Melanesia," *Oceania* 23 (1952–53): 241–276; 24 (1953–54): 58–76.

sovereignties of two thousand or three thousand are run-of-the-mill, and the most advanced chiefdoms, as in Tonga or Hawaii, might claim ten thousand, even tens of thousands. Varying step by step with such differences in size of the polity are differences in territorial extent: from a few square miles in western Melanesia to tens or even hundreds of square miles in Polynesia.

The Polynesian advance in political scale was supported by advance over Melanesia in political structure. Melanesia presents a great array of social-political forms: here political organization is based upon patrilineal descent groups, there on cognatic groups, or men's club-houses recruiting neighborhood memberships, on a secret ceremonial society, or perhaps on some combination of these structural principles. Yet a general plan can be discerned. The characteristic western Melanesian "tribe," that is, the ethnic-cultural entity, consists of many autonomous kinship-residential groups. Amounting on the ground to a small village or a local cluster of hamlets, each of these is a copy of the others in organization, each tends to be economically self-governing, and each is the equal of the others in political status. The tribal plan is one of politically unintegrated segments — segmental. But the political geometry in Polynesia is pyramidal. Local groups of the order of self-governing Melanesian communities appear in Polynesia as subdivisions of a more inclusive political body. Smaller units are integrated into larger through a system of intergroup ranking, and the network of representative chiefs of the subdivisions amounts to a coordinating political structure. So instead of the Melanesian scheme of small, separate, and equal political blocs, the Polynesian polity is an extensive pyramid of groups capped by the family and following of a paramount chief. (This Polynesian political upshot is often, although not always, facilitated by the development of ranked lineages. Called *conical clan* by Kirchhoff, at one time *ramage* by Firth and *status lineage* by Goldman, the Polynesian ranked lineage is the same in principle as the so-called *obok* system widely distributed in Central Asia, and it is at least analogous to the Scottish clan, the Chinese clan, certain Central African Bantu lineage systems, the housegroups of Northwest Coast Indians, perhaps even the "tribes" of the Israelites. Genealogical ranking is its distinctive feature: members of the same descent unit are ranked by genealogical distance from the common ancestor; lines of the same group become senior and cadet branches on this principle; related corporate lineages are relatively ranked, again by genealogical priority.)

Here is another criterion of Polynesian political advance: historical performance. Almost all of the native peoples of the South Pacific were brought up against intense European cultural pressure in the late eighteenth and the nineteenth centuries. Yet only the Hawaiians, Tahitians,

Tongans, and to a lesser extent the Fijians, successfully defended themselves by evolving countervailing, native-controlled states. Complete with public governments and public law, monarchs and taxes, ministers and minions, these nineteenth-century states are testimony to the native Polynesian political genius, to the level and the potential of indigenous political accomplishments.

Embedded within the grand differences in political scale, structure and performance is a more personal contrast, one in quality of leadership. An historically particular type of leader-figure, the "big-man" as he is often locally styled, appears in the underdeveloped settings of Melanesia. Another type, a chief properly so-called, is associated with the Polynesian advance. Now these are distinct sociological types, that is to say, differences in the powers, privileges, rights, duties, and obligations of Melanesian big-men and Polynesian chiefs are given by the divergent societal contexts in which they operate. Yet the institutional distinctions cannot help but be manifest also in differences in bearing and character, appearance and manner — in a word, personality. It may be a good way to begin the more rigorous sociological comparison of leadership with a more impressionistic sketch of the contrast in the human dimension. Here I find it useful to apply characterizations — or is it caricature? — from our own history to big-men and chiefs, however much injustice this does to the historically incomparable backgrounds of the Melanesians and Polynesians. The Melanesian big-man seems so thoroughly bourgeois, so reminiscent of the free-enterprising rugged individual of our own heritage. He combines with an ostensible interest in the general welfare a more profound measure of self-interested cunning and economic calculation. His gaze, as Veblen might have put it, is fixed unswervingly to the main chance. His every public action is designed to make a competitive and invidious comparison with others, to show a standing above the masses that is product of his own personal manufacture. The historical caricature of the Polynesian chief, however, is feudal rather than capitalist. His appearance, his bearing is almost regal; very likely he just *is* a big man — " 'Can't you see he is a chief? See how big he is?' "[2] In his every public action is a display of the refinements of breeding, in his manner always that *noblesse oblige* of true pedigree and an incontestable right of rule. With his standing not so much a personal achievement as a just social due, he can afford to be, and he is, every inch a chief.

In the several Melanesian tribes in which big-men have come under anthropological scrutiny, local cultural differences modify the expression of their personal powers. But the indicative quality of big-man authority

[2] Edward Winslow Gifford, *Tongan Society* (Honolulu: Bernice P. Bishop Museum Bulletin 61, 1926).

is everywhere the same: it is *personal* power. Big-men do not come to office; they do not succeed to, nor are they installed in, existing positions of leadership over political groups. The attainment of big-man status is rather the outcome of a series of acts which elevate a person above the common herd and attract about him a coterie of loyal, lesser men. It is not accurate to speak of "big-man" as a political title, for it is but an acknowledged standing in interpersonal relations — a "prince among men" so to speak as opposed to "The Prince of Danes." In particular Melanesian tribes the phrase might be "man of importance" or "man of renown," "generous rich-man," or "center-man," as well as "big-man."

A kind of two-sidedness in authority is implied in this series of phrases, a division of the big-man's field of influence into two distinct sectors. "Center-man" particularly connotes a cluster of followers gathered about an influential pivot. It socially implies the division of the tribe into political in-groups dominated by outstanding personalities. To the in-group, the big-man presents this sort of picture:

> The place of the leader in the district group [in northern Malaita] is well summed up by his title, which might be translated as "center-man." . . . He was like a banyan, the natives explain, which, though the biggest and tallest in the forest, is still a tree like the rest. But, just because it exceeds all others, the banyan gives support to more lianas and creepers, provides more food for the birds, and gives better protection against sun and rain.[3]

But "man of renown" connotes a broader tribal field in which a man is not so much a leader as he is some sort of hero. This is the side of the big-man facing outward from his own faction, his status among some or all of the other political clusters of the tribe. The political sphere of the big-man divides itself into a small internal sector composed of his personal satellites — rarely over eighty men — and a much larger external sector, the tribal galaxy consisting of many similar constellations.

As it crosses over from the internal into the external sector, a big-man's power undergoes qualitative change. Within his faction a Melanesian leader has true command ability, outside of it only fame and indirect influence. It is not that the center-man rules his faction by physical force, but his followers do feel obliged to obey him, and he can usually get what he wants by haranguing them — public verbal suasion is indeed so often employed by center-men that they have been styled "harangueutans." The orbits of outsiders, however, are set by their own center-men. " 'Do it yourself. I'm not *your* fool,' " would be the char-

---

[3] H. Ian Hogbin, "Native Councils and Courts in the Solomon Islands," *Oceania* 14 (1943–44): 258–283.

acteristic response to an order issued by a center-man to an outsider among the Siuai.[4] This fragmentation of true authority presents special political difficulties, particularly in organizing large masses of people for the prosecution of such collective ends as warfare or ceremony. Big-men do instigate mass action, but only by establishing both extensive renown and special personal relations of compulsion or reciprocity with other center-men.

Politics is in the main personal politicking in these Melanesian societies, and the size of a leader's faction as well as the extent of his renown are normally set by competition with other ambitious men. Little or no authority is given by social ascription: leadership is a creation — a creation of followership. "Followers," as it is written of the Kapauku of New Guinea, "stand in various relations to the leader. Their obedience to the headman's decisions is caused by motivations which reflect their particular relations to the leader."[5] So a man must be prepared to demonstrate that he possesses the kinds of skills that command respect — magical powers, gardening prowess, mastery of oratorical style, perhaps bravery in war and feud. Typically decisive is the deployment of one's skills and efforts in a certain direction: towards amassing goods, most often pigs, shell monies and vegetable foods, and distributing them in ways which build a name for cavalier generosity, if not for compassion. A faction is developed by informal private assistance to people of a locale. Tribal rank and renown are developed by great public giveaways sponsored by the rising big-man, often on behalf of his faction as well as himself. In different Melanesian tribes, the renown-making public distribution may appear as one side of a delayed exchange of pigs between corporate kinship groups; a marital consideration given a bride's kinfolk; a set of feasts connected with the erection of a big-man's dwelling, or of a clubhouse for himself and his faction, or with the purchase of higher grades of rank in secret societies; the sponsorship of a religious ceremony; a payment of subsidies and blood compensations to military allies; or perhaps the giveaway is a ceremonial challenge bestowed on another leader in the attempt to outgive and thus outrank him (a potlatch).

The making of the faction, however, is the true making of the Melanesian big-man. It is essential to establish relations of loyalty and obligation on the part of a number of people such that their production can be mobilized for renown-building external distribution. The bigger the faction the greater the renown; once momentum in external distribution has been generated the opposite can also be true. Any ambitious

[4] Douglas Oliver, *A Solomon Islands Society* (Cambridge: Harvard University Press, 1955).

[5] Leopold Pospisil, *Kapauku Papuans and Their Law* (New Haven: Yale University Press, Yale University Publications in Anthropology, no. 54, 1958).

man who can gather a following can launch a societal career. The rising big-man necessarily depends initially on a small core of followers, principally his own household and his closest relatives. Upon these people he can prevail economically: he capitalizes in the first instance on kinship dues and by finessing the relation of reciprocity appropriate among close kinsmen. Often it becomes necessary at an early phase to enlarge one's household. The rising leader goes out of his way to incorporate within his family "strays" of various sorts, people without familial support themselves, such as widows and orphans. Additional wives are especially useful. The more wives a man has the more pigs he has. The relation here is functional, not identical: with more women gardening there will be more food for pigs and more swineherds. A Kiwai Papuan picturesquely put to an anthropologist in pidgin the advantages, economic and political, of polygamy: " 'Another woman go garden, another woman go take firewood, another woman go catch fish, another woman cook him — husband he sing out plenty people come kaikai [i.e., come to eat].' "[6] Each new marriage, incidentally, creates for the big-man an additional set of in-laws from whom he can exact economic favors. Finally, a leader's career sustains its upward climb when he is able to link other men and their families to his faction, harnessing their production to his ambition. This is done by calculated generosities, by placing others in gratitude and obligation through helping them in some big way. A common technique is payment of bridewealth on behalf of young men seeking wives.

The great Malinowski used a phrase in analyzing primitive political economy that felicitously describes just what the big-man is doing: amassing a "fund of power." A big-man is one who can create and use social relations which give him leverage on others' production and the ability to siphon off an excess product — or sometimes he can cut down their consumption in the interest of the siphon. Now although his attention may be given primarily to short-term personal interests, from an objective standpoint the leader acts to promote long-term societal interests. The fund of power provisions activities that involve other groups of the society at large. In the greater perspective of that society at large, big-men are indispensable means of creating supralocal organization: in tribes normally fragmented into small independent groups, big-men at least temporarily widen the sphere of ceremony, recreation and art, economic collaboration, of war too. Yet always this greater societal organization depends on the lesser factional organization, particularly on the ceilings on economic mobilization set by relations between center-men and followers. The limits and the weaknesses of the

---

[6] Gunnar Landtman, *The Kiwai Papuans of British New Guinea* (London: Macmillan, 1927).

political order in general are the limits and weaknesses of the factional in-groups.

And the personal quality of subordination to a center-man is a serious weakness in factional structure. A personal loyalty has to be made and continually reinforced; if there is discontent it may well be severed. Merely to create a faction takes time and effort, and to hold it, still more effort. The potential rupture of personal links in the factional chain is at the heart of two broad evolutionary shortcomings of western Melanesian political orders. First, a comparative instability. Shifting dispositions and magnetisms of ambitious men in a region may induce fluctuations in factions, perhaps some overlapping of them, and fluctuations also in the extent of different renowns. The death of a center-man can become a regional political trauma: the death undermines the personally cemented faction, the group dissolves in whole or in part, and the people re-group finally around rising pivotal big-men. Although particular tribal structures in places cushion the disorganization, the big-man political system is generally unstable over short terms: in its superstructure it is a flux of rising and falling leaders, in its substructure of enlarging and contracting factions. Secondly, the personal political bond contributes to the containment of evolutionary advance. The possibility of their desertion, it is clear, often inhibits a leader's ability to forceably push up his followers' output, thereby placing constraints on higher political organization, but there is more to it than that. If it is to generate great momentum, a big-man's quest for the summits of renown is likely to bring out a contradiction in his relations to followers, so that he finds himself encouraging defection — or worse, an egalitarian rebellion — by encouraging production.

One side of the Melanesian contradiction is the initial economic reciprocity between a center-man and his followers. For his help they give their help, and for goods going out through his hands other goods (often from outside factions) flow back to his followers by the same path. The other side is that a cumulative build-up of renown forces center-men into economic extortion of the faction. Here it is important that not merely his own status, but the standing and perhaps the military security of his people depend on the big-man's achievements in public distribution. Established at the head of a sizeable faction, a center-man comes under increasing pressure to extract goods from his followers, to delay reciprocities owing them, and to deflect incoming goods back into external circulation. Success in competition with other big-men particularly undermines internal-factional reciprocities: such success is precisely measurable by the ability to give outsiders more than they can possibly reciprocate. In well delineated big-man polities, we find leaders negating the reciprocal obligations upon which their following had been predicated. Substituting extraction for reciprocity, they must compel their people to "eat the leader's renown," as one Solomon Island group puts it, in return for productive efforts. Some center-men appear more able than others to dam the inevitable tide of discontent that mounts within their factions, perhaps because of charismatic personalities, perhaps because of the particular social organizations in which they operate. But paradoxically the ultimate defense of the center-man's position is some slackening of his drive to enlarge the funds of power. The alternative is much worse. In the anthropological record there are not merely instances of big-man chicanery and of material deprivation of the faction in the interests of renown, but some also of overloading of social relations with followers: the generation of antagonisms, defections, and in extreme cases the violent liquidation of the center-man. Developing internal constraints, the Melanesian big-man political order brakes evolutionary advance at a certain level. It sets ceilings on the intensification of political authority, on the intensification of household production by political means, and on the diversion of household outputs in support of wider political organization. But in Polynesia these constraints were breached, and although Polynesian chiefdoms also found their developmental plateau, it was not before political evolution had been carried above the Melanesian ceilings. The fundamental defects of the Melanesian plan were overcome in Polynesia. The division between small internal and larger external political sectors, upon which all big-man politics hinged, was suppressed in Polynesia by the growth of an enclaving chiefdom-at-large. A chain of command subordinating lesser chiefs and groups to greater, on the basis of inherent societal rank, made local blocs or personal followings (such as were independent in Melanesia) merely dependent parts of the larger Polynesian chiefdom. So the nexus of the Polynesian chiefdom became an extensive set of offices, a pyramid of higher and lower chiefs holding sway over larger and smaller sections of the polity. Indeed the system of ranked and subdivided lineages (conical clan system), upon which the pyramid was characteristically established, might build up through several orders of inclusion and encompass the whole of an island or group of islands. While the island or the archipelago would normally be divided into several independent chiefdoms, high-order lineage connections between them, as well as kinship ties between their paramount chiefs, provided structural avenues for at least temporary expansion of political scale, for consolidation of great into even greater chiefdoms.

The pivotal paramount chief as well as the chieftains controlling parts of a chiefdom were true office holders and title holders. They were not, like Melanesian big-men, fishers of men: they held positions of authority over permanent groups. The honorifics of Polynesian chiefs likewise did not refer to a standing in interpersonal relations, but to their leadership of political divisions — here "The Prince of Danes" *not* "the prince among men." In western Melanesia the personal superiorities and inferiorities arising in the intercourse of particular men largely defined the political bodies. In Polynesia there emerged suprapersonal structures of leadership and followership, organizations that continued independently of the particular men who occupied positions in them for brief mortal spans.

And these Polynesian chiefs did not make their positions in society — they were installed in societal positions. In several of the islands, men did struggle to office against the will and stratagems of rival aspirants. But then they came *to* power. Power resided in the office; it was not made by the demonstration of personal superiority. In other islands, Tahiti was famous for it, succession to chieftainship was tightly controlled by inherent rank. The chiefly lineage ruled by virtue of its genealogical connections with divinity, and chiefs were succeeded by first sons, who carried "in the blood" the attributes of leadership. The important comparative point is this: the qualities of command that had to reside in men in Melanesia, that had to be personally demonstrated in order to attract loyal followers, were in Polynesia socially assigned to office and rank. In Polynesia, people of high rank and office *ipso facto* were leaders, and by the same token the qualities of leadership were automatically lacking — theirs was not to question why — among the underlying population. Magical powers such as a Melanesian big-man might acquire to sustain his position, a Polynesian high chief inherited by divine descent as the *mana* which sanctified his rule and protected his person against the hands of the commonalty. The productive ability the big-man laboriously had to demonstrate was effortlessly given Polynesian chiefs as religious control over agricultural fertility, and upon the ceremonial implementation of it the rest of the people were conceived dependent. Where a Melanesian leader had to master the compelling oratorical style, Polynesian paramounts often had trained "talking chiefs" whose voice was the chiefly command.

In the Polynesian view, a chiefly personage was in the nature of things powerful. But this merely implies the objective observation that his power was of the group rather than of himself. His authority came from the organization, from an organized acquiescence in his privileges and organized means of sustaining them. A kind of paradox resides in evolutionary developments which detach the exercise of authority from the necessity to demonstrate personal superiority: organizational power actually extends the role of personal decision and conscious planning, gives it greater scope, impact, and effectiveness. The growth of a political system such as the Polynesian constitutes advance over Melanesian orders of interpersonal dominance in the human control of human affairs. Especially significant for society at large were privileges accorded Polynesian chiefs which made them greater architects of funds of power than ever was any Melanesian big-man.

Masters of their people and "owners" in a titular sense of group resources, Polynesian chiefs had rights of call upon the labor and agricultural produce of households within their domains. Economic mobilization did not depend on, as it necessarily had for Melanesian big-men, the *de novo* creation by the leader of personal loyalties and economic obligations. A chief need not stoop to obligate this man or that man, need not by a series of individual acts of generosity induce others to support him, for economic leverage over a group was the inherent chiefly due. Consider the implications for the fund of power of the widespread chiefly privilege, related to titular "ownership" of land, of placing an interdiction, a tabu, on the harvest of some crop by way of reserving its use for a collective project. By means of the tabu the chief directs the course of production in a general way: households of his domain must turn to some other means of subsistence. He delivers a stimulus to household production: in the absence of the tabu further labors would not have been necessary. Most significantly, he has generated a politically utilizable agricultural surplus. A subsequent call on this surplus floats chieftainship as a going concern, capitalizes the fund of power. In certain islands, Polynesian chiefs controlled great storehouses which held the goods congealed by chiefly pressures on the commonalty. David Malo, one of the great native custodians of old Hawaiian lore, felicitously catches the political significance of the chiefly magazine in his well-known *Hawaiian Antiquities:*

> It was the practice for kings [i.e., paramount chiefs of individual islands] to build store-houses in which to collect food, fish, tapas [bark cloth], malos [men's loin cloths] pa-us [women's loin skirts], and all sorts of goods. These store-houses were designed by the Kalaimoku [the chief's principal executive] as a means of keeping the people contented, so they would not desert the king. They were like the baskets that were used to entrap the *hinalea* fish. The *hinalea* thought there was something good within the basket, and he hung round the outside of it. In the same way the people thought there was food in the store-houses, and they kept their eyes on the king. As the rat will not desert the pantry . . . where he thinks food is, so the people will not desert the king while they think there is food in his store-house.[7]

Redistribution of the fund of power was the supreme art of Polynesian politics. By well-planned *noblesse oblige* the large domain of a paramount

[7] David Malo, *Hawaiian Antiquities* (Honolulu: Hawaiian Gazette Co., 1903).

chief was held together, organized at times for massive projects, protected against other chiefdoms, even further enriched. Uses of the chiefly fund included lavish hospitality and entertainments for outside chiefs and for the chief's own people, and succor of individuals or the underlying population at large in times of scarcities — bread and circuses. Chiefs subsidized craft production, promoting in Polynesia a division of technical labor unparalleled in extent and expertise in most of the Pacific. They supported also great technical construction, as of irrigation complexes, the further returns to which swelled the chiefly fund. They initiated large-scale religious construction too, subsidized the great ceremonies, and organized logistic support for extensive military campaigns. Larger and more easily replenished than their western Melanesian counterparts, Polynesian funds of power permitted greater political regulation of a greater range of social activities on greater scale.

In the most advanced Polynesian chiefdoms, as in Hawaii and Tahiti, a significant part of the chiefly fund was deflected away from general redistribution towards the upkeep of the institution of chieftainship. The fund was siphoned for the support of a permanent administrative establishment. In some measure, goods and services contributed by the people precipitated out as the grand houses, assembly places, and temple platforms of chiefly precincts. In another measure, they were appropriated for the livelihood of circles of retainers, many of them close kinsmen of the chief, who clustered about the powerful paramounts. These were not all useless hangers-on. They were political cadres: supervisors of the stores, talking chiefs, ceremonial attendants, high priests who were intimately involved in political rule, envoys to transmit directives through the chiefdom. There were men in these chiefly retinues — in Tahiti and perhaps Hawaii, specialized warrior corps — whose force could be directed internally as a buttress against fragmenting or rebellious elements of the chiefdom. A Tahitian or Hawaiian high chief had more compelling sanctions than the harangue. He controlled a ready physical force, an armed body of executioners, which gave him mastery particularly over the lesser people of the community. While it looks a lot like the big-man's faction again, the differences in functioning of the great Polynesian chief's retinue are more significant than the superficial similarities in appearance. The chief's coterie, for one thing, is economically dependent upon him rather than he upon them. And in deploying the cadres politically in various sections of the chiefdom, or against the lower orders, the great Polynesian chiefs sustained command where the Melanesian big-man, in his external sector, had at best renown.

This is not to say that the advanced Polynesian chiefdoms were free of internal defect, of potential or actual malfunctioning. The large political-military apparatus indicates something of the opposite. So does the recent work of Irving Goldman[8] on the intensity of "status rivalry" in Polynesia, especially when it is considered that much of the status rivalry in developed chiefdoms, as the Hawaiian, amounted to popular rebellion against chiefly despotism rather than mere contest for position within the ruling-stratum. This suggests that Polynesian chiefdoms, just as Melanesian big-man orders, generate along with evolutionary development countervailing anti-authority pressures, and that the weight of the latter may ultimately impede further development.

The Polynesian contradiction seems clear enough. On one side, chieftainship is never detached from kinship moorings and kinship economic ethics. Even the greatest Polynesian chiefs were conceived superior kinsmen to the masses, fathers of their people, and generosity was morally incumbent upon them. On the other side, the major Polynesian paramounts seemed inclined to "eat the power of the government too much," as the Tahitians put it, to divert an undue proportion of the general wealth toward the chiefly establishment. The diversion could be accomplished by lowering the customary level of general redistribution, lessening the material returns of chieftainship to the community at large — tradition attributes the great rebellion of Mangarevan commoners to such cause. Or the diversion might — and I suspect more commonly did — consist in greater and more forceful exactions from lesser chiefs and people, increasing returns to the chiefly apparatus without necessarily affecting the level of general redistribution. In either case, the well-developed chiefdom creates for itself the dampening paradox of stoking rebellion by funding its authority.

In Hawaii and other islands cycles of political centralization and decentralization may be abstracted from traditional histories. That is, larger chiefdoms periodically fragmented into smaller and then were later reconstituted. Here would be more evidence of a tendency to overtax the political structure. But how to explain the emergence of a developmental stymie, of an inability to sustain political advance beyond a certain level? To point to a chiefly propensity to consume or a Polynesian propensity to rebel is not enough: such propensities are promoted by the very advance of chiefdoms. There is reason to hazard instead that Parkinson's notable law is behind it all: that progressive expansion in political scale entailed more-than-proportionate accretion in the ruling apparatus, unbalancing the flow of wealth in favor of the apparatus. The ensuing unrest then curbs the chiefly impositions, sometimes by reducing chiefdom scale to the nadir of the periodic cycle.

[8] Irving Goldman, "Status Rivalry and Cultural Evolution in Polynesia," *American Anthropologist* 57 (1957): 680–697; "Variations in Polynesian Social Organization," *Journal of the Polynesian Society* 66 (1957): 374–390.

Comparison of the requirements of administration in small and large Polynesian chiefdoms helps make the point.

A lesser chiefdom, confined say as in the Marquesas Islands to a narrow valley, could be almost personally ruled by a headman in frequent contact with the relatively small population. Melville's partly romanticized — also for its ethnographic details, partly cribbed — account in *Typee* makes this clear enough. But the great Polynesian chiefs had to rule much larger, spatially dispersed, internally organized populations. Hawaii, an island over four thousand square miles with an aboriginal population approaching one hundred thousand, was at times a single chiefdom, at other times divided into two to six independent chiefdoms, and at all times each chiefdom was composed of large subdivisions under powerful subchiefs. Sometimes a chiefdom in the Hawaiian group extended beyond the confines of one of the islands, incorporating part of another through conquest. Now, such extensive chiefdoms would have to be coordinated; they would have to be centrally tapped for a fund of power, buttressed against internal disruption, sometimes massed for distant, perhaps overseas, military engagements. All of this to be implemented by means of communication still at the level of word-of-mouth, and means of transportation consisting of human bodies and canoes. (The extent of certain larger chieftainships, coupled with the limitations of communication and transportation, incidentally suggests another possible source of political unrest: that the burden of provisioning the governing apparatus would tend to fall disproportionately on groups within easiest access of the paramount.) A tendency for the developed chiefdom to proliferate in executive cadres, to grow top-heavy, seems in these circumstances altogether functional, even though the ensuing drain on wealth proves the chiefdom's undoing. Functional also, and likewise a material drain on the chiefdom at large, would be widening distinctions between chiefs and people in style of life. Palatial housing, ornamentation and luxury, finery and ceremony, in brief, conspicuous consumption, however much it seems mere self-interest always has a more decisive social significance. It creates those invidious distinctions between rulers and ruled so conducive to a passive — hence quite economical! — acceptance of authority. Throughout history, inherently more powerful political organizations than the Polynesian, with more assured logistics of rule, have turned to it — including in our time some ostensibly revolutionary and proletarian governments, despite every pre-revolutionary protestation of solidarity with the masses and equality for the classes.

In Polynesia then, as in Melanesia, political evolution is eventually shortcircuited by an overload on the relations between leaders and their people. The Polynesian tragedy, however, was somewhat the opposite of the Melanesian. In Polynesia, the evolutionary ceiling was set by extraction from the population at large in favor of the chiefly faction, in Melanesia by extraction from the big-man's faction in favor of distribution to the population at large. Most importantly, the Polynesian ceiling was higher. Melanesian big-men and Polynesian chiefs not only reflect different varieties and levels of political evolution, they display in different degrees the capacity to generate and to sustain political progress.

Especially emerging from their juxtaposition is the more decisive impact of Polynesian chiefs on the economy, the chiefs' greater leverage on the output of the several households of society. The success of any primitive political organization is decided here, in the control that can be developed over household economies. For the household is not merely the principal productive unit in primitive societies, it is often quite capable of autonomous direction of its own production, and it is oriented towards production for its own, not societal consumption. The greater potential of Polynesian chieftainship is precisely the greater pressure it could exert on household output, its capacity both to generate a surplus and to deploy it out of the household towards a broader division of labor, cooperative construction, and massive ceremonial and military action. Polynesian chiefs were the more effective means of societal collaboration on economic, political, indeed all cultural fronts. Perhaps we have been too long accustomed to perceive rank and rule from the standpoint of the individuals involved, rather than from the perspective of the total society, as if the secret of the subordination of man to man lay in the personal satisfactions of power. And then the breakdowns too, or the evolutionary limits, have been searched out in men, in "weak" kings or megalomaniacal dictators — always, "who is the matter?" An excursion into the field of primitive politics suggests the more fruitful conception that the gains of political developments accrue more decisively to society than to individuals, and the failings as well are of structure not men.

26

Psychological preparations for war

ANTHONY F. C. WALLACE

*Wars are violent disputes that take place between different political
groups. They reflect conflicts for which there are no political
remedies. But the pain and hardship of war leads to the question,
How can people be induced to fight? The answer, according to
Anthony F. C. Wallace in this selection, lies in mobilization for
emergencies, a process found in all societies. The mobilized state
characterized by a high degree of order and obedience to authority
rather than hatred of an enemy is the key to participation in conflict.
Prevention of war, however, will depend not on a change in human
nature or the eradication of the mobilization process, but on the
creation of political processes and structures that manage the disputes
or perceived threats that lead societies into conflict.*

War is the sanctioned use of lethal weapons by members of one society
against members of another. It is carried out by trained persons working
in teams that are directed by a separate policy-making group and supported in various ways by the noncombatant population. Generally, but
not necessarily, war is reciprocal. There are few, if any, societies that
have not engaged in at least one war in the course of their known history,
and some have been known to wage wars continuously for generations
at a stretch.

Because war is apparently perverse, being both painful and sought
after, people frequently give psychological explanations for it. Those
who think about it with resignation, or with favor, conclude that making
war is part of human nature, like making love; others are equally convinced that nothing so evil can be explained except as the result of social-

From *War: The Anthropology of Armed Conflict and Aggression* ed. by Marvin Harris, Morton
Fried, and Robert Murphy. Copyright © 1967 by the Museum of Natural History; copyright
© 1968 by Doubleday & Company, Inc. Reprinted by permission of the publisher.

or psychopathology. In this discussion, however, we shall not be concerned to answer the ultimate question, but a more limited one: What, if any, psychological preparation is required for a society to enter *a* war?

THE STATE OF MOBILIZATION

The principal psychological preparation for war is the training of all members of the society to participate efficiently in a social process that I shall call mobilization. I do not refer here simply to military mobilization in the modern sense of calling up reservists and drafting hitherto uncommitted men and resources to a war, although that is one instance of the larger phenomenon. Rather, I refer to the fact that all human societies, and the societies of many of the higher primates below man, are observed to exist alternately in two states. In one of these, lone individuals and a variety of subgroups occupy themselves in resting and in diversified and complexly coordinated economic, sexual, educational, and other activities. In the other state, the population arranges itself precisely into three well-defined groups — the policymakers, the young males, and the females and children — and the entire society coordinates its activities under the leadership of recognized authority toward the achievement of a single task. The former state I shall call the relaxed state; the latter, the mobilized state; and mobilization is the process of transformation from the relaxed to the mobilized state.

· Among the lower primates, the baboon troops described by DeVore (1965), and DeVore and Washburn (1963), and others are the most obvious example of this alternation of states. In the relaxed state, the troop is dispersed: an aggregate of individuals and small groups engaged in feeding, grooming, sleeping, sex, and play. In the mobilized state — which is assumed while the troop is traveling — there is an exact partition of the troop into three groups, which occupy different and traditional positions in the line of march: the lesser males are at the front and rear, where they can confront challenges from predators; the dominant males and females carrying infants are in the center; and the other females and juveniles surround the central group. Similar formal traveling, hunting, and defensive dispositions have been described for a number of other social species. The capacity to mobilize is a widespread feature of animal behavior.

In man, the mobilized state, and its contrast to the relaxed state, has also been described in detail for many societies, although the large size and complexity of human groups often obscure the generality of the distinction. Gearing (1958) clearly conceptualized the difference in Cherokee culture between what he called the structural pose of peace and the structural pose of war and described the institutional arrangements associated with each. These two structural poses for peace and war, in similar institutional form, are assumed by a number of North American Indian tribes. One thinks also of the elegant and rigid arrangements of camp circle and police developed by the Plains Indians when they were hunting buffalo. In band and tribal societies generally, travel, hunting, and war require the state of mobilization. But in modern societies, characterized by urbanism, the nation-state, and complex and powerful technology, the alternation between the relaxed state and the mobilized state in matters of transportation, food getting, civil defense, and so on must proceed on different schedules for different institutions and localities. The whole nation still mobilizes only for a revitalization movement (a movement whose aim is to reform and reinvigorate a culture) and for war.

THE PROCESS OF MOBILIZATION

In order for a society to shift from the relaxed to the mobilized state, the population must receive a releasing stimulus, in response to which everyone promptly disposes himself according to a plan. Obviously the stimulus must be broadcast in order that all members of the population receive it quickly, correctly, and simultaneously. For a small band, most of whose members are always within earshot of one another, this is relatively easy. But the larger the group, the more difficult it is to prevent the communication from being distorted in transmission, from reaching individuals at different times, and from being seriously delayed in reaching some. Hence, as a society increases in size and as its territorial boundaries enlarge, cultural innovations are required that will ensure speed and reliability in communication of the releasing stimulus and any associated instructions. This requirement has probably prompted many tribal and early urban societies to invent special language codes, systems of graphic symbols, broadcast devices, and roads and other transportation methods, and to train men in the arts of precise memorization of messages and of rapid and careful travel.

It is also obviously desirable, although not necessary, that the releasing stimulus not merely elicit a disciplined response but evoke a motivational system appropriate to the action to be taken. Here the society enters into a kind of conspiracy with itself to combine the alerting signal with symbolic content that, given a certain distribution of modal personality variables, will arouse maximum desirable emotion. The releasing stimulus is therefore apt to be — particularly in the case of mobilization for war — a report that a certain kind of event has occurred to which people with that character type will respond with anger, determination, fear, or whatever affective state is desired by the communicating group. For Iroquois Indians, this symbolically arousing stimulus was always a report that a kinsman had been killed and that a survivor demanded revenge. For twentieth-century Americans, the symbolically arousing stimulus is apt to be the report that helpless Americans or their allies are being held prisoner or are under attack, and must be rescued.

It is important to note, however, that this embellishment of the releasing stimulus is not, and cannot be, necessary to ensure mobilization. A population is composed of persons with a variety of character structures and personal motives, many with limited intelligence and others suffering from greater or lesser degrees of psychopathology, and mobilization must proceed independent of private motive. Hence, atrocity stories, scare reports, and the like are never adequate to ensure mobilization; indeed, in some situations, such as medical emergencies, they appear to interfere with it. Thus the intensity of the emotion aroused must not be so high as to preoccupy the person being mobilized; the symbol must function more as a rationalization for personal sacrifice than as a stimulus toward unrestrained violence or flight.

TRAINING FOR MOBILIZATION

It is apparent that the shift from the relaxed to the mobilized state must be taken by people who have already learned what to do in response to the releasing stimulus. In all societies this learning probably occurs very early in life, and very largely without didactic instruction, in the course of the child's living through the alternating states of relaxation and mobilization. He learns, while acquiring the language, and by constant observation and participation, the difference between the two states and the nature of the three main status groups characteristic of the mobilized state. And as he grows older, he is trained more and more explicitly to recognize the releasing stimulus, to take orders, and to play specific roles in one of the groups.

One critically necessary feature of this learning is the development of a readiness to move from a situation characterized by considerable personal freedom and democratic, consensual decision making to a hierarchical and authoritarian structural pose. In many band and tribal cultures there is little in the way of coercive authority exercised in the making of decisions during the relaxed state but a very high degree of it in states of mobilization. Thus, among the Iroquois daily life in the village was largely managed by tradition, supplemented by consensual decision when alternative policies had to be chosen, and children were generally given a great deal of freedom. The Iroquois were famous, at least among European observers, for their intolerance of personal constraint. But when a war party mobilized, the participants suddenly assumed a posture of rigorous discipline under the command of a captain who had unquestioned and absolute authority during the military mission. At the end of the expedition, however, this authority terminated, and the captain's influence after that depended entirely on the willingness of other citizens to take his advice in council.

How the early Iroquois trained their children to be able to switch structural pose is not clear from the records available to us now. But a great deal of information is at hand to reveal how our own children are trained to switch poses. A classic example is the school fire drill, which, in addition to improving the chances of evacuating a school quickly in case of fire, provides a general model of how to mobilize in an emergency. At the sound of the alarm, the physical disposition and social relationships of the children abruptly change from the relaxed order characteristic of class or play group to the exact discipline of the fire drill line of march. Similar training in mobilization is given in athletic activities and in popular literature and film, where the training takes the form of play and spectator sport. The principle that is communicated in such exercises, apart from their specific utility, is that when the mobilization signal is heard, automatic obedience to recognized authority is required and assumes priority over other motives.

THE IMPERSONALITY OF WAR

So far, we have discussed the phenomenon of mobilization as the central theme in psychological preparation for war. But what of the fear, suspicion, and hatred of "the enemy," traditionally believed to be prerequisites for war, that are often invoked by the releasing signal? It is my contention that far from being necessary, these attitudes are almost irrelevant to war except as rationalizations. Human beings generally reserve their settled fears, suspicions, and hatreds for those closest to them: kinsmen, neighbors, and colleagues. Today's enemy in war is yesterday's stranger and tomorrow's ally. The psychological target of lethal weapons in war is an abstraction rather than a person (as the saying goes, "I have nothing against you personally"); hence any member of a society that at the moment happens to be classified as an enemy is apt, in one way or another, to be fair game (with "no hard feelings," of course). Few soldiers ever personally kill anybody; those who kill often do not actually see what they hit; and most never push a button, pull a trigger, or throw a grenade in combat.

War is never really total; its aim is never the absolute annihilation of the enemy and all his works; death and destruction are limited by more or less arbitrary restraints concerning the weapons to be used, the treatment of prisoners, civilians, and nonmilitary targets, and the goals of military action. Thus, being removed from hate, war is also relatively free of guilt. This is not to say that some persons may not displace domestic hate upon foreign enemies by psychiatrically familiar mechanisms of defense, nor that bereaved persons, or those who have suffered personal threat or injury, do not experience, at least for a time, a very personal hatred. But such feelings are not a reliable indicator of efficiency in combat, where an ability to maintain cognitive orientation and a commitment to task-completion in noisy, fatiguing, and dangerous surroundings may be much more important than a high level of primitive urges to fight-or-flight.

Nor can war usefully be regarded as essentially an outgrowth of mass hysteria or mass movements, although some wars, and some events in most wars, are affected by such contagious enthusiasms. A religiously dedicated population, for instance, is likely to be easy to mobilize and difficult to defeat. But the action of a mob in sacking a building or in lynching a neighbor is almost the opposite of war, for it is directed toward the matériel and persons of one's own community, and by definition is carried out without communication of the releasing signal by authority.

Thus, in our technologically sophisticated society, it is readily apparent that it is possible for half of the national budget and a substantial proportion of our young men to be mobilized to fight an enemy seen by few and rarely recognized even when seen. Lethal weapons are employed by technicians who never set eyes on their human targets. Nor can the other side claim a much more personal focus of their military activities. War is an extremely impersonal business conducted by persons whose private motives — apart from the motive of efficient participation in the state of mobilization — are highly diversified.

THE INTERESTS SERVED BY WAR

We have, so far, discussed the psychological preparations required for a people as a whole to conduct war effectively and have argued that little more is required than a population trained to respond affirmatively to the mobilization signal and to carry out orders from recognized authority. But what determines the communication of this signal?

The signal must be given by a person or group recognized as having the responsibility to do so when the situation requires it. This, in contemporary industrial societies, is apt to include at least some of the persons who will make policy during the mobilization state, but in general it is not necessary that the body that gives the signal for war be the body that directs the conduct and arranges the termination of the war. It is obvious enough that this signal will be given when an authorized person perceives that a threat exists to the continued functioning of the system that cannot be met by the society without shifting to the mobilized state and using lethal weapons against members of another society. When the society is under physical attack itself, the danger is obvious, and war may be the only alternative to abandoning hope of maintaining, or returning to, the traditional form of relaxed state; it may even be the only alternative to destruction. But sometimes even when no serious attack is threatened, the authorized body communicates the releasing signal, the society mobilizes, begins to use lethal weapons, and initiates an extremely costly and, sometimes, fatal conflict.

I have already suggested that war is often perverse. It is well known to pacifist and soldier alike that many wars are unnecessary, disastrous, even catastrophic mistakes. They do not serve the purpose, whatever it may be, for which the society has mobilized, and they cause immense suffering and damage. The sense of moral outrage that such events arouse does not carry us far, however, in trying to understand how these disasters happen. Political witch-hunting and accusations of psychopathology and criminal conspiracy may simply obscure the facts. In one minor war whose inception is very well documented — the Black Hawk War between the United States and the Sac and Fox Indians in 1832 — the record clearly shows that the responsible policy-making bodies on both sides were *not* in favor of war. An irresponsible insistence by an Indian faction on crossing the Mississippi River to join forces with a religious prophet, and lack of discipline in an Illinois militia detachment, precipitated the first firing of guns, and a sequence of events followed mechanically that resulted in the death, from disease, starvation, and bullets, of several hundred Indians and whites. The critical event was a misunderstanding. The Indians, disillusioned with their prophet, attempted to surrender to the militia before a shot was fired in order to gain free passage back across the Mississippi to their tribal territory. The militia were drunk, had no interpreter, and were unaccustomed to discipline, and fired on the peace party. In the ensuing melee the militia were defeated by the Indian warriors, who then fled with their women and children in an effort to escape across the river by a different route. But the use of lethal weapons on a militia detachment automatically set in motion a sequence of communications that resulted in the mobilization signal being given by the President of the United States. The Sac and Fox council, however, refused to broadcast *their* signal, and the fighting was restricted to the east bank of the Mississippi; the Indian territory across the river was not attacked.

Such examples could, of course, be multiplied *ad nauseam*. The point they illustrate is that unwanted wars — and most wars are now unwanted — occur as a result of a perversion of administrative process rather than as a result of popular folly. The types and sources of such perversions are complex. In some cases, the psychopathology of administrative personnel is evidently responsible (the case of Nazi Germany is the best example of this type). In other cases, responsible and intelligent administrators attempting to act in the best long-term interests of their society are precipitated by misinformation, communication failures, and a rigid, poorly designed system of decision making into unnecessarily mobilizing the society for war.

From this point of view, it would appear that the administrative structure of any society — and every society has an administrative structure at least latent during the relaxation phase and active during its mobilization phases — is extraordinarily vulnerable to perversion in regard to war decisions.

THE PREVENTION OF WAR

There are few people who take the position that *all* war is a mistake or is morally wrong, and who refuse therefore to mobilize for war on behalf of their society in any role and under any circumstance whatever. Most pacifists refuse to kill personally but support mobilization in other ways. Generally speaking, organized opposition to war is opposition to *a* war that is believed to be morally wrong or, practically, a mistake. These opponents of war are willing to fight if mobilized in what they regard as a good cause. Nonetheless, despite the rarity of true and radical pacifism, there are few persons in industrial countries today who would deny that preventing war from occurring is a task of paramount importance. It has come to be recognized as one of the principal unsolved problems of mankind.

Short of universal pacifism or the inclusion of all countries in one state, the means of preventing war would seem to lie in the invention and diffusion of more effective political and administrative processes. It is, to put it crudely, a problem of developing a number of interrelated "fail-safe" systems that will reduce the probability of mistakes (in technology, in intergroup relations, in communication, and in personality function) from precipitating a war while other means of resolving conflicts of interest are being employed. The kind of fail-safe devices to which I refer are not merely sophisticated electronic systems, which control the weapons themselves. They are also principles in human relationships that, making use of what we already know about human beings, minimize the likelihood of any society perceiving itself as being in a situation of external threat so dire that war or destruction are seen as the only alternatives. Not all such intersocietal threats are economic and military; perhaps the most dangerous threats of all are threats to self-respect and threats to interfere with local revitalization movements.

It is not very likely, in the immediate future, that universal disarmament or a single world state will come into being. Nor is it desirable, even if it were possible, to eliminate the principal psychological preparation for war — training for mobilization — for societies must be able to mobilize for other purposes, even if not for war. And it is irrelevant to propose that undeluded, nonhating, freely loving young people be raised and nourished, for they will be the best fighters of all. If the last century has taught us anything about human nature, it is that good persons can do impersonal evil and that war does not require hate.

CONCLUSION

In conclusion, my argument may be summarized briefly as the assertion that the main process of preparing a people for war is simply training them to participate obediently in mobilization for concerted action in emergencies. War does not require training a people to hate an external enemy. Since training for mobilization is unavoidable, and the elimination of intergroup hostility would be irrelevant, it is clear that the prevention of war will not be accomplished either by eliminating its basis in psychological preparation or by improving human nature. Rather, the problem of ensuring peace must be approached by the innovation of political and administrative safeguards that guarantee that alternative processes of conflict resolution are not interrupted by war-by-mistake.

IX

Religion, magic, and world view

People seem most content when they are confident about themselves and the order of things around them. Uncertainty breeds debilitating anxiety; insecurity saps people's sense of purpose and their willingness to participate in social activity. Most of the time our usual cultural institutions serve as a lens through which we can reliably view and interpret the world and respond to its demands. But from time to time the unexpected or the contradictory intervenes to shake our assurance. A farmer may wonder about his skill when a properly planted and tended crop fails to grow. A wife may feel bewildered when the man she has treated with tenderness and justice for many years runs off with another woman. Death, natural disaster, and countless other forms of adversity strike without warning, eating away at the foundations of our confidence.

At these crucial points in life, we often fill the gap in our knowledge with answers of another kind. We employ a religious dimension to help account for the vagaries of our experience. Religion is cultural knowledge, often associated with the supernatural, that people use to cope with the ultimate problems of their existence. Its use gives us a sense of understanding and control. A crop failure takes on meaning if it can be attributed to the will of God. Unfaithfulness in a spouse makes sense when it is thought to be the outcome of love magic. Adversity, if not controllable, may seem less threatening when we identify the spirit, deity, or witch causing it.

People may deal with misfortune and uncertainty through magic or religious ritual. Magic consists of the strategies used to control supernatural power. Specialists in magic, often referred to as shamans, possess their own power or know sayings and rituals that control supernatural force. They seek to produce clearly defined ends, such as the healing of a patient or the growth of a crop. During the ritual, the magician may imitate the desired result, may draw power to effect it from some sacred fetish such as a rabbit's foot, or may minister to a piece of the object or person he wishes to influence.

Religious ritual most often entails the worship of deities or spirits. Supplicants seek to influence supernatural beings through prayer, sacrifice, and several other forms of religious expression. Worshippers do not control the gods, but they do achieve a sense of well-being in the belief that their world is in friendly, or at least trustworthy, hands.

World view refers to a system of comprehensive concepts and often unstated assumptions about life. It usually contains a cosmology about the way things are and a mythology concerning how things have come to be that way. World view presents answers to some of the more general questions and contradictions surrounding our lives. Death, conflicting values, and the meaning of human existence may all find explanation in a group's world view.

Religion, magic, and world view also serve a social function. Human societies are fragile, complex entities, continuously bombarded by disruptive changes and strained by the individual ambitions of their members. Important values are easily forgotten or ignored; significant social conventions may disappear or meet with a variety of interpretations. Religion and magic regularly dramatize important features of the social structure. In our society, preachers of many denominations and faiths regularly remind us of our social responsibilities, emphasize the importance of our relationships by conducting baptisms and weddings, and review what was laudable about us at our funerals. Such social consequences go hand in hand with religion's psychological functions.

27

When technology fails:
Magic and religion in New Guinea

PHILIP L. NEWMAN

All people experience anxiety when confronted with situations they cannot control, and in many societies natural methods of influencing and predicting events work only part of the time. In such instances, supernatural forces are invoked to account for such events and our relation to them. In this article, Philip Newman describes the use of magic and witchcraft by a highland New Guinea people and shows that they employ such practices throughout their lives whenever faced with uncertainty. He suggests that magical procedures can be ranked according to their ability to release tension, and that the choice of particular magical practices correlates with the degree of anxiety to be reduced.

Man has created many forms in his quest for means of dealing with the world around him. Whether these forms be material tools, social groups, or intangible ideas, they are all, in a sense, "instruments": each is a means to some end; each has a purpose that it fulfills. When we think of such things as magical rites, a belief in ghosts, or accusations of sorcery, however, the matter of purpose becomes less obvious. In the descriptions and in the case history that follow, we will try both to show something of the magical and religious beliefs of a New Guinea people and to demonstrate the purposes that these beliefs have for the men who hold them.

In the mountainous interior of Australian New Guinea, the Asaro River has its headwaters some thirty miles to the north of Goroka, a European settlement that serves as the administrative center for the

Originally published as "Sorcery, Religion, and the Man." With permission from *Natural History*, Vol. 71, No. 2; Copyright the American Museum of Natural History, 1962.

Central Highlands District. Near Goroka, the Asaro flows through a wide valley where the ground cover is mostly grasses and reeds. In its upper reaches, this valley narrows into a gorge where steep, heavily forested ridges reach out toward the river from mountain masses on either side. Some 12,000 people live on this part of the river, occupying an area of approximately 200 square miles. While these people are culturally and linguistically similar, they do not form a single political unit. Indeed, before contact with Europeans, the area was characterized by incessant intertribal warfare. Even now, when active warfare is no longer part of their lives, the pattern of alliances and animosities among the tribes is a factor in social intercourse.

Except for the cessation of warfare, life in the valley today is little changed from what it was before the Australian government began active pacification of the area after the end of World War II. Almost daily, the people climb up from the valley floor to enter the dense forest on the mountain slopes. It is here that building wood is gathered; birds and small marsupials are shot for meat, plumage, or fur; plants that provide for many needs are collected.

Below an altitude of some 7,000 feet, the forest has been cut back to make room for gardens that cling to the sides of steep ridges and crowd together in the narrow valley floors. These gardens provide the people's staple foods — sweet potatoes, yams, sugar cane, and a variety of green vegetables. A woman spends most of her time at garden work, preparing new planting areas, weeding the crop, and harvesting the mature plants. In fallow areas nearby she can turn loose the pigs her husband has entrusted to her care. If they wander too far afield by evening, her call will bring them back on the run. They know that a meal awaits them, as well as a snooze by the fire in their "mother's" house.

While each family may have one or more houses near the forest or in their garden, the center of social life is the village. The villages are located on the tops of ridges in spots usually selected with an eye to their defensibility against enemies. The fifteen to twenty houses that compose each village usually march in single file along the narrow ridge. But, if space permits, they are formed into a square. All the houses are much alike — round, about fifteen feet in diameter, made of double rows of five-foot stakes. The space between the stakes is filled with grass and the outside covered with strips of bark. The roof is thatched and topped with a long, tasseled pole.

Two or three houses always stand out. They are larger, they are not in line with the rest, and they may have as many as eight poles protruding through their roofs. These are the men's houses. As a rule, men and women do not live together, for the men fear that too much contact with women is weakening. For this reason, a man builds a house for his wife — or each of them, if he has more than one — and then helps in the construction of the larger house where he and the other men of the village will sleep apart. Ideally, all the men who live together in a single house can trace their descent back to a known, common ancestor. They thus constitute a lineage. Such a lineage is connected to the other village men's houses by descent links, but in many cases the links are so amorphous that no one can actually tell what they are. Similarly, several villages will be linked together into a clan, but genealogical ties may be more imputed than real.

Just as the forest and the garden represent the physical framework within which each individual lives, so too these various orders of grouping — the lineage, the village, the clan, and the tribe — represent the social framework of existence. The members of these groups are the people with whom each individual is in daily contact. They nurture him, teach him, and assist him in times of crisis. It is from these groups that he derives such things as his name, his rights to the land for gardening and hunting, and the financial help that he needs when it is time to purchase a wife. They hail his birth and mourn his death.

In turn, each individual has obligations to the other members of these groups. He acts as a representative of his group when dealing with outsiders. In this way, he enters into a whole series of relationships with individuals and groups outside his own immediate circle. He may visit a neighboring clan to help one of his own clansmen win the admiration of a prospective bride by sitting up all night near the hot fire singing love songs to her. Or a trip may take him to a nearby tribe, where he dances mightily with other men to show that his group is appreciative of the gift of food and valuables they are about to receive. He may walk several days over difficult ground to reach a completely alien group, where he can barter for shells, plumes, or foodstuffs not available in his own group. As in all societies, the groups comprising the society provide for the individual, while the individual, in turn, contributes some of his efforts to the life of the group.

Man not only has his tools and his society to help cope with the world: he also has his ideas. There are some problems presented by the environment for which the people of the upper Asaro have not yet devised a mechanical or technical solution. There are other problems for which a technical solution seems not enough. Finally, there are problems for which an idea seems to be an inherently better solution than a physical or social tool. It is here that we enter the realm of magic and religion.

A great many of the activities among the upper Asaro people have a magical or religious component. When a child is born, it is cleaned, fed, and covered with grease to help protect it from the cool mountain air. It is also protected, nonphysically, by burying its umbilical cord in some secluded spot — so that sorcerers cannot later use this piece of the newformed being to cause illness or death by magical means. During the first few days of life, the infant is also made to accept, via magic, his first social responsibility — not to cry at night and disturb its mother. A small bundle of sweet-smelling grass is placed on the mother's head and her desire for uninterrupted slumber is blown into the grass by an attendant. The grass is then crushed over the head of the child and its pungent odor released so that the infant will breathe in the command along with the scent of the plant.

Throughout an individual's life there will be magical rites to protect him from various dangers, to overcome difficulties, and to assist his growth. When a young boy kills his first animal, his hand will be magically "locked" in the position that first sent an arrow on a true course. When he reaches puberty and moves out of his mother's house to begin his life in the men's house, he will be ritually cleansed of the contamination he has been subjected to during his years of association with women. If he were not so cleansed, he would never become strong enough to engage in men's activities. During the years when a young man is trying to win the favor of a girl, he not only relies on his prowess in singing love songs and his decorations, but on his knowledge of love magic as well. If all the usual spells and potions fail, he may utilize one especially powerful form that is thought to make him appear to his beloved with an entirely new face — the face of someone he knows she likes.

In his mature years, when a man's attention turns to the growth of pigs and gardens, he will have magical as well as technical skills to help him. Gardens are not difficult to grow in this fertile land, but it is still wise to put a certain series of leaves across one's fences, so that any thief will find his arms and legs paralyzed should he decide to raid the garden. It also behooves one whose gardens are near the main trails and settlements to give them magical assistance, for a slow-growing garden in such a conspicuous place could be an embarrassment.

The raising of pigs is a more difficult matter, and it is here that magical and religious rites become greatly elaborated. Some of these rites are performed by an individual for his own pigs. It may be a simple performance, as when smoke is blown into the ear of a wild pig to tame it. The theory is that the smoke cools and dries the pig's "hot" disposition. On the other hand, these individual rites may attain considerable complexity, as in the propitiation of forest spirits called *nokondisi*. These spirits are capricious in nature — sometimes playing malicious tricks on men and sometimes performing acts of kindness. Each man, therefore, maintains a small, fenced enclosure in which he builds a miniature earth oven and a tiny house. By placing food in the earth oven he may be able to entice a *nokondisi* to come live near his pigs and watch after them. In return for the food, the spirit will help bring in lost pigs, protect the herd from thieves, and carry the animals safely across flooded streams during the rainy season.

In addition to the magic performed by an individual on behalf of his own pigs, some rather elaborate rites are performed by the lineage and clan for all the pigs belonging to these groups. The largest of these is the *gerua* ceremony, performed at intervals of from five to seven years. In this ritual, hundreds of pigs are killed and used to pay off various kinds of economic obligations to other clans. It is a time for feasting and dancing, for courting and reunion. It is also a time for propitiating the ghosts of the dead in the hope that they will help the living grow their pigs. All the pigs are killed in the name of particular ghosts. The songs are pleas for ghostly assistance. The wooden *gerua* boards, with their colorful geometric designs, are visible symbols to the ghosts that they have not been forgotten. It is not tender sentiment that motivates this display, however. Rather, it is the fear that failure to do so will engender the wrath of the ever watchful dead.

The magical and religious beliefs that we have so far examined are all used in conjunction with other practices of a nonmagical nature. There are some areas, however, where no purely technical solutions are available, and where magic and religion are the only "tools" available. One such area is sickness. The people of the upper Asaro are not generally aware of modern medical practices, although efforts are being made in that direction. The nonmagical techniques available to them, such as inhaling the steam from fragrant plants to relieve a stopped-up nose, are few. These remedies do not extend to more serious maladies. When serious illness strikes, the only recourse is to magic.

The magical solutions available are many and varied. There are herbs with magical properties that are administered in much the same way as are medicines in our own society. I made a cursory check, however, which seems to show that few of the plants possess any curative value.

Ghosts and forest spirits are frequently thought to be the causes of illness, for they are deemed capable of entering the body and devouring a person's inner organs. Cures for such illnesses usually involve propitiation of the offending supernatural.

Witches and sorcerers are believed to be another major cause of illness, for they are supposedly capable of injecting foreign bodies into a victim, or performing black magic on objects that have been in association with the victim. To cure illness caused in this way involves calling in a magical specialist who can either extract the foreign bodies or retrieve the objects being operated upon.

While the ideas and rites listed here do not exhaust the entire inventory available to the group under discussion, they give some sense of the variety that exists. The notions are interesting in themselves, but the question of how an individual makes use of these notions is even more fascinating. Let us look at a crisis in the life of one of these people, and see how he picks and chooses among the various "tools" at his disposal.

Ombo was a young man in his early thirties. He had been married for about five years, but was childless. Early one April, it was announced in the traditional style that his wife, Magara, was with child. On such an occasion, a food distribution is held in the village and the announcement, along with gifts of food, was sent out to related villages. Ombo was instructed in the food taboos he would have to undergo during the period of his wife's pregnancy to protect himself from her increased contamination.

All went well for the first few weeks and then Magara became ill. It is doubtful that her illness was associated with her pregnancy, for her symptoms were the classic signs of malaria — a rather rare disease in this part of the highlands. The first attempts to cure her involved a variety of highly regarded pseudomedications.

A potion of sweet-smelling leaves was administered. A command to the effect that the illness should depart was blown into the leaves, and the leaves were eaten. It was thought that the command, thus internalized, would drive out the illness.

At various other times, attempts were made to relieve her headaches and body pains by rubbing the afflicted areas with stinging nettles. It was held that when the welts and the pain caused by the nettles subsided, the pains in her body would also leave. On one occasion her husband blew smoke over her during a period of fever because, as we have seen, smoke is held to have a cooling and drying effect. He also painted various parts of her body with mud in an effort to cause the pain to dry up at the same time the mud dried.

This kind of treatment continued until early May without any noticeable improvement in Magara's condition. After almost a month had passed and it became apparent that the illness was not going away, Ombo began to speculate on a possible cause. During the next few weeks he came up with several solutions. While he had been away from the village, working for Europeans in Goroka, he had acquired some charms to help him win at a card game popular among the sophisticated younger men.

One of these charms was fairly new and he was worried that he might not have gained sufficient control over it. Since he kept it hidden in his wife's house, his conclusion was that the charm was exerting its influence on her and causing the illness. He therefore removed it from her house and sent it away to a friend in another tribe. There was no improvement in his wife's condition.

Ombo's next action was to destroy his spirit house. He had not kept it in good repair and had not been diligent in feeding the *nokondisi* that lived there. His father suggested that the angered spirit was taking revenge on Magara. By destroying the house of the spirit, Ombo caused it to retreat to the forest where it could do no harm. Finally, he burned the costly paraphernalia of a potent sorcery technique he had purchased some years before, fearing it affected his wife.

By now it was late in May. Magara had become so ill that she stopped all but the most minimal work in her garden. Concern about her illness began to increase, and people outside the immediate family began to speculate about its cause. Ombo's older brother mentioned one day that a malevolent ghost might be behind it. It was not long after this that a meeting was held in the men's house and Fumai, a member of the lineage, recounted a dream he had had the night before. In it, he had seen the ghost of Ombo's great-grandmother sitting in the forest near the spot where *gerua* boards are displayed for the ancestors. She had covered herself with ashes and, in a fit of self-pity, was wailing loudly because no one had made a *gerua* board in her honor at the last *gerua* ceremony, and no one had killed a pig in her name. Since ashes are put on at the death of a near relative as a sign of mourning, while clay is put on if the deceased is more distantly related, and since ghosts are thought to be capable of causing death, it was concluded that the dream was prophetic. It implied the imminent death of Magara at the great-grandmother's hands unless something were done.

The next day, Ombo and his wife, along with his parents and siblings, set out for the spot where the ghost had been "seen." A pig was killed there in honor of the ghost. It was cooked in an earth oven filled with valued food items — the largest sweet potatoes, the most succulent yams, and the most highly prized varieties of taro. While water was being poured into the oven, a speech was addressed to the ghost. It was pointed out that the food had been prepared and donated in her honor at considerable trouble to those present. The feeling was expressed that she should be satisfied with the amount and the quality of the offering. She was then told to refrain from causing trouble in the future. As the food steamed in the oven, a *gerua* board was made in the ghost's honor and placed among others in a nearby tree. Some of the food was eaten and the rest was later distributed among members of the lineage.

Things seemed to go well for the next few weeks. Magara improved and was able to return to her work in the garden. Discussion of the topic was dropped. Then, late in June, she suddenly became ill again. Ombo was greatly upset. I suggested to him that she might have malaria and should be taken to the medical aid post. But Ombo did not want to do this, for by now he was convinced that his wife was being attacked by a sorcerer. To deal with this threat, a magical specialist had to be called in. It was several days before he arrived, for he lived some distance away in another tribe. As with any good "doctor," his first acts were aimed at relieving his patient's pain and fever. With much physical strain, he literally pulled the pain from her body and cast it into the ground where it could do no further harm. His next task was to find out what was causing her illness. For over two hours he sat chatting with Ombo and Magara, discussing the history of the illness, the treatments that had been used, and their own life histories. All the while, he puffed on a tobacco pipe made of a bamboo tube. The degree of irritation caused by the smoke in his throat signalized the appearance in the conversation of significant diagnostic events. Finally, he announced his conclusion — illness by black magic.

To eliminate the effects of the imputed black magic, the object being manipulated by the sorcerer had to be recovered. To do this, the magical specialist first had a bundle of long, thin leaves prepared. Into the bundle were put cooked pork and a variety of plants with magical properties. The specialist never directly touched the bundle himself, but directed Ombo in its preparation. When the bundle was completed, it and a specially prepared bamboo tube were both carried into Magara's house. She was given the tube to hold and the bundle was hung in the rafters near the center pole. After a rite to protect her from further sorcery, Ombo and Magara were locked together in the house.

The specialist remained outside. He walked round and round the house, reciting spells and whirling a special plant around his head. He was pulling the unknown object away from the sorcerer and bringing it back home. The ceremony became a real struggle: the object would come tantalizingly close, only to slip away. Then the specialist announced that the object had arrived. Magara was instructed to open the bundle in the rafters. Inside, among the bits of meat, were a small spider and a piece of string of the type used to hang ornaments around the neck.

The spider, Magara and Ombo were told, was an assistant to the specialist. It had taken the string out of the sorcerer's house and into the open where the specialist could reach it with his powers. The sorcerer was thought to be a young man who had once wanted to marry Magara. The existence of a disappointed suitor was one fact that had come out during the specialist's long interview. When Magara had married Ombo, the suitor had become angry and cut a bit of her necklace string to use for sorcery. The specialist placed the recovered string in the bamboo tube that Magara had been holding, and the tube was then hidden away among the thatch.

From that time until late September, when I left the area, Magara did not experience any further attacks of illness, although she was not in the best of health. The community considered her cured. Significantly, her child was born prematurely in September and died two days later, but no one saw any connection between this death and her illness.

What, then, can we say about the purpose of such ideas and behavior patterns? A situation such as Magara's creates a great deal of tension in an individual who experiences it. If magic does nothing more, it allows the bearer of this tension to act. Both the patient and those concerned feel that something is being done. The pioneer anthropologist Bronislaw Malinowski long ago made the point: "Magic expresses the greater value for man of confidence over doubt, of steadfastness over vacillation, of optimism over pessimism."

It is a rare man indeed, however, who can maintain his confidence and optimism in the face of repeated failure. The question then arises, why is it that magic is not more readily given up? Three answers have traditionally been given to this question, all of them valid. In the first place, for people such as these, there is no alternative. Secondly, for the believer in the efficacy of magic, the occasional chance successes are more significant than repeated failure. Finally, explanations for failures are always at hand. Inadvertent errors in spells or formulas that must be performed precisely, or imagined countermagic, are ready explanations that are necessarily built into the very nature of magic.

The case history we have seen suggests still a fourth answer. This answer becomes apparent, however, only if we examine the way in which an individual makes use of the magical notions available to him. In the progression of the various magical techniques and explanations employed by Ombo, we can see that they call for behavior patterns allowing for increasingly aggressive release of the tension built up in him by the failure of previously selected techniques.

The simple pseudomedicinal rites, such as rubbing with nettles and painting with mud, were enough to reduce the tension of the initial crisis. The treatment was symptomatic and there was no attempt to identify the cause of the illness. When it became apparent that these techniques had failed, we find Ombo resorting to the more drastic measure of destroying valuable property. The frustration was not yet great enough to cause him to seek outlets in other people: that which he destroyed and removed from his use belonged only to him. In the next phase, we find that a ghost is predicated as the causative agent. One need not be nice to ghosts. They, like the living, are thought to be a mercenary lot who do not much care what is said about them as long as they get their just due. The speech made to the great-grandmother was studded with commands and expressions of anger at the trouble the ghost had caused. This was an excellent mechanism for the release of tension, just as was the physical act of killing the pig.

Finally, we see the most aggressive act of all — accusing a specific individual of sorcery. The accused individual was a member of an enemy tribe and lived some distance away. It was, therefore, unlikely that accuser and accused would often meet. But if the two had come together, a fight would have been inevitable. In former times, this could have led to open warfare. Thus, Ombo not only used magic as a tool against disease, but also selected the magical tools in such an order that his own increasing anxiety was relieved by increasingly aggressive actions. It is thus not only the forms created by man that enable him to cope with the world he meets, but the very way in which he manipulates those forms that are available to him.

28

Baseball magic

GEORGE J. GMELCH

Americans pride themselves on their "scientific" approach to life and problem solving. But as George Gmelch demonstrates in this article, American baseball players, much like the New Guinea Highlanders described by Philip Newman in the previous section, also depend to a great extent on supernatural forces to ensure success in their athletic endeavors. He demonstrates that the findings of anthropologists in distant cultures shed light on our own cultural practices.

> We find magic wherever the elements of chance and accident, and the emotional play between hope and fear have a wide and extensive range. We do not find magic wherever the pursuit is certain, reliable, and well under the control of rational methods. — Bronislaw Malinowski.

Professional baseball is a nearly perfect arena in which to test Malinowski's hypothesis about magic. The great anthropologist was not, of course, talking about sleight of hand but of rituals, taboos and fetishes that men resort to when they want to ensure that things go their own way. Baseball is rife with this sort of magic, but, as we shall see, the players use it in some aspects of the game far more than in others.

Everyone knows that there are three essentials of baseball — hitting, pitching and fielding. The point is, however, that the first two, hitting and pitching, involve a high degree of chance. The pitcher is the player least able to control the outcome of his own efforts. His best pitch may be hit for a bloop single while his worst pitch may be hit directly to one of his fielders for an out. He may limit the opposition to a single hit and lose, or he may give up a dozen hits and win. It is not uncommon for pitchers to perform well and lose, and vice versa; one has only to look at the frequency with which pitchers end a season with poor won-

Published by permission of Transaction, Inc., from *Transaction*, Vol. 8, #8. Copyright © 1971 by Transaction, Inc.

lost percentages but low earned run averages (number of runs given up per game). The opposite is equally true: some pitchers play poorly, giving up many runs, yet win many games. In brief, the pitcher, regardless of how well he performs, is dependent upon the proficiency of his teammates, the inefficiency of the opposition and the supernatural (luck).

But luck, as we all know, comes in two forms, and many fans assume that the pitcher's tough losses (close games in which he gave up very few runs) are eventually balanced out by his "lucky" wins. This is untrue, as a comparison of pitchers' lifetime earned run averages to their overall won-lost records shows. If the player could apply a law of averages to individual performance, there would be much less concern about chance and uncertainty in baseball. Unfortunately, he cannot and does not.

Hitting, too, is a chancy affair. Obviously, skill is required in hitting the ball hard and on a line. Once the ball is hit, however, chance plays a large role in determining where it will go, into a waiting glove or whistling past a falling stab.

With respect to fielding, the player has almost complete control over the outcome. The average fielding percentage or success rate of .975, compared to a .245 success rate for hitters (the average batting average), reflects the degree of certainty in fielding. Next to the pitcher or hitter, the fielder has little to worry about when he knows that better than 9.7 times in ten he will execute his task flawlessly.

If Malinowski's hypothesis is correct, we should find magic associated with hitting and pitching, but none with fielding. Let us take the evidence by category — ritual, taboo and fetish.

RITUAL

After each pitch, ex-major leaguer Lou Skeins used to reach into his back pocket to touch a crucifix, straighten his cap and clutch his genitals. Detroit Tiger infielder Tim Maring wore the same clothes and put them on exactly in the same order each day during a batting streak. Baseball rituals are almost infinitely various. After all, the ballplayer can ritualize any activity he considers necessary for a successful performance, from the type of cereal he eats in the morning to the streets he drives home on.

Usually, rituals grow out of exceptionally good performances. When the player does well he cannot really attribute his success to skill alone. He plays with the same amount of skill one night when he gets four hits as the next night when he goes hitless. Through magic, such as ritual, the player seeks greater control over his performance, actually control over the elements of chance. The player, knowing that his ability is fairly constant, attributes the inconsistencies in his performance to some form of behavior or a particular food that he ate. When a player get four hits in a game, especially "cheap" hits, he often believes that there must have been something he did, in addition to his ability, that shifted luck to his side. If he can attribute his good fortune to the glass of iced tea he drank before the game or the new shirt he wore to the ballpark, then by repeating the same behavior the following day he can hope to achieve similar results. (One expression of this belief is the myth that eating certain foods will give the ball "eyes," that is, a ball that seeks the gaps between the fielders.) In hopes of maintaining a batting streak, I once ate fried chicken every day at 4:00 P.M., kept my eyes closed during the national anthem and changed sweat shirts at the end of the fourth inning each night for seven consecutive nights until the streak ended.

Fred Caviglia, Kansas City minor league pitcher, explained why he eats certain foods before each game: "Everything you do is important to winning. I never forget what I eat the day of a game or what I wear. If I pitch well and win I'll do it all exactly the same the next day I pitch. You'd be crazy not to. You just can't ever tell what's going to make the difference between winning and losing."

Rituals associated with hitting vary considerably in complexity from one player to the next, but they have several components in common. One of the most popular is tagging a particular base when leaving and returning to the dugout each inning. Tagging second base on the way to the outfield is habitual with some players. One informant reported that during a successful month of the season he stepped on third base on his way to the dugout after the third, sixth and ninth innings of each game. Asked if he ever purposely failed to step on the bag he replied, "Never! I wouldn't dare, it would destroy my confidence to hit." It is not uncommon for a hitter who is playing poorly to try different combinations of tagging and not tagging particular bases in an attempt to find a successful combination. Other components of a hitter's ritual may include tapping the plate with his bat a precise number of times or taking a precise number of warm-up swings with the leaded bat.

One informant described a variation of this in which he gambled for a certain hit by tapping the plate a fixed number of times. He touched the plate once with his bat for each base desired: one tap for a single, two for a double and so on. He even built in odds that prevented him from asking for a home run each time. The odds of hitting a single with one tap were one in three, while the chances of hitting a home run with four taps were one in 12.

Clothing is often considered crucial to both hitters and pitchers.

They may have several athletic supporters and a number of sweat shirts with ritual significance. Nearly all players wear the same uniform and undergarments each day when playing well, and some even wear the same street clothes. In 1954, the New York Giants, during a 16-game winning streak, wore the same clothes in each game and refused to let them be cleaned for fear that their good fortune might be washed away with the dirt. The route taken to and from the stadium can also have significance; some players drive the same streets to the ballpark during a hitting streak and try different routes during slumps.

Because pitchers only play once every four days, the rituals they practice are often more complex that the hitters', and most of it, such as tugging the cap between pitches, touching the rosin bag after each bad pitch or smoothing the dirt on the mound before each new batter, takes place on the field. Many baseball fans have observed this behavior never realizing that it may be as important to the pitcher as throwing the ball.

Dennis Grossini, former Detroit farmhand, practiced the following ritual on each pitching day for the first three months of a winning season. First, he arose from bed at exactly 10:00 A.M. and not a minute earlier or later. At 1:00 P.M. he went to the nearest restaurant for two glasses of iced tea and a tuna fish sandwich. Although the afternoon was free, he observed a number of taboos such as no movies, no reading and no candy. In the clubhouse he changed into the sweat shirt and jock he wore during his last winning game, and one hour before the game he chewed a wad of Beechnut chewing tobacco. During the game he touched his letters (the team name on his uniform) after each pitch and straightened his cap after each ball. Before the start of each inning he replaced the pitcher's rosin bag next to the spot where it was the inning before. And after every inning in which he gave up a run he went to the clubhouse to wash his hands. I asked him which part of the ritual was most important. He responded: "You can't really tell what's most important so it all becomes important. I'd be afraid to change anything. As long as I'm winning I do everything the same. Even when I can't wash my hands [this would occur when he must bat] it scares me going back to the mound. . . . I don't feel quite right."

One ritual, unlike those already mentioned, is practiced to improve the power of the baseball bat. It involves sanding the bat until all the varnish is removed, a process requiring several hours of labor, then rubbing rosin into the grain of the bat before finally heating it over a flame. This ritual treatment supposedly increases the distance the ball travels after being struck. Although some North Americans prepare their bats in this fashion it is more popular among Latin Americans. One informant admitted that he was not certain of the effectiveness of the treatment. But, he added, "There may not be a God, but I go to church just the same."

Despite the wide assortment of rituals associated with pitching and hitting, I never observed any ritual related to fielding. In all my 20 interviews only one player, a shortstop with acute fielding problems, reported any ritual even remotely connected to fielding.

TABOO

Mentioning that a no-hitter is in progress and crossing baseball bats are the two most widely observed taboos. It is believed that if the pitcher hears the words "no-hitter" his spell will be broken and the no-hitter lost. As for the crossing of bats, that is sure to bring bad luck; batters are therefore extremely careful not to drop their bats on top of another. Some players elaborate this taboo even further. On one occasion a teammate became quite upset when another player tossed a bat from the batting cage and it came to rest on top of his. Later he explained that the top bat would steal hits from the lower one. For him, then, bats contain a finite number of hits, a kind of baseball "image of limited good." Honus Wagner, a member of baseball's Hall of Fame, believed that each bat was good for only 100 hits and no more. Regardless of the quality of the bat he would discard it after its 100th hit.

Besides observing the traditional taboos just mentioned, players also observe certain personal prohibitions. Personal taboos grow out of exceptionally poor performances, which a player often attributes to some particular behavior or food. During my first season of professional baseball I once ate pancakes before a game in which I struck out four times. Several weeks later I had a repeat performance, again after eating pancakes. The result was a pancake taboo in which from that day on I never ate pancakes during the season. Another personal taboo, born out of similar circumstances, was against holding a baseball during the national anthem.

Taboos are also of many kinds. One athlete was careful never to step on the chalk foul lines or the chalk lines of the batter's box. Another would never put on his cap until the game started and would not wear it at all on the days he did not pitch. Another had a movie taboo in which he refused to watch a movie the day of a game. Often certain uniform numbers become taboo. If a player has a poor spring training or a bad year, he may refuse to wear the same uniform number again. I would not wear double numbers, especially 44 and 22. On several occasions, teammates who were playing poorly requested a change of uniform during the middle of the season. Some players consider it so important that they will wear the wrong size uniform just to avoid a certain number or to obtain a good number.

Again, with respect to fielding, I never saw or heard of any taboos being observed, though of course there were some taboos, like the uniform numbers, that were concerned with overall performance and so included fielding.

FETISHES

These are standard equipment for many baseball players. They include a wide assortment of objects: horsehide covers of old baseballs, coins, bobby pins, protective cups, crucifixes and old bats. Ordinary objects are given this power in a fashion similar to the formation of taboos and rituals. The player during an exceptionally hot batting or pitching streak, especially one in which he has "gotten all the breaks," credits some unusual object, often a new possession, for his good fortune. For example, a player in a slump might find a coin or an odd stone just before he begins a hitting streak. Attributing the improvement in his performance to the new object, it becomes a fetish, embodied with supernatural power. While playing for Spokane, Dodger pitcher Alan Foster forgot his baseball shoes on a road trip and borrowed a pair from a teammate to pitch. That night he pitched a no-hitter and later, needless to say, bought the shoes from his teammate. They became his most prized possession.

Fetishes are taken so seriously by some players that their teammates will not touch them out of fear of offending the owner. I once saw a fight caused by the desecration of a fetish. Before the game, one player stole the fetish, a horsehide baseball cover, out of a teammate's back pocket. The prankster did not return the fetish until after the game, in which the owner of the fetish went hitless, breaking a batting streak. The owner, blaming his inability to hit on the loss of the fetish, lashed out at the thief when the latter tried to return it.

Rube Waddel, an old-time Philadelphia Athletic pitching great, had a hairpin fetish. However, the hairpin he possessed was only powerful as long as he won. Once he lost a game he would look for another hairpin, which had to be found on the street, and he would not pitch until he found another.

The use of fetishes follows the same pattern as ritual and taboo in that they are connected only with hitting or pitching. In nearly all cases the player expressed a specific purpose for carrying a fetish, but never did a player perceive his fetish as having any effect on his fielding.

I have said enough, I think, to show that many of the beliefs and practices of professional baseball players are magical. Any empirical connection between the ritual, taboo and fetishes and the desired event is quite absent. Indeed, in several instances the relationship between the cause and effect, such as eating tuna fish sandwiches to win a ball game, is even more remote than is characteristic of primitive magic. Note, however, that unlike many forms of primitive magic, baseball magic is usually performed to achieve one's own end and not to block someone else's. Hitters do not tap their bats on the plate to hex the pitcher, but to improve their own performance.

Finally, it should be plain that nearly all the magical practices that I participated in, observed or elicited, support Malinowski's hypothesis that magic appears in situations of chance and uncertainty. The large amount of uncertainty in pitching and hitting best explains the elaborate magic practices used for these activities. Conversely, the high success rate in fielding, .975, involving much less uncertainty, offers the best explanation for the absence of magic in this realm.

29

Religion and culture:
God's saviours in the Sierra Madre

WILLIAM L. MERRILL

One of the most important functions of religion is to reconcile life's contradictions. Life and death, good and evil, good fortune and adversity, all constitute paradoxes that people seek to explain, and it is often religion that deals with these basic oppositions. Yet the ways in which religion structures the answers to these questions vary markedly from one society to another, reflecting adaptive concerns and other cultural assumptions about life. Religious beliefs that work well for one society may seem incomprehensible to members of another. In this article by William Merrill, we see that Catholic beliefs about God and Christ, introduced to the Rarámuri Indians of Mexico by Jesuit missionaries, have been transformed to fit traditional religious beliefs and a world view that predate contact with the West. The Rarámuri have transformed the Christian definitions of God and the Devil, and especially the events that surround Easter, to fit their own concerns for balance, for a continued harmony between people and their social and natural world.

In 1607 the Catalan Jesuit Juan Fonte intervened in a conflict involving members of two Indian groups, the Tarahumaras and the Tepehuanes, who lived in the rugged Sierra Madre of northern New Spain, where the Mexican states of Chihuahua and Durango meet today. These Indians had previously remained beyond the influence of the Jesuits, except for missions established in the previous decade among the more

Originally published as "God's Saviours in the Sierra Madre." With permission from *Natural History*, Vol. 93, No. 3; Copyright the American Museum of Natural History, 1983.

southerly Tepehuanes. For the next nine years, Fonte devoted himself to converting them to Christianity, until the Tepehuanes revolted and killed him and five of his fellow missionaries. Almost immediately, other Jesuits arrived to replace the martyrs, and a vigorous mission system gradually spread throughout the region.

From the outset, converting the Tarahumaras required some modification of the strict orthodox line. The early missionaries apparently took Catholic doctrine and ritual, combined them with European folk beliefs and dances of the day, added their own innovations, adapted the whole to what they concluded the Tarahumaras would understand and accept, and presented it to them as the word and will of God. For their part, the Tarahumaras interpreted this complex of beliefs and actions in terms of their own ideas, adopting and modifying portions of it as they saw fit. In 1767 Charles III of Spain, distrustful of them, expelled the Jesuits from his New World domains. The Franciscans inherited the Tarahumara mission system, but financial difficulties and the disruptions of war and revolution led to its decline and abandonment by the mid-nineteenth century. Responsibility for their religious affairs reverted entirely to the Tarahumaras, who then developed, in their own fashion, the beliefs and rituals inherited from the mission period.

In 1900 the Jesuits reestablished the mission system, but in the years since, they have not attempted to force orthodoxy upon the Tarahumaras. The priests are peripheral to the Indians' religious life, performing baptisms and an occasional mass but little else, and few actually live in Tarahumara communities. Today the priests actively support the Tarahumaras in the practice of their own brand of Catholicism because they consider it a key element of Tarahumara cultural identity, which they hope to preserve. There is considerable pressure on the Tarahumaras to adopt the culture of the Mexicans who have settled in their area and who now number about 200,000, four times the Indian population. The Tarahumaras have maintained control of their religion, however. The settlers — joined in recent years by tourists from abroad — participate almost exclusively as onlookers at the Indians' elaborate holy day ceremonies, particularly those of Christmas and Easter.

The people whom outsiders have for centuries called Tarahumaras refer to themselves as Rarámuri, a word that means, on increasingly specific levels, human beings in distinction to nonhumans, Indians as opposed to non-Indians, the Rarámuri proper rather than some other Indian group, and finally, Rarámuri men in contrast to Rarámuri women. The Rarámuri version of the origin of their religion differs radically from the one just outlined. They maintain that almost everything they have and do, say and believe, was communicated by God to their ancestors soon after this world began. God, they say, is their father and they associate him with the sun. His wife, their mother, is affiliated with the moon and identified as the Virgin Mary. God's elder brother, and thus the Rarámuri's uncle, is the Devil. The Devil is the father of all non-Indians, whom the Rarámuri call *chabóchi*, "whiskered ones," an apt label since Rarámuri men have little facial hair. The Devil and his wife care for the *chabóchi* just as God and his wife care for the Rarámuri. At death, the souls of the Rarámuri ascend to heaven while those of the *chabóchi* join their parents on the bottom-most level of the universe, three levels below the earth.

The Rarámuri believe that people who commit misdeeds during their lives will be punished when they die, but they worry very little about their fate in the afterlife. They are far more concerned with the here and now and consider that their well-being depends almost entirely upon their ability to maintain proper relations with the other beings in their universe, particularly God and the Devil. God, as befits a parent, is benevolently inclined toward the Rarámuri, but he will withhold his beneficence if they fail to reciprocate his attentions adequately. The Devil's tendencies are just the opposite: he will send illness and misfortune to torment the Rarámuri unless they give him food.

The nineteenth-century Norwegian explorer and anthropologist Carl Lumholtz wrote of the Rarámuri, "The only wrong toward the gods of which he may consider himself guilty is that he does not dance enough." By "dance" Lumholtz meant that whole complex of dancing, chanting, feasting, and offerings that constitutes a Rarámuri religious fiesta. It is primarily through these fiestas that the Rarámuri balance accounts with God, who is pleased by the beauty of their performances and appreciates the offerings of food and maize beer they send to him. Typically they also bury bits of food during these fiestas to placate the Devil and deflect his malevolence.

Any Rarámuri with the resources and inclination can stage a fiesta any time of the year. People sometimes sponsor fiestas because God instructs them in their dreams to do so or because they feel in special need of his protection. They also hold them to send food, tools, clothing, and other goods to recently deceased relatives; to compensate Rarámuri doctors for curing the living; or to petition God to end a drought. There are also certain times of the year when fiestas or, at least, special rituals are required, particularly at points in the life cycle of the maize upon which the Rarámuri rely for their existence and on or near the more prominent holy days in the Catholic ritual calendar.

The fiestas associated with the maize crop take place in the hamlets where the Rarámuri live rather than at the churches around which the early missionaries had intended for them to settle. When the maize is a month or two old, neighboring households jointly sponsor a fiesta, during which a Rarámuri doctor and several assistants pass through the fields curing the maize. The doctor waves a knife and wooden cross to prevent hail from destroying the crop, while his assistants sprinkle a variety of medicines to protect the plants from pests and to enhance their growth. Periodically, the doctor stops to deliver a speech encouraging the maize to grow well and to have strength because the rains will soon commence. Later, in August, when the green ears of maize are ready to be eaten, a second fiesta is staged to offer the first fruits of the year to God, for he provided the Rarámuri with their first domesticated plants.

Despite these flurries of ritual activity during the maize-growing season, the major ceremonial activity does not get under way until the end of harvest. The most elaborate ritual events between harvest and planting are the Catholic holy day ceremonies, which begin in early December and follow one another in quick succession: Immaculate Conception (December 8), then Virgin of Guadalupe Day (December 12), Christmas Eve, and Epiphany (January 6), leading up to Candlemas (February 2), which marks for the Rarámuri the beginning of the Easter season (they do not observe Lent). The predominant theme of this winter round of celebration is the perpetuation of proper relations with God by recognizing and reciprocating his blessings. Although individual households may sponsor fiestas at their homes in conjunction with these holy days, the principal ritual activities on most take place at the thirty or so churches scattered across the 20,000 square miles of Rarámuri country.

Each fiesta is sponsored by one or more individuals who, at the conclusion of the same fiesta the year before, volunteered or were asked by others in the community to provide the food and maize beer. Together with the community's political and religious leaders, these fiesta sponsors direct the events. Men, women, and children, sometimes in the hundreds, converge on the local church from hamlets as much as fifteen miles away. Most of these people help by preparing or offering food, performing the often strenuous dances and rituals that are required, or providing encouragement and moral support to the major participants. Typically, a fiesta begins on the eve of the holy day in question and lasts all night long. If a Catholic priest arrives, mass is celebrated once or twice; if not, Rarámuri ritualists recite standard prayers. In most cases, large quantities of food and maize beer are distributed and consumed after first being offered to God.

The Rarámuri regard these celebrations as opportunities for socializing and having a good time. They joke with one another and often parody the leading ritual performers, but their frivolity does not detract from the importance they ascribe to the undertaking. They expect their efforts and even their jokes to please and satisfy God so that he will give them long lives, abundant crops, and healthy children. They also hope that their activities will convince him to postpone replacing the present world with a new one, an event that many Rarámuri, influenced by some of their Mexican neighbors, anticipate will come in the year 2000.

At this time of year, between February 2 and Easter, the theme of Rarámuri ritual begins to shift from an emphasis on the relationship between the Rarámuri and God to a concern with the relationship between God and the Devil. God and the Devil are brothers but, although they occasionally interact on a friendly basis, the Devil usually is bent on God's destruction. Most of the time God fends the Devil off, but each year the Devil succeeds by trick or force in rendering God dangerously vulnerable. Invariably this occurs immediately prior to Holy Week. From the Rarámuri point of view, their elaborate Easter ceremonies are intended to protect and strengthen God so that he can recover and prevent the Devil from destroying the world. (The description that follows applies specifically to the community of Basíhuare, Chihuahua, where, more than in some other communities, the ceremonies deviate considerably from orthodox Catholicism. There is substantial regional variation in Rarámuri religion, owing to the different impact of Catholic missionaries in different areas and the rugged terrain, which has discouraged interaction among Rarámuri of separate regions.)

Soon after February 2, the men in Basíhuare assemble at the local church to appoint four of their number to the office of Pharisee. Each of the new Pharisees is paired with one of the four community officials known as Captains, who serve year-round as keepers of the peace and messengers for the top community officials. From the day of their selection until Easter Day, when their term of office ends, the Pharisees share police and messenger duties with the Captains and join with them as the principal organizers and performers of the Holy Week pageantry. The Pharisees, regarded as the Devil's allies, carry wooden swords painted white with ocher designs; the Captains, the allies of God, bear quivers made of coatis, the entrails replaced by bows and arrows.

In the weeks leading up to Easter, most men and older boys agree to assist either the Pharisees or the Captains during Holy Week. The reasons they join one group or the other are usually personal. For example, a man may choose to be a Pharisee this year because last year he was a Soldier, as the people who help the Captains are called. Or he may prefer the ceremonial roles or accouterments of one side to those of the other. Or he may follow the lead of friends or relatives. The usual outcome is a more or less equal division of the male community between the two groups.

The central theme of the Rarámuri's Holy Week — the conflict between God and the Devil and the Rarámuri's role as God's protector — is first expressed in a major way during the fiesta held in conjunction with Palm Sunday. A Palm Sunday ceremony I attended in Basíhuare gives some idea of the activities that will be taking place this year beginning on March 26. The preparations for the fiesta began at dusk on Saturday as, near the church, a bull was butchered by the men and its flesh, bones, and blood set to boiling by the women. Close by, several men removed stones and trash from a plot of ground to create what the Rarámuri call an *awírachi*, meaning "dance space" or "patio." Other men brought a bench about ten feet long from inside the church and placed it along the east side of the patio to hold the food that was to be offered to God. Behind it three crosses were erected and draped with necklaces, some of which bore small wooden crosses or metal crucifixes.

About 10:30 P.M., an old Rarámuri man wrapped in a hand-woven wool blanket stood at the western edge of the patio and began shaking a rattle and intoning the wordless phrases of the *tutubúri*, an indigenous rite thanking God for caring and providing for the Rarámuri and asking that he continue to bless them. Soon after the *tutubúri* got under way, a second, rather different kind of dance began on the opposite side of the patio. Known as the *matachín*, a term possibly of Arabic origin, this dance presumably derives from one or more Renaissance European folk dances, but no one knows exactly when or in what form Catholic missionaries introduced it to the Rarámuri. The *matachín* dancers wear long capes and mirrored crowns and dance in two lines, whirling and crossing to the accompaniment of violins and guitars in a manner reminiscent of the Virginia reel. The *matachín* dance is said to please God because it is so beautiful. The same is true of the *tutubúri*, but, unlike the *matachín*, it is never performed within the church walls.

In the intervals between *matachín* and *tutubúri* performances, two troops of mostly young men and boys, designated as Pharisees and Soldiers, enacted the Pharisee dance, characterized by high, skipping steps executed in sinuous lines to the pounding of drums and the melody of sweet-sounding reed whistles. Some Soldiers carried bayonet-tipped staves while the Pharisees, who earlier had smeared their bodies with white earth, dragged wooden swords at their sides. The leading Pharisees donned twilled hats adorned with turkey feathers; the Rarámuri point out that the Pharisee dance bears certain similarities to the mating ritual of the turkey gobbler, but they are uncertain if the relationship is derivative or only coincidental.

About midnight, a Jesuit priest, who had arrived especially for the occasion, celebrated mass in Rarámuri and Spanish. The men knelt on the left side of the church, the women and small children on the right, and a few Mexicans stood at the rear. No Rarámuri partook of Holy Communion — in Basíhuare, they seldom do — but before and after the service, the *matachín* was danced in front of the altar.

Soon after sunrise, the first phase of the fiesta concluded. Earthen bowls of beef stew, together with stacks of tortillas and tamales and bundles of ground, parched maize, were taken to the patio and placed on the bench in front of the crosses. Seven men lifted the food to the cardinal directions, allowing the aroma and steam from the food to waft heavenward to be consumed by God. In this way, the Rarámuri acknowledged their debt to him and compensated for the sustenance he had provided them. The women then distributed the food among the people present so that all would be strengthened for the remaining activities and the journey home.

At mid-morning, one of the Rarámuri officials called *méstro*, who recite Catholic prayers and care for the accouterments of the church, rang the church bell three times. As they had done for as many years as anyone can remember, the Soldiers and Pharisees, working on opposite sides of the churchyard, began setting up wooden crosses at appropriate distances, marking the stations of the cross. Then all filed into the church for mass. At the conclusion of the service, the priest distributed palm leaves among the members of the congregation, who followed him in a procession around the churchyard, commemorating, in accordance with Catholic doctrine, Christ's entry into Jerusalem, when palm branches were strewn before him.

The Rarámuri attribute somewhat different significance to the palm. After bearing the fronds like scepters in the procession, they carry them home, for the leaves can be burned to prevent hail from destroying a crop or decocted and drunk to cure chest pains. They say the palm owes its special qualities to an event that occurred in the distant past. God, God's wife, and the Devil had been drinking maize beer for several hours when God fell asleep and the Devil succeeded in seducing God's wife, largely through his accomplished guitar playing. God awoke, catching them *in flagrante delicto*, and a fight ensued. The Devil pulled a knife and God fled, with the Devil in close pursuit. God would surely have been slain had a palm not offered its thick leaves as a hiding place. This event sealed an enduring friendship between God and the palm and established the palm's usefulness to the Rarámuri; however, it also determined that humans would fight and commit adultery in imitation of their deities.

Drums and reed whistles alternated with liturgy as the Palm Sunday procession passed through the various stations of the cross. At circuit's end, the priest retired to the house in which he stays during his visits to Basíhuare. The others assembled facing the front of the church, where their community leaders stood, grasping the wooden canes that signify their authority. The principal Rarámuri official called before him several men known to be accomplished dreamers and requested that they relate what their recent dreams had revealed about the coming year and especially the impending Holy Week. The dreamers reported that, as in years past at this time, God was in a weak and vulnerable state, this year because the Devil forced him to drink a great deal of maize beer and he had not yet recovered. The Rarámuri people must protect God and his wife until he was well again, they said, or the Devil would destroy them and the world. The official acknowledged the dreamers' advice and in a loud voice urged everyone to return to the church in three days for the Easter ceremonies to care for their parents, God and God's wife.

By mid-morning on Holy Wednesday, the Captains, Pharisees, and a few of their helpers were busy at work in the churchyard, making preparations for the Easter ceremonies. With saplings, leaves, and fibers gathered from nearby hills and canyons, they constructed archways, crosses, wreaths, and rosettes, positioning them in and around the church to mark the processional route, on two adjacent hilltops, and at the cemetery. A woman swept the church with a bundle of long grass stems while three men attended to the altar and its adornments: four candlesticks, two crosses, and a statue and portrait of the Virgin Mary. Another man cleared stones, branches, and trash from the processional path encircling the church.

The principal community officials and their families set themselves up in nearby huts and rockshelters, all of which are abandoned except on such ritual occasions. There they cleared dance patios, erected arches and crosses, and prepared the food and maize beer they would be obliged to serve in the days ahead. Like the other Rarámuri who were going to participate in the ceremony, they made sure that the clothes they would be wearing were either new or sparkling clean, as is expected during Holy Week.

The Rarámuri call Holy Week *Norírawachi,* meaning "when we walk in circles," because they spend much of Maundy Thursday, Good Friday, and Holy Saturday morning circumscribing the church in formal procession. The point of the procession is to protect the church, and, by extension, God and God's wife. The fate of the universe rests on the Rarámuri's shoulders during this period, for they must prevent the Devil from vanquishing God and destroying the world. Their every action takes on cosmic significance. They must fast until past noon on Maundy Thursday and Good Friday because to eat would bloat God's stomach. Until Friday afternoon, fighting or chopping wood would bruise or cut

God, so they must avoid both. They must dance and offer food to strengthen God, and they must guard the church and its paraphernalia, particularly the reproduction, hanging above the altar, of the miraculous portrait of the Virgin of Guadalupe, who is God's wife and their mother. Four Soldiers with bayonet-bearing staves are posted in front of the altar inside the church while a drum and whistle play behind them. Four Pharisees, wooden swords in hand, keep watch on the church steps. Replacements arrive every hour or so, and the guard is maintained much of Thursday and Friday.

Despite their efforts in guarding the church, the Pharisees are cast as the Devil's allies and as the opponents of the Soldiers, who are allied with God. The Pharisees reveal their association with the Devil most dramatically on Good Friday afternoon, when they appear with three figures made of wood and long grasses representing Judas, Judas's wife, and their dog. The Rarámuri say Judas is one of the Devil's relatives, and they call him Grandfather and his wife Grandmother. They also assign personal names to them each year: one recent Easter in Basíhuare, Judas was known as Ramón, his wife was María, and the dog, Monje, or Monk. Judas and his wife wear elements of Mexican-style clothing, as befits the Devil's kin, and display their oversized genitalia prominently. The Pharisees parade the figures around the church and dance before them, then turn them over to the Soldiers who do the same. The Pharisees then hide the figures away for the night.

In Basíhuare, as in many other Rarámuri communities, the Easter ceremonies conclude on Holy Saturday, not Easter Sunday. In the morning, the Soldiers and Pharisees engage in wrestling matches, battling symbolically for control of Judas. Regardless of the outcome, the Soldiers take possession, shooting arrows into the three figures and setting them afire. Then all remaining Easter paraphernalia is dismantled or destroyed. Such destruction is necessary, the Rarámuri say, to avert strong winds in the coming months. For the same reason, they place food and maize beer at ceremonial arches on two hilltops near the church, offerings to engender the good will of the Devil and the Wind, which they personify. By noon the church and its yard lie silent, deserted in favor of the many maize beer drinking parties being held in the surrounding countryside.

The Catholic missionaries who introduced Easter ceremonies to the Rarámuri presumably intended them to be reenactments of Christ's crucifixion and resurrection and dramatizations of the conflict between good and evil. The priests themselves probably adapted their teachings somewhat to what they knew of Rarámuri religion, but their original messages have been radically transformed by the Rarámuri to conform more closely to indigenous rituals, beliefs, and values. The Christian Trinity of Father, Son, and Holy Spirit has become in Rarámuri Catholicism a Duality of Father and Mother associated with the sun and moon, respectively. The Holy Spirit is never mentioned, and the events of Christ's life of which the Rarámuri are aware are attributed to God the Father. Because God created their ancestors, the Rarámuri regard themselves as his children, but they also maintain that God and his wife have many natural offspring who live with them in heaven. They apply the term "Jesus Christ" to all the males among these children and "Saint" to all the females, identifying the robes of saints (even male ones) as dresses.

The idea that Christ died on the cross to redeem the sins of humankind makes little sense to the Rarámuri. Ethnic affiliation rather than acceptance or rejection of Christ as Saviour determines a person's fate in the afterlife: the Rarámuri ascend to heaven after death to be with their parents, God and his wife, while the *chabóchi* (non-Indians) join the Devil and his wife below. According to the Rarámuri, *chabóchi* people want to live out eternity in the Devil's realm because it is a pleasant place to live, and the Devil and his wife are their parents. On the other hand, the souls of people who commit serious crimes such as murder or grand theft are completely destroyed soon after death. There is punishment for ill deeds in the Rarámuri cosmos, but no eternal damnation with its concomitant suffering.

To some degree God and the Devil personify good and evil for the Rarámuri, but in a much less absolute way than in Christian theology. Both God and the Devil can help or harm the Rarámuri depending on how the Rarámuri act toward them. The Rarámuri endeavor to perpetuate good relations with God and to placate the Devil by performing fiestas and making food offerings to them. By so doing they repay God for caring and providing for them and encourage the Devil to refrain from attacking them. If they fail in these obligations and overtures, God and the Devil will turn against them.

The basic purpose of their fiestas and offerings and of so much else the Rarámuri do, both in and outside their rituals, is to maintain balance in the world. This orientation, which almost certainly existed among the Rarámuri before Western contact, seems to have had a substantial impact on how they interpreted and adapted the Easter ceremonies that the missionaries taught them. Implicit throughout the Easter proceedings are expressions of the complementarity and mutual obligations that exist among various segments of Rarámuri society, between males and females, for example, or community officials and the people they lead and represent. While the most obvious message in the Easter celebration is the confrontation between God and the Devil, the Rarámuri have not followed the more orthodox Christian line of desiring the complete destruction of the Devil and his influence. Instead, their goal is to produce good relations between the Devil and themselves and to restore the balance between God and the Devil that existed before God fell victim to the Devil's machinations.

30

Urban witches

EDWARD J. MOODY

Witchcraft is usually seen as a feature of underdeveloped societies, but it is also present in the urban centers of the United States. Edward Moody presents empirical data on the person who uses black magic, and analyzes the function it has for the magician. Even in "civilized" societies, some people try to explain events in their lives and to compensate for personal inadequacies and anxieties by a belief in witchcraft.

Every Friday evening just before midnight, a group of men and women gathers at a home in San Francisco; and there, under the guidance of their high priest, a sorcerer or magus sometimes called the "Black Pope of Satanism," they study and practice the ancient art of black magic. Precisely at midnight they begin to perform Satanic rituals that apparently differ little from those allegedly performed by European Satanists and witches at least as early as the seventh century. By the dim and flickering light of black candles, hooded figures perform their rites upon the traditional Satanic altar — the naked body of a beautiful young witch — calling forth the mysterious powers of darkness to do their bidding. Beneath the emblem of Baphomet, the horned god, they engage in indulgences of flesh and sense for whose performance their forebears suffered death and torture at the hands of earlier Christian zealots.

Many of these men and women are, by day, respected and responsible citizens. Their nocturnal or covert practice of the black art would, if exposed, make them liable to ridicule, censure, and even punishment. Even though we live in an "enlightened" age, witches are still made a focus of a community's aggression and anxiety. They are de-

This article was written especially for this book. Copyright © 1971 by Little, Brown and Company (Inc.). The research on which this article is based was conducted during the period from October 1967 to August 1969.

nounced from the pulpit, prosecuted to the limit of the law, and subjected to extralegal harassment by the fearful and ignorant.

Why then do the Satanists persist? Why do they take these risks? What benefits do they derive from membership in a Satanic church, what rewards are earned from the practice of witchcraft? What indulgences are enjoyed that they could not as easily find in one of the more socially acceptable arenas of pleasure available in our "permissive" society?

The nearly universal allegation of witchcraft in the various cultures of the world has excited the interest of social scientists for years and the volume of writing on the topic is staggering. Most accounts of witchcraft, however, share the common failing of having been written from the point of view of those who do not themselves practice the black art. Few, if any, modern authors have had contact with witches, black magicians, or sorcerers, relying instead on either the anguished statements of medieval victims of inquistion torture, or other types of secondhand "hearsay" evidence for their data. To further confuse the issue, authoritative and respected ethnologists have reported that black magic and witchcraft constitute an imaginary offense because it is impossible — that because witches cannot do what they are supposed to do, they are nonexistent.

WITCHES AND MAGICIANS

But the witches live. In 1965 while carrying out other research in San Francisco, California, I heard rumors of a Satanic cult which planned to give an All-Hallows Eve blessing to a local chamber of horrors. I made contact with the group through its founder and high priest and thus began over two years of participant-observation as a member of a contemporary black magic group. As a member of this group I interacted with my fellow members in both ritual and secular settings. The following description is based on the data gathered at that time.

The witches and black magicians who were members of the group came from a variety of social class backgrounds. All shades of political opinion were represented from Communist to American Nazi. Many exhibited behavior identified in American culture as "pathological," such as homosexuality, sadomasochism, and transvestism. Of the many characteristics that emerged from psychological tests, extensive observations, and interviews, the most common trait, exhibited by nearly all Satanic novices, was a high level of general anxiety related to low self-esteem and a feeling of inadequacy. This syndrome appears to be related to intense interpersonal conflicts in the nuclear family during socialization. Eighty-five percent of the group, the administrative and magical hierarchy of the church, reported that their childhood homes were split by alcoholism, divorce, or some other serious problem. Their adult lives were in turn marked by admitted failure in love, business, sexual, or social relationships. Before entering the group each member appeared to have been battered by failure in one or more of the areas mentioned, rejected or isolated by a society frightened by his increasingly bizarre and unpredictable behavior, and forced into a continuing struggle to comprehend or give meaning to his life situation.

Almost all members, prior to joining the group, had made some previous attempt to gain control over the mysterious forces operating around them. In order to give their environment some structure, in order to make it predictable and thus less anxiety-provoking, they dabbled in astrology, the Tarot, spiritualism, or other occult sciences, but continued failure in their everyday lives drove them from the passive and fatalistic stance of the astrologer to consideration of the active and manipulative role of sorcerer or witch. In articles in magazines such as *Astrology* and *Fate*, the potential Satanist comes into direct contact with magic, both white and black. Troubled by lack of power and control, the pre-Satanist is frequently introduced to the concept of magic by advertisements which promise "Occult power . . . now . . . for those who want to make real progress in understanding and working the forces that rule our Physical Cosmos . . . a self-study course in the practice of Magic." Or, Ophiel will teach you how to "become a power in your town, job, club, etc.," how to "create a familiar [a personal magic spirit servant] to help you through life," how to "control and dominate others." "The Secret Way" is offered free of charge, and the Esoteric Society offers to teach one how herbs, roots, oils, and rituals may be used, through "white magic," to obtain love, money, power, or a peaceful home. They will also teach one self-confidence and how to banish "unwanted forces." The reader is invited to join the Brotherhood of the White Temple, Inc.; the Monastery of the Seven Rays (specializing in sexual magic); the Radiant School; and numerous other groups that promise to reveal the secrets of success in business, sex, love, and life — the very secrets the potential or pre-Satanist feels have eluded him. Before joining the group, the pre-Satanist usually begins to perform magic ceremonies and rituals whose descriptions he receives for a fee from one of the various groups noted above, from magical wholesale houses, or from occult book clubs. These practices reinforce his "magical world view," and at the same time bring him in contact with other practitioners of the magical arts, both white and black.

Although most of the mail-order magic groups profess to practice "white" magic — benevolent magic designed only to benefit those involved and never aggressive or selfish, only altruistic — as opposed to "black," malevolent, or selfish magic, even white magic rituals require ingredients that are rare enough so they can be bought only at certain specialty stores. These stores, usually known to the public as candle shops although some now call themselves occult art supply houses, provide not only the raw materials — oils, incenses, candles, herbs, parchments, etc. — for the magical workings, but serve as meeting places for those interested in the occult. A request for some specific magic ingredient such as "John the Conqueror oil," "Money-come" powder, "crossing" powder, or black candles usually leads to a conversation about the magical arts and often to introductions to other female witches and male warlocks. The realization that there are others who privately practice magic, white or black, supports the novice magician in his new-found interest in magical manipulation. The presence of other witches and magicians in his vicinity serves as additional proof that the problems he has personally experienced may indeed be caused by witchcraft, for the pre-Satanist has now met, firsthand, witches and warlocks who previously were only shadowy figures, and if there are a few known witches, who knows how many there might be practicing secretly?

Many witches and magicians never go beyond the private practice of white or black magic, or at most engage in a form of magic "recipe" swapping. The individual who does join a formal group practicing magic may become affiliated with such groups in one of several ways. In some cases he has been practicing black magic with scant success. Perhaps he has gone no further than astrology or reading the designs on the ancient Tarot cards, a type of socially acceptable magic which the leader of the Satanic church disparagingly calls "god in sport clothes." But the potential Satantist has come to think of the cosmos as being ordered, and ordered according to magical — that is, imperceptible — principles. He is prompted by his sense of alienation and social inadequacy to try to gain control of the strange forces that he feels influence or control him and, hearing of a Satanic church, he comes to learn magic.

Others join because of anxiety and inadequacy of a slightly different nature. They may be homosexual, nymphomaniac, sadist, or masochist. They usually have some relatively blatant behavioral abnormality which, though they personally may not feel it wrong, is socially maladaptive and therefore disruptive. As in many "primitive" societies, magic and witchcraft provide both the "disturbed" persons and, in some cases, the community at large with a ready and consistent explanation for those "forces" or impulses which they themselves have experienced. Seeking control, or freedom, the social deviants come ultimately to the acknowledged expert in magic of all kinds, the head of the Satanic church, to have their demons exorcised, the spells lifted, and their own powers restored.

Others whose problems are less acute come because they have been brought, in the larger religious context, to think of themselves as "evil." If their struggle against "evil" has been to no avail, many of the individuals in question take this to mean that the power of "evil" is greater than the power of "good" — that "God is dead" — and so on. In their search for a source of strength and security, rather than continue their vain struggle with that "evil" force against which they know themselves to be powerless, they seek instead to identify themselves with evil, to join the "winning" side. They identify with Satan — etymologically the "opposition" — and become "followers of the left-hand path," "walkers in darkness."

Finally, there are, of course, those who come seeking thrills, or titillation, lured by rumors of beautiful naked witches, saturnalian orgies, and other strange occurrences. Few of these are admitted into the group.

BLACK MAGIC

For the novice, initial contact with the Satanists is reassuring. Those assisting the "Prince of Darkness" who heads the church are usually officers in the church, long-term members who have risen from the rank and file to positions of trust and authority. They are well-dressed, pleasant persons who exude an aura of confidence and adequacy. Rather than having the appearance of wild-eyed fanatics or lunatics, the Satanists look like members of the middle-class, but successful middle-class. The Prince of Darkness himself is a powerfully built and striking individual with a shaven head and black, well-trimmed beard. Sitting among the implements of magic, surrounded by books that contain the "secrets of the centuries," he affirms for those present what they already know: that there is a secret to power and success which can and must be learned, and that secret is black magic.

All magic is black magic according to the Satanists. There is no altruistic or white magic. Each magician intends to benefit from his magical manipulation, even those workings performed at someone else's behest. To claim to be performing magic only for the benefit of others is either hypocrisy — the cardinal sin in Satanic belief — or naiveté, another serious shortcoming. As defined by the Satanists, magic itself is a surprisingly common-sense kind of phenomenon: "the change in situations or events in accordance with one's will, which would, using normally accepted methods, be unchangeable." Magic can be divided into two categories: ritual (ceremonial) and nonritual (manipulative).

Ritual, or "the greater magic," is performed in a specified ritual area and at a specific time. It is an emotional, not an intellectual act. Although the Satanists spend a great deal of time intellectualizing and

rationalizing magic power, they state specifically that "any and all intellectual activity must take place *before* the ceremony, not during it."[1]

The "lesser magic," nonritual (manipulative) magic, is, in contrast,
a type of transactional manipulation based upon a heightened awareness
of the various processes of behavior operative in interaction with others,
a Satanic "games people play." The Satanist in ritual interaction is taught
to analyze and utilize the motivations and behavioral Achilles' heels of
others for his own purposes. If the person with whom one is interacting
has masochistic tendencies, for example, the Satanist is taught to adopt
the role of sadist, to "indulge" the other's desires, to be dominant,
forceful, and even cruel in interaction with him.

Both the greater and the lesser magic is predicated upon a more
general "magical" world view in which all elements of the "natural
world" are animate, have unique and distinctive vibrations that influence
the way they relate to other natural phenomena. Men, too, have vibrations, the principal difference between men and inanimate objects being
that men can alter their pattern of vibrations, sometimes consciously
and at will. It is the manipulation and the modification of these vibrations, forces, or powers that is the basis of all magic. There are "natural
magicians," untrained and unwitting manipulators of magic power. Some,
for example, resonate in harmony with growing things; these are people
said to have a "green thumb," gardeners who can make anything grow.
Others resonate on the frequency of money and have the "Midas touch"
which turns their every endeavor into a profit-making venture. Still
others are "love magnets"; they automatically attract others to them,
fascinate and charm even though they may be physically plain themselves. If one is a "natural magician," he does some of these things
unconsciously, intuitively, but because of the intellectual nature of our
modern world, most people have lost their sensitivity to these faint
vibrations. Such individuals may, if they become witches, magicians or
Satanists, regain contact with that lost world just as tribal shamans are
able to regain contact with another older world where men communicated with animals and understood their ways. It is this resensiti-
zation to the vibrations of the cosmos that is the essence of magical
training. It takes place best in the "intellectual decompression chamber"
of magical ritual, for it is basically a "subjective" and "nonscientific"
phenomenon.

Those who have become members of the inner circle learn to make
use of black magic, both greater and lesser, in obtaining goals which are

[1] The official doctrine of several Satanic groups within the continental United States
is contained in the *Satanic Bible* by Anton Szandor LaVey (New York: Avon Books, 1969),
p. 111.

the antithesis of Christian dogma. The seven deadly sins of Christian teaching — greed, pride, envy, anger, gluttony, lust, and sloth — are depicted as Satanic virtues. Envy and greed are, in the Satanic theology, natural in man and the motivating forces behind ambition. Lust is necessary for the preservation of the species and not a Satanic sin. Anger is the force of self-preservation. Instead of denying natural instincts the Satanist learns to glory in them and turn them into power.

Satanists recognize that the form of their ritual, its meanings and its functions are largely determined by the wider society and its culture. The novitiate in the Satanic cult is taught, for example, that the meaning of the word "Satan" etymologically is "the opposition," or "he who opposes," and that Satanism itself arose out of opposition to the demeaning and stultifying institutions of Christianity. The cult recognizes that had there been no Christianity there would be no Satanism, at least not in the form it presently takes, and it maintains that much of the Satanic ritual and belief is structured by the form and content of Christian belief and can be understood only in that larger religious context. The Satanists choose black as their color, not white, precisely because white is the symbol of purity and transcendence chosen by Christianity, and black therefore has come to symbolize the profane earthy indulgences central to Satanic theodicy. Satanists say that their gods are those of the earth, not the sky; that their cult is interested in making the sacred profane, in contrast to the Judeo-Christian cults which seek to make the profane sacred. Satanism cannot, in other words, be understood as an isolated phenomenon, but must be seen in a larger context.

The Satanic belief system, not surprisingly, is the antithesis of Christianity. Their theory of the universe, their cosmology, is based upon the notion that the desired end state is a return to a pagan awareness of the mystical forces inhabiting the earth, a return to an awareness of their humanity. This is in sharp contrast to the transcendental goals of traditional Christianity. The power associated with the pantheon of gods is also reversed: Satan's power is waxing; God's, if he still lives, waning. The myths of the Satanic church purport to tell the true story of the rise of Christianity and the fall of paganism, and there is a reversal here too. Christ is depicted as an early "con man" who tricked an anxious and powerless group of individuals into believing a lie. He is typified as "pallid incompetence hanging on a tree."[2] Satanic novices are taught that early church fathers deliberately picked on those aspects of human desire that were most natural and made them sins, in order to use the inevitable transgressions as a means of controlling the populace, promising them salvation in return for obedience. And finally, their substan-

[2] LaVey 1969:31.

tive belief, the very delimitation of what is sacred and what is profane, is the antithesis of Christian belief. The Satanist is taught to "be natural; to revel in pleasure and in self-gratification. To emphasize indulgence and power in this life."

The opposition of Satanists to Christianity may be seen most clearly in the various rituals of greater magic. Although there are many different types of rituals all aimed at achieving the virtues that are the inverted sins of the Christian, we shall examine briefly only two of these: blasphemy and the invocation of destruction. By far the most famous of Satanic institutions, the Black Mass and other forms of ritual blasphemy serve a very real and necessary function for the new Satanist. In many cases the exhortations and teachings of his Satanic colleagues are not sufficient to alleviate the sense of guilt and anxiety he feels when engaging in behavior forbidden by Judeo-Christian tradition. The novice may still cower before the charismatic power of Christian symbols; he may still feel guilty, still experience anxiety and fear in their presence. It is here that the blasphemies come into play, and they take many forms depending on the needs of the individuals involved.

A particular blasphemy may involve the most sacred Christian rituals and objects. In the traditional Black Mass powerful Christian symbols such as the crucifix are handled brutally. Some Black Masses use urine or menstrual flow in place of the traditional wine in an attempt to evoke disgust and aversion to the ritual. If an individual can be conditioned to respond to a given stimulus, such as the communion wafer or wine, with disgust rather than fear, that stimulus's power to cause anxiety is diminished. Sexuality is also used. A young man who feared priests and nuns was deliberately involved in a scene in which two witches dressed as nuns interacted with him sexually; his former neurotic fear was replaced by a mildly erotic curiosity even in the presence of real nuns. The naked altar — a beautiful young witch — introduces another deliberate note of sexuality into a formerly awe-inspiring scene.

By far the most frequently used blasphemy involves laughter. Awe-inspiring or fear-producing institutions are made the object of ridicule. The blasphemous rituals, although still greater magic, are frequently extremely informal. To the outsider they would not seem to have any structure; the behavior being exhibited might appear to be a charade, or a party game. The Satanists decide ahead of time the institution to be ridiculed and frequently it is a Christian ritual. I have seen a group of Satanists do a parody of the Christmas manger scene, or dress in clerical garb while performing a satire of priestly sexual behavior. The target of blasphemy depends upon the needs of the various Satanists. If the group feels it is necessary for the well-being of one member, they will gladly, even gleefully, blaspheme anything from psychiatry to psychedelics.

In the invocation of destruction black magic reaches its peak. In some cases an individual's sense of inadequacy is experienced as victimization, a sense of powerlessness before the demands of stronger and more ruthless men. The Satanic Bible, in contrast to Christian belief, teaches the fearful novice that "Satan represents vengeance instead of turning the other cheek." In the Third Chapter of the Book of Satan, the reader is exhorted to "hate your enemies with a whole heart, and if a man smite you on one cheek, SMASH him on the other . . . he who turns the other cheek is a cowardly dog."[3]

One of the most frequently used rituals in such a situation is the Conjuration of Destruction, or Curse. Contrary to popular belief, black magicians are not indiscriminately aggressive. An individual must have harmed or hurt a member of the church before he is likely to be cursed. Even then the curse is laid with care, for cursing a more powerful magician may cause one's curse to be turned against oneself. If, in the judgment of the high priest and the congregation, a member has been unjustly used by a non-Satanist, even if the offender is an unaffiliated witch or magician, at the appropriate time in the ritual the member wronged may step forward and, with the aid and support of the entire congregation, ritually curse the transgressor. The name of the intended "sacrifice" is usually written on parchment made of the skin of unborn lamb and burned in the altar flame while the member himself speaks the curse; he may use the standard curse or, if he so desires, prepare a more powerful, individualistic one. In the curse he gives vent to his hostility and commands the legions of hell to torment and sacrifice his victim in a variety of horrible ways. Or, if the Satanist so desires, the High Priest will recite the curse for him, the entire group adding their power to the invocation by spirited responses.

The incidence of harmful results from cursing is low in the church of Satan because of two factors: first, one does not curse other members of the church for fear that their superior magic might turn the curse back upon its user; second, victims outside the congregation either do not believe in the power of black magic or do not recognize the esoteric symbols that should indicate to them they are being cursed.

On only one occasion was I able to see the effect of a curse on a "victim." A member attempted to use the church and its members for publicity purposes without their permission. When the leader of the group refused to go along with the scheme, the man quit — an action that would normally have brought no recrimination — and began to

---

[3] LaVey 1969:33.

slander the church by spreading malicious lies throughout San Francisco social circles. Even though he was warned several times to stop his lies, the man persisted; so the group decided to level the most serious of all curses at him, and a ritual death rune was cast.

Casting a death rune, the most serious form of greater magic, goes considerably beyond the usual curse designed to cause only discomfort or unhappiness, but not to kill. The sole purpose of the death rune is to cause the total destruction of the victim. The transgressor's name is written in blood (to the Satanist, blood is power — the very power of life) on special parchment, along with a number of traditional symbols of ceremonial magic. In a single-minded ritual of great intensity and ferocity, the emotional level is raised to a peak at which point the entire congregation joins in ritually destroying the victim of the curse. In the case in question, there was an orgy of aggression. The lamb's-wool figurine representing the victim was stabbed by all members of the congregation, hacked to pieces with a sword, shot with a small calibre pistol, and then burned.

A copy of the death rune was sent to the man in question, and every day thereafter an official death certificate was made out in his name and mailed to him. After a period of weeks during which the "victim" maintained to all who would listen that he "did not believe in all that nonsense," he entered the hospital with a bleeding ulcer. Upon recovery he left San Francisco permanently.

In fairness, I must add that the "victim" of the curse had previously had an ulcer, was struggling with a failing business, and seemed hypertense when I knew him. His knowledge of the "curse" may have hastened the culmination of his difficulties. The Satanic church, however, claimed it as a successful working, a victory for black magic, and word of it spread among the adherents of occult subculture, enhancing the reputation of the group.

CONCLUSION

Contemporary America is presently undergoing a witchcraft revival. On all levels, from teenagers to octogenarians, interest in, or fear of, witchcraft has increased dramatically over the past two years. It is hardly possible to pass a popular magazine rack without seeing an article about the revival of the black arts. Covens and cults multiply, as does the number of exorcisms and reconsecrations. England, France, Germany, and a host of other countries all report a rebirth of the black art. Why? Those who eventually become Satanists are attempting to cope with the everyday problems of life, with the here and now, rather than with some transcendental afterlife. In an increasingly complex world which they do not fully understand, an anxiety-provoking world, they seek out a group dedicated to those mysterious powers that the sufferers have felt moving them. Fearful of what one witch calls "the dark powers we all feel moving deep within us," they come seeking either *release* or *control*. They give various names to the problems they bring, but all, anxious and afraid, come to the Satanic cult seeking help in solving problems beyond their meager abilities. Whatever their problem — bewitchment, business failure, sexual impotence, or demonic possession — the Satanists, in the ways I have mentioned and many more, *can* and *do* help them. Witchcraft, the witches point out, "is the most practical of all beliefs. According to its devotees, its results are obvious and instantaneous. No task is too high or too lowly for the witch." Above all, the beliefs and practices provide the witch and the warlock with a sense of power, a feeling of control, and an explanation for personal failure, inadequacy, and other difficulties.

Moreover, a seeker's acceptance into the Inner Circle provides a major boost for his self-esteem; he has, for the first time, been accepted into a group as an individual despite his problems and abnormalities. Once within the Inner Circle that support continues. The Satanic group is, according to the cultural standards of his society, amoral, and the Satanist frequently finds himself lauded and rewarded for the very impulses and behavior that once brought shame and doubt.

Each Satanist is taught, and not without reason, that the exposure of his secret identity, of the fact that he is a powerful and adequate black magician, means trouble from a fearful society. Therefore, in keeping with the precepts of lesser magic, he learns to transform himself magically by day (for purposes of manipulation) into a bank clerk, a businessman, or even a college professor. He wears the guise and plays the role expected by society in order to manipulate the situation to his own advantage, to reach his desired goals. Members of society at large, aware only of his "normal" role behavior and unaware of the secret person within, respond to him positively instead of punishing him or isolating him. Then, in the evening, in the sanctity of his home, or when surrounded by his fellow magicians, he revert to his "true" role, that of Satanic priest, and becomes himself once again. Inadequate and anxious persons, guilty because of socially disapproved impulses, are accepted by the Satanists and taught that the impulses they feel are natural and normal, but must be contained within certain spatial and temporal boundaries — the walls of the ritual chamber, the confines of the Inner Circle.

X

Culture change

Nowhere in the world do human affairs remain precisely constant from year to year. Although others may speak of tradition-bound, conservative, changeless societies, new ways of doing things mark the history of even the most stable groups. Change occurs when an Australian aboriginal dreams about a new myth and teaches it to the members of his band; when a loader in a restaurant kitchen invents a way to stack plates more quickly in the dishwasher; or when a New Guinea big-man cites the traditional beliefs about ghosts to justify the existence of a new political office devised by a colonial government. Wherever people interpret their natural and social worlds in a new way, social change has occurred. Broad or narrow, leisurely or rapid, such change is part of life in every society.

Culture change is extremely complex and is not well understood by social scientists. Although people may alter the way they live for variety or aesthetic pleasure, they most often change their behavior in response to problems or to better fulfill traditional goals. Most culture change begins with innovation or borrowing by one or more individuals. Many changes die early because they fail to gain acceptance by the society at large or even a significant segment of the group. For culture change to occur, innovations or borrowed elements must be accepted and eventually integrated into the existing culture pattern.

In the contemporary world the most important stimulus to change is contact among people with different cultures. All the processes of interaction, exchange of ideas, borrowing, and change under these conditions are called *acculturation*. A salient feature of acculturation situations that anthropologists investigate is the relative power over natural resources held by the groups in contact which often determines the course of change. Most non-Western tribal societies have been forced to change by the powerful onslaught of the emissaries of the West. Often this has meant serious cultural loss and social disorganization, conditions which may stimulate nativistic movements or movements for national liberation.

The articles in this section are studies of the effects of culture contact and people's attempts to cope with new and different objects, activities, and ideas. Often welcomed initially, such changes set off a chain reaction of consequences which themselves require adjustment or, if that fails, an entire reordering of world view.

31

Steel axes for stone-age Australians

LAURISTON SHARP

*Technology and social structure are closely linked in every society. In
this article, Lauriston Sharp shows how the introduction of an
apparently insignificant, hatchet-sized steel axe to Australian
aborigines can alter the relationship among family members, change
patterns of economic exchange, and threaten the very meaning
of life itself.*

I.

Like other Australian aboriginals, the Yir Yoront group which lives
at the mouth of the Coleman River on the west coast of Cape York
Peninsula originally had no knowledge of metals. Technologically their
culture was of the old stone age or paleolithic type. They supported
themselves by hunting and fishing, and obtained vegetables and other
materials from the bush by simple gathering techniques. Their only
domesticated animal was the dog; they had no cultivated plants of any
kind. Unlike some other aboriginal groups, however, the Yir Yoront did
have polished stone axes hafted in short handles which were most important in their economy.

Towards the end of the 19th century metal tools and other European artifacts began to filter into the Yir Yoront territory. The flow
increased with the gradual expansion of the white frontier outward from
southern and eastern Queensland. Of all the items of western technology
thus made available, the hatchet, or short handled steel axe, was the
most acceptable to and the most highly valued by all aboriginals.

In the mid 1930's an American anthropologist lived alone in the
bush among the Yir Yoront for 13 months without seeing another white
man. The Yir Yoront were thus still relatively isolated and continued to
live an essentially independent economic existence, supporting them-

Reproduced by permission of the Society for Applied Anthropology from *Human Organization* 11 (2):17–22, 1952.

selves entirely by means of their old stone age techniques. Yet their polished stone axes were disappearing fast and being replaced by steel axes which came to them in considerable numbers, directly or indirectly, from various European sources to the south.

What changes in the life of the Yir Yoront still living under aboriginal conditions in the Australian bush could be expected as a result of their increasing possession and use of the steel axe?

II. THE COURSE OF EVENTS

Events leading up to the introduction of the steel axe among the Yir Yoront begin with the advent of the second known group of Europeans to reach the shores of the Australian continent. In 1623 a Dutch expedition landed on the coast where the Yir Yoront now live.[1] In 1935 the Yir Yoront were still using the few cultural items recorded in the Dutch log for the aboriginals they encountered. To this cultural inventory the Dutch added beads and pieces of iron which they offered in an effort to attract the frightened "Indians." Among these natives metal and beads have disappeared, together with any memory of this first encounter with whites.

The next recorded contact in this area was in 1864. Here there is more positive assurance that the natives concerned were the immediate ancestors of the Yir Yoront community. These aboriginals had the temerity to attack a party of cattle men who were driving a small herd from southern Queensland through the length of the then unknown Cape York Peninsula to a newly established government station at the northern tip.[2] Known as the "Battle of the Mitchell River," this was one of the rare instances in which Australian aboriginals stood up to European gunfire for any length of time. A diary kept by the cattle men records that:

> . . . 10 carbines poured volley after volley into them from all directions, killing and wounding with every shot with very little return, nearly all their spears having already been expended. . . . About 30 being killed, the leader thought it prudent to hold his hand, and let the rest escape. Many more must have been wounded and probably drowned, for 59 rounds were counted as discharged.

The European party was in the Yir Yoront area for three days; they then disappeared over the horizon to the north and never returned. In the almost three-year long anthropological investigation conducted some 70

[1] An account of this expedition from Amboina is given in R. Logan Jack, *Northmost Australia* (2 vols.), London, 1921, vol. 1, pp. 18–57.
[2] R. Logan Jack, *op. cit.*, pp. 298–335.

years later — in all the material of hundreds of free association interviews, in texts of hundreds of dreams and myths, in genealogies, and eventually in hundreds of answers to direct and indirect questioning on just this particular matter — there was nothing that could be interpreted as a reference to this shocking contact with Europeans.

The aboriginal accounts of their first remembered contact with whites begin in about 1900 with references to persons known to have had sporadic but lethal encounters with them. From that time on whites continued to remain on the southern periphery of Yir Yoront territory. With the establishment of cattle stations (ranches) to the south, cattle men made occasional excursions among the "wild black-fellows" in order to inspect the country and abduct natives to be trained as cattle boys and "house girls." At least one such expedition reached the Coleman River where a number of Yir Yoront men and women were shot for no apparent reason.

About this time the government was persuaded to sponsor the establishment of three mission stations along the 700-mile western coast of the Peninsula in an attempt to help regulate the treatment of natives. To further this purpose a strip of coastal territory was set aside as an aboriginal reserve and closed to further white settlement.

In 1915, an Anglican mission station was established near the mouth of the Mitchell River, about a three-day march from the heart of the Yir Yoront country. Some Yir Yoront refused to have anything to do with the mission, others visited it occasionally while only a few eventually settled more or less permanently in one of the three "villages" established at the mission.

Thus the majority of the Yir Yoront continued to live their old self-supporting life in the bush, protected until 1942 by the government reserve and the intervening mission from the cruder realities of the encroaching new order from the south. To the east was poor, uninhabited country. To the north were other bush tribes extending on along the coast to the distant Archer River Presbyterian mission with which the Yir Yoront had no contact. Westward was the shallow Gulf of Carpentaria on which the natives saw only a mission lugger making its infrequent dry season trips to the Mitchell River. In this protected environment for over a generation the Yir Yoront were able to recuperate from shocks received at the hands of civilized society. During the 1930's their raiding and fighting, their trading and stealing of women, their evisceration and two- or three-year care of their dead, and their totemic ceremonies continued, apparently uninhibited by western influence. In 1931 they killed a European who wandered into their territory from the east, but the investigating police never approached the group whose members were responsible for the act.

As a direct result of the work of the Mitchell River mission, all Yir Yoront received a great many more western artifacts of all kinds than ever before. As part of their plan for raising native living standards, the missionaries made it possible for aboriginals living at the mission to earn some western goods, many of which were then given or traded to natives still living under bush conditions; they also handed out certain useful articles gratis to both mission and bush aboriginals. They prevented guns, liquor, and damaging narcotics, as well as decimating diseases, from reaching the tribes of this area, while encouraging the introduction of goods they considered "improving." As has been noted, no item of western technology available, with the possible exception of trade tobacco, was in greater demand among all groups of aboriginals than the short handled steel axe. The mission always kept a good supply of these axes in stock; at Christmas parties or other mission festivals they were given away to mission or visiting aboriginals indiscriminately and in considerable numbers. In addition, some steel axes as well as other European goods were still traded in to the Yir Yoront by natives in contact with cattle stations in the south. Indeed, steel axes had probably come to the Yir Yoront through established lines of aboriginal trade long before any regular contact with whites had occurred.

III. RELEVANT FACTORS

If we concentrate our attention on Yir Yoront behavior centering about the original stone axe (rather than on the axe — the object — itself) as a cultural trait or item of cultural equipment, we should get some conception of the role this implement played in aboriginal culture. This, in turn, should enable us to foresee with considerable accuracy some of the results stemming from the displacement of the stone age by the steel axe.

The production of a stone axe required a number of simple technological skills. With the various details of the axe well in mind, adult men could set about producing it (a task not considered appropriate for women or children). First of all a man had to know the location and properties of several natural resources found in his immediate environment: pliable wood for a handle, which could be doubled or bent over the axe head and bound tightly; bark, which could be rolled into cord for the binding; and gum, to fix the stone head in the haft. These materials had to be correctly gathered, stored, prepared, cut to size and applied or manipulated. They were in plentiful supply, and could be taken from anyone's property without special permission. Postponing consideration of the stone head, the axe could be made by any normal man who had a simple knowledge of nature and of the technological skills involved, together with fire (for heating the gum), and a few simple cutting tools — perhaps the sharp shells of plentiful bivalves.

The use of the stone axe as a piece of capital equipment used in producing other goods indicates its very great importance to the subsistence economy of the aboriginal. Anyone — man, woman, or child — could use the axe; indeed, it was used primarily by women, for theirs was the task of obtaining sufficient wood to keep the family campfire burning all day, for cooking or other purposes, and all night against mosquitoes and cold (for in July, winter temperature might drop below 40 degrees). In a normal lifetime a woman would use the axe to cut or knock down literally tons of firewood. The axe was also used to make other tools or weapons, and a variety of material equipment required by the aboriginal in his daily life. The stone axe was essential in the construction of the wet season domed huts which keep out some rain and some insects; of platforms which provide dry storage; of shelters which give shade in the dry summer when days are bright and hot. In hunting and fishing and in gathering vegetable or animal food the axe was also a necessary tool, and in this tropical culture, where preservatives or other means of storage are lacking, the natives spend more time obtaining food than in any other occupation — except sleeping. In only two instances was the use of the stone axe strictly limited to adult men: for gathering wild honey, the most prized food known to the Yir Yoront; and for making the secret paraphernalia for ceremonies. From this brief listing of some of the activities involving the use of the axe, it is easy to understand why there was at least one stone axe in every camp, in every hunting or fighting party, and in every group out on a "walk-about" in the bush.

The stone axe was also prominent in interpersonal relations. Yir Yoront men were dependent upon interpersonal relations for their stone axe heads, since the flat, geologically recent, alluvial country over which they range provides no suitable stone for this purpose. The stone they used came from quarries 400 miles to the south, reaching the Yir Yoront through long lines of male trading partners. Some of these chains terminated with the Yir Yoront men, others extended on farther north to other groups, using Yir Yoront men as links. Almost every older adult man had one or more regular trading partners, some to the north and some to the south. He provided his partner or partners in the south with surplus spears, particularly fighting spears tipped with the barbed spines of sting ray which snap into vicious fragments when they penetrate human flesh. For a dozen such spears, some of which he may have obtained from a partner to the north, he would receive one stone axe head. Studies have shown that the sting ray barb spears increased in value as they move south and farther from the sea. One hundred and fifty miles south of Yir Yoront one such spear may be exchanged for one stone axe head. Although actual investigations could not be made, it was presumed that farther south, nearer the quarries, one sting ray barb spear would bring several stone axe heads. Apparently people who acted as links in the middle of the chain and who made neither spears nor axe heads would receive a certain number of each as a middleman's profit.

Thus trading relations, which may extend the individual's personal relationships beyond that of his own group, were associated with spears and axes, two of the most important items in a man's equipment. Finally, most of the exchanges took place during the dry season, at the time of the great aboriginal celebrations centering about initiation rites or other totemic ceremonials which attracted hundreds and were the occasion for much exciting activity in addition to trading.

Returning to the Yir Yoront, we find that adult men kept their axes in camp with their other equipment, or carried them when travelling. Thus a woman or child who wanted to use an axe — as might frequently happen during the day — had to get one from a man, use it promptly, and return it in good condition. While a man might speak of "my axe," a woman or child could not.

This necessary and constant borrowing of axes from older men by women and children was in accordance with regular patterns of kinship behavior. A woman would expect to use her husband's axe unless he himself was using it; if unmarried, or if her husband was absent, a woman would go first to her older brother or to her father. Only in extraordinary circumstances would she seek a stone axe from other male kin. A girl, a boy, or a young man would look to a father or an older brother to provide an axe for their use. Older men, too, would follow similar rules if they had to borrow an axe.

It will be noted that all of these social relationships in which the stone axe had a place are pair relationships and that the use of the axe helped to define and maintain their character and the roles of the two individual participants. Every active relationship among the Yir Yoront involved a definite and accepted status of superordination or subordination. A person could have no dealings with another on exactly equal terms. The nearest approach to equality was between brothers, although the older was always superordinate to the younger. Since the exchange of goods in a trading relationship involved a mutual reciprocity, trading partners usually stood in a brotherly type of relationship, although one was always classified as older than the other and would have some advantage in case of dispute. It can be seen that repeated and widespread conduct centering around the use of the axe helped to generalize and standardize these sex, age, and kinship roles both in their normal benevolent and exceptional malevolent aspects.

The status of any individual Yir Yoront was determined not only by sex, age, and extended kin relationships, but also by membership in one of two dozen patrilineal totemic clans into which the entire community was divided.[3] Each clan had literally hundreds of totems, from one or two of which the clan derived its name, and the clan members their personal names. These totems included natural species or phenomena such as the sun, stars, and daybreak, as well as cultural "species": imagined ghosts, rainbow serpents, heroic ancestors; such eternal cultural verities as fires, spears, huts; and such human activities, conditions, or attributes as eating, vomiting, swimming, fighting, babies and corpses, milk and blood, lips and loins. While individual members of such totemic classes or species might disappear or be destroyed, the class itself was obviously ever-present and indestructible. The totems, therefore, lent permanence and stability to the clans, to the groupings of human individuals who generation after generation were each associated with a set of totems which distinguished one clan from another.

The stone axe was one of the most important of the many totems of the Sunlit Cloud Iguana clan. The names of many members of this clan referred to the axe itself, to activities in which the axe played a vital part, or to the clan's mythical ancestors with whom the axe was prominently associated. When it was necessary to represent the stone axe in totemic ceremonies, only men of this clan exhibited it or pantomimed its use. In secular life, the axe could be made by any man and used by all; but in the sacred realm of the totems it belonged exclusively to the Sunlit Cloud Iguana people.

Supporting those aspects of cultural behavior which we have called technology and conduct, is a third area of culture which includes ideas, sentiments, and values. These are most difficult to deal with, for they are latent and covert, and even unconscious, and must be deduced from overt actions and language or other communicating behavior. In this aspect of the culture lies the significance of the stone axe to the Yir Yoront and to their cultural way of life.

The stone axe was an important symbol of masculinity among the Yir Yoront (just as pants or pipes are to us). By a complicated set of ideas the axe was defined as "belonging" to males, and everyone in the society (except untrained infants) accepted these ideas. Similarly spears, spear throwers, and fire-making sticks were owned only by men and were also symbols of masculinity. But the masculine values represented

[3] The best, although highly concentrated, summaries of totemism among the Yir Yoront and the other tribes of north Queensland will be found in R. Lauriston Sharp, "Tribes and Totemism in Northeast Australia," *Oceania*, Vol. 8, 1939, pp. 254–275 and 439–461 (especially pp. 268–275); also "Notes on Northeast Australian Totemism," in *Papers of the Peabody Museum of American Archaeology and Ethnology*, Vol. 20, *Studies in the Anthropology of Oceania and Asia*, Cambridge, 1943, pp. 66–71.

by the stone axe were constantly being impressed on all members of society by the fact that females borrowed axes but not other masculine artifacts. Thus the axe stood for an important theme of Yir Yoront culture: the superiority and rightful dominance of the male, and the greater value of his concerns and of all things associated with him. As the axe also had to be borrowed by the younger people it represented the prestige of age, another important theme running through Yir Yoront behavior.

To understand the Yir Yoront culture it is necessary to be aware of a system of ideas which may be called their totemic ideology. A fundamental belief of the aboriginal divided time into two great epochs: (1) a distant and sacred period at the beginning of the world when the earth was peopled by mildly marvelous ancestral beings or culture heroes who are in a special sense the forebears of the clans; and (2) a period when the old was succeeded by a new order which includes the present. Originally there was no anticipation of another era supplanting the present. The future would simply be an eternal continuation and reproduction of the present which itself had remained unchanged since the epochal revolution of ancestral times.

The important thing to note is that the aboriginal believed that the present world, as a natural and cultural environment, was and should be simply a detailed reproduction of the world of the ancestors. He believed that the entire universe "is now as it was in the beginning" when it was established and left by the ancestors. The ordinary cultural life of the ancestors became the daily life of the Yir Yoront camps, and the extraordinary life of the ancestors remained extant in the recurring symbolic pantomimes and paraphernalia found only in the most sacred atmosphere of the totemic rites.

Such beliefs, accordingly, opened the way for ideas of what *should be* (because it supposedly *was*) to influence or help determine what actually *is*. A man called Dog-chases-iguana-up-a-tree-and-barks-at-him-all-night had that and other names because he believed his ancestral alter ego had also had them; he was a member of the Sunlit Cloud Iguana clan because his ancestor was; he was associated with particular countries and totems of this same ancestor; during an initiation he played the role of a dog and symbolically attacked and killed certain members of other clans because his ancestor (conveniently either anthropomorphic or kynomorphic) really did the same to the ancestral alter egos of these men; and he would avoid his mother-in-law, joke with a mother's distant brother, and make spears in a certain way because his and other people's ancestors did these things. His behavior in these specific ways was outlined, and to that extent determined for him, by a set of ideas concerning the past and the relation of the present to the past.

But when we are informed that Dog-chases-etc. had two wives

from the Spear Black Duck clan and one from the Native Companion clan, one of them being blind, that he had four children with such and such names, that he had a broken wrist and was left handed, all because his ancestor had exactly these same attributes, then we know (though he apparently didn't) that the present has influenced the past, that the mythical world has been somewhat adjusted to meet the exigencies and accidents of the inescapably real present.

There was thus in Yir Yoront ideology a nice balance in which the mythical was adjusted in part to the real world, the real world in part to the ideal pre-existing mythical world, the adjustments occurring to maintain a fundamental tenet of native faith that the present must be a mirror of the past. Thus the stone axe in all its aspects, uses, and associations was integrated into the context of Yir Yoront technology and conduct because a myth, a set of ideas, had put it there.

IV. THE OUTCOME

The introduction of the steel axe indiscriminately and in large numbers into the Yir Yoront technology occurred simultaneously with many other changes. It is therefore impossible to separate all the results of this single innovation. Nevertheless, a number of specific effects of the change from stone to steel axes may be noted, and the steel axe may be used as an epitome of the increasing quantity of European goods and implements received by the aboriginals and of their general influence on the native culture. The use of the steel axe to illustrate such influences would seem to be justified. It was one of the first European artifacts to be adopted for regular use by the Yir Yoront, and whether made of stone or steel, the axe was clearly one of the most important items of cultural equipment they possessed.

The shift from stone to steel axes provided no major technological difficulties. While the aboriginals themselves could not manufacture steel axe heads, a steady supply from outside continued; broken wooden handles could easily be replaced from bush timbers with aboriginal tools. Among the Yir Yoront the new axe was never used to the extent it was on mission or cattle stations (for carpentry work, pounding tent pegs, as a hammer, and so on); indeed, it had so few more uses than the stone axe that its practical effect on the native standard of living was negligible. It did some jobs better, and could be used longer without breakage. These factors were sufficient to make it of value to the native. The white man believed that a shift from steel to stone axe on his part would be a definite regression. He was convinced that his axe was much more efficient, that its use would save time, and that it therefore represented technical "progress" towards goals which he had set up for the native. But this assumption was hardly borne out in aboriginal practice. Any leisure time the Yir Yoront might gain by using steel axes or other western tools was not invested in "improving the conditions of life," nor, certainly, in developing aesthetic activities, but in sleep — an art they had mastered thoroughly.

Previously, a man in need of an axe would acquire a stone axe head through regular trading partners from whom he knew what to expect, and was then dependent solely upon a known and adequate natural environment, and his own skills or easily acquired techniques. A man wanting a steel axe, however, was in no such self-reliant position. If he attended a mission festival when steel axes were handed out as gifts, he might receive one either by chance or by happening to impress upon the mission staff that he was one of the "better" bush aboriginals (the missionaries' definition of "better" being quite different from that of his bush fellows). Or, again almost by pure chance, he might get some brief job in connection with the mission which would enable him to earn a steel axe. In either case, for older men a preference for the steel axe helped change the situation from one of self-reliance to one of dependence, and a shift in behavior from well-structured or defined situations in technology or conduct to ill-defined situations in conduct alone. Among the men, the older ones whose earlier experience or knowledge of the white man's harshness made them suspicious were particularly careful to avoid having relations with the mission, and thus excluded themselves from acquiring steel axes from that source.

In other aspects of conduct or social relations, the steel axe was even more significantly at the root of psychological stress among the Yir Yoront. This was the result of new factors which the missionary considered beneficial: the simple numerical increase in axes per capita as a result of mission distribution, and distribution directly to younger men, women, and even children. By winning the favor of the mission staff, a woman might be given a steel axe which was clearly intended to be hers, thus creating a situation quite different from the previous custom which necessitated her borrowing an axe from a male relative. As a result a woman would refer to the axe as "mine," a possessive form she was never able to use of the stone axe. In the same fashion, young men or even boys also obtained steel axes directly from the mission, with the result that older men no longer had a complete monopoly of all the axes in the bush community. All this led to a revolutionary confusion of sex, age, and kinship roles, with a major gain in independence and loss of subordination on the part of those who now owned steel axes when they had previously been unable to possess stone axes.

The trading partner relationship was also affected by the new situation. A Yir Yoront might have a trading partner in a tribe to the south whom he defined as a younger brother and over whom he would therefore have some authority. But if the partner were in contact with the mission or had other access to steel axes, his subordination obviously decreased. Among other things, this took some of the excitement away from the dry season fiesta-like tribal gatherings centering around initiations. These had traditionally been the climactic annual occasions for exchanges between trading partners, when a man might seek to acquire a whole year's supply of stone axe heads. Now he might find himself prostituting his wife to almost total strangers in return for steel axes or other white man's goods. With trading partnerships weakened, there was less reason to attend the ceremonies, and less fun for those who did.

Not only did an increase in steel axes and their distribution to women change the character of the relations between individuals (the paired relationships that have been noted), but a previously rare type of relationship was created in the Yir Yoront's conduct towards whites. In the aboriginal society there were few occasions outside of the immediate family when an individual would initiate action to several other people at once. In any average group, in accordance with the kinship system, while a person might be superordinate to several people to whom he could suggest or command action, he was also subordinate to several others with whom such behavior would be tabu. There was thus no overall chieftainship or authoritarian leadership of any kind. Such complicated operations as grass-burning animal drives or totemic ceremonies could be carried out smoothly because each person was aware of his role.

On both mission and cattle stations, however, the whites imposed their conception of leadership roles upon the aboriginals, consisting of one person in a controlling relationship with a subordinate group. Aboriginals called together to receive gifts, including axes, at a mission Christmas party found themselves facing one or two whites who sought to control their behavior for the occasion, who disregarded the age, sex, and kinship variables of which the aboriginals were so conscious, and who considered them all at one subordinate level. The white also sought to impose similar patterns on work parties. (However, if he placed an aboriginal in charge of a mixed group of post-hole diggers, for example, half of the group, those subordinate to the "boss," would work while the other half, who were superordinate to him, would sleep.) For the aboriginal, the steel axe and other European goods came to symbolize this new and uncomfortable form of social organization, the leader-group relationship.

The most disturbing effects of the steel axe, operating in conjunction with other elements also being introduced from the white man's several sub-cultures, developed in the realm of traditional ideas, sentiments, and values. These were undermined at a rapidly mounting rate, with no new conceptions being defined to replace them. The result was the erection of a mental and moral void which foreshadowed the collapse and destruction of all Yir Yoront culture, if not, indeed, the extinction of the biological group itself.

From what has been said it should be clear how changes in overt behavior, in technology and conduct, weakened the values inherent in a reliance on nature, in the prestige of masculinity and of age, and in the various kinship relations. A scene was set in which a wife, or a young son whose initiation may not yet have been completed, need no longer defer to the husband or father who, in turn, became confused and insecure as he was forced to borrow a steel axe from them. For the woman and boy the steel axe helped establish a new degree of freedom which they accepted readily as an escape from the unconscious stress of the old patterns — but they, too, were left confused and insecure. Ownership became less well defined with the result that stealing and trespassing were introduced into technology and conduct. Some of the excitement surrounding the great ceremonies evaporated and they lost their previous gaiety and interest. Indeed, life itself became less interesting, although this did not lead the Yir Yoront to discover suicide, a concept foreign to them.

The whole process may be most specifically illustrated in terms of totemic system, which also illustrates the significant role played by a system of ideas, in this case a totemic ideology, in the breakdown of a culture.

In the first place, under pre-European aboriginal conditions where the native culture has become adjusted to a relatively stable environment, few, if any, unheard of or catastrophic crises can occur. It is clear, therefore, that the totemic system serves very effectively in inhibiting radical cultural changes. The closed system of totemic ideas, explaining and categorizing a well-known universe as it was fixed at the beginning of time, presents a considerable obstacle to the adoption of new or the dropping of old culture traits. The obstacle is not insurmountable and the system allows for the minor variations which occur in the norms of daily life. But the inception of major changes cannot easily take place.

Among the bush Yir Yoront the only means of water transport is a light wood log to which they cling in their constant swimming of rivers, salt creeks, and tidal inlets. These natives know that tribes 45 miles further north have a bark canoe. They know these northern tribes can thus fish from midstream or out at sea, instead of clinging to the river banks and beaches, that they can cross coastal waters infested with crocodiles, sharks, sting rays, and Portuguese men-of-war without danger. They know the materials of which the canoe is made exist in their own environment. But they also know, as they say, that they do not have canoes because their own mythical ancestors did not have them. They assume that the canoe was part of the ancestral universe of the northern tribes. For them, then, the adoption of the canoe would not be simply a matter of learning a number of new behavioral skills for its manufacture and use. The adoption would require a much more difficult procedure; the acceptance by the entire society of a myth, either locally developed or borrowed, to explain the presence of the canoe, to associate it with some one or more of the several hundred mythical ancestors (and how decide which?), and thus establish it as an accepted totem of one of the clans ready to be used by the whole community. The Yir Yoront have not made this adjustment, and in this case we can only say that for the time being at least, ideas have won out over very real pressures for technological change. In the elaborateness and explicitness of the totemic ideologies we seem to have one explanation for the notorious stability of Australian cultures under aboriginal conditions, an explanation which gives due weight to the importance of ideas in determining human behavior.

At a later stage of the contact situation, as has been indicated, phenomena unaccounted for by the totemic ideological system begin to appear with regularity and frequency and remain within the range of native experience. Accordingly, they cannot be ignored (as the "Battle of the Mitchell" was apparently ignored), and there is an attempt to assimilate them and account for them along the lines of principles inherent in the ideology. The bush Yir Yoront of the mid-thirties represent this stage of the acculturation process. Still trying to maintain their aboriginal definition of the situation, they accept European artifacts and behavior patterns, but fit them into their totemic system, assigning them to various clans on a par with original totems. There is an attempt to have the myth-making process keep up with these cultural changes so that the idea system can continue to support the rest of the culture. But analysis of overt behavior, of dreams, and of some of the new myths indicates that this arrangement is not entirely satisfactory, that the native clings to his totemic system with intellectual loyalty (lacking any substitute ideology), but that associated sentiments and values are weakened. His attitude towards his own and towards European culture are found to be highly ambivalent.

All ghosts are totems of the Head-to-the-East Corpse clan, are thought of as white, and are of course closely associated with death. The white man, too, is closely associated with death, and he and all things pertaining to him are naturally assigned to the Corpse clan as totems. The steel axe, as a totem, was thus associated with the Corpse clan. But as an "axe," clearly linked with the stone axe, it is a totem of the Sunlit Cloud Iguana clan. Moreover, the steel axe, like most European goods, has no distinctive origin myth, nor are mythical ancestors associated with it. Can anyone, sitting in the shade of a *ti* tree one afternoon, create a myth to resolve this confusion? No one has, and the horrid suspicion arises as to the authenticity of the origin myths, which failed to take into account this vast new universe of the white man. The steel axe, shifting hopelessly between one clan and the other, is not only replacing the stone axe physically, but is hacking at the supports of the entire cultural system.

The aboriginals to the south of the Yir Yoront have clearly passed beyond this stage. They are engulfed by European culture, either by the mission or cattle station sub-cultures or, for some natives, by a baffling, paradoxical combination of both incongruent varieties. The totemic ideology can no longer support the inrushing mass of foreign culture traits, and the myth-making process in its native form breaks down completely. Both intellectually and emotionally a saturation point is reached so that the myriad new traits which can neither be ignored nor any longer assimilated simply force the aboriginal to abandon his totemic system. With the collapse of this system of ideas, which is so closely related to so many other aspects of the native culture, there follows an appallingly sudden and complete cultural disintegration, and a demoralization of the individual such as has seldom been recorded elsewhere. Without the support of a system of ideas well devised to provide cultural stability in a stable environment, but admittedly too rigid for the new realities pressing in from outside, native behavior and native sentiments and values are simply dead. Apathy reigns. The aboriginal has passed beyond the realm of any outsider who might wish to do him well or ill.

Returning from the broken natives huddled on cattle stations or on the fringes of frontier towns to the ambivalent but still lively aboriginals settled on the Mitchell River mission, we note one further devious result of the introduction of European artifacts. During a wet season stay at the mission, the anthropologist discovered that his supply of tooth paste was being depleted at an alarming rate. Investigation showed that it was being taken by old men for use in a new tooth paste cult. Old materials of magic having failed, new materials were being tried out in a malevolent magic directed towards the mission staff and some of the younger aboriginal men. Old males, largely ignored by the missionaries, were seeking to regain some of their lost power and prestige. This mild aggression proved hardly effective, but perhaps only because confidence in any kind of magic on the mission was by this time at a low ebb.

For the Yir Yoront still in the bush, a time could be predicted when personal deprivation and frustration in a confused culture would produce an overload of anxiety. The mythical past of the totemic ancestors would disappear as a guarantee of a present of which the future was supposed to be a stable continuation. Without the past, the present could be meaningless and the future unstructured and uncertain. Insecurities would be inevitable. Reaction to this stress might be some form of symbolic aggression, or withdrawal and apathy, or some more realistic approach. In such a situation the missionary with understanding of the processes going on about him would find his opportunity to introduce his forms of religion and to help create a new cultural universe.

32

Cargo cults

PETER M. WORSLEY

When one cultural group becomes dominated by another, its original meaning system may seem thin, ineffective, and contradictory. The resulting state of deprivation often causes members to rebuild their culture along more satisfying lines. In this article Peter Worsley describes such a movement among the peoples of New Guinea and adjacent islands, an area where Western influence has caused cultural disorientation and where cargo cults have provided the basis for reorganization.

Patrols of the Australian Government venturing into the "uncontrolled" central highlands of New Guinea in 1946 found the primitive people there swept up in a wave of religious excitement. Prophecy was being fulfilled: The arrival of the Whites was the sign that the end of the world was at hand. The natives proceeded to butcher all of their pigs — animals that were not only a principal source of subsistence but also symbols of social status and ritual preeminence in their culture. They killed these valued animals in expression of the belief that after three days of darkness "Great Pigs" would appear from the sky. Food, firewood, and other necessities had to be stockpiled to see the people through to the arrival of the Great Pigs. Mock wireless antennae of bamboo and rope had been erected to receive in advance the news of the millennium. Many believed that with the great event they would exchange their black skins for white ones.

This bizarre episode is by no means the single event of its kind in the murky history of the collision of European civilization with the indigenous cultures of the southwest Pacific. For more than one hundred

From "Cargo Cults," *Scientific American* 200 (May 1959): 117–128. Reprinted with permission of W. H. Freeman and Company. Copyright © 1959 by Scientific American, Inc. All rights reserved. Illustrations are omitted.

years traders and missionaries have been reporting similar disturbances among the peoples of Melanesia, the group of Negro-inhabited islands (including New Guinea, Fiji, the Solomons, and the New Hebrides) lying between Australia and the open Pacific Ocean. Though their technologies were based largely upon stone and wood, these peoples had highly developed cultures, as measured by the standards of maritime and agricultural ingenuity, the complexity of their varied social organizations, and the elaboration of religious belief and ritual. They were nonetheless ill prepared for the shock of the encounter with the Whites, a people so radically different from themselves and so infinitely more powerful. The sudden transition from the society of the ceremonial stone ax to the society of sailing ships and now of airplanes has not been easy to make.

After four centuries of Western expansion, the densely populated central highlands of New Guinea remain one of the few regions where the people still carry on their primitive existence in complete independence of the world outside. Yet as the agents of the Australian Government penetrate into ever more remote mountain valleys, they find these backwaters of antiquity already deeply disturbed by contact with the ideas and artifacts of European civilization. For "cargo" — Pidgin English for trade goods — has long flowed along the indigenous channels of communication from the seacoast into the wilderness. With it has traveled the frightening knowledge of the white man's magical power. No small element in the white man's magic is the hopeful message sent abroad by his missionaries: the news that a Messiah will come and that the present order of Creation will end.

The people of the central highlands of New Guinea are only the latest to be gripped in the recurrent religious frenzy of the "cargo cults." However variously embellished with details from native myth and Christian belief, these cults all advance the same central theme: the world is about to end in a terrible cataclysm. Thereafter God, the ancestors, or some local culture hero will appear and inaugurate a blissful paradise on earth. Death, old age, illness, and evil will be unknown. The riches of the white man will accrue to the Melanesians.

Although the news of such a movement in one area has doubtless often inspired similar movements in other areas, the evidence indicates that these cults have arisen independently in many places as parallel responses to the same enormous social stress and strain. Among the movements best known to students of Melanesia are the "Taro Cult" of New Guinea, the "Vailala Madness" of Papua, the "Naked Cult" of Espiritu Santo, the "John Frum Movement" of the New Hebrides, and the "Tuka Cult" of the Fiji Islands.

At times the cults have been so well organized and fanatically persistent that they have brought the work of government to a standstill. The outbreaks have often taken the authorities completely by surprise and have confronted them with mass opposition of an alarming kind. In the 1930's, for example, villagers in the vicinity of Wewak, New Guinea, were stirred by a succession of "Black King" movements. The prophets announced that the Europeans would soon leave the island, abandoning their property to the natives, and urged their followers to cease paying taxes, since the government station was about to disappear into the sea in a great earthquake. To the tiny community of Whites in charge of the region, such talk was dangerous. The authorities jailed four of the prophets and exiled three others. In yet another movement, that sprang up in declared opposition to the local Christian mission, the cult leader took Satan as his god.

Troops on both sides in World War II found their arrival in Melanesia heralded as a sign of the Apocalypse. The G.I.'s who landed in the New Hebrides, moving up for the bloody fighting on Guadalcanal, found the natives furiously at work preparing airfields, roads, and docks for the magic ships and planes that they believed were coming from "Rusefel" (Roosevelt), the friendly king of America.

The Japanese also encountered millenarian visionaries during their southward march to Guadalcanal. Indeed, one of the strangest minor military actions of World War II occurred in Dutch New Guinea, when Japanese forces had to be turned against the local Papuan inhabitants of the Geelvink Bay region. The Japanese had at first been received with great joy, not because their "Greater East Asia Co-Prosperity Sphere" propaganda had made any great impact upon the Papuans, but because the natives regarded them as harbingers of the new world that was dawning, the flight of the Dutch having already given the first sign. Mansren, creator of the islands and their peoples, would now return, bringing with him the ancestral dead. All this had been known, the cult leaders declared, to the crafty Dutch, who had torn out the first page of the Bible where these truths were inscribed. When Mansren returned, the existing world order would be entirely overturned. White men would turn black like Papuans, Papuans would become Whites; root crops would grow in trees, and coconuts and fruits would grow like tubers. Some of the islanders now began to draw together into large "towns"; others took Biblical names such as "Jericho" and "Galilee" for their villages. Soon they adopted military uniforms and began drilling. The Japanese, by now highly unpopular, tried to disarm and disperse the Papuans; resistance inevitably developed. The climax of this tragedy came when several canoe-loads of fanatics sailed out to attack Japanese warships, believing themselves to be invulnerable by virtue of the holy water with which they had sprinkled themselves. But the bullets of the Japanese did not turn to water, and the attackers were mowed down by machine-gun fire.

Behind this incident lay a long history. As long ago as 1857 missionaries in the Geelvink Bay region had made note of the story of Mansren. It is typical of many Melanesian myths that became confounded with Christian doctrine to form the ideological basis of the movements. The legend tells how long ago there lived an old man named Manamakeri ("he who itches"), whose body was covered with sores. Manamakeri was extremely fond of palm wine, and used to climb a huge tree every day to tap the liquid from the flowers. He soon found that someone was getting there before him and removing the liquid. Eventually he trapped the thief, who turned out to be none other than the Morning Star. In return for his freedom, the Star gave the old man a wand that would produce as much fish as he liked, a magic tree, and a magic staff. If he drew in the sand and stamped his foot, the drawing would become real. Manamakeri, aged as he was, now magically impregnated a young maiden; the child of this union was a miracle-child who spoke as soon as he was born. But the maiden's parents were horrified, and banished her, the child, and the old man. The trio sailed off in a canoe created by Mansren ("The Lord"), as the old man now became known. On this journey Mansren rejuvenated himself by stepping into a fire and flaking off his scaly skin, which changed into valuables. He then sailed around Geelvink Bay, creating islands where he stopped, and peopling them with the ancestors of the present-day Papuans.

The Mansren myth is plainly a creation myth full of symbolic ideas relating to fertility and rebirth. Comparative evidence — especially the shedding of his scaly skin — confirms the suspicion that the old man is, in fact, the Snake in another guise. Psychoanalytic writers argue that the snake occupies such a prominent part in mythology the world over because it stands for the penis, another fertility symbol. This may be so, but its symbolic significance is surely more complex than this. It is the "rebirth" of the hero, whether Mansren or the Snake, that exercises such universal fascination over men's minds.

The nineteenth-century missionaries thought that the Mansren story would make the introduction of Christianity easier, since the concept of "resurrection," not to mention that of the "virgin birth" and the "second coming," was already there. By 1867, however, the first cult organized around the Mansren legend was reported.

Though such myths were widespread in Melanesia, and may have sparked occasional movements even in the pre-White era, they took on a new significance in the late nineteenth century, once the European powers had finished parceling out the Melanesian region among themselves. In many coastal areas the long history of "blackbirding" — the seizure of islanders for work on the plantations of Australia and Fiji — had built up a reservoir of hostility to Europeans. In other areas, however, the arrival of the Whites was accepted, even welcomed, for it meant access to bully beef and cigarettes, shirts and paraffin lamps, whisky and bicycles. It also meant access to the knowledge behind these material goods, for the Europeans brought missions and schools as well as cargo.

Practically the only teaching the natives received about European life came from the missions, which emphasized the central significance of religion in European society. The Melanesians already believed that man's activities — whether gardening, sailing canoes, or bearing children — needed magical assistance. Ritual without human effort was not enough. But neither was human effort on its own. This outlook was reinforced by mission teaching.

The initial enthusiasm for European rule, however, was speedily dispelled. The rapid growth of the plantation economy removed the bulk of the able-bodied men from the villages, leaving women, children, and old men to carry on as best they could. The splendid vision of the equality of all Christians began to seem a pious deception in face of the realities of the color bar, the multiplicity of rival Christian missions and the open irreligion of many Whites.

For a long time the natives accepted the European mission as the means by which the "cargo" would eventually be made available to them. But they found that acceptance of Christianity did not bring the cargo any nearer. They grew disillusioned. The story now began to be put about that it was not the Whites who made the cargo, but the dead ancestors. To people completely ignorant of factory production, this made good sense. White men did not work; they merely wrote secret signs on scraps of paper, for which they were given shiploads of goods. On the other hand, the Melanesians labored week after week for pitiful wages. Plainly the goods must be made for Melanesians somewhere, perhaps in the Land of the Dead. The Whites, who possessed the secret of the cargo, were intercepting it and keeping it from the hands of the islanders, to whom it was really consigned. In the Madang district of New Guinea, after some forty years' experience of the missions, the natives went in a body one day with a petition demanding that the cargo secret should now be revealed to them, for they had been very patient.

So strong is this belief in the existence of a "secret" that the cargo cults generally contain some ritual in imitation of the mysterious European customs which are held to be the clue to the white man's extraordinary power over goods and men. The believers sit around tables with bottles of flowers in front of them, dressed in European clothes, waiting for the cargo ship or airplane to materialize; other cultists feature magic pieces of paper and cabalistic writing. Many of them deliberately turn their backs on the past by destroying secret ritual objects, or exposing them to the gaze of uninitiated youths and women, for whom formerly even a glimpse of the sacred objects would have meant the severest penalties, even death. The belief that they were the chosen people is further reinforced by their reading of the Bible, for the lives and customs of the people in the Old Testament resemble their own lives rather than those of the Europeans. In the New Testament they find the Apocalypse, with its prophecies of destruction and resurrection, particularly attractive.

Missions that stress the imminence of the Second Coming, like those of the Seventh Day Adventists, are often accused of stimulating millenarian cults among the islanders. In reality, however, the Melanesians themselves rework the doctrines the missionaries teach them, selecting from the Bible what they themselves find particularly congenial in it. Such movements have occurred in areas where missions of quite different types have been dominant, from Roman Catholic to Seventh Day Adventist. The reasons for the emergence of these cults, of course, lie far deeper in the life-experience of the people.

The economy of most of the islands is very backward. Native agriculture produces little for the world market, and even the European plantations and mines export only a few primary products and raw materials: copra, rubber, gold. Melanesians are quite unable to understand why copra, for example, fetches thirty pounds sterling per ton one month and but five pounds a few months later. With no notion of the workings of world-commodity markets, the natives see only the sudden closing of plantations, reduced wages and unemployment, and are inclined to attribute their insecurity to the whim or evil in the nature of individual planters.

Such shocks have not been confined to the economic order. Governments, too, have come and gone, especially during the two world wars: German, Dutch, British, and French administrations melted overnight. Then came the Japanese, only to be ousted in turn largely by the previously unknown Americans. And among these Americans the Melanesians saw Negroes like themselves, living lives of luxury on equal terms with white G.I.'s. The sight of these Negroes seemed like a fulfillment of the old prophecies to many cargo cult leaders. Nor must we forget the sheer scale of this invasion. Around a million U.S. troops passed through the Admiralty Islands, completely swamping the inhabitants. It was a world of meaningless and chaotic changes, in which anything was possible. New ideas were imported and given local twists. Thus in the Loyalty Islands people expected the French Communist Party to bring the millennium. There is no real evidence, however, of any Communist influence in these movements, despite the rather hysterical belief among Solomon Island planters that the name of the local "Masinga Rule" movement was derived from the word "Marxian"! In reality the name comes from a Solomon Island tongue, and means "brotherhood."

Europeans who have witnessed outbreaks inspired by the cargo cults are usually at a loss to understand what they behold. The islanders throw away their money, break their most sacred taboos, abandon their gardens, and destroy their precious livestock; they indulge in sexual license or, alternatively, rigidly separate men from women in huge communal establishments. Sometimes they spend days sitting gazing at the horizon for a glimpse of the long-awaited ship or airplane; sometimes they dance, pray, and sing in mass congregations, becoming possessed and "speaking with tongues."

Observers have not hesitated to use such words as "madness," "mania," and "irrationality" to characterize the cults. But the cults reflect quite logical and rational attempts to make sense out of a social order that appears senseless and chaotic. Given the ignorance of the Melanesians about the wider European society, its economic organization and its highly developed technology, their reactions form a consistent and understandable pattern. They wrap up all their yearning and hope in an amalgam that combines the best counsel they can find in Christianity and their native belief. If the world is soon to end, gardening or fishing is unnecessary; everything will be provided. If the Melanesians are to be part of a much wider order, the taboos that prescribe their social conduct must now be lifted or broken in a newly prescribed way.

Of course the cargo never comes. The cults nonetheless live on. If the millennium does not arrive on schedule, then perhaps there is some failure in the magic, some error in the ritual. New breakaway groups organize around "purer" faith and ritual. The cult rarely disappears, so long as the social situation which brings it into being persists.

At this point it should be observed that cults of this general kind are not peculiar to Melanesia. Men who feel themselves oppressed and deceived have always been ready to pour their hopes and fears, their aspirations and frustrations, into dreams of a millennium to come or of a golden age to return. All parts of the world have had their counterparts of the cargo cults, from the American Indian ghost dance to the Communist-millenarist "reign of the saints" in Münster during the Reformation, from medieval European apocalyptic cults to African "witch-finding" movements and Chinese Buddhist heresies. In some situations men have been content to wait and pray; in others they have sought to hasten the day by using their strong right arms to do the Lord's work. And always the cults serve to bring together scattered groups, notably the peasants and urban plebeians of agrarian societies and the peoples of "stateless" societies where the cult unites separate (and often hostile) villages, clans, and tribes into a wider religio-political unity.

Once the people begin to develop secular political organizations, however, the sects tend to lose their importance as vehicles of protest. They begin to relegate the Second Coming to the distant future or to the next world. In Melanesia ordinary political bodies, trade unions and native councils are becoming the normal media through which the islanders express their aspirations. In recent years continued economic prosperity and political stability have taken some of the edge off their despair. It now seems unlikely that any major movement along cargo-cult lines will recur in areas where the transition to secular politics has been made, even if the insecurity of prewar times returned. I would predict that the embryonic nationalism represented by cargo cults is likely in future to take forms familiar in the history of other countries that have moved from subsistence agriculture to participation in the world economy.

33

Psychotherapy in Africa

THOMAS ADEOYE LAMBO

*There was a time when many people thought Western medicine in all
its forms would eventually displace the indigenous medical practices
of Africa and Asia. Although Western medicine continues to exert a
strong influence in changing cultures, its role has changed. It is
widely recognized now that medicine for the mind and body depends
on the culture in which it is practiced. In this article Thomas Lambo
shows how psychotherapy in Africa is more effective when
psychiatrists and traditional healers work as a team. He argues that
treatment of all kinds must begin with a people's indigenous beliefs.
And throughout this study is the implicit message that Western
medicine has much to learn from the socially oriented therapies of
non-Western cultures.*

Some years ago, a Nigerian patient came to see me in a state of extreme
anxiety. He had been educated at Cambridge University and was, to all
intents and purposes, thoroughly "Westernized." He had recently been
promoted to a top-level position in the administrative service, by-passing
many of his able peers. A few weeks after his promotion, however, he
had had an unusual accident from which he barely escaped with his
life. He suddenly became terrified that his colleagues had formed a
conspiracy and were trying to kill him.

His paranoia resisted the usual methods of Western psychiatry,
and he had to be sedated to relieve his anxiety. But one day he came
to see me, obviously feeling much better. A few nights before, he said,
his grandfather had appeared to him in a dream and had assured him
of a long and healthy life. He had been promised relief from fear and
anxiety if he would sacrifice a goat. My patient bought a goat the fol-

lowing day, carried out all of the detailed instructions of his grandfather, and quickly recovered. The young man does not like to discuss this experience because he feels it conflicts with his educational background, but occasionally, in confidence, he says: "There is something in these native things, you know."

To the Western eye, such lingering beliefs in ritual and magic seem antiquated and possibly harmful — obstacles in the path of modern medicine. But the fact is that African cultures have developed indigenous forms of psychotherapy that are highly effective because they are woven into the social fabric. Although Western therapeutic methods are being adopted by many African therapists, few Africans are simply substituting new methods for traditional modes of treatment. Instead, they have attempted to combine the two for maximum effectiveness.

The character and effectiveness of medicine for the mind and the body always and everywhere depend on the culture in which the medicine is practiced. In the West, healing is often considered to be a private matter between patient and therapist. In Africa, healing is an integral part of society and religion, a matter in which the whole community is involved. To understand African psychotherapy one must understand African thought and its social roots.

It seems impossible to speak of a single African viewpoint because the continent contains a broad range of cultures. The Ga, the Masai, and the Kikuyu, for example, are as different in their specific ceremonies and customs as are the Bantus and the Belgians. Yet in sub-Saharan black Africa the different cultures do share a consciousness of the world. They have in common a characteristic perception of life and death that makes it possible to describe their overriding philosophy. (In the United States, Southern Baptists and Episcopalians are far apart in many of their rituals and beliefs, yet one could legitimately say that both share a Christian concept of life.)

The basis of most African value systems is the concept of the unity of life and time. Phenomena that are regarded as opposites in the West exist on a single continuum in Africa. African thought draws no sharp distinction between animate and inanimate, natural and supernatural, material and mental, conscious and unconscious. All things exist in dynamic correspondence, whether they are visible or not. Past, present, and future blend in harmony; the world does not change between one's dreams and the daylight.

Essential to this view of the world is the belief that there is continuous communion between the dead and the living. Most African cultures share the idea that the strength and influence of every clan is anchored by the spirits of its deceased heroes. These heroes are omnipotent and indestructible, and their importance is comparable to that of the Catholic saints. But to Africans, spirits and deities are ever present in human affairs; they are the guardians of the established social order.

The common element in rituals throughout the continent — ancestor cults, deity cults, funeral rites, agricultural rites — is the unity of the people with the world of spirits, the mystical and emotional bond between the natural and supernatural worlds.

Because of the African belief in deities and ancestral spirits, many Westerners think that African thought is more concerned with the supernatural causes of events than with their natural causes. On one level this is true. Africans attribute nearly all forms of illness and disease, as well as personal and communal catastrophes, accidents, and deaths to the magical machinations of their enemies and to the intervention of gods and ghosts. As a result there is a deep faith in the power of symbols to produce the effects that are desired. If a man finds a hair, or a piece of material, or a bit of a fingernail belonging to his enemy, he believes he has only to use the object ritualistically in order to bring about the enemy's injury or death.

As my educated Nigerian patient revealed by sacrificing a goat, the belief in the power of the supernatural is not confined to uneducated Africans. In a survey of African students in British universities conducted some years ago, I found that the majority of them firmly believed that their emotional problems had their origin in, or could at least be influenced by, charms and diabolical activities of other African students or of people who were still in Africa. I recently interviewed the student officers at the Nigeria House in London and found no change in attitude.

The belief in the power of symbols and magic is inculcated at an early age. I surveyed 1,300 elementary-school children over a four-year period and found that 85 percent used native medicine of some sort — incantations, charms, magic — to help them pass exams, to be liked by teachers, or to ward off the evil effects of other student "medicines." More than half of these children came from Westernized homes, yet they held firmly to the power of magic ritual.

Although most Africans believe in supernatural forces and seem to deny natural causality, their belief system is internally consistent. In the Western world, reality rests on the human ability to master things, to conquer objects, to subordinate the outer world to human will. In the African world, reality is found in the soul, in a religious acquiescence to life, not in its mastery. Reality rests on the relations between one human being and another, and between all people and spirits.

The practice of medicine in Africa is consistent with African philosophy. Across the African continent, sick people go to acknowledged diviners and healers — they are often called witch doctors in the West — in order to discover the nature of their illness. In almost every instance, the explanation involves a deity or an ancestral spirit. But this is only one aspect of the diagnosis, because the explanation given by the diviner is also grounded in natural phenomena. As anthropologist Robin Horton observes:

> The diviner who diagnoses the intervention of a spiritual agency is also expected to give some acceptable account of what moved the agency in question to intervene. And this account very commonly involves reference to some event in the world of visible, tangible happenings. Thus if a diviner diagnoses the action of witchcraft influence or lethal medicine spirits, it is usual for him to add something about the human hatreds, jealousies, and misdeeds that have brought such agencies into play. Or, if he diagnoses the wrath of an ancestor, it is usual for him to point to the human breach of kinship morality which has called down this wrath.

The causes of illness are not simply attributed to the unknown or dropped into the laps of the gods. Causes are always linked to the patient's immediate world of social events. As Victor Turner's study of the Ndembu people of central Africa revealed, diviners believe a patient "will not get better until all the tensions and aggressions in the group's interrelationships have been brought to light and exposed to ritual treatment." In my work with the Yoruba culture, I too found that supernatural forces are regarded as the agents and consequences of human will. Sickness is the natural effect of some social mistake — breaching a taboo or breaking a kinship rule.

African concepts of health and illness, like those of life and death, are intertwined. Health is not regarded as an isolated phenomenon but reflects the integration of the community. It is not the mere absence of disease but a sign that a person is living in peace and harmony with his neighbors, that he is keeping the laws of the gods and the tribe. The practice of medicine is more than the administration of drugs and potions. It encompasses all activities — personal and communal — that are directed toward the promotion of human well-being. As S. R. Burstein wrote, to be healthy requires

> averting the wrath of gods or spirits, making rain, purifying streams or habitations, improving sex potency or fecundity or the fertility of fields and crops — in short, it is bound up with the whole interpretation of life.

Native healers are called upon to treat a wide range of psychiatric disorders, from schizophrenia to neurotic syndromes. Their labels may not be the same, but they recognize the difference between an incapacitating psychosis and a temporary neurosis, and between a problem that can be cured (anxiety) and one that cannot (congenital retardation or idiocy). In many tribes a person is defined as mad when he talks nonsense, acts foolishly and irresponsibly, and is unable to look after himself.

It is often assumed that tribal societies are a psychological paradise and that mental illness is the offspring of modern civilization and its myriad stresses. The African scenes in Alex Haley's *Roots* tend to portray a Garden of Eden, full of healthy tribesmen. But all gardens have snakes. Small societies have their own peculiar and powerful sources of mental stress. Robin Horton notes that tribal societies have a limited number of roles to be filled, and that there are limited choices for individuals. As a result each tribe usually has a substantial number of social misfits. Traditional communities also have a built-in set of conflicting values: aggressive ambition versus a reluctance to rise above one's neighbor; ruthless individualism versus acceptance of one's place in the lineage system. Inconsistencies such as these, Horton believes,

> are often as sharp as those so well known in modern industrial societies. . . . One may even suspect that some of the young Africans currently rushing from the country to the towns are in fact escaping from a more oppressive to a less oppressive psychological environment.

Under typical tribal conditions, traditional methods are perfectly effective in the diagnosis and treatment of mental illness. The patient goes to the tribal diviner, who follows a complex procedure. First the diviner (who may be a man or a woman) determines the "immediate" cause of the illness — that is, whether it comes from physical devitalization or from spiritual possession. Next he or she diagnoses the "remote" cause of the ailment: Had the patient offended one of his ancestor spirits or gods? Had a taboo been violated? Was some human agent in the village using magic or invoking the help of evil spirits to take revenge for an offense?

The African diviner makes a diagnosis much as a Western psychoanalyst does: through the analysis of dreams, projective techniques, trances, and hypnotic states (undergone by patient and healer alike), and the potent power of words. With these methods, the diviner defines the psychodynamics of the patient and gains insight into the complete life situation of the sick person.

One projective technique of diagnosis — which has much in common with the Rorschach test — occurs in *Ifa* divination, a procedure used by Yoruba healers. There are 256 *Odus* (incantations) that are poetically structured; each is a dramatic series of words that evoke the patient's emotions. Sometimes the power of the *Odus* lies in the way the words are used, the order in which they are arranged, or the stark-ness with which they express a deep feeling. The incantations are used to gain insight into the patient's problem. Their main therapeutic value, as is the case with the Rorschach ink blots, is to interpret omens, bring up unconscious motives, and make unknown desires and fears explicit.

Once the immediate and remote causes are established, the diag-nosis is complete and the healer decides on the course of therapy. Usu-ally this involves an expiatory sacrifice meant to restore the unity between man and deity. Everyone takes part in the treatment; the ritual involves the healer, the patient, his family, and the community at large. The group rituals — singing and dancing, confessions, trances, storytelling, and the like — that follow are powerful therapeutic measures for the patient. They release tensions and pressures and promote positive men-tal health by tying all individuals to the larger group. Group rituals are effective because they are the basis of African social life, an essential part of the lives of "healthy" Africans.

Some cultures, such as the N'jayei society of the Mende in Sierra Leone and the Yassi society of the Sherbro, have always had formal group therapy for their mentally ill. When one person falls ill, the whole tribe attends to his physical and spiritual needs.

Presiding over all forms of treatment is the healer, or *nganga*. My colleagues and I have studied and worked with these men and women for many years, and we are consistently impressed by their abilities. Many of those we observed are extraordinary individuals of great com-mon sense, eloquence, boldness, and charisma. They are highly re-spected within their communities as people who through self-denial, dedication, and prolonged meditation and training have discovered the secrets of the healing art and its magic (a description of Western healers as well, one might say).

The traditional *nganga* has supreme self-confidence, which he or she transmits to the patient. By professing an ability to commune with supernatural beings — and therefore to control or influence them — the healer holds boundless power over members of the tribe. Africans regard the *nganga*'s mystical qualities and eccentricities fondly, and with awe. So strongly do people believe in the *nganga*'s ability to find out which ancestral spirit is responsible for the psychological distress of the patient, that pure suggestion alone can be very effective.

For centuries the tribal practice of communal psychotherapy served African society well. Little social stigma was attached to mental illness; even chronic psychotics were tolerated in their communities and were able to function at a minimal level. (Such tolerance is true of many rural cultures.) But as the British, Germans, French, Belgians, and Portuguese colonized many African countries, they brought a European concept of mental illness along with their religious, economic, and educational systems.

They built prisons with special sections set aside for "lunatics" — usually vagrant psychotics and criminals with demonstrable mental disorders — who were restricted with handcuffs and ankle shackles. The African healers had always drawn a distinction between mental illness and criminality, but the European colonizers did not.

In many African cultures today, the traditional beliefs in magic and religion are dying. Their remaining influence serves only to create anxiety and ambivalence among Africans who are living through a period of rapid social and economic change. With the disruption and disorganization of family units, we have begun to see clinical problems that once were rare: severe depression, obsessional neurosis, and emotional incapacity. Western medicine has come a long way from the shackle solution, but it is not the best kind of therapy for people under such stress. In spite of its high technological and material advancement, modern science does not satisfy the basic metaphysical and social needs of many people, no matter how sophisticated they are.

In 1954 my colleagues and I established a therapeutic program designed to wed the best practices of traditional and contemporary psychology. Our guiding premise was to make use of the therapeutic practices that already existed in the indigenous culture, and to recognize the power of the group in healing.

We began our experiment at Aro, a rural suburb of the ancient town of Abeokuta, in western Nigeria. Aro consists of four villages that lie in close proximity in the beautiful rolling countryside. The villages are home to Yoruba tribesmen and their relatives, most of whom are peasant farmers, fishermen, and craftsmen.

Near these four villages we built a day hospital that could accommodate up to 300 patients, and then we set up a village care system for their treatment. Our plan was to preserve the fundamental structure of African culture: closely knit groups, well-defined kin networks, an interlocking system of mutual obligations and traditional roles.

Patients came to the hospital every morning for treatment and spent their afternoons in occupational therapy, but they were not confined to the hospital. Patients lived in homes in the four villages or, if necessary, with hospital staff members who lived on hospital grounds — ambulance drivers, clerks, dispensary attendants, and gardeners. (This boarding-out procedure resembles a system that has been practiced for several hundred years in Gheel, a town in Belgium, where the mentally ill live in local households surrounding a central institution.)

We required the patients, who came from all over Nigeria, to arrive at the village hospital with at least one relative — a mother, sister, brother, or aunt — who would be able to cook for them, wash their clothes, take them to the hospital in the morning, and pick them up in the afternoon.

These relatives, along with the patients, took part in all the social activities of the villages: parties, plays, dances, storytelling. Family participation was successful from the beginning. We were able to learn about the family influences and stresses on the patient, and the family members learned how to adjust to the sick relative and deal with his or her emotional needs.

The hospital staff was drawn from the four villages, which meant that the hospital employees were the "landlords" of most of the patients, in constant contact with them at home and at work. After a while, the distinction between the two therapeutic arenas blurred and the villages became extensions of the hospital wards.

Doctors, nurses, and superintendents visited the villages every day and set up "therapy" groups — often for dancing, storytelling, and other rituals — as well as occupational programs that taught patients traditional African crafts.

It is not enough to treat patients on a boarding-out or outpatient basis. If services are not offered to them outside of the hospital, an undue burden is placed on their families and neighbors. This increases the tension to which patients are exposed. An essential feature of our plan was to regard the villages as an extension of the hospital, subject to equally close supervision and control.

But we neither imposed the system on the local people nor asked them to give their time and involvement without giving them something in return. We were determined to inflict no hardships. The hospital staff took full responsibility for the administration of the villages and for the health of the local people. They held regular monthly meetings with the village elders and their councils to give the villagers a say in the system. The hospital also arranged loans to the villagers to expand, repair, or build new houses to take care of the patients; it paid for the installation of water pipes and latrines; it paid for a mosquito eradication squad; it offered jobs to many local people and paid the "landlords" a small stipend.

Although these economic benefits aided the community, no attempt was ever made to structure the villages in any way, or to tell the villagers what to do with the patients or how to treat them. As a result of economic benefits, hospital guidance, and a voice in their own management, village members supported the experiment.

In a study made after the program began, we learned that patients who were boarded out under this system adapted more quickly and responded more readily to treatment than patients who lived in the hospital. Although the facilities available in the hospital were extensive — drug medication, group therapy sessions, modified insulin therapy, electroconvulsive shock treatments — we found that the most important therapeutic factor was the patient's social contacts, especially with people who were healthier than the patient. The village groups, unlike the hospital group, were unrehearsed, unexpected, and voluntary. Patients could choose their friends and activities; they were not thrown together arbitrarily and asked to "work things out." We believe that the boarded-out patients improved so quickly because of their daily contact with settled, tolerant, healthy people. They learned to function in society again without overwhelming anxiety.

One of the more effective and controversial methods we used was to collaborate with native healers. Just as New Yorkers have faith in their psychoanalysts, and pilgrims have faith in their priests, the Yoruba have faith in the *nganga*; and faith, as we are learning, is half the battle toward cure.

Our unorthodox alliance proved to be highly successful. The local diviners and religious leaders helped many of the patients recover, sometimes through a simple ceremony at a village shrine, sometimes in elaborate forms of ritual sacrifice, sometimes by interpreting the spiritual or magical causes of their dreams and illnesses.

At the beginning of the program patients were carefully selected for admission, but now patients of every sort are accepted: violent persons, catatonics, schizophrenics, and others whose symptoms make them socially unacceptable or emotionally withdrawn. The system is particularly effective with emotionally disturbed and psychotic children, who always come to the hospital with a great number of concerned relatives. Children who have minor neurotic disorders are kept out of the hospital entirely and treated exclusively and successfully in village homes.

The village care system was designed primarily for the acutely ill and for those whose illness was manageable, and the average stay for patients at Aro was, and is, about six months. But patients who were chronically ill and could not recover in a relatively short time posed a problem. For one thing, their relatives could not stay with them in the villages because of family and financial obligations in their home communities. We are working out solutions for such people on a trial-and-error basis. Some of the incapacitated psychotic patients now live on special farms; others live in Aro villages near the hospital and earn their keep while receiving regular supervision. The traditional healers keep watch over these individuals and maintain follow-up treatment.

We have found many economic, medical, and social advantages to our program. The cost has been low because we have concentrated on using human resources in the most effective and strategic manner. Medically and therapeutically, the program provides a positive environment for the treatment of character disorders, sociopathy, alcoholism, neuroses, and anxiety. Follow-up studies show that the program fosters a relatively quick recovery for these problems and that the recidivism rate and the need for aftercare are significantly reduced. The length of stay at Aro, and speed of recovery, is roughly one third of the average stay in other hospitals, especially for all forms of schizophrenia. Patients with neurotic disorders respond most rapidly. Because of its effectiveness, the Aro system has been extended to four states in Nigeria and to five countries in Africa, including Kenya, Ghana, and Zambia. At each new hospital the program is modified to fit local conditions.

Some observers of the Aro system argue that it can operate only in nonindustrial agrarian communities, like those in Africa and Asia, where families and villages are tightly knit. They say that countries marked by high alienation and individualism could not import such a program. Part of this argument is correct. The Aro approach to mental health rests on particularly African traditions, such as the *nganga*, and on the belief in the continuum of life and death, sickness and health, the natural and the supernatural.

But some lessons of the Aro plan have already found their way into Western psychotherapy. Many therapists recognize the need to place the sick person in a social context; a therapist cannot heal the patient without attending to his beliefs, family, work, and environment. Various forms of group therapy are being developed in an attempt to counteract the Western emphasis on curing the individual in isolation. Lately, family therapy has been expanded into a new procedure called network therapy in which the patient's entire network of relatives, coworkers, and friends become involved in the treatment.

Another lesson of Aro is less obvious than the benefits of group support. It is the understanding that treatment begins with a people's indigenous beliefs and their world view, which underlie psychological functioning and provide the basis for healing. Religious values that give meaning and coherence to life can be the healthiest route for many people. As Jung observed years ago, religious factors are inherent in the path toward healing, and the native therapies of Africa support his view.

A supernatural belief system, Western or Eastern, is not a sphere of arbitrary dreams but a sphere of laws that dictate the rules of kinship, the order of the universe, the route to happiness. The Westerner sees only part of the African belief system, such as the witch doctor, and wonders how wild fictions can take root in a reasonable mind. (His own fictions seem perfectly reasonable, of course.) But to the African, the religious-magical system is a great poem, allegorical of human experience, wise in its portrayal of the world and its creatures. There is more method, more reason, in such madness than in the sanity of most people today.

34

Highways and the future of the Yanomamö

SHELTON H. DAVIS

History is replete with examples of national expansion at the expense of less powerful neighbors. Scores of North American Indian nations, to say nothing of numerous groups in other parts of the world, have succumbed to more powerful neighbors. In this article, Shelton H. Davis describes how the Yanomamö, one of the last unacculturated groups in Brazil, face cultural extinction at the hands of intruders. Attracted by the discovery of uranium, geologists and miners travel along a new road that bisects tribal territory. Without an adequate reservation set aside for their protection, argues Davis, the Yanomamö have little chance to survive.

This is a promise that I can strongly make: we are going to create a policy of integrating the Indian population into Brazilian society as rapidly as possible. . . . We think that the ideals of preserving the Indian population within its own "habitat" are very beautiful, but unrealistic. — Sr. Mauricio Rangel Reis, Brazilian Minister of the Interior, March 1974.

The Yanomamö (also referred to as the Yanoáma, Shiriana, Xiriana, Guaharinbo, and Waika) are the largest unacculturated Indian tribe in South America. The tribe is estimated to number between 10,000 and 25,000 people, who live in hundreds of small villages skirting the border between Venezuela and Brazil. The Yanomamö men love to participate in highly ritualized chest-pounding duels, intervillage fueds, and warfare. The women of the tribe are expert gardeners, and cultivate magical

This article was written especially for this book. Copyright © 1976 by Shelton H. Davis. Printed by permission. For a more detailed discussion of the events described in this article see the author's book, *Victims of the Miracle: Development and the Indians of Brazil* (Cambridge University Press, 1977).

charms to ward off the violence and the aggression of their men. Yanomamö shamans possess a vast knowledge of medical plants, many of which remain unknown to modern pharmacological science. During special curing ceremonies, these shamans blow an hallucinogenic drug called *ebene* in order to produce spiritual and visionary experiences.

For at least a century, the Yanomamö have been forced to retreat defensively into a vast jungle refuge area between the Orinoco and Marauia rivers. To the south, they were attacked by Brazilian rubber collectors and settlers. To the north, they fought off the expanding cattle frontier in Venezuela and the more acculturated and rifle-bearing Makiritare tribe. Until recently, however, the only major threats to the independence and territorial integrity of the Yanomamö came from inquisitive anthropologists, Italian priests, and North American evangelical missionaries. Unlike other Indian tribes of the Amazon Basin, the Yanomamö had successfully escaped the contamination of Western man, his civilization, his society, and his lethal diseases.

In 1974 and 1975, two events occurred that critically upset the former socio-environmental adaptations of the Brazilian section of the Yanomamö tribe. The first event was the construction of the 2,500-mile Northern Perimeter Highway (a major artery in the highly publicized Trans-Amazonic road system) through the tribe's territory. The second was the announcement in February 1975 that one of the world's largest uranium deposits had been discovered in Yanomamö territory. Both events have already had their effects on the physical and cultural well-being of the Yanomamö tribe. A narrative account of what has happened to the Yanomamö since these events should provide the reader with insight into the controversial question of Indian policy and development policy in the Amazon Basin region of Brazil.

THE ABORIGINES PROTECTION SOCIETY REPORT OF 1973

In the summer of 1972, a four-member investigating team of the Aborigines Protection Society of London (APS) visited the Amazon Basin on the invitation of the recently created National Indian Foundation of Brazil (FUNAI). One place visited by the APS team was the far northern territory of Roraima, the major home of the estimated 5,000 to 10,000 people who make up the Brazilian section of the Yanomamö tribe.

Initially, the APS team was impressed by the situation of the Yanomamö relative to other tribal groups in Brazil. Contacts with outsiders had begun only in the previous decade, and the Indians, according to the APS team, seemed to be "still largely insulated from the colonizing and commercial interests of Brazil." The Indians' main contacts during this period were with foreign missionaries (the Salesian Fathers, and the New Tribes and Unevangelized Field Missions of the United States) who had established several mission stations in the Yanomamö area, but who seemed to pose little threat to the integrity of the tribe. "The Yanomamö," the APS team wrote in their report published in 1973, "seemed to be content with their culture, and had proved strong enough to resist the converting zeal of missionaries."

The APS team was also impressed by the fact that FUNAI was planning to intervene in the Yanomamö area, and envisioned the creation of a federally recognized Indian reserve for the tribe. To the surprise of the APS team, however, it was discovered that the proposed reserve would only contain an area sufficient for 300 members of the tribe, and would exclude almost every Yanomamö village identified by FUNAI itself.

The APS team noted that none of the experienced missionaries in the Yanomamö area had been consulted about the reserve, and that its proposed limits would significantly endanger the tribe. "We consider," the APS team wrote, "that a major extension of this Reserve is both necessary and justified and furthermore that discussions should be opened with the Venezuelan authorities to see what forms of liaison and coordination of Indian policy are possible along the frontier."

In September 1972, meeting with the then-president of FUNAI, General Oscar Jeronimo Bandeira de Melo, the APS team suggested that negotiations should be carried out between the Brazilian and Venezuelan governments for the creation of an international Yanomamö reserve. The president of FUNAI responded to this suggestion by claiming that for reasons of "national security" it would be impossible for the government to create an Indian reserve or park along the borders of Brazil. In addition, he said that an international reserve established in collaboration with the government of Venezuela would be extremely difficult to create because it would have to be negotiated through the foreign offices of both governments, and might be taken advantage of by the Yanomamö for purposes of "smuggling gold across the frontier." Members of the APS team questioned these arguments, and when they left Brazil they had severe doubts about whether the physical and cultural integrity of the Yanomamö would be maintained.

THE NORTHERN PERIMETER HIGHWAY

In 1973, it became known that the Brazilian government was planning to build a major highway along its northern frontier. The new road was called the Northern Perimeter Highway, and was to be completed by 1975. Unlike the Trans-Amazonic Highway to the south which was built for purposes of agrarian colonization, the new Northern Perimeter Highway was to be the major minerals transportation link in the Amazon Basin of Brazil. It would begin on the Atlantic coast, and pass westward through the large manganese mining operation of Bethlehem Steel Corporation in Amapa. Then it would cut to the north, passing above the huge multimillion dollar bauxite project of Alcan Aluminum Company along the Trombetas River in Para. Finally it would proceed south and westward, skirting the borders of Colombia and Peru and passing through one of the potentially largest oil fields in Brazil. It was estimated that over 50,000 Indians were living in nearly a hundred isolated tribal groups along the path of the new road. Among the groups were the still hostile and unpacified Yanomamö, Waimiri-Atroari, and Marubo tribes.

In May 1974, Edwin Brooks, a member of the APS team, published a report indicating how this new highway network could affect the Yanomamö tribe. Brooks's report contained a series of recent Brazilian government maps which showed that two highways were being planned to pass through the proposed, but still to be demarcated, Yanomamö Indian reserve. One of these was the Northern Perimeter Highway. The other was a smaller territorial road that would join the mission stations at Catrimani and Surucucus. Both highways, Brooks claimed, would jeopardize the territorial integrity of the Yanomamö tribe. The construction of these highways, he predicted, would be as devastating in their effects upon Indians as the highly publicized BR-080 highway invasion of the northern part of the Xingu National Park, which in 1972 brought a measles epidemic and nearly destroyed the once safe and thriving Txukahamei tribe.

URANIUM DISCOVERIES IN 1975

In February 1975, the critical event occurred that would eventually determine the future of the Yanomamö tribe. At that time, Brazil's Minister of Mines and Energy, Shigeaki Ueki, announced the discovery of an immense uranium field in the Surucucus region of Roraima Territory. This was claimed to be one of the largest uranium fields in the world and it was located in the major territory of the Brazilian section of the Yanomamö tribe.

The existence of radioactive minerals in this region was known as far back as 1951, but exploration for uranium did not begin until 1970 when the Brazilian government allocated significant amounts of monies for development of the nuclear sector. By 1974, over 150 technicians were working in the Surucucus region of Roraima alone, including members of the military, Project Radam (the large aerial photographic and mineral reconnaissance survey of the Amazon), the state-owned mineral exploration company (CPRM), and Nuclebras, the new state-owned company created to promote uranium exploration and nuclear research in Brazil.

At the time of the announcement of the Surucucus uranium discoveries, it also became known that Brazil was holding secret negotiations with several European countries for the provision of long-term deliveries of natural uranium in exchange for the most advanced nuclear technology. In May 1975, these negotiations became public when it was revealed that West Germany would be constructing eight nuclear power plants in Brazil at a cost of four billion dollars in exchange for the development of new sources of uranium and the construction of several uranium enrichment and nuclear fuel recycling plants.

Most international observers viewed the nuclear deal between West Germany and Brazil in purely geopolitical and economic terms. Not unexpectedly, none of these observers noted the more immediate implications of the Surucucus uranium discoveries for the survival of the Yanomamö and neighboring Indian tribes.

ONCHOCERCIASIS STRIKES YANOMAMÖ TRIBE

In the weeks immediately following the announcement of the Surucucus uranium discoveries, reports about uprooting and contamination of the Yanomamö tribe began to appear. The most shocking of these reports was the revelation that a FUNAI medical team, headed by Dr. Jose Alfredo Guimarães, had found several new foci of the dreaded disease onchocerciasis (African river blindness) throughout the northwest Amazon region.

Onchocerciasis, which is carried by blackflies of the Simuliid family and whose symptoms include fibrous tumors on skin and eyes as well as blindness, was first reported in the Western Hemisphere in Guatemala in 1916. By 1965 the disease had spread to Colombia, and in the early 1970s the presence of the disease was reported in the Amazon region of Brazil. In 1973 several Brazilian doctors warned the government about the growing incidence of onchocerciasis in the Amazon, and cautioned against plans for the building of the Northern Perimeter Highway.

These warnings were repeated in a report by two American scientists, Drs. R. J. A. Goodland and Howard S. Irwin, published in October 1974. Goodland and Irwin noted that the only hope for containing the spread of onchocerciasis in the Amazon was to discontinue or reroute the Northern Perimeter Highway. Onchocerciasis, they claimed, was possibly the most serious health threat in the Amazon, and was spreading along the margins of the Northern Perimeter Highway. "If the road planned to pierce the main focus is not realigned," they wrote, "disaster as rife as in Africa must be expected."

Unfortunately, the report of the FUNAI medical team in early 1975 confirmed these predictions. According to this report, onchocerciasis, which was previously localized in the area surrounding the Venezuelan-Brazilian border, had now spread beyond Roraima, and was reaching as far south as Para, Acre, and the center-west of Brazil. In the state of Amazonas alone, in a sample of 310 people investigated, Dr. Guimarães found 94 (30.23 percent) to be infected with the disease.

The most serious incidence of the disease had occurred among the Indian tribes of the northwestern part of the Amazon Basin. Along the Marauia River, one band of Yanomamö Indians was found to have a 100 percent incidence of the disease. In the Upper Solimoes region, the Tikuna tribe revealed an incidence of 87.5 percent. Along the Demini and Mapulau rivers, five Indian tribes (the Uxi-u-theli, Waiho-ko-a-theli, Welihessipi-u-theli, Pakidai, and Tucano) were all reported to have been infected. Lower incidences of onchocerciasis were found among Tucano and Maku tribes of the Waupes River, and the Baniwa tribe of the Içana River region.

In revealing these statistics to the Brazilian press, the president of FUNAI, General Ismarth de Araujo Oliveira (nominated to replace General Bandeira de Melo in March 1974), claimed that control of onchocerciasis was extremely difficult because it involved the intervention of several ministries besides the Indian Foundation, and required an expensive movement of people involved in the execution of development projects along the Northern Perimeter Highway. Onchocerciasis, he went on to note, was virtually "flying on the wings of the fly," and the only combatant known was an expensive French remedy which, according to the General, when applied to Indians killed them because of lack of physical resistance.

INDIAN POLICY ALONG THE NORTHERN PERIMETER HIGHWAY

Following news of the epidemic, a picture of what Indian policy would be like along the Northern Perimeter Highway started to emerge. In March 1975, for example, a young Indian agent named Benamour Fontes revealed that he had abandoned his position as the leader of a FUNAI pacification expedition along the Yanomamö front. Speaking at a press interview in Manaus, Fontes explained his actions by claiming that he had not received the necessary strategic and financial support from the central offices of FUNAI in Brasilia. The salaries of his coworkers were not paid promptly, and hunters and lumbermen along with government geologists had already begun to invade the territory of the Yanomamö tribe.

In addition, Fontes revealed that all strategic support was being given to the more publicized Waimiri-Atroari pacification expedition to the south. He said that he wanted to avoid what happened to fellow Indian agent Gilberto Pinto, who had spent more than eight years asking for men and supplies and who was tragically killed by angered Waimiri-Atroari tribesmen in December of the previous year. A state of chaos,

Fontes concluded, existed along the route of the Northern Perimeter Highway, and this could only prove disastrous for the Yanomamö and other Indian tribes.

During this period, reporters increasingly sought an official statement of government Indian policy in the northern Amazon region from high authorities within FUNAI. The event which precipitated such a statement occurred on the same day as the resignation of Benamour Fontes, when the governor of Roraima Territory, Fernando Ramos Pereira, went before the Brazilian press and declared that in his opinion an "area as rich as this — with gold, diamonds, and uranium — could not afford the luxury of conserving half a dozen Indian tribes who are holding back the development of Brazil."

The governor's statement caused a sort of miniscandal in Brazil, and the president of FUNAI responded immediately by saying that there was nothing contradictory between the protection of the Indian tribes of Roraima, such as the large Yanomamö tribe, and the development of the country. Citing Article 45 of the new Brazilian Indian Statute, which gives the government the right to administer and lease Indian mineral resources, the president said that "the Indian can only benefit from the mineral wealth discovered on the lands which he inhabits." The Indian Statute, he claimed, calls for the "integration" of the Indians into the Brazilian economy, and provides for their "participation," as owners of property, in the exploitation of mineral resources contained on their lands.

At the same time, the president of FUNAI revealed that a contract had been signed with two anthropologists associated with the University of Brasilia for the creation of Project Perimetral-Yanomami, a far-reaching program for the integration of the Yanomamö tribe. The purpose of Project Perimetral-Yanomami would be to set the groundwork for the economic integration of the Yanomamö into the expanding penetration and colonization fronts in the far northern part of Brazil. The Indians, according to the president, would be inoculated against disease and provided with new economic skills to trade the products of their labor with colonists who were beginning to settle along the Northern Perimeter Highway. One of the anthropologists contracted by FUNAI said that the goal of Project Perimetral-Yanomami was "to implant a system of *direct integration* [italics added] that would permit economic advantages for both groups."

GENERAL IMPLICATIONS

To conclude, three points about the general significance of the foregoing events are important. First, the official government policy of integrating Indian tribes into the expanding economy, instead of protecting them in their aboriginal territories through the creation of closed Indian parks and reserves, has been tried in several other areas of the Amazon Basin, and has proved devastating for Indian tribes. The policy most recently failed with the Aripuana Indian Park in Rondonia, home of the 5,000-member Cintas Largas and Surui tribes. A brief description of conditions in the Aripuana Indian Park provides a forecast of what may happen to the Yanomamö tribe.

The Cintas Largas received considered international publicity because of the brutal massacre at Parallel Eleven in 1963. In 1968, FUNAI proposed an Indian park for the Cintas Largas and neighboring Surui tribes, but then in 1970, it began to lease lands in the park to a large Saõ Paulo colonization company, to seven international cassiterite (tin) mining firms, and to the state government for the purpose of building a series of interior roads.

By 1973, these encroachments on the Aripuana Indian Park had begun to take their toll on the Indians. Geologists from Project Radam and private companies were searching for minerals in every part of the park. Numerous landing strips were constructed in the area. Two roads effectively destroyed the territorial integrity of the park. Game was beginning to become critically scarce, and Indians were abandoning their gardens to outside settlers and colonists.

In 1975, under the auspices of the International Work Group for Indigenous Affairs, Dr. Jean Chiappino, a French physician who had recently spent several months in Aripuana Indian Park, published a report describing the conditions of the Cintas Largas and Surui tribes. These Indians received no effective protection from FUNAI, and were suffering from disease, hunger, and apathy. An epidemic of tuberculosis, carried by outsiders, had struck all age groups in one Surui band, bringing death to the Indians within the short space of two months. The initial symptom of the disease was a hoarse cough. This was followed by a "pussy expectoration . . . which exhausted the patient," and a "permanent fever." This syndrome developed fastest among Indian children, and "carried off its victims in terminal cachexia." The spread of the epidemic, Dr. Chiappino noted, "distressed, disoriented, and destroyed" Indian families and the social group. According to his calculations, over 60 percent of the Surui population observed was affected by this epidemic alone.

Most important, Dr. Chiappino claimed that this epidemic, as well as the general state of despair and disorganization among the Cintas Largas and Surui tribes, could be directly related to the "integrationist" policies of FUNAI. Although land protection is stipulated in the Brazilian constitution, these Indians were without any effective protection of their lands, and were suffering the worst effects of uncontrolled contact with outsiders. Economic integration was merely a convenient euphemism for hiding the nasty facts of physical and cultural death for these Indians. According to Dr. Chiappino, their survival could only be ensured through a concerted program of medical assistance and the creation of a closed and well-protected Indian reserve.

Second, Brazilian Indian policy must be seen within the context of the wider national program for the rapid economic development and occupation of the Amazon region. Despite the sincere and humanitarian intentions of some of its employees and the openness to outside suggestions and assistance from its present director, FUNAI is still an agency within the Brazilian Ministry of the Interior, and hence is substantially constrained in its protectionist functions by the larger developmentalist objectives of the federal government.

In certain recent cases, FUNAI has been able to protect Indian land and territorial rights, and there are some areas of central Brazil where Indian tribes are experiencing a demographic and cultural renaissance. However, in areas like the more populated northern part of the Amazon Basin, where Indian land rights conflict with the interests of large, multinational or state-owned mining companies, or with the plans of the National Highway Department, FUNAI has been unable to fulfill its constitutional mandate to Indian tribes.

Perhaps most significantly, the new Indian Statute passed in December 1973 provides FUNAI with the right to administer and lease Indian mineral resources. In the near future these mineral leasing provisions could provide the conditions for the total collaboration of FUNAI with powerful economic and developmentalist interests in Brazil. These provisions are particularly dangerous because of the recent discoveries of uranium and petroleum deposits in the Amazon Basin.

Third, Brazil alone must not be held responsible for the social and environmental consequences of the Amazon development program. What is taking place in the Amazon region today is a classic case of a high technology and dependency model of economic development being applied to one of the last and largest frontier regions of the world. For example, Project Radam, the huge aerial photographic survey that has been uncovering most of the mineral wealth of the Amazon, was substantially developed with technical assistance from government agencies and private corporations in the United States. Almost all heavy earthmoving equipment used to clear jungle for the Trans-Amazonic roads was supplied by European, North American, and Japanese multinational firms. The Amazon program received substantial financial inputs for hydroelectric and agribusiness development projects from international lending institutions such as the World Bank. Even more relevant to this discussion is the recent discovery of uranium on Yanomamö lands, which must be seen within the context of the entire global scramble for nuclear technologies, power plants, and fuels.

The tragedy of the destruction of the Yanomamö and other aboriginal tribes is that these unique peoples may provide an alternative and indigenous model for the socially and ecologically sound development of the Amazon region. By bringing pressure to bear for the creation of an international Yanomamö reserve, as suggested by the APS in 1973, we could provide the basis not only for the survival of these peoples, but also for the survival of the entire planet and ourselves.

35

Rites of desecration:
Tourists as Bali's new gods

COLIN TURNBULL

*We have come to expect that political domination by one group over
another will result in change, particularly among those who have
been subordinated. But in today's world there is another kind of
invasion that may also dramatically affect the lives of those who
experience it. It is the affluent tourist, once largely confined to the
cultural and vacation centers of the industrialized nations, who
wades eagerly ashore on lands only recently made accessible to his
hunger for esoteric sights and colorful photographs. The effect of
tourists on the social fabric and basic beliefs of a people who have
been recently "discovered" is the topic of this article by Colin
Turnbull. He describes how tourists have descended on the once quiet
and beautiful island of Bali, showing disrespect for all that its people
hold sacred.*

To the Balinese their home is known as Pulau Dewata, or "Island of the
Gods." But sometimes it seems that in the last few years the gods of
Bali have descended in the form of tourists. With swimsuits and cameras
as their sacred symbols, they appear to hold the power of both desecration and consecration.

The Balinese have traditionally considered their island to be safe
as well as sacred, but tourism has changed that too; from tourism and
tourists there is little safety. The government of Indonesia has done its
best to contain the damage, both social and environmental, by confining
tourists to the southern point of the island. But Bali is not much more
than a hundred miles long and since it is both encircled and traversed

Originally published as "Bali's New Gods." With permission from *Natural History*, Vol.
91, No. 1; Copyright the American Museum of Natural History, 1982.

by motor roads, only the western jungles are effectively free from the pollution that tourism brings. Even there, however, the people are not untouched. On this small and densely populated island (approaching three million people for its two thousand square miles), every village, if not every family, has somehow been affected by the massive influx of tourists, an influx so sudden and rapid, the islanders have had little time to adapt.

It would be easy enough to paint a totally negative picture of the impact of tourism on Bali. The once beautiful sandy beach at Kuta, for instance, is now littered with bodies in various stages of undress, interspersed with pimps, hawkers, and masseurs who move from body to body, plying their services. When I was there last year the beach was patrolled by two well-dressed prostitutes riding on scooters for ready pickup and delivery. Even the water was not entirely safe; to reach it one ran the risk of being run down by tourist youths racing and trick riding on motorcycles. And once in the water there was the danger of being hit by speedboats, towing large rubber dinghies loaded with shrieking tourists who seemed to have come thousands of miles to do what they could have done at home.

Yet the local fishermen, whose beach it used to be, continued to go about their business as though none of these intrusions were going on. And sunset was still a beautiful time of day. Kuta Beach is renowned for its sunsets, but apart from some scattered photographers, few tourists are to be found there in the twilight; after all it is cocktail time, and sunsets look just as good from a comfortable lounge, with drink in hand.

Bali's modernization, urban development, and extraordinary economic growth, with all the corresponding benefits of medical, social, and educational services that had previously not existed, also have their negative aspects. It could be argued that prior to the descent of the tourist gods, for whose benefit the island seems largely to be administered, some of these services were not needed; they are needed now to combat problems brought by tourism itself. The economic benefits touch only a few, and the cost to all is high in terms of damage to the social fabric. How high might be measured by the increase in the rate of teenage suicide.

Nevertheless, tourism is of major, often paramount, economic and even political importance in many remote parts of the world, and one of the major issues that has to be faced is how to weigh the complex advantages against the equally complex disadvantages. Here my focus is on one small segment of the overall problem of the social change induced by tourism: the interaction between the tourist and what is sacred to the people of the place he is visiting. In a vast subcontinent such as India even the most profane tourists are likely to have little effect on what is sacred to the Indian; on a small island like Bali, it is another matter. The Balinese people's way of life is intimately bound up with their religious belief and practice, and there are some 30,000 temples on the island, so the possibility and danger of desecration are very real. But in looking at the desecration and how it takes place, most often unconsciously at the hands of tourists, we find there is also a kind of consecration taking place.

In line with my ongoing analogy between tourism and pilgrimage, of all tourist meccas surely Bali is one that is truly sacred. The quest of most tourists going there involves an ideal of perfection, of beauty and goodness — which, incidentally, are qualities by which the Balinese religion defines the sacred. Since for the Balinese the land itself is sacred, the very environmental and ecological changes wrought in the name of tourism or by tourists are a form of desecration. And since reciprocity in human relationships is also sacred in their essentially egalitarian traditional way of life, the abuse of money is also a form of desecration. With money they have learned to "purchase" human services for individual gain, without involving any further reciprocal personal obligation. Money all too easily and subtly short-circuits mutual concern and consideration. This effect of tourism is perhaps most insidious and most pervasive in a cultural setting such as Bali. What is a small amount of money for the tourist may be a small fortune to the Balinese. Individual wealth in such measure, together with other material appurtenances of Western civilization brought by tourism, readily lures young men and women, even boys and girls, away from their homes and villages. Too late, they discover they have also been lured away from the security their traditions offered and from the ideals their lives were built around.

At the individual level, desecration by tourists may be conscious or unconscious. On Bali it is most often the latter; vandalism, such as the scarification of sacred monuments by graffiti and pilferage from sacred sites, is not yet as common as elsewhere. But it is curious that the most conscious, blatant, and offensive insults are given at the most sacred places and on the most sacred occasions. Sometimes it is the tourist industry itself, through the initiative of local entrepreneurs, that overtly desecrates what is holiest, but individual tourists do their share of conscious profanation. For instance, even at Pura Besakih (the Mother Temple) on Mount Agung, probably the holiest shrine in Bali, I saw some tourists openly ignore polite requests not to enter certain areas. They swaggered wherever they wished, openly ridiculing the sense of propriety so sacred to the Balinese, making loud and coarse jokes concerning customs of modesty in dress and nonadmission of women during their menstrual period. And down the coast at Goa Lawah, the sacred home of the mythical serpent Basuki is noted by most tourists merely for the quantity of bats that infest the cave. The associated temple, a holy place reserved largely for death ceremonies, is ignored or paid scant courtesy at best. Crowds of tourists press through worshipers to see and photograph the bats or push among mourners to take snapshots of a funerary ritual. I saw three particularly unkempt and scantily dressed youths force their way up the steps, ignoring requests to put on the required ritual waist sash readily available to all foreign visitors and ridiculing the offered wraparound apron that would have concealed the immodesty of their very short shorts. They burst among the mourners with whoops and jeers, and one tried to throw stones into the cave to dislodge the bats. Eventually a little old Balinese priest came up to them and politely asked them to leave. There was something about that tiny man that stopped them in their tracks. They looked at each other in surprise, then with a few more self-conscious gymnastics and coarse comments they bounded down the long flight of steps, laughing as they knocked people aside.

I caught up with them on the nearby beach of volcanic lava. All their bounce and bravado had gone; they were arguing about just why they had listened to that silly little old man. After all, they had come all that way to see the bats and they had as much right to be there as anyone else. But none of them suggested turning around and going back. They had been touched by something — and stopped. The Balinese might say that the youths had been stopped by the gods. It was certainly no threat of physical coercion that had prevented them from "having their fun"; and plainly they had no respect for the "silly little old man" or the religion he professed. But evidently he somehow commanded an air of authority that was just as effective as that of any armed policeman or bouncer. I will not insist that the authority was sacred in the sense that any supernatural force was at work, but whatever the source, it was powerful enough to prevent an act of desecration. It touched the desecraters, too, and for a moment compelled them to acknowledge the existence of something sacred to others.

The abusive and offensive behavior of these three young men also affected the rest of us. It annoyed the photographers and those trying to film the mourning ceremony, particularly when one of the three bearded, bandannaed heads popped into a viewfinder. It caused a few to stop taking photographs. What it did to the Balinese I cannot say; apart from the priest who intervened they seemed to pay no attention. Perhaps it merely heightened their awareness of the sanctity of the place and the worship they were about; perhaps that is what it did for all of us.

For those who are uncomfortable with the word *sacred*, some Balinese whom I talked with about this and similar incidents use the word *respect*. The young manager of a beach resort was very clear and emphatic. He did not object to the behavior itself; Basuki, after all, was perfectly capable of looking after himself and could have struck the youths dead. It was rather the lack of human consideration that offended him. More than this overt act of desecration or, only slightly less overt, the insulting condescension of tourists in his hotel, on the beach, or on the streets, he found their manner of dress objectionable. This for him was true desecration. To attack the gods directly is merely foolhardy and ignorant. But to attack the sanctity of "proper human relationships" is an insult and a threat that is as real as it is mortal. Much of Balinese social structure is built around the concept of propriety, and despite the outward appearance of freedom and relaxation, there is an underlying code, which is specific and rigorous, concerning mutual relationships. That code clearly defines the acceptable limits of behavior, and dress is an important element. Other than when bathing, men in shorts are indecent, and without shirts they offer open insult; the same is true for women. On the beach, the pimps, hawkers, masseurs, and even the two motorized prostitutes were all impeccably dressed, the women with blouses buttoned up to the neck and the men in long trousers and open-neck shirts fastened as high as they would go. Even the totally naked fishermen somehow gave the appearance of being fully clad, in respectability at least, as they entered or emerged from the water casually concealing their genitals with the left hand, their neat piles of clothes close to the water's edge.

The hotel manager came from the north coast of Bali and talked longingly and lovingly of "the other side of the island," of its beauty and safety. By "safety" he was not referring to physical safety. His home was only a few hours drive away, but he had never been back and said he could not return there. "Like the rest of us who have left our homes, I am not clean. Look at how I dress." He was considerably better dressed than I was, but in Western style. Yet he was in no way bitter or hostile to tourism. He was grateful for the new horizons it had opened up to him and to the island, and while aware of the damage being done to the traditional way of life, he pointed out that he and others were now more aware that they had something to lose. When I asked him what he had gained, other than this knowledge, his Western clothes and dark glasses, his home without a family, and his scooter (all things that he listed), he gave an odd answer. He said, "Now I know there is even more for me to respect."

At the beginning I referred to tourists as the new gods of Bali, with swimsuits and cameras as their sacred symbols, holding the power of desecration and consecration. This was not entirely flippant. One brochure in front of me describes Bali, not as "Island of the Gods," but as a "Photographer's Paradise." And under "Emergencies" it lists four: police, hospital, ambulance, and finally, camera troubles. Since so many of us take cameras with us when we travel abroad we should be aware of the possible sacral power of this device and the way that we handle it.

One could do an amusing study of the ritual behavior of photographers, but that is not what I have in mind. I have in mind what is very clearly in the minds of Muslims when they prohibit photography of the human form, and what the Jewish scriptures had in mind when they forbade graven images. It is the ancient idea of "quintessence," that fifth and *essential* ingredient that was thought to be latent in all being — the stuff of the stars, some thought, the stuff of sanctity and divinity. No representation of man (or God) that does not show that inner reality can do justice to man or God. Since the quintessence is invisible, any pictorial or graven image is wanting, and failing to do justice to a divinity is a desecration.

I think most of us — even the most profane, the most irreligious — have something that to us is sacred. I doubt if many could put their finger on what the invisible quintessence of that sacredness is, any more than the ancients could when they coined the word. But we are aware of its presence. It is what sometimes motivates us to take photographs, and it is very definitely what sometimes motivates us *not* to take photographs. Probably most of us have had moments when, camera in hand, we have seen something deeply moving, so beautiful that it seemed made for photography, yet somehow we came away with the shutter still cocked, the camera unused. The Balinese would call that an act of "respect." We might say it was because the light was not right, but even that excuse is to say that our mechanical apparatus was, at that moment, incapable of making a perfect image of what we "saw."

Or we might recognize that what we saw with our eyes was not really what we wished to capture, that any photographic rendition without the smell, the touch, the feeling, without that indefinable quintessence, would be a failure. Like most other tourists at Kuta Beach I watched sunsets. I watched *every* sunset, and I watched from the beach, bare feet in the sand. And like others I took photographs. They are probably like those everyone else took, and while they are spectacular, they do not have that essential that made some moments standing on the beach in the warm air, with the smell and sound of the surf, sacred. All the photographs do is to help recall the sunsets that were sacred because they occurred when I deliberately went out to the beach *without* my camera, to be part of the sunset instead of a detached, objective observer.

So it was at the temples of Bali (and of course elsewhere). The act

of photography seems on the one hand to diminish what is being photographed by making it commonplace or to insult it by the futility of
trying to capture its invisible essence; on the other hand the photographer is demeaned if he or she doesn't realize that there *is* an invisible
essence. I observed Balinese noting with obvious approval or disapproval the manner and mood of the photographer. There were times
when a cluck of disapproval was heard as a tourist took a quick snapshot
of something particularly sacred, hurrying on with hardly a pause or
second glance. Then there were times when the photographer's intense
concentration, and rigid requirements for perfect conditions, conveyed
a sense of respect and brought a quiet sigh of approval; for respect,
whatever its origin, can only serve to heighten rather than diminish
what is sacred. The drawback is that the act of taking a photograph too
often puts a distance between the photograph and the object being
photographed. For the tourist in particular there is often neither the time
nor the opportunity to empathize and identify in a way that makes for
outstanding photography, which is a true art. The snapshot is literally
a "taking" and may serve to remove the tourist even further from the
very thing he most wants to approach and share.

The cost of using the lure of photography to attract tourists to Bali
can be high. The narrow streets of Kuta are lined with indigenous tourist
agencies, car hire firms, and bus operators. Outside their one-room
offices are blackboards and posters advertising their "specials." The
sacred gets top priority and commands the highest price, but how long
can the sacred remain intact when subject to such commercialization?
Even death is not immune. The most lurid and colorful posters call
tourists to come and enjoy cremations — one advertised a mass cremation. For many Balinese the cost of living has grown so enormously
that they can no longer afford to finance a cremation for a single family
member, so the dead are pooled, so to speak, and the conflagration is
made even more dramatic by the glare of floodlights, the explosion of
flashbulbs, and the presence of the new gods.

There was even an "underground" tourist traffic in death, surrep-
titious visits to a lakeside beach where the bodies of the dead are laid
out in the open. I wonder how many have the stomach to show such
photographs to their friends, and what they say about the custom. I
found I did not have the stomach to go and find out. I confined most
of my photography thereafter to the profane; mainly to photographs of
other tourists at work with their cameras.

To the Student:

To make *Conformity and Conflict* a better book in its next edition, we need to know what you think of the book as it is now. Please help us by filling out this questionnaire and returning it to: *Conformity and Conflict*, Little, Brown and Co., College Division, 34 Beacon Street, Boston, Mass. 02106.

School: _____ Course title: _____

Instructor's name: _____

I.   Please give us your reactions to the selections:

		Keep	Drop	Didn't Read
1.	Lee, Eating Christmas in the Kalahari	——	——	——
2.	Bohannan, Shakespeare in the bush	——	——	——
3.	Briggs, Kapluna daughter: Adopted by the Eskimo	——	——	——
4.	Spradley, Trouble in the tank: Ethics in urban fieldwork	——	——	——
5.	Eschholz and Rosa, Student slang for college courses	——	——	——
6.	Nash, Odds and Endos: The language of bicycle motocross racing	——	——	——
7.	Hall and Hall, The sounds of silence	——	——	——
8.	Turner, Cosmetics: The language of bodily adornment	——	——	——
9.	Rynkiewich, Matrilineal kinship: Coming home to Bokelab	——	——	——
10.	Wolf, Uterine families and the women's community	——	——	——
11.	Starr and Alamuddin, The marriage contract: Bridewealth in Lebanon	——	——	——
12.	Scott, Sororities and the husband game	——	——	——
13.	Friedl, Society and sex roles	——	——	——
14.	Stein, Male and female: The doctor-nurse game	——	——	——
15.	Gregor, Men's clubs: No girls allowed	——	——	——
16.	Benderly, Rape-free or rape prone	——	——	——
17.	Lee, The hunters: Scarce resources in the Kalahari	——	——	——
18.	Harris, India's sacred cow	——	——	——
19.	Farb and Armelagos, The food connection	——	——	——

	Keep	Drop	Didn't Read
20. Bohannan, The impact of money on an African subsistence economy	___	___	___
21. McCurdy and Carlson, The shrink-wrap solution: Anthropology in business	___	___	___
22. Schildkrout, Young traders of northern Nigeria	___	___	___
23. Spradley, Beating the drunk charge	___	___	___
24. Chagnon, Yanomamö: The fierce people	___	___	___
25. Sahlins, Poor man, rich man, big-man, chief	___	___	___
26. Wallace, Psychological preparations for war	___	___	___
27. Newman, When technology fails: Magic and religion in New Guinea	___	___	___
28. Gmelch, Baseball magic	___	___	___
29. Merrill, Religion and culture: God's saviours in the Sierra Madre	___	___	___
30. Moody, Urban witches	___	___	___
31. Sharp, Steel axes for stone-age Australians	___	___	___
32. Worsley, Cargo cults	___	___	___
33. Lambo, Psychotherapy in Africa	___	___	___
34. Davis, Highways and the future of the Yanomamö	___	___	___
35. Turnbull, Rites of desecration: Tourists as Bali's new gods	___	___	___

II. Was the general introduction (Chapter I) helpful? How might it be improved?

_____

III. Were the chapter and article introductions helpful? _____
How might they be improved?

_____

IV. Please add any comments or suggestions. _____

_____

_____

_____

May we quote you in our promotional efforts for this book? __ Yes __ No

_____   _____
Date   Signature

_____
Mailing address